international
review of
social history

Supplement 11

Uncovering Labour in Information Revolutions, 1750–2000

Edited by Aad Blok and Greg Downey

CAMBRIDGE
UNIVERSITY PRESS

Shaftesbury Road, Cambridge CB2 8EA, United Kingdom

One Liberty Plaza, 20th Floor, New York, NY 10006, USA

477 Williamstown Road, Port Melbourne, VIC 3207, Australia

314–321, 3rd Floor, Plot 3, Splendor Forum, Jasola District Centre, New Delhi – 110025, India

103 Penang Road, #05–06/07, Visioncrest Commercial, Singapore 238467

Cambridge University Press is part of Cambridge University Press & Assessment, a department of the University of Cambridge.

We share the University's mission to contribute to society through the pursuit of education, learning and research at the highest international levels of excellence.

www.cambridge.org
Information on this title: www.cambridge.org/9780521543538

A catalogue record for this publication is available from the British Library

ISBN   978-0-521-54353-8   Paperback

CONTENTS

Uncovering Labour in Information Revolutions, 1750–2000

Edited by
Aad Blok and Greg Downey

NOTES ON CONTRIBUTORS

Chris Benner Department of Geography and Labor Studies and Industrial Relations, 302 Walker Building, Pennsylvania State University, University Park, PA 16803, USA; e-mail: cbenner@psu.edu

Aad Blok Internationaal Instituut voor Sociale Geschiedenis, Cruquiusweg 31, 1019 AT Amsterdam, The Netherlands; e-mail: abl@iisg.nl

Deep Kanta Lahiri Choudhury Wellcome Unit for the History of Medicine, University of Oxford, 45-47 Banbury Road, Oxford OX2 6PE, UK; e-mail: deep.lahirichoudhury@wuhmo.ox.ac.uk

Greg Downey School of Journalism & Mass Communication, School of Library & Information Studies, University of Wisconsin-Madison, 5115 Vilas Hall, 821 University Avenue Madison, WI 53706, USA; e-mail: gdowney@wisc.edu

Bernard Dubbeld University of Chicago, 1414 East 59th Street #374, Chicago, IL 60637, USA; e-mail: bdubbeld@uchicago.edu

Nathan Ensmenger History & Sociology of Science Department, 303 Logan Hall, University of Pennsylvania, Philadelphia, PA 19063, USA; e-mail: nathanen@sas.upenn.edu

Hector Postigo Center for Cultural Design, Rensselaer Polytechnic Institute, Troy, NY 12180, USA; e-mail: postih@rpi.edu

Eve Rosenhaft School of Modern Languages, University of Liverpool, Modern Languages Building, Liverpool L69 7ZR, UK; e-mail: dan85@liverpool.ac.uk

Helen Sampson Seafarers' International Research Centre, Cardiff University, PO Box 907, Cardiff CF10 3YP, UK; e-mail: SampsonH@Cardiff.ac.uk

Aristotle Tympas Philosophy and History of Science Department, University of Athens, PO Box 80501, 18510 Piraeus, Greece; e-mail: tympas@phs.uoa.gr

Bin Wu Seafarers' International Research Centre, Cardiff University, PO Box 907, Cardiff CF10 3YP, UK; e-mail: WuB@Cardiff.ac.uk

IRSH 48 (2003), Supplement, pp. 1–11 DOI: 10.1017/S002085900300124X
© 2003 Internationaal Instituut voor Sociale Geschiedenis

Introduction*

AAD BLOK

The last few decades of the twentieth century witnessed a rapid develop-ment in information and communication technologies (ICT), which has contributed to such drastic economic, social, and cultural changes that they are commonly referred to as the "Information Revolution". This Informa-tion Revolution is believed by many to be so influential and comprehensive that it is bringing about an epochal rupture in global economic, social, cultural, and political history comparable to the previous major historical shifts of the Agrarian Revolution and the Industrial Revolution. Naturally, a development so pervasive has been analysed by a great number of scholars from various disciplines, among whom social theorists, in all their diversity, have been the most numerous. Here is not the place for even a concise overview of the rich variety of theorizing and analysis of the Information Revolution and the resulting Information Society,[1] but much of the theorization of the relationship between work and the most recent information revolution can still be traced to the initial statements about "postindustrial society", "de-industrialization" and "globalization".[2]

Fundamental to much of this work is the underlying question: is global society at large leaving the age of industrialism behind and entering an age of postindustrialism? Depending on the theoretical perspective, the terms

---

* I would like to thank Greg Downey for his suggestions and for joining in this "virtual" project; Lex Heerma van Voss and Ursula Langkau-Alex for their suggestions; and Marcel van der Linden for his advice and for giving the initial impetus for the project.

1. A very comprehensive and lucid overview of theories of the Information Revolution and the Information Society is given by Frank Webster, *Theories of the Information Society*, 2nd edn (London [etc.], 2002); for a critical overview from a distinctly neo-Marxist perspective see Nick Dyer-Witheford, *Cyber-Marx: Cycles and Circuits of Struggle in High-Technology Capitalism* (Urbana, IL [etc.], 1999); for a recent concise critical theoretical overview see François Fortier, *Virtuality Check: Power Relations and Alternative Strategies in the Information Society* (London [etc.], 2001).
2. Daniel Bell, *The Coming of Post-Industrial Society: A Venture in Social Forecasting* (New York, 1973); the classic study on deindustrialization is Barry Bluestone and B. Harrison, *The Deindustrialization of America: Plant Closings, Community Abandonment, and the Dismantling of Basic Industries* (New York, 1982); for a recent historical overview of the relation between deindustrialization and globalization, see Christopher Johnson, "Introduction: De-industriali-zation and Globalization", in Bert Altena and Marcel van der Linden (eds), *De-Industrialization: Social, Cultural, and Political Aspects*, *International Review of Social History*, Supplement 10 (Cambridge [etc.], 2002), pp. 3–33.

industrialism/postindustrialism can be substituted by modernism/post-modernism, Fordism/post-Fordism, industrial capitalism/informational capitalism, or industrialism/informationalism. Following Frank Webster,[3] theorists in this field may be divided into clearly separated camps: those who believe that the rapid technological developments in information and communication technology over the past decades are causing such drastic changes in modern capitalist society that history is indeed entering a distinct new phase, and we are therefore living through an epochal change; and those who stress elements of continuity in the technological, economic, and social developments which are generally labelled as the Information Revolution. On one side of the line Webster places, among others, theorists of postindustrialism (Daniel Bell and his many followers), of postmodernism (Jean Baudrillard, Mark Poster), and Manuel Castells, with his theory of the informational mode of capitalist development. On the other side, he includes neo-Marxists, such as Herbert Schiller; Anthony Giddens's theory of reflexive modernization; Jürgen Habermas's theory of the public sphere; and David Harvey's theory of flexible accumulation.

The consequences of the Information Revolution for labour have been an important theme in many of the theories and analyses that have been developed on both sides of the line between continuity and change. The initial utopian enthusiasm about "electronic cottages"[4] and the general idea that automation and ICTs would increasingly allow machines to take over unattractive, tedious labour soon found its dystopian backlash in the form of a fear of "electronic sweatshops", a "jobless future", the "end of work", a growing digital divide and an increasing contingency of jobs.[5] One the most influential analysts of the Information Revolution in the past decade to endorse this idea of a radical change is Manuel Castells, whose magnum opus, *The Information Age*, is no doubt among the most fundamental analyses. Castells gives the subject of work and labour relations ample attention: in the first volume of his trilogy, *The Rise of the Network Society* (1996), he devotes almost one-quarter of the book to

---

3. Webster, *Theories of the Information Society*, p. 6.
4. Alvin Toffler, *The Third Wave* (New York, 1980).
5. Barbara Garson, *The Electronic Sweatshop: How Computers Are Transforming the Office of the Future into the Factory of the Past* (New York, 1988); Ursula Huws, *The New Homeworkers: New Technology and the Changing Location of White-Collar Work* (London, 1984); idem, "The Making of a Cybertariat? Virtual Work in a Real World", *The Socialist Register: A Survey of Moments and Ideas* (2001), pp. 1–23; Stanley Aronowitz and W. DiFazio, *The Jobless Future: Sci-Tech and the Dogma of Work* (Minneapolis, MN, 1994); Amy Sue Bix, *Inventing Ourselves Out of Jobs? America's Debate Over Technological Unemployment, 1929–1981* (Baltimore, MD, 2000); Jeremy Rifkin, *The End of Work: The Decline of the Global Labor Force and the Dawn of the Post-Market Era* (New York, 1995); Pippa Norris, *Digital Divide? Civic Engagement, Information Poverty, and the Internet Worldwide* (Cambridge, 2001); Richard S. Belous, *The Contingent Economy: The Growth of the Temporary, Part-Time and Subcontracted Workforce* (Washington DC, 1989).

"The Transformation of Work and Employment".[6] Aside from transformations in employment and occupational structure, Castells also analyses the transformations of labour itself. Flexibilization and social division seem to be inextricably connected with the rise of the new informational mode of development: "The prevailing model for labor in the new, information-based economy is that of a core labor force, formed by information-based managers and by [...] 'symbolic analysts', and a disposable labor force, that can be automated and/or hired/fired/off-shored, depending upon market demand and labor costs."[7] According to Castells, it is not so much a question of social division of labour, but of "the disaggregation of labor",[8] an ongoing individualization of labour, which leads to an increasing weakening of international and national labour movements.

Castells's analysis can clearly be classified as one of the more pessimistic views on labour in the Information Revolution, but what he shares with many others analysts of the Information Revolution is the primacy he gives to technological development as the essence of the Information Revolution. In such analyses technological development, or rather technological progress, is conceived as an essentially autonomous process and the Information Revolution, thus conceived, is seen as an essentially technological revolution. This conception has become dominant in the conventional, "orthodox" discourse on the consequences of the rapid developments in ICTs, and has had a strong influence on popular understanding of the Information Revolution. At the same time, it has given rise to various criticisms, which regard Castells's analysis as being based on a form of technological reductionism or determinism.[9] Given this technological determinism, many analysts are more focused on the *consequences* of the Information Revolution for labour and labour relations, than on the *role* and *position* of labour in this process.

Another important analogy between Castells's theory and many other theories endorsing the idea of a historical rupture of the Information Revolution is the apparent lack of a longer-term historical perspective. The focus on technological development, in this case that of the microchip, personal computer, and digital network technologies, as the decisive force driving societal change has led to a, sometimes very explicit, lack of interest in any historical comparison.[10] Yet, to be able to make a critical assessment

---

6. Manuel Castells, *The Rise of the Network Society*, vol. 1 of *The Information Age: Economy, Society and Culture* (London [etc.], 1996), pp. 201–326.

7. *Ibid.*, p. 272.

8. *Ibid.*, p. 279.

9. Webster, *Theories of the Information Society*, p. 120.

10. Castells is quite explicit about this at the end of the third volume of his trilogy, when he indicates what his reaction is to the question of what is essentially so new about the developments he has analysed: "What is new about all this? Why is this a new world? I do believe

of the validity of the concept of revolutionary change brought about by the technological developments in the realm of information and communication, the longer-term historical dimensions of these developments must be taken into consideration. In other words: to be able to assess just how revolutionary this Information Revolution is, a distinct historical perspective seems indispensable.

This Supplement to the *International Review of Social History* is not, of course, the first to urge for a more historical perspective on the present-day Information Revolution. In recent historiography, a number of scholars have looked into a variety of historical roots of the present-day Information Revolution and Information Age, from the development of literacy, through the printing revolution, the scientific revolution, to the development of the postal system, and telegraph and telephone networks.[11] Daniel Headrick has argued that, whereas information is as old as mankind, throughout history there have been periods of sharp acceleration, or revolution, in the amount of information that people had access to and in the creation of information systems to deal with it: "The appearance of writing, the alphabet, double-entry book-keeping, the printing press, the telegraph, the transistor, and the computer – each has contributed mightily to the acceleration of information in their time. In short, there have been many information revolutions."[12] These revolutions have occurred both in the development of material technologies, such as the printing press, telegraph, and personal computers, and in the development of more abstract, immaterial information systems, such as were developed during the scientific revolution in the late seventeenth to the nineteenth centuries.[13]

However useful this attention to the historical roots of the present-day Information Revolution is, the main unit of analysis in most of this work remains either the information and information systems as such (for

that there is a new world emerging in this end of the millennium. In the three volumes of this book I have tried to provide information and ideas in support of this statement [...] *Yet, this is not the point I want to make.* My main statement is that it does not really matter if you believe that this world, or any of its features, is new or not. My analysis stands by itself. This is our world, the world of the Information Age. And this is my analysis of this world, which must be understood, used, judged by itself, by its capacity, or incapacity, to identify and explain the phenomena that we observe and experience, regardless of its newness." Manuel Castells, *End of Millennium*, vol. 3 of *The Information Age: Economy, Society and Culture* (Malden, MA [etc.], 1999), p. 356, fn. 1.

11. Asa Briggs and P. Burke, *A Social History of the Media: From Gutenberg to the Internet* (Oxford, 2002); Peter Burke, *A Social History of Knowledge: From Gutenberg to Diderot* (Cambridge, 2000); Adrian Johns, *The Nature of the Book: Print and Knowledge in the Making* (Chicago, IL [etc.], 1998); Daniel R. Headrick, *When Information Came of Age: Technologies of Knowledge in the Age of Reason and Revolution, 1700–1850* (New York [etc.], 2000); Michael E. Hobart and Z.S. Schiffman, *Information Ages: Literacy, Numeracy, and the Computer Revolution* (Baltimore, MD, 2000).

12. Headrick, *When Information Came of Age*, p. 8.

13. *Ibid.*

example, the development of the periodical press, encyclopaedias, and statistics) or the related technological infrastructure (such as the development of the postal system and the telegraph). If, in this respect, any attention is given to labour, it is focused mainly on the highly skilled "knowledge work" of inventors, innovators, and system-builders. The role and position of labour in these information revolutions has been mostly overlooked until now.

In his recent article "Virtual Webs, Physical Technologies, and Hidden Workers: The Spaces of Labor in Information Networks", one of the two editors of the present volume has argued that labour is almost by definition the least obvious aspect in information revolutions to analyse, where the unit of analysis in historical analyses hitherto has mostly been either technology or information.[14] Much of the labour involved in the development, maintenance, and production of information and communication technologies and networks has remained hidden by the focus on technological development, which has caused historians to look predominantly at the inventors, the successful entrepreneurs, the engineers or system-builders. The focus on information and its transmission, and, more particularly, on the growing importance, quantitatively and qualitatively, of information and communication in economic processes – both as a commodity and as an essential precondition for the functioning of increasingly complex production and administrative processes – has left the human labour involved in the production, transmission and usage of information on a daily basis largely underexposed. The major exception to this is the large body of recent work done on the position of women in the present-day Information Revolution.[15]

In order to fill what we see as a lacuna, we have taken labour as the central unit of analysis for this volume: it is from a distinctly social and historical understanding of both the role and position of labour in this

14. Greg Downey, "Virtual Webs, Physical Technologies, and Hidden Workers: The Spaces of Labor in Information Networks", *Technology and Culture*, 42 (2001), pp. 209–235.

15. For examples of studies of the position of women and the role of women's work in the field of technology and engineering in the period before the development of the electronic computer, see fn. 70 of Aristotle Tympas's contribution to this volume; on the role of women in the early development of the electronic computer, see Jennifer S. Light, "When Computers Were Women", *Technology and Culture*, 40 (1999), pp. 455–483; for a recent overview of studies on women and contemporary information technology, see Linda Shult, *Information Technology and Women's Lives: A Bibliography* (Madison, WI, 1996); for an example of the numerous studies on the position of women vis-à-vis information technology in developing countries, see Swasti Mitter and S. Rowbotham (eds), *Women Encounter Information Technology: Perspectives of the Third World* (London [etc.], 1995); other examples include Carla S. Freeman, *High Tech and High Heels in the Global Economy: Women, Work, and Pink-Collar Identities in the Caribbean* (Durham, NC, 2000); and Juliet Webster, *Shaping Women's Work: Gender, Employment and Information Technology* (London [etc.], 1996). An example of a study in which "ordinary" labour does take centre stage is Gregory J. Downey, *Telegraph Messenger Boys: Labor, Technology and Geography, 1850–1950* (New York [etc.], 2002).

latest and earlier information revolutions, and of the consequences of these information revolutions for labour, in terms of social, spatial and temporal divisions, that this volume has been compiled. Mapping out a trajectory for this project, we have formulated a number of fundamental questions:

(1) What has been the role and position of human labour in the development of various information revolutions, where one might make a distinction at the level of the shopfloor (be it a clerk's desk, a typesetter's or printer's room, a telegraph office, telephone switchboard, or a high-tech office space)?

(2) How have the technologies and practices of these information revolutions in turn influenced work and labour relations, both informational work, and noninformational work?

(3) How have spatial and temporal divisions of labour changed together with new technology-enabled spatial and temporal flows of capital and commodities? In this respect, globalization can be considered to be an inextricable phenomenon of the increasing role of information technologies (or vice versa).

The contributions brought together here explore various forms of labour in relation to developing information and communication technologies during both this latest and earlier information revolutions. Both the role of various forms and divisions of labour in these developments and the consequences of these developments for labour are dealt with in this volume. The chronological scope is the twentieth century, with the exception of Eve Rosenhaft's contribution on a particular form of white-collar, clerical work in the emerging life-insurance funds in eighteenth-century Germany. The geographical focus is predominantly on the United States. This is a direct result of the increasing US dominance in information and communication technologies in the course of the twentieth century, a dominance which has, according to many analysts of the present-day Information Revolution, contributed considerably to US dominance in the world economy over the past century.[16]

To uncover both the role and position of labour in this last and in earlier information revolutions, and the consequences of these revolutions for labour, it is useful to look at the various ways labour is (or can become) involved with developing information and communication technologies. The following subdivision might prove useful:

(1) labour involved in the invention, development, construction and maintenance of the informational infrastructures of the present-day

16. Castells, for instance, attributes the Soviet Union's failure from the 1950s onward to keep up economically with the US in large part to the fact that the Soviets missed the boat with the PC revolution; Castells, *End of Millennium*, pp. 26–37.

and earlier internetworks, such as postal, telegraph, telephone, and digital networks;[17]

(2) labour involved, in the context and structure of any one of these internetworks, in producing, using, transforming, and transmitting information;

(3) labour that is not directly involved in producing and reproducing information in the sense above, but which changes as a result of the development of information and communication technologies, particularly in the sense of being degraded or becoming redundant.

This division is schematic, and forms of labour might fall into the first two categories at the same time or develop from one category into another as a result of technological change and/or of changing social or cultural circumstances. In each of the essays in this collection, one or more of these forms of labour are dealt with.

In "Hands and Minds: Clerical Work in the First 'Information Society'", Eve Rosenhaft explores the careers of the German clerk, Anton Dies, and his successors, who were involved in the development and management of one of the survivors' pension funds that emerged in the middle of the eighteenth century. Rosenhaft situates her biographical study of these clerks in the context of a newly emerging information regime, in which governments in Germany and elsewhere in Europe attached increasing importance to collecting and processing data for administrative and governance purposes. At the same time, information came to play an increasing role in the development of mercantile capitalism. These developments led to the demand for a new information system,[18] in which the role and position of clerical work changed radically. Rosenhaft shows how the application of recently developed complex statistical techniques to generate information vital for commercial success in a high-risk commercial enterprise, the need to transmit this information, through advertisements, to the larger public while at the same time being subjected to demands of secrecy and scrutiny, and attacks from competitors aimed at personal reputations, all made for working conditions with occupational hazards comparable to the present-day dangers of repetitive strain injuries and burnout.

Another example of labour in an information revolution before this latest one is found in Deep Kanti Lahiri Choudhury's account of the Indian Telegraph General Strike of 1908. Choudhury's analysis of the strike in its larger context of a colonial state-owned telegraph industry with a racially divided labour force not only offers a nice comparison and contrast with previous work done on labour organizing and unrest in the

---

17. For the origins of the term "internetwork" see Downey, *Telegraph Messenger Boys*, p. 211, fn. 6.

18. Headrick, *When Information Came of Age*, pp. 9–11.

North American for-profit telegraph industry,[19] but also points to another
interesting phenomenon: the ability (however short-lived) of information
workers to use the information and communication technology and
infrastructure, which they operate on a daily basis, for their own purposes
in organizing and propagating a strike. Choudhury's sketch of what he
labels "India's first virtual community" points ahead to present-day
optimism among some pundits of this information revolution about the
possibilities of achieving real democracy, if not even liberation, through
the realization of the Internet's virtual promises.[20]

Going back to a period when computers were still human,[21] Aristotle
Tympas, in his contribution "Perpetually Laborious: Computing Electric
Power Transmission before the Electronic Computer", explores the
dependency on human computing labour to perform the necessary and
increasingly complex computations for the development of electric power
networks (itself a prerequisite for the electronic age that was yet to come)
in the United States in the first decades of the twentieth century. Following
on from recent work on the role of women in the development of the early
electronic computers,[22] Tympas points to the tendency within the
orthodox historiography of technology to mythologize the technical
development and underexpose the human labour involved. Focusing on
the contemporary technical literature, he shows how, paradoxically, the
desire to eliminate what was perceived as a computing labour crisis by
mechanizing computing through the development of new forms of
(mechanical and electrical) analysers, only led to new, more complex
networks, which in turn rendered the analysers obsolete and left the
dependency on human computing labour (perceived of as a computing
labour crisis) intact.

These first three contributions look either at labour involved in
producing and reproducing information infrastructures and information
systems before our present electronic information age, or at labour
producing information which exists in and through these infrastructures
and systems on a daily basis. In Bernard Dubbeld's contribution,
"Breaking the Buffalo: The Transformation of Stevedoring Work in
Durban between 1970 and 1990", the focus is on labour becoming
redundant in the present information age as a result of a technological
development in transport inextricably connected with this contemporary
Information Revolution: containerization. Dubbeld analyses the hard fate
of the Durban stevedores, whose work became increasingly casualized,

---

19. See, in this respect, especially Downey, *Telegraph Messenger Boys*.
20. See, for example, Dyer-Witheford, *Cyber-Marx*, and Fortier, *Virtuality Check*.
21. Paul Ceruzzi, "When Computers Were Human", *Annals of the History of Computing*, 13
(1991), pp. 237–244.
22. Light, "When Computers Were Women".

marginalized, and ultimately redundant as the result of the interplay between the labour politics of a racial state, the far-reaching and often contradictory consequences of technological change, and the developments and fierce competition among the international ports and in the shipping industry under late twentieth-century, neoliberal capitalism. Contrasting the situation of the Durban stevedores with that of dock labourers and other industrial workers worldwide, Dubbeld argues that the generalizing term "globalization" does insufficient justice to the importance of local conditions and contingencies in shaping technological change and its impact on labour. The same might well apply to the use of that concomitant generalization of "informatization".

The impact of containerization and ICT is also explored in the contribution by Helen Sampson and Bin Wu, who focus on the work process on board ships in the global shipping industry and the changing position and working conditions of international seafarers. Using an ethnographic, micro approach, they demonstrate how a generalizing geographical theory – David Harvey's concepts of "turnover time of capital" and "time-space compression"[23] – may fruitfully be used to analyse the experiences of the modern international seafarers.

The last three case studies in this volume all focus on the historical and geographical core of the latest Information Revolution, the late twentieth-century United States. Nathan Ensmenger explores the emergence of the computer programmer as a central figure in an ongoing debate from the 1960s onward about the role of information technology in organizational transformation. Focusing on the conflict between the craft-centred practices of the computer programmers and the "scientifically" oriented management techniques of their corporate managers, he argues that the skills and expertise that computer programmers possessed transcended traditional boundaries between business knowledge and technical expertise. With that, programmers constituted a substantial challenge to established corporate hierarchies and power structures. The debate among industrial and governmental managers on the supposed existence and persistence of a "software crisis" from the early 1960s onward – itself an interesting parallel with the idea of a computing labour crisis as described by Tympas – and the seemingly unrelenting quest of these managers to develop a software development methodology that would finally eliminate corporate dependence on the craft knowledge of individual programmers, can best be understood, according to Ensmenger, in light of this struggle over workplace authority.

Chris Benner explores the activities of "guilds" and other occupational

---

23. David Harvey, *The Condition of Postmodernity: An Enquiry into the Origins of Cultural Change* (Oxford [etc.], 1989).

communities, where skilled information technology workers in Silicon Valley, the digital Information Revolution's heartland, come together in order to share knowledge, improve career opportunities, and protect themselves from insecurity. Benner evaluates the effectiveness and the broader implications of these organizations for worker representation in the information economy. Given the rapidly changing skill requirements associated with the volatility of the information economy, these guild-like structures have a difficult time affecting labour supply or regulating standards in their occupations, and thus lack the monopoly strength that sustained their medieval and early modern antecedents. But, as the decline of workplace stability continues to undermine worksite-based representation, the attractiveness of these guild-type structures increases, and thus can be an important component of broader strategies aimed at building security for workers in the information economy.

Finally, Hector Postigo offers an intriguing story of the changing position and perception of volunteer and hobbyist work on the Internet. Against the background of the specific relationship volunteers and hobbyists historically have had with the evolution of the Net, with its idiosyncratic culture of virtuality and digital communitarism, Postigo shows how the understanding of labour, leisure, and volunteer and hobbyist labour became problematized, as the work of volunteer and hobbyists groups came to be harnessed by corporations. A number of America Online (AOL) volunteers who worked in chat-rooms, forums, and bulletin boards gradually became aware that their activities have made a shift from leisure to work and, therefore, some members of this group have started to demand compensation for their unwaged labour.

As the legal process around the claims of these AOL volunteers has still not been resolved, the story of this form of information labour connects this volume to topical issues, and with that, the history of labour in information revolutions as brought together in this volume turns full circle, from labour in an earlier era of revolutionary changes in information systems – the eighteenth century – to the present digital Information Revolution and the Internet. In the concluding contribution to this volume, the co-editor of this *IRSH* Supplement, Greg Downey, gives a commentary on the place of labour in the history and the existing historiography of information revolutions. Focusing on the US context, he analyses how the history of information-technology labour has been studied hitherto, particularly from within the fields of history of technology and human geography, and concludes that "overall the notion of 'information labor' as a historical unit of analysis is lacking any secondary synthesis or coherent body of theory", as it constantly remains hidden behind technology and/or information as units of analysis, and is often assumed to be technologically determined. The contributions to this volume, we hope, show that the history of information revolutions can be fruitfully written with labour as a historical unit of analysis. Such an approach is useful, we believe, not only to uncover the role and position of labour in historical and contemporary manifestations of revolutionary developments in information and communication technologies, but also as a much needed critical perspective on the present-day Information Revolution.

IRSH 48 (2003), Supplement, pp. 13–43 DOI: 10.1017/S0020859003001251
© 2003 Internationaal Instituut voor Sociale Geschiedenis

Hands and Minds: Clerical Work in the First "Information Society"*

Eve Rosenhaft

This article examines some aspects of the labour involved in generating, recording and transmitting information in eighteenth-century Europe. It centres on the study of a particular occupational group: the men involved in the day-to-day operations of the schemes for the marketing of life-contingent pensions which would develop into modern life insurance, a form of enterprise whose growth was deeply implicated in the emerging "information society". The bulk of the work these men did was what we would now call clerical work: keeping and processing records and accounts, managing correspondence, preparing reports for publication. It was in the nature of the information regimes within which they worked and the kind of information they were handling, though, that the responsibilities and demands placed on them went beyond those associated with the mechanical function of recording and reproducing. This made for an occupational profile which was relatively fluid, and only gradually came to be distinguishable from other contemporary forms of middle-class employment, in terms of the disciplines peculiar to it and the hazards it incurred. Among the hazards were forms of mental and physical strain that accompanied rapid increases in the volume of data that had to be handled and in the speed of its circulation, as a direct consequence of its character as "information". While the account focuses on the study of a particular kind of enterprise in a particular place, northwest Germany, it draws on comparative data for officers and staff in analogous forms of commercial and administrative employment in Britain. The article concludes with a consideration of how their occupational profile might fit into an extended account of the historical development of information work.

* This article is based on research towards a wider study of life insurance and middle-class culture in eighteenth-century Germany. Research to date has been funded by the British Academy, the German Academic Exchange Service, and the University of Liverpool. I am grateful to William J. Ashworth, Jürgen Schlumbohm, and Richard Waller for their advice and comments, and to Sylvia Möhle for inspired assistance with genealogical research on Anton Dies.

AN INFORMATION SOCIETY IN THE EIGHTEENTH CENTURY

In the conclusion to an article of 1999 outlining the work and mentality of British revenue officers in the eighteenth century, John Brewer issued an appeal for "more study of the routine work of minor functionaries".[1] This was in the context of a volume comparing German and English manifestations of the eighteenth-century state. Brewer's call was accordingly an invitation to examine "minor functionaries" in terms of their role in governance. As commonly happens when British and German historians meet, it presumed that the most interesting result of the study would be the differences it exposed, between servants of an absolutist garrison state orchestrating change in an ordered corporative society, and those of a fiscal-military state engaged in permanent negotiation with a population at best "polite and commercial" and at worst "ungovernable". If we think about the work that those "functionaries" did in generic terms, however, the similarities are equally striking. The service of British revenue officers involved collecting and processing information – discrete data about individual people, places, and things which were of use in specific practical applications that interested the state. It also required the deployment of particular forms of knowledge – weights and measures, the qualities of chemical compounds, systems of calculation. Even if we confine our view to the category of servants of the state, it is clear that the emergence of this kind of work was an international phenomenon; in the German case, historians have begun to analyse cameral government in terms of the ways in which administrative innovation depended on both the self-conscious engagement with new scientific and technical knowledges and new ways of managing data.[2]

What is equally clear is that in collecting and processing data for administrative purposes and communicating their intentions in the course of governance, states in both Britain and Germany (and not only there) contributed in different degrees to developments in the wider culture that merit the characterization "information society". Accounts of the information society inspired by late-twentieth-century developments

---

1. John Brewer, "Servants of the Public – Servants of the Crown: Officialdom of Eighteenth-Century English Central Government", in John Brewer and Eckhart Hellmuth (eds), *Rethinking Leviathan: The Eighteenth-Century State in Britain and Germany* (Oxford, 1999), pp. 127–147.
2. Henry E. Lowood, "The Calculating Forester: Quantification, Cameral Science, and the Emergence of Scientific Forestry Management in Germany", in Tore Frängsmyr, J.L. Heilbron and Robin E. Rider (eds), *The Quantifying Spirit in the 18th Century* (Berkeley, CA, 1990), pp. 315–341; R. Andre Wakefield, "The Apostles of Good Police: Science, Cameralism, and the Culture of Administration in Central Europe, 1656–1800", unpublished Ph.D. dissertation, University of Chicago, 1999; *idem*, "Chemical Police", *Science in Context*, 13 (2000), pp. 231–267.

centre on the way in which new technologies have facilitated the circulation of data, but conceive the social impact of technological change in terms both of the forms of social organization necessary to produce and sustain the technology and of changing expectations and demands on the part of its users; at each of these stages – social and material infrastructure and user demand (or consumption) – a whole range of agents is implicated, including state agencies, commercial and industrial organizations, and members of the public as individuals or in association with others.[3] "Information" in this context is something distinct from knowledge; it refers to discrete bits of knowledge, and implies an expectation of easy and relatively indiscriminate access on the presumption of their potential usefulness, such that information appears to become a commodity and the generation of information an end in itself.[4] Daniel Headrick, locating an information revolution in the eighteenth century, has accordingly described its key components in terms of organizational, computational, and representational practices which reduced complex knowledges to transparent assemblages of manageable data.[5] Organized into tables, taxonomies, and encyclopedias, these data then became available for application in the development of new knowledges and techniques – but also as items of curiosity and circulation in their own right. The sign and engine of a new information regime was the expansion of the periodical press. At differing paces in different national and regional contexts, developments in the transport and communications infrastructure responded to the demand that information be able to move as quickly as it was generated.[6] The social infrastructure, too, was transformed. Although the impetus for collecting and disseminating data might originate with the state, circulation was promoted by new social institutions which could have a purely "civil society" or a hybrid character. Reading circles and clubs merged into circulating libraries, which abandoned the vision of the library as a storehouse of knowledge for that of a place where the public could access the latest in opinions, emotional sensations, or scientific discoveries. In the German case, the same informal circles also have been

3. David Lyon, *The Information Society: Issues and Illusions* (Cambridge, 1988); John Feather, *The Information Society: A Study of Continuity and Change* (London, 1988).
4. Cf. Thomas Richards, *The Imperial Archive: Knowledge and the Fantasy of Empire* (London, 1993), p. 5 – a work which otherwise emphasizes the arcane and secretive aspects of information management in modern states.
5. Daniel Headrick, *When Information Came of Age: Technologies of Knowledge in the Age of Reason and Revolution, 1700–1850* (Oxford [etc.], 2000).
6. On the links between press circulation, postal services and road-building, see Margot Lindemann, *Deutsche Presse bis 1815* (Berlin, 1969), p. 38; Michael Harris, *London Newspapers in the Age of Walpole* (Rutherford, NJ [etc.], 1987), pp. 19–32.

described as forming the basis of a potentially political associational culture.[7]

With the rise of public finance and the growth of popular investment and speculation, the need for accurate (or plausible) information was shared by states, entrepreneurs, and private individuals. Commercial data ceased to be something communicated between merchants and brokers in a fixed geographical location (the exchange) and became a matter of public interest; information (and misinformation) about events in the realms of politics, exploration, and science and technology increasingly played a material role in individual commercial decisions which cumulatively affected the fates of nations. Information also became an object of consumption in developing consumer economies, depending as they did on the dissemination of advice about both what was to be had and what people ought to want. The "furious itch of novelty" produced an "immoderate appetite of intelligence",[8] and the passion for refining and disseminating useful knowledge associated with popular Enlightenment found its voice in the same media organs that carried advertising and a delightfully undifferentiated category: "news".[9]

INFORMATION WORK

These developments led to changes in familiar kinds of work and also to new forms of employment. As has been pointed out, the work of "minor functionaries" like revenue officers, mines inspectors, or foresters involved

7. Jürgen Habermas, *Strukturwandel der Öffentlichkeit* (Darmstadt [etc.], 1962). For examples of the extensive discussions around Habermas's concept of "public-sphere" work, see Craig Calhoun (ed.), *Habermas and the Public Sphere* (Cambridge, MA, 1992); Peter Uwe Hohendahl (ed.), *Öffentlichkeit. Geschichte eines kritischen Begriffs* (Stuttgart [etc.], 2000).
8. From *The British Mercury* of 1712, cited by Robert Iliffe, "Author-Mongering: The 'Editor' between Producer and Consumer", in Ann Bermingham and John Brewer (eds), *The Consumption of Culture 1600–1800: Image, Object, Text* (London [etc.], 1995), pp. 166–192, 166.
9. On the role of commercial information in the emergence of modern capitalism, see Larry Neal, *The Rise of Financial Capitalism* (Cambridge, 1993), pp. 20–43. For studies that emphasize the centrality of broadly commercial impulses to the development of a "print-based public sphere", see Colin Jones, "The Great Chain of Buying: Medical Advertisement, the Bourgeois Public Sphere, and the Origins of the French Revolution", in Ronald Schechter (ed.), *The French Revolution: The Essential Readings* (London, 2001), pp. 138–174; Shelley Costa, "Marketing Mathematics in Early Eighteenth-Century England: Henry Beighton, Certainty and the Public Sphere", *History of Science*, 40 (2002), pp. 211–232. See also Peter Burke, *A Social History of Knowledge: From Gutenberg to Diderot* (Cambridge, 2000), pp. 149–176. On early advertising in Germany, see Heidrun Homburg, "Werbung – 'eine Kunst, die gelernt sein will'. Aufbrüche in eine neue Warenwelt 1750–1850", *Jahrbuch für Wirtschaftsgeschichte*, (1997:1), pp. 11–52. For an anthropologist's interpretation of consumption as an "information system", see Mary Douglas and Baron Isherwood, *The World of Goods: Towards an Anthropology of Consumption*, 2nd edn (London, 1996).

specialist knowledges and techniques for recording and managing data which were new and subject to the expectation of continuous refinement. Other kinds of workers found their ancient duties supplemented by the needs of the state to inform and be informed: German Protestant ministers had always been responsible for a certain amount of record-keeping, maintaining the parish register and keeping the minutes of church consistories. In eighteenth-century rural parishes, their responsibilities were enlarged by having to extract vital statistics from the register for the use of public officials and supervise the circulation and cataloguing of official notices sent from the centres of government.[10] In banking and mercantile enterprises, the routine work of record-keeping expanded in volume with the multiplication of the categories of relevant information and the growth in the number of users,[11] while new forms of enterprise emerged that depended entirely on the collection and management of information from a wide range of sources; the best example of this is insurance. Beyond this, the demand for information and its multifarious uses, the widening awareness of what was knowable combined with the increasing ease of circulation, generated an information regime in which all actors in the public realm were subject to a new degree of scrutiny. The result was that information control was added to the work of clerical and administrative staff in both state and private employment.

Greg Downey has commented on the tendency of both academic and popular discussions of today's information society to overlook or suppress the human labour involved in information networks.[12] In the case of contemporary information systems, this blindness is a function of a technology so advanced that it seems to "do" itself. Paradoxically, the labour that sustained the first information society has also remained largely invisible in the literature, but (I suspect) largely because of its "low-tech" quality. Unlike telegraphers and telephonists, whose work has been

---

10. David Warren Sabean, "Peasant Voices and Bureaucratic Texts: Narrative Structures in Early Modern German Protocols", in Peter Becker and William Clark (eds), *Little Tools of Knowledge: Historical Essays on Academic and Bureaucratic Practices* (Ann Arbor, MI, 2001), pp. 67–93; Reiner Prass, "Die Brieftasche des Pfarrers. Wege der Übermittlung von Informationen in ländlichen Kirchengemeinden des Fürstentums Minden", in Ralf Pröve and Norbert Winnige (eds), *Wissen ist Macht. Herrschaft und Kommunikation in Brandenburg-Preußen 1600–1850* (Berlin, 2001), pp. 69–82.

11. H.M. Boot, "Salaries and Career Earnings in the Bank of Scotland, 1730–1880", *Economic History Review*, 4 (1991), pp. 629–653, 631. Boot comments that, in spite of the increased volume of business, the number of tellers only doubled, while clerks more than trebled and domestic and portering staff increased five-fold; the differential degrees of increase suggest that there was a multiplier effect such that an increase in the volume of "front office" business led to a still greater growth in the demands on internal record-keeping, external accountability, and correspondence.

12. Greg Downey, "Virtual Webs, Physical Technologies, and Hidden Workers: The Spaces of Labor in Information Networks", *Technology and Culture*, 42 (2001), pp. 209–235.

the subject of historical research, early modern information workers cannot be perceived as directly subject to the rhythms of a new mechanical or technical process. Even printing was no longer new in the eighteenth century. Nor did all public communication take printed form. Robert Darnton has described mid-eighteenth-century Paris as an "information society", in spite of the paucity of printed news media that resulted from a tight government controls; in France a considerable part of the eighteenth-century hunger for news was fed by manuscript sheets produced in workshops full of copyists.[13] The more important innovations were the "technologies of knowledge" (Headrick) which made information into something available and desirable. It was the pressure placed on familiar resources (both muscles and nerves)[14] by changing demand that made the handling of information a new kind of work.

Recent work in the history of modern science has taught us to see the production of knowledge in this period in terms of labour process. We now see the laboratory as a space in which both the actions of scientists and their cognitive consequences are mediated through contingent forms of social organization, within the scientific workplace and in the wider community of those interested in the "product".[15] It has been shown how the observation and recording of data required not only collective effort but the imposition of new disciplines on the body of the observer, and new controls on those charged with keeping records.[16] Conversely, we have learned that the emergence of modern machine calculation or cybernetics involved self-conscious reflection on the character of mental calculation as a laborious process, in terms that echoed the discourses of labour discipline generated by emergent industrialism.[17] All of these approaches remind us

13. Robert Darnton, "An Early Information Society: News and Media in Eighteenth-Century Paris", *American Historical Review*, 105 (2000), pp. 1–35. On the persistence of manuscript culture, see François Moureau, "La plume et le plomb", in F. Moureau (ed.), *De bonne main. La communication manuscrite au XVIIIe siècle* (Oxford, 1993), pp. 5–16. On the social impact of printing before mechanization, see most recently the exchange between Elizabeth L. Eisenstein and Adrian Johns, "AHR Forum: How Revolutionary was the Print Revolution?", *American Historical Review*, 107 (2002), pp. 84–128.
14. Cf. Laura Levine Frader, "From Muscles To Nerves: Gender, 'Race', and the Body at Work in France 1919–1939", *International Review of Social History*, 44 (1999), Supplement 7, pp. 123–147.
15. The *locus classicus* for this approach to the "scientific revolution" is still Steven Shapin and Simon Schaffer, *Leviathan and the Air Pump: Hobbes, Boyle and the Experimental Life* (Princeton, NJ, 1985).
16. Simon Schaffer, "Astronomers Mark Time: Discipline and the Personal Equation", *Science in Context*, 2 (1988), pp. 115–145; William J. Ashworth, "The Calculating Eye: Baily, Herschel, Babbage and the Business of Astronomy", *British Journal of the History of Science*, 27 (1994), pp. 409–441, 434–437.
17. Andrew Warwick, "The Laboratory of Theory, or What's Exact About the Exact Sciences?", in Norton Wise (ed.), *The Values of Precision* (Princeton, NJ, 1995), pp. 311–351; William J. Ashworth, "Memory, Efficiency and Symbolic Analysis: Charles Babbage, John Herschel and the Industrial Mind", *Isis*, 87 (1996), pp. 629–653.

that there is work going on in what we always pictured as a sweat-free zone, and draw our attention also to the way in which knowledge-based discourse is productive of new realities, what Theodore Porter (in a discussion of the "craft dimension of quantification") refers to as "the administrative creation of new things".[18] Similarly, research on early modern print culture has moved from an exclusive focus on the texts to consider the social and material infrastructure for their production and circulation.[19] Studies of both laboratory and "literatory" (Adrian Johns) life, as also of the business of public administration, are thus increasingly giving attention to "how things worked". In the process they are beginning to illuminate the spaces in which the quotidian labour took place that made innovation possible.[20]

THE CALENBERG

This essay looks into one of those spaces, to examine the ordinary but indispensable work of generating, storing, and moving bits of knowledge using (mainly) pen and paper. It examines the situation of a particular group of "minor functionaries": clerical workers in the emerging life-insurance business. Specifically, these were men involved in schemes for the provision of survivors' pensions, or widows' funds. Widows' funds were created all over northern Europe, beginning in the late seventeenth century; in Germany, there were two waves of founding, one around 1700 and a second at mid-century. They were typically created on an associational basis by groups of middle-class men (in the first instance, usually clergy), although in the German lands some of them were promoted by territorial governments. They offered pensions for widows, at levels guaranteed in advance, on the basis of a cash deposit and regular contributions over the lifetime of the husband. Their operations were more

18. Theodore M. Porter, *Trust in Numbers: The Pursuit of Objectivity in Science and Public Life* (Princeton, NJ, 1995), p. 47.
19. Adrian Johns, *The Nature of the Book: Print and Knowledge in the Making* (Chicago [etc.], 1998); Pamela E. Selwyn, *Everyday Life in the German Book Trade: Friedrich Nicolai as Bookseller and Publisher in the Age of Enlightenment 1750–1810* (University Park, PA, 2000); Robert Darnton, *The Business of Enlightenment: A Publishing History of the Encyclopédie 1775–1800* (Cambridge, MA, 1979). In continental library history, attention to the day-to-day work of the staff of circulating libraries remains a desideratum; see Roger Chartier, *The Order of Books: Readers, Authors and Libraries in Europe between the Fourteenth and Eighteenth Centuries*, Lydia G. Cochrane (transl.) (Cambridge, 1994); Jeffrey Garrett, "Redefining Order in the German Library 1775–1825", *Eighteenth-Century Studies*, 33 (1999), pp. 103–123; Kurt Habitzel and Günter Mühlberger, "Die Leihbibliotheksforschung in Deutschland, Österreich und der Schweiz: Ergebnisse und Perspektiven", *Internationales Archiv für Sozialgeschichte der deutschen Literatur*, 22 (1997), pp. 66–108.
20. See, for example, Steven Shapin's chapter on Robert Boyle's technicians and servants: Steven Shapin, *A Social History of Truth: Civility and Science in Seventeenth-Century England* (Chicago [etc.], 1994), pp. 355–408; Wakefield, "The Apostles of Good Police", pp. 1–42.

primitive than those of the modern life insurance schemes that succeeded them. Indeed their almost universal experience of financial failure has been seen as the necessary precondition for the emergence of full-blown premium insurance in the late eighteenth century. In the German case, it is clear that the collapse of a number of large funds in the glare of nationwide publicity from the late 1770s onwards spurred the reception of statistical probabilism there. But their founders did practise a form of actuarial accounting, scaling contributions to the ages of husband and wife on the basis of principles gleaned from the study of tables of mortality. In this sense, the widows' funds, like premium life insurance, were highly information-sensitive; they depended on the effective application of accurate data, and the men who worked for them from mid-century onwards were continuously involved in studying new mortality statistics and devising new ways of reading and applying them. Widows' funds were also implicated in information networks by virtue of their dependence on advertising and publicity. What distinguished these funds from more traditional forms of mutual provision for social security was that they recruited from the general public and increasingly relied on continuous recruiting, or continuous growth, to sustain their operations. This implied both a convincing address to the public and competition among funds for customers as well as for information and technical expertise.[21]

The present account is based on the manuscript and published records of the largest of the German funds, the Calenbergische Witwen-Verpflegungs-Gesellschaft, or Calenberg, and focuses on the men who made their careers in the new enterprise. Founded in Hanover in 1766, the Calenberg was exceptional among contemporary widows' funds, but in ways that make it useful as an extreme exemplar of the features set out above. It was created and operated by an organ of state, the territorial estates (*Landschaft*) of the Hanoverian Principality of Calenberg. The fund was administered by the Treasury Committee of the *Landschaft*, and all decisions were subject to ratification by the Crown Office, King George III's viceregal deputies in Hanover. At the same time it was a highly public enterprise. For complicated operational reasons, it was peculiarly reliant on continuous growth, and adopted an exceptionally adventurous approach to recruitment, being the only fund in Germany to recruit not only beyond the borders of the Hanoverian territory but all

---

21. J.C. Riley, "'That Your Widows May Be Rich': Providing for Widowhood in Old Regime Europe", *Economisch- en sociaal-historisch jaarboek*, 45 (1982), pp. 58–76; Bernd Wunder, "Pfarrwitwenkassen und Beamtenwitwen-Anstalten vom 16.–19. Jahrhundert", *Jahrbuch für historische Forschung*, 12 (1985), pp. 429–498; Geoffrey Wilson Clark, *Betting on Lives: Life Insurance in English Society and Culture 1695–1775* (Manchester, 1999); Ludwig Arps, *Auf sicheren Pfeilern. Deutsche Versicherungswirtschaft vor 1914* (Göttingen, 1965); Peter Borscheid, *Mit Sicherheit leben. Die Geschichte der deutschen Lebensversicherungswirtschaft und der Provinzial-Lebensversicherungsanstalt von Westfalen* (Greven, 1989).

over Europe.²² It was consequently the largest widows' fund in Germany (possibly in Europe) at the point when it went into crisis in 1779–1780, but one that was exposed both to intense competition and, once the crisis set in, to scrutiny from many quarters.

ANTON DIES: A CAREER IN INFORMATION MANAGEMENT

The first man to carry significant responsibility for the day-to-day operation of the Calenberg was Anton Dies. All the indications are that he was a self-made man.²³ He was born in Hanover 1726, the youngest of seven children of an invalid soldier. There is no evidence that he attended any university, and his lack of higher education is further suggested by the fact that he married at the age of twenty-two; his bride, the daughter of a corporal, was in an advanced stage of pregnancy at the time. Dies was someone whose entire life was defined by his involvement with information in its various forms, as his career took him from one innovative institution to another.

Dies's first recorded appointment was in the Hanover Intelligenz-Comtoir, or information office, which opened in 1750.²⁴ Information offices were characteristic institutions of enlightened territorial government in Germany: clearing-houses for official notices, news, job offers and enquiries, notices of goods for sale, items lost and found, and so on. Of uncertain genealogy, the Intelligenz-Comtoir was surrounded in public discourse with the aura that reflected the hopes of a new information age.

22. On the history of the Calenberg widows' fund, see Reinhard Oberschelp, *Niedersachsen 1760–1820*, 2 vols (Hildesheim, 1982), vol. 1, pp. 230–237; William Boehart, *"[...] nicht brothlos und nothleidend zu hinterlassen"* (Hamburg, 1985). I have dealt with aspects of demand, recruitment, operation, and crisis in the Calenberg and other German widows' funds in two forthcoming articles: Eve Rosenhaft, "But the Heart Must Speak for the Widows: The Origins of Life Insurance in Germany and the Gender Implications of Actuarial Science", in Marion Gray and Ulrike Gleixner (eds), *Gender in Transmission: Breaks and Continuities in German-Speaking Europe 1750–1850* (Ann Arbor, MI, 2003); idem, "Did Women Invent Life Insurance? Widows and the Demand for Financial Services in Eighteenth-Century Germany", in David R. Green and Alastair Owens (eds), *Family Welfare: Gender, Property and Inheritance Since the Seventeenth Century* (Westport, CT, 2003).
23. Heinrich Wilhem Rotermund, *Das gelehrte Hannover*, vol. 1 (Hanover, 1823) (as cited in *Deutsches Biographisches Archiv*). For data on Dies's family, see Jürgen Ritter (ed.), *Garnison-Kirchenbuch Hannover 1690–1811*, vols 3 and 4 (Hanover, 1990–1991), entries 7951 (Pape) and 10752 (Ties); entries in the registers of St Aegidien, Marktkirche, and Neustädter Hof- und Stadtkirche, Evangelisches Kirchenbuchamt Hanover.
24. Preface to bound volume of first half-year (1750) of *Hannoverische Gelehrte Anzeigen*. The records of the Hanover Intelligenz-Comtoir were destroyed in 1943, along with other holdings of the Niedersächsisches Hauptstaatsarchiv, Hanover; the original files began in 1732, suggesting that the institution was under consideration from a relatively early date; see letter from the Archives to the author, 30 September 2002.

The earliest German proposal for the creation of an Intelligenz-Comtoir, published by Wilhelm von Schröder in 1683, began as an exercise in cameralist thinking, but culminated in the utopian vision of a single, universal market in which the rapid and unimpeded flow of information would promote the free circulation of goods and money.[25] Eighteenth-century writers celebrated the Intelligenz-Comtoir as an agency for social integration; it could both aid strangers to find their way in the city and bind together the citizens who participated in the sharing of information, translating a common curiosity into a common interest.[26] The principal means by which the latter effect was to be achieved was the publication of printed intelligencers. Some 220 separate regionally circulating intelligencers (*Intelligenzblätter* or *Anzeiger*) formed the basis for a popular press in eighteenth-century Germany, as many expanded to include longer critical and scientific articles while others remained essentially news-sheets but increased their frequency of publication.[27] In some towns, the Intelligenz-Comtoir also operated a circulating library.[28] Working in the Intelligenz-Comtoir, Dies might thus have had any one (or more) of a number of functions: receiving and registering items of information delivered from Crown or local administrative offices or brought into the office or posted by individuals; keeping accounts; writing up or editing copy for the intelligencer; fetching books, recording loans and returns, or corresponding about unpaid fees or lost or damaged books in the library. This involved an interface with the information-hungry and information-sensitive public which could be problematic. Order had to be maintained

25. Wilhelm Freyherr von Schröder, *Fürstliche Schatz- und Rent-Kammer* (Leipzig, 1704), pp. 393–407.
26. E, "Über das Intelligenzwesen", *Braunschweigisches Magazin*, 1788/1, col. 1–16: reprinted in Reinhard Oberschelp, *Niedersächsische Texte 1756–1820* (Hildesheim, 1983), pp. 320–327; "Kurze Nachricht von dem vermuthlich ersten Vorschlag, ein Intelligenz-Comtoir anzulegen", *Hannoverisches Magazin*, 1764/2, col. 1463–68. Cf. Homburg, "Werbung", pp. 20–25; Lindemann, *Deutsche Presse*, pp. 248–255. Peter Burke cites developments of this kind outside Germany, noting the intimate historical relationship between the rise of urbanism and the anonymity and uncertainty of city life and the demand for information (in practice, the intelligencers also brought information generated in the urban centres to the rural elites); see Burke, *Social History*, pp. 70–74. Gilles Feyel, *L'Annonce et la nouvelle. La presse d'information en France sous l'Ancien Régime (1630–1788)* (Oxford, 2000), provides a sketch of the the operation of French information offices (pp. 454–456 and 796–814), and outlines the mutual influence of English, French and German models (pp. 605–629) for the information office and the printed intelligencer.
27. Holger Böning, "Das Intelligenzblatt – eine literarisch-publizistische Gattung des 18. Jahrhunderts", *Internationales Archiv für die Sozialgeschichte der deutschen Literatur*, 19 (1994), pp. 22–32 (review article); Bernd Wunder, "Vom Intelligenzblatt zum Gesetzblatt. Zur Zentralisierung inner- und außeradministrativer Normkommunikation in Deutschland (17./18. Jahrhundert)", *JEV – Jahrbuch für europäische Verwaltungsgeschichte*, 9 (1997), pp. 29–82.
28. *Verzeichniss derjenigen [...] Bücher und neuesten deutschen Schriften, welche in der im hiesigen Intelligenz-Comtoir [...] ausgeliehen werden* (Göttingen, 1769).

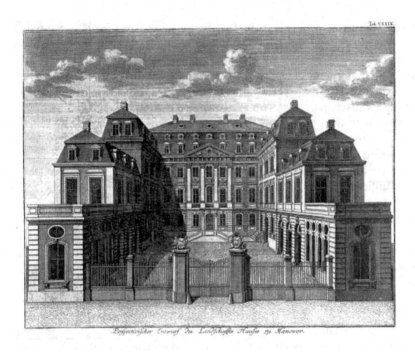

Figure 1. The Landschaftshaus in Hanover, built 1712. The office provided for the Registrator in the original plans was on the first floor (Bel-étage) at the rear, overlooking a garden.
From: Johann Friedrich von Penther, Vierter Theil einer ausführlichen Anleitung zur bürgerlichen Bau-Kunst *(Augsburg, 1748).*
Reproduction courtesy of Historisches Museum Hannover.

among people who gathered inside and outside the office, sometimes to complain about something that had been published. And individuals placing or responding to advertisements would persist in corresponding via the Intelligenz-Comtoir, thus adding to the already considerable business of writing and forwarding letters.[29]

For a man with intellectual ambitions and the urge to serve the public good, there were advantages to being at the nexus of public communication, too. That Dies was such a one is evidenced by his participation in a kind of actuarial quiz run by the Hanover intelligencer in 1760.[30] Dies's

29. For examples of problems, see Decrees of Karl, Duke of Braunschweig and Lüneburg, on the management of the Braunschweig Intelligenz-Comtoir, 29 November 1745 and 31 January 1746, in Staats- und Universitätsbibliothek Göttingen; "Nachricht, die Hannoverischen Anzeigen betreffend", *Nützliche Sammlungen vom Jahre 1757*, 3, not paginated.
30. A. Dies, "Fünfte Beantwortung des ausserordentlichen Gerichtsvorfalls", *Hannoverische Beyträge zum Nutzen und Vergnügen*, 1760/2, no. 61 (1 August 1760), col. 971f. The task was to solve a problem involving the distribution of an inheritance in the unanticipated case of twins being born.

appointment to a position at the Intelligenz-Comtoir probably dates from that year; it took place at the instance of the manager of the office, Albrecht Christoph von Wüllen, who had known Dies at least since 1755, when he stood as godfather to Dies's first-born son.[31] In Hanover, the Intelligenz-Comtoir was administered by the *Landschaft* and housed in its assembly house (*Landschaftshaus*). The annual prize essay competitions promoted by the Göttingen Scientific Society were sponsored by the *Landschaft* from the income of the Intelligenz-Comtoir. In 1763 and 1764, at the prompting of the *Landschaft*, the Society selected as the topic for the prize in economics the best way to organize a widows' fund. Dies submitted an essay under the title *Patriae sacrum* for the second round, and, while he failed to win the prize, the essay was deemed worthy of publication.[32] Through the continuing patronage of von Wüllen, Dies was drawn into the process of planning what would become the Calenberg, carrying out all the necessary calculations.[33] In April 1767, the fund went into operation. On 7 May, Dies was appointed keeper of accounts (*Rechnungs-Führer*) to the new widows' fund, with the formal title of Registrator.[34]

Von Wüllen had already approached Dies about taking up the post in November 1766. Dies's reply is an illuminating document of both the material circumstances and the mentality of eighteenth-century information-tion workers. He avowed that the question of the size of his salary had made for a sleepless night. His response was to enumerate his household, beginning with his six children, "who thank God are fresh and healthy and like to eat. My desire to raise them to fortune and see that they are taught as much as will go into their heads is as strong as a father's can be".[35] He "costed" them at 50 Rtl a head, as he did the nurse and housemaid in his employ, and himself and his wife at 100 Rtl each. Five of his children were under twelve, and this meant that any landlord in a desirable neighbour-hood would charge a premium for the disturbance. If a separate office were needed, too, he would need 60 Rtl for rent and 40 Rtl for fuel. While he

31. This is clear from a letter of Dies written in 1766; see Pro Memoria (Dies to von Wüllen), 1 November 1766, Niedersächsisches Hauptstaatsarchiv Hannover (HStAHann), Dep. 7B, vol. 326I, pp. 130–132.
32. On the prize competition: *Göttingische Anzeigen von gelehrten Sachen* 1763, no. 138, p. 1116; 1764, no. 89, pp. 714–715; 1765, no. 95/96, pp. 769–771; 1766, no. 154, p. 1226; Johann David Michaelis, "Nöthige Aufmerksamkeit, die man bey Vorschlägen zu Einlegung guter Witwencassen beobachten muß", in *idem*, *Vermischte Schriften*, 2 vols (Frankfurt a. M., 1766–1769), vol. 2, pp. 99–117.
33. Minutes of a meeting of the Treasury Committee 26 March 1767, HStAHann, Dep. 7B, vol. 326II, pp. 339–342.
34. "Instruction für den zu der Calenbergischen allgemeinen Witwen Verpflegungsgesellschaft bestellten Rechnungsführer Registrator Dies", HStAHann, Hann. 93, vol. 3706, pp. 316–320.
35. At least one of Dies's children proved a disappointment in this respect, but became more famous than his father: Albert Christoph, born in 1755, abandoned the academic path marked out for him and apprenticed himself to a painter; he became a well-known landscape artist: *Deutsches Biographisches Archiv*.

conceded the principle that two could live as cheaply as one, he also pointed out that his estimate took no account of the need to save for "christenings, sickness, death and the like". His conclusion aimed at the right balance of humility and firmness, inviting his patron to acknowledge that "in the past few years I really have earned as much, and more", while recognizing the grace of God in providing him with a patron who had given him the opportunity to do so – "even against my will". Grateful to have been given the chance to serve his country, and wanting nothing more than the means to continue, he closed with an expression of guarded confidence in the Treasury Committee, "of which I am assured that it knows how to set a wage according to the workload and the circumstances of the time, *which is no longer the last century*".[36]

In the event, Dies was awarded not the 700 Rtl he had claimed, but 500 Rtl a year payable semi-annually – a middling income which placed him financially among postmasters, provincial non-graduate physicians, other clerical and administrative staff in state service, and the highest-earning skilled tradesmen.[37] The members of the Treasury Committee regarded this as relatively generous, but were prepared to recommend it to the Crown on the grounds that they intended to forbid Dies from undertaking any other form of paid work without their express permission, "lest he be distracted in his work". Nor was he permitted to act as an agent for any subscriber (policyholder) or group of subscribers. Dies's *Caution* – the surety required of all staff charged with the handling of money – was set at 3,000 Rtl, two-thirds of which was guaranteed in the first instance by a certain Johann Christoph Eisendecker.[38]

Dies's duties were spelled out in a set of instructions. He was to process applications for membership and the supporting documents (proof of age and health of both husband and wife); keep minutes of the meetings which considered applications; correspond with applicants and their agents; and fill in the membership certificates. Dies had to be present on the occasions when the Treasurer received and returned subscribers' deposits to keep a record of all payments. He was to keep a careful record of all those joining the fund and of all who left, whether through resignation, remarriage, or death, to work out what was owing to them in returned contributions or dowry payments (widows were offered a lump sum in lieu of dowry as incentive to remarry), to draw down the money from the Treasurer and pay it out. Every six months he was to produce an account of pensions owed for the Committee, and, on their authorization, draw down the required funds and pay the pensions directly to the widows or their agents,

36. Pro Memoria (Dies to von Wüllen), 1 November 1766, emphasis mine.
37. *Anhang zu der Personensteuer-Verordnung für die Fürstentümer Calenberg und Göttingen vom 9. August 1763*, in Oberschelp, *Niedersächsische Texte*, pp. 148–158.
38. PM Brandes, 10 August 1767 and Crown Office to *Landschaft*, 19 April 1768, HStAHann, Hann. 93, vol. 3706, pp. 337–338, 361.

who came to the *Landschaftshaus* to collect them; here too he was to maintain a journal and a file of receipts. Once the pensions had been disbursed, Dies had to work out the subscribers' contributions for the next half-year: In the Calenberg, subscribers contracted for a certain number of units, or *Simpla*, reflecting both the size of the pension contracted for and the ages of husband and wife. The money value of the *Simplum* was recalculated every six months in the light of current charges on the fund (notably the size of the last pensions bill) and predicted income.[39] When a rate was approved, subscribers had to be notified. Notification of the contribution rates took place in the context of a general account, published twice a year, which reported on current membership numbers, pensions owing, income, and outgoings, and also included news of changes in regulations. These *Avertissements*, which in Dies's time could be up to eight pages long, were issued as separate publications for posting to subscribers; the Treasury Committee also made a point of seeing that the reports, or digests of them, were placed in the principal intelligencers.[40] Beyond simply calculating the rate for the *Simplum*, then, Dies had to draw up semi-annual tabulations of membership, income, and outgoings and to draft the *Avertissements* for publication. The original instructions provided for him to produce in duplicate semi-annual lists of all individual subscribers, wives and widows and their details, showing (as appropriate) their ages, number of *Simpla* or pension payable, and dates of death or remarriage, with all supporting documentation attached. Once the contributions rates were known, subscribers or their agents had to come to the *Landschaftshaus* to make payment, and it was Dies's job to take the payments in, record them, and pass the money on to the Treasurer. He was responsible for keeping a record of subscribers whose contributions were in arrears, issuing reminders, and making arrangements for persistent defaulters to be expelled from the fund. He was strictly forbidden to hold more than 3,000 Rtl at any one time, or to handle fund money at home. During the six months of the year designated for admitting new subscribers and making and receiving payments, he was obliged to spend every morning from 9 am to 12 noon in an office in the *Landschaftshaus*. Beyond these specific tasks, the document prescribed a wider duty of care; the very first obligation laid on Dies, after the injunction to follow the orders and instructions of the *Landschaft* Treasury Committee which administered the fund, was "to foster the interests of the society according to the best of his knowledge and conscience, and as far as is in his power forestall any damage or disadvantage".

---

39. *Verordnung, behuef der von Calenbergischer Landschaft anzulegenden Witwen-Verpflegungs-Gesellschaft* (14 October 1766), HStAHann, Cal. Br. 23b, vol. 579 (n.p.).
40. See, for example, a letter from the publisher of the *Hamburgischer Correspondent* to the Treasury Committee, 23 May 1767, and attached copy of the *Hamburgischer Correspondent* for 9 May 1767, HStAHann, Dep. 7B, vol. 326II, pp. 208–210.

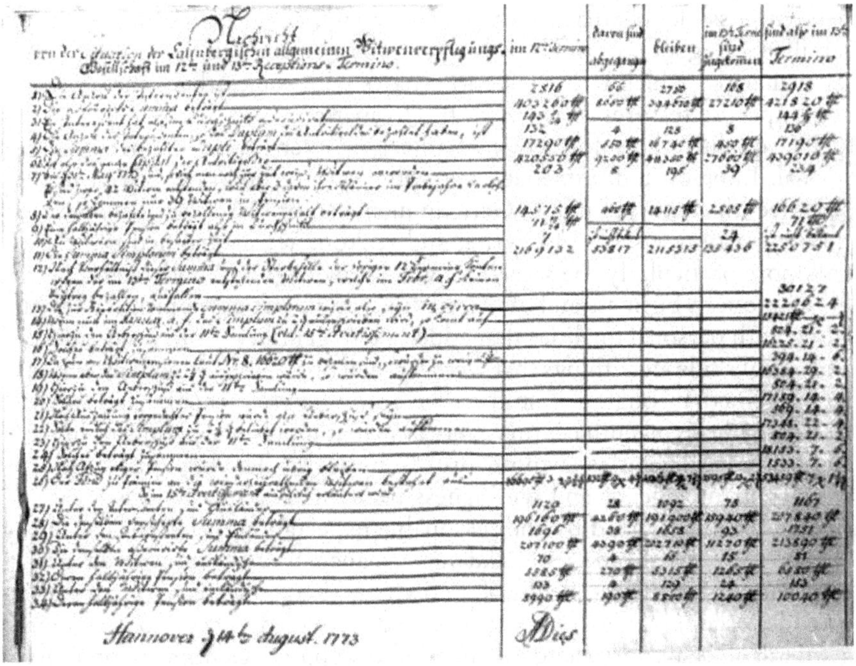

Figure 2. The Calenberg semi-annual report for August 1783, in Anton Dies's hand. *Niedersächsisches Hauptstaatsarchiv Hannover. Reproduced with permission.*

DIES AMONG INFORMATION WORKERS, INFORMATION WORKERS AMONG CLERICAL WORKERS

Before going on to relate how Dies's job developed, it is worthwhile pausing to consider the occupational and career profile represented by the terms and method of his employment. His experience in this respect offers points of comparison with that of some contemporary groups on which published data are available. These include clerks, secretaries, and minor officials in more conventional forms of public service in Germany, and employees in merchant houses, insurance offices, and banks. They also include the employees and officers of two British institutions which in some respects mark the poles between which Dies's work was situated: the Excise and the Royal Society.[41] There are many points of overlap which

41. What follows is based on: Luise Schorn-Schütte, *Evangelische Geistlichkeit in der Frühneuzeit* (Gütersloh, 1996); Stefan Brakensiek, *Fürstendiener – Staatsbeamte – Bürger. Amtsführung und Lebenswelt der Ortsbeamten in niederhessischen Kleinstädten (1750–1830)* (Göttingen, 1999); Hartmut Dahlweid, "Verwaltung und Verwaltungspersonal in Lippe im 18. Jahrhundert", in Neithart Bulst, Jochen Hoock, and Wolfgang Kaiser (eds), *Die Grafschaft Lippe im 18. Jahrhundert. Bevölkerung, Wirtschaft und Gesellschaft eines deutschen Kleinstaates* (Bielefeld, 1993), pp. 303–369; Jacob M. Price (ed.), "Directions for the Conduct of a Merchant's Counting House, 1766" (a document from the records of Herries & Company, London),

make it possible to situate Dies in a broad and, to the eighteenth century, familiar category of middle-class employment. There are also some particularities which Dies's situation shares with some others, that suggest some specific features of work with information.

The qualifications for work of this kind were as much personal as formal. Literacy and numeracy were obvious preconditions. Even in the seventeenth century, though, German manuals for secretaries emphasized that any artisan could read, write, and reckon. What qualified the clerk, and more particularly the secretary, was knowledge and understanding of his employer's business and of the methods and practices appropriate to it, along with personal qualities that added up to gentility. Both occupational and social skills were things that were learned on the job, though much was to be gained through self-study. The formularies, manuals, and advice books of the eighteenth century were aimed as much at aspirants to higher clerical employment as at those already in post.[42] The key qualifications were thus intelligence and willingness to learn. The reward was a career structure characterized by the reasonable expectation of internal promotion on the basis of experience and performance. Work that involved direct engagement with new fields of knowledge and new technologies also provided scope for self-realization, and provided access to the more gentlemanly status associated with membership in a scientific community. Dies's ambition to combine his accounting duties with more speculative or inventive work in applied mathematics echoes the experience of officers of the Royal Society. Edmond Halley, for example, began his career in 1685/1686 as clerk to the Society. The position involved nothing more eminent than assisting the secretaries, fair-copying letters and minutes, and transcribing letters received, and he took it on in the midst of a crisis incurred by the secretaries' increasing workload. Halley not only successfully fulfilled his clerical duties, but managed at the same time to

Business History, 28 (1986), pp. 134–150; *Merkwürdige Lebensbeschreibungen verschiedener Kaufleute und Handlungsdiener nach ihren glücklichen und unglücklichen Gebegenheiten*, 3 vols (Hamburg [etc.], 1771, 1772, 1780). Boot, "Salaries and Career Earnings"; *idem*, "Real Incomes of the British Middle Class, 1760–1850: The Experience of the East India Company", *Economic History Review* 52 (1999), pp. 636–668; John Brewer, *The Sinews of Power: War, Money and the English State 1688–1783* (Cambridge, MA, 1990), pp. 80, 108–112; *idem*, "Servants of the Public"; H.W. Robinson, "The Administrative Staff of the Royal Society 1663–1861", *Notes and Records of the Royal Society of London*, 4 (1946), pp. 193–205; Henry Horwitz, "Record-Keepers in the Court of Chancery and Their 'Record' of Accomplishment in the Seventeenth and Eighteenth Centuries", *Historical Research*, 70, no. 171 (1997), pp. 34–51; P.G.M. Dickson, *The Sun Insurance Office 1710–1960* (London, 1960), pp. 32–61; Rolf Engelsing, "Die wirtschaftliche und soziale Differenzierung der deutschen kaufmännischen Angestellten in In- und Ausland 1690–1900", in *Zur Sozialgeschichte deutscher Mittel- und Unterschichten* (Göttingen, 1978), pp. 55–111.

42. One example for many: *Teutsche Sekretariat-Kunst [...] herausgegeben von dem Spaten*, 4 parts in 2 vols (Jena, 1681), part 1, p. 7. This book of instructions for secretaries went into four editions, the last published in 1726.

carry out the scientific investigations and publishing activities which would qualify him for later posts at the Mint and as Astronomer Royal.[43]

The formal disciplines imposed on workers generally reflect the absence of a fixed division of labour, rather than being obviously designed to enforce one. One discipline common to all of these occupations was discretion; it was common for men with administrative responsibilities in public service to be formally sworn to secrecy, and this was also the practice in eighteenth-century German pension funds. Dies's promise to defend the fund from harm implied that he would not reveal vital information. Secrecy, of course, protected the employer (as well as the customers to whose private circumstances a worker might be privy). At the same time, the expectation of confidentiality was a natural concomitant of the understanding that workers of this kind were more than simply operatives, and that the quality of their contribution to the enterprise depended on their understanding of its internal operations. Control of their own public utterance was part of the price they paid in turn for the prospect of promotion. Similarly, employers' exhortations to method and order implied a continuing degree of individual discretion in the management of tasks. In Dies's case, the stipulation of times for attendance in the office related directly and solely to his responsibilites for meeting the public. Contemporary instructions for merchants' clerks were firmer about attendance, but describe relatively informal systems of time-keeping associated with an expectation of collegiality and work-sharing among employees. One exception here is the work of British excise officers who, working in the field without direct supervision, were subject to an elaborate regime of self-accounting. This regime can be seen as a function, among other things, of the Excise's character as a machine for generating information – both knowledge directly relevant to the raising of public finance and, increasingly, statistical data for general administrative purposes. At the same time, (by John Brewer's account) these officers successfully resisted seeing themselves as "cogs", and indeed the fact that much depended on their personal responsibility and their skill and inventiveness in the application of technical knowledge demanded that discipline be balanced with leeway.[44]

Excise officers shared with Dies a relatively unusual feature of his terms of employment, namely the ban on supplementary sources of income. In other respects, the financial arrangements on which Dies's employment was grounded were characteristic of middle-class employment more generally. The *Caution*, or surety, was both a marker and an enforcer of one's position in the society outside of the workplace. Since it was normally a sum exceeding the actual assets of the employee, raising a

---

43. Robinson, "Administrative Staff", pp. 195–196.
44. Brewer, "Servants of the Public", p. 146.

surety depended on the his being able to find fellow-citizens who would in turn act as guarantors; it was thus a material guarantee of the employee's probity and a test of his standing in the community, and at the same time served to reinforce his dependence on local networks of obligation. Johann Christoph Eisendecker, who acted as guarantor for Dies's Caution, would be the next man to be appointed to a position of responsibility in the Calenberg, and his standing surety for Dies probably marked the beginning of a tacit "expectancy" on his part. Whatever an individual's qualification, formal and informal arrangements such as expectancy and patronage remained key steps in a career in public service or administration.[45] In terms of systems of emolument, though, Dies's situation seems to signal something relatively new. The supplementing of nominal salaries through fees (from the public), perquisites or payments in kind, piece-rates such as page-rates for copyists and clerks, and cash gratuities for supplementary services was standard practice in all nonmanual occupations in the eighteenth century, including in all areas of public service. The British Excise pioneered fixed salaries as early as the seventeenth century, but in other occupations these began to be introduced only in the last third of the century, in both Britain and the German lands. In the German context, the introduction of regular salaries is generally associated with moves towards the regularization of public service in a set of legal categories (*Beamtenrecht*), which was beginning in Prussia in the late eighteenth century, but took off effectively after 1800 under the influence of the Napoleonic occupation. As a set of privileges and a marker of status, *Beamtenrecht* was something that German employees in the private sector would aspire to over the succeeding century and a half. But the implications of this regularization were ambivalent. In Dies's case, the ban on outside earnings represented an acknowledgement of the worker's key function as a handler of both money and information, and the time and mental independence that these functions demanded. It promised to free them from the efforts involved in piecing together a decent income. At the same time, it made them entirely dependent on their employers. This could have material disadvantages. Where (as in the German lands) there were no fixed salary scales and no formal arrangements for adjustment, real incomes became more sensitive to the vagaries of price and currency inflation (both endemic in the 1770s). Moreover, in Dies's case no arrangement had been made by which his income would rise with the workload. As the expanding workload led to a crisis in Dies's circumstances, the tenuousness of the security provided by a guaranteed salary would become clear.

---

45. Cf. K. Malettke (ed.), *Ämterkäuflichkeit. Aspekte sozialer Mobilität im europäischen Vergleich* (Berlin, 1980).

THE DEMANDS OF THE JOB 1: PUBLICITY, COMPETITION, AND INFORMATION CONTROL

The catalogue of Dies's accounting duties set out above suggests that he had a lot to do, but both the volume of work and the stress associated with it were given a particular character by the way in which they interacted with a changing information regime. The growth of widows' funds was characterized by competition at two levels: the institutions themselves were in competition with one another for subscribers (as well as sometimes for licenses or official patronage), and the men who devoted themselves to devising schemes and systems of calculation for their operation – whether as free-lancers or in the pay of the funds – were in competition for both prestige and the prospect of being paid for their advice. The injunction on Dies to defend the interests of the fund meant that the keeping of secrets had to be balanced with the judicious release of information, in the form of public relations. As early as 1766 Dies was called on to defend the fund. When the Göttingen City Treasurer, Johann Augustin Kritter, circulated a manuscript claiming that the new plan dangerously underestimated the future pensions commitment, it was Dies who drafted two detailed refutations for the attention of the Committee. These were documents covering forty-three pages, in which Dies (like Kritter) drew on published mortality tables and speculation about the remarriage prospects of widows to project the maximum number of widows that might have to be supported by the fund.[46] Once the fund was up and running, he would be engaged in a more or less continuous interface with the public and with "experts" who continued to challenge the Calenberg's claims to stability, warding off and responding to publicly expressed doubts in print. The regular *Avertissements* were designed to instigate customer trust as much through the show of transparency and statistical expertise as through any evidence of solidity contained in the figures themselves. In their production, Dies's role was behind the scenes. But Dies also risked his own and the Calenberg's reputation by defending his employers in print. Any work of information or argument launched in the press could expect a response not only from the competitors themselves but also from the public.

In the case of the Calenberg, the tendency of publicity to avenge itself on the people who produced it is well illustrated by the press and pamphlet war around the question of how stable the fund was, which brought to public attention the debate that had been going on in private correspondence since the fund was first proposed. In late 1768, a short piece entitled "Thoughts about the Calenberg Widows' Fund" ran over two weekly

---

46. "Bemerkungen über die von Herr Kritter, wider die von Sr. Königl. Majestät von Groß-Britannien allergnädigst bestätigte Calenbergische Witwencasse, eingesandte Rechnung, nebst angehengter Gegenrechnung" (22 February 1767), and "Noch ein paar Anmerkungen gegen Herr Kritter" (12 March 1767), HStAHann, Hann. 93, vol. 3706, pp. 182–200, 215–218.

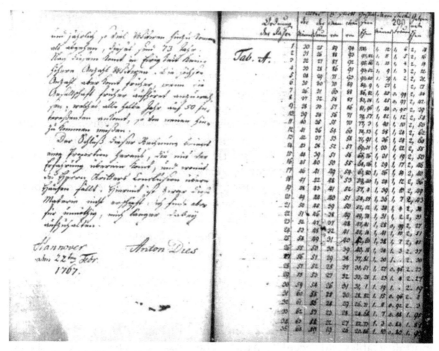

Figure 3. Page 22 of Anton Dies's manuscript response to Kritter, and the beginning of a tabular appendix. The table traces the mortality of a cohort of married couples, in order to establish the long-term relationship of the number of widows to paying subscribers in a widows' fund. *Niedersächsisches Hauptstaatsarchiv Hannover. Reproduced with permission.*

issues of the *Göttingische Gelehrte Beyträge*. The author was (or purported to be) a subscriber to the fund, and began by setting out the considerations that had moved him to make a financial sacrifice to buy a pension for his wife. He had, he wrote, not bothered to make a detailed analysis of the fund's operation himself; relying on "the honesty and skill" of its founders and the "happy success of other public institutions in which I believed them to have been involved", he had been confident of its soundness – "until yesterday evening, when I read issue 31 of the *Göttingische Gelehrte Beyträge*, and fell into a doubt which destroyed my ease of mind". He was referring to an earlier article, itself cast as a commentary by a Calenberg subscriber, which enumerated in detail the statistical claims of the Calenberg founders and their gadfly, Kritter.[47] This

47. "Gedancken über die Calenbergische Witwen-Verpflegungs-Gesellschaft", *Göttingische Gelehrte Beyträge*, 1768, nos 37 and 38 (17 and 24 December), cols 464–469; "Unvorgreiffliche Gedanken über das berühmte Calenbergische Institum [*sic*] einer allgemeinen Witwenver-pflegungsgesellschaft", *Göttingische Gelehrte Beyträge*, 1768, no. 31 (5 November), cols 354–369. A similar 'reader's letter', directed this time at Kritter and citing Dies's counter-attack: "Disconto mit Hrn Camerarius Kritters Conto-Courant von der Bremischen Witwen-

was no lightning exchange; seven weeks elapsed between the publication of
the two articles. But their tone conveys a sense of immediacy of reception
and response, of being in the middle of a constantly flowing stream of data.
The original piece had been published not only in Göttingen's learned
weekly but in intelligencers in Braunschweig and Hamburg, where four
well-established widows' funds were waiting to accommodate any
subscribers who lost faith in the Calenberg; this provoked von Wüllen
himself into an irritable defence of his fund.[48] Generally, though, it fell to
Dies to channel and harness the stream of information, and during 1768
and 1769 he engaged in an exchange of press articles and pamphlets with
Kritter, in which he proved himself the more vitriolic polemicist, if not
unequivocally the better statistician.[49]

THE DEMANDS OF THE JOB 2: THE VOLUME OF DOCUMENTATION

While the information management aspect of pension-fund work constituted a source of emotional and moral pressure in itself, the generating of
public-relations material added to a volume of routine internal documentation that expanded as the enterprise grew. It was the size of the workload
that Dies and his successors in the Calenberg complained about. A progress
report (apparently unsolicited) to von Wüllen dated 7 October 1767 "in the
evening" shows Dies hard at work justifying the confidence placed in him,
though still with a relatively leisurely and varied routine. He reports (in
tabular form) on the new subscribers he has registered and on those who
have died or resigned, with a commentary on the consequences for the
fund's current and future income. He asks that the Committee consider a
question of principle that has occurred to him, for "as I work all sorts of
fancies [*Grillen*] come into my head". He comments on news about the
royal family, reports on the problems he still faces with working out tables
of *Simpla*, interrupts to report that an agent has "just sent me three new
young subscribers" and comments "the flow of documents is increasing

Pflegeschaft", *Hannoverisches Magazin*, 1768, no. 99 (9 December), cols 1569–1583 [= whole number].

48. v. W., "Ueber die Gedanken, so das Calenbergische Institutum einer allgemeinen Wittwenverpflegungsgesellschaft betreffen", *Hannoverisches Magazin*, 1769, no. 22 (17 March), cols 337–351.

49. [A. Dies], "Beweis, dass alle getaufte Kinder in Paris von solchen Ehefrauen geboren werden, die keine Männer haben, nach Süssmilchischen Grundsätzen geführet", *Hannoverisches Magazin*, 1768, no. 1 (7 October), cols 1281–1296 [= whole number]. Cf. A. Dies, *Briefe an den Herrn Senator und Cämmerer Kritter in Göttingen, die Grundsätze von Wittwencassen betreffend* (Frankfurt [etc.], 1769) (38 pp.); Johann Augustin Kritter, *Beweis, daß die Männer in den Wittwenverpflegungsgesellschaften über 135 Jahre alt werden, mit einem Schreiben an Herrn Dies* (Göttingen, 1769).

every day".[50] In the following years, the sheer volume of clerical work – most of which was carried by Dies – grew steadily as a function of the fund's success. By the summer of 1773 the fund had more than 2,900 married couples on its books and was paying pensions to 234 widows. At the same time the need for calculation, recalculation, and strategic planning became more urgent; 1773 was the first year in which the imbalance between spending on pensions and contributions income placed before the Committee the strategic decision of whether to raise the price of the *Simplum* to an unpopular level or call on the *Landschaft* for subsidy. In July, it was agreed that Dies needed help. Johann Christoph Eisendecker was appointed with the title of cashier to assist Dies, particularly in the administration of contributions. In an arrangement entirely characteristic for the period, Eisendecker was to be paid a salary of 100 Rtl, half of which was to come out of Dies's salary. Moreover, Eisendecker undertook to find 675 Rtl to make up a deficit in Dies's accounts, with the right to claim reimbursement in instalments out of Dies's salary; in return Eisendecker was promised that he would take over the post of Registrator when Dies died or retired.[51]

Dies was explicitly enjoined when he was hired to be aware that his accounts might be inspected at any time, and so to keep his records "in such an order that the [information] required is immediately apparent". In December 1774, it became apparent that he had failed to do so, and indeed that he was still unable to keep up with the pace of the job. It emerged that he had accepted 650 Rtl worth of deposits from subscribers in a private capacity but had failed to pay them into the fund. The Chairman of the Treasury Committee was uncertain whether this was an example of embezzlement or simply an oversight; in any case it represented a breach of the rules, and Dies submitted his resignation. The letter of resignation made no direct mention of the actual occasion of its writing, but its wording suggests that he had indeed diverted the deposit money to other uses. He was at pains to explain that he simply could not keep up with the six-monthly reporting cycle, and added that there was no way to make up work which had fallen behind except "with outside assistance" – which would have had to be financed out of his own pocket. The letter as a whole, which climaxes with the dramatic announcement of Dies's intention to seek his fortune in foreign parts, sets out vividly the impact that the spiralling demands of the job had had on somebody who had invested identity and reputation in the business of information management. Of the moral consequences of his situation, he wrote: "I could not bear it if the institute's documentation under so many headings could not be effectively completed under my responsibility [*unter meinen Händen*], leaving the

50. Dies to von Wüllen, 7 October 1767, HtAHann, Dep. 7B, vol. 326I, pp. 86–87.
51. Crown Office to Landschaft, 8 July 1773, HStAHann, Hann. 93, vol. 3707, p. 17; Eisendecker to Treasury Committee, 9 January 1783, HStAHann, Hann. 93, vol. 3708, pp. 262–265.

blame to fall on me after my death." The letter opened with an account of "frequent embarrassments [...] worries and strife [which] on several occasions have led to illness"; in particular, Dies complained of a paralysis of the right arm which had dogged him for nearly a year and made work impossible for days and weeks at a time.[52]

Dies's only request of his former employers was that a pension of 100 Rtl be provided for his wife, to assist her with the care of their children. The negotiations around this question underline the ambivalence of Dies's position as a key worker in an information-sensitive enterprise. It took the authorities almost two years to make up their minds. When Dies contacted the Treasury Committee in November 1775 to renew his request, he reported that he had been without any source of income since his resignation except what he could get by selling his furniture, and he had now run out of things to sell. Clearly, his salary from the Calenberg had not been sufficient to allow for savings. Moreover, he pointed out, as a result of eight years' work for the Calenberg he had "lost connection with the best houses in Hanover"; the exclusive focus on a demanding job which required that he hold himself aloof from his wealthy and influential neighbours had robbed him of opportunities for networking and patronage. And he still could not do much with his arm. He nevertheless expressed a desire to be re-employed in widows' fund work on some basis or other. In fact he had done work for the Committee in the preceding months, some of which had been paid for, and his completion of a particularly impressive exercise of calculation (comparing the Calenberg with the newly founded Berlin widows' fund) prompted the Treasury Committee in July 1776 to renew its original recommendation to the Crown Office that the pension be granted. The reason for their original recommendation was that Dies was privy to inside knowledge about the operation of the Calenberg, and that if he were not tied to the kingdom (*vinculiert*) he might set up a competing fund somewhere else. By 1776 it was clear that he did not have any serious plans to emigrate, but also that his services (and loyalty) were still worth retaining on a consultancy basis. The Crown Office remained unconvinced about the security issue, but agreed that the family should not be allowed to fall into destitution. While Dies continued to do occasional work for the Calenberg, his wife received an annual stipend of 100 Rtl for the rest of her life.[53]

A similar set of conditions faced Johann Christoph Eisendecker when he succeeded Dies as Registrator. His duties continued to include the work of cashier, but this was not reflected in his salary, which was fixed at 500 Rtl.

52. Christoph Chapuzeau, Abbot of Loccum to Crown Office, 14 December 1774 and attached letter of Dies to Treasury Committee, 6 December 1774, HStAHann, Hann. 93, vol. 3707, pp. 95–99.
53. Correspondence between the Treasury Committee and the Crown Office, December 1774 and July 1776, HStAHann, Hann. 93, vol. 3707, pp. 100–103, 189–192.

Like Dies's salary, Eisendecker's was now subject to impositions; Dies's wife's pension came out of it. By the end of 1774, only 275 of the 675 Rtl which he had borrowed in order to lend it on to the Calenberg had been repaid, and the rest was still outstanding in 1783, when Frau Dies died and Eisendecker wrote to the Treasury Committee to ask that he now be allowed to enjoy his full salary.[54] Eisendecker took this occasion to comment on his own workload, which he estimated at more than three times what Dies's had been. This estimate was realistic. The parlous state of the Calenberg's accounts had become public in 1780, when the fund had over 3,700 married couples and more than 700 widows on its books. This led to a spiralling crisis which required not only rapid policy decisions based on constantly revised calculations, but also readiness to respond at any time to what had now become a maelstrom of data and polemic. Both subscribers and widows organized themselves and engaged in private and public protestations against plans to reduce pensions and raise contributions, competing groups of subscribers demanding and being granted the right to negotiate formally with the Treasury Committee about the terms on which the fund might be rescued. All of the leading mathematicians in the German lands were called on for advice, formally or informally, as were the law faculties of four universities. Argument and counter-argument circulated in manuscript correspondence, in printed pamphlets and handbills, and in the intelligencers and the scholarly press, alongside more reasoned (though not always disinterested) disputations about the uses of mortality tables and methods of calculation. The Treasury Committee was in more or less permanent session from the beginning of 1781 onwards, in minuted sessions and via memoranda criss-crossing the town and environs of Hanover at all hours of the day and night.

By 1783 the crisis was approaching a provisional resolution, in the form of a plan for a reformed fund which, when it was published in July, would leave nobody very happy. Justifying the reforms to subscribers, widows and the watching general public required that the officers of the Calenberg engage with all the arguments in circulation; the first *Avertissement* issued following the publication of the reform plan came with a twenty-four-page actuarial table.[55] In the process of reform, each new factor taken into account, each mechanism devised to improve the security of the enterprise, introduced a new set of arithmetical operations that needed to be carried out. In a period when compound interest, for example, was normally worked out at length by calculating a year at a time, this incurred a

---

54. Eisendecker to Treasury Committee, 9 January 1783, HStAHann, Hann. 93, vol. 3708, pp. 262–265.

55. *41stes Avertissement, die Calenbergische Witwen-Verpflegungs-Gesellschaft betreffend*, 9 July 1783, HStAHann, Hann. 93, vol. 3705, pp. 81–92. The tables show the average duration of marriage for couples according to the respective ages of husband and wife.

multiplier effect on both the manual and the mental work required.[56] None of this could proceed without the effort of men like Eisendecker. The only change in Eisendecker's conditions of service, however, had been an increase in the *Caution* he was liable for – not a compensation, but a further imposition. In his letter of January 1783 he explicitly reminded his employers "that I do not have the least side income, which could be expected in almost any [other] employment", and concluded with the assertion that he could no longer support his family on what he was being paid. Like Dies, he also complained of the effect on his health of the growth in his workload.

A final exchange of correspondence from the Calenberg files suggests that Eisendecker was provided with some clerical assistance in the crisis, but also confirms the impression of a pathogenically expanding workload. In March 1784 one of the regular employees of the *Landschaft*, a clerk (*Kanzellist*) named Rath who had apparently been seconded to do some work for the Calenberg, wrote to the Treasury Committee to request that he be paid. When no action had been taken by the summer, his wife wrote again to present his case: The work he had done for the widows' fund had been additional to his normal duties, she argued. Moreover, not only had he not been paid anything extra for "many years' extraordinary work", but he had also had to pay out of his own pocket for clerical assistance in order to keep up with the increased workload. In July the Committee proposed that he be made a discretionary grant, but Maria Rath was not satisfied, and reasserted her husband's claim to formal and substantial acknowledgement of his efforts. Receiving no further response, she again took up the cudgels in December. At the centre of her pleas was the fact that her husband had since the spring been suffering from a mental disorder (*Gemüthskrankheit*). She found her husband's condition "uncommonly oppressive", and was renewing her husband's petition

> [...] because the burden is too much for me, and I cannot see any way I can continue to fulfil the many and heavy obligations for which my unfortunate husband's regular income – already considerably reduced – is no longer sufficient, and meet the needs of myself and my three young children.

At the same time she reported that before her husband's breakdown, she had dissuaded him from presenting his employers with a catalogue of all the documents he had prepared for the widows' fund, urging him to

---

56. Dies amused himself in his retirement with trying to find an alternative method for calculating compound interest, in his case using a table; see [Anton] Dies, "Anatocismus inversus. Oder: Regul, Zinse auf Zinse auf eine verkehrte, jedoch auf die kürzeste und leichteste Art auszurechnen", *Hannoverisches Magazin* 1781, no. 1, cols 167–170. Cf. Andrew Warwick's comment on how the reception of mechanical computational aids by actuaries in the 1860s and 1870s exposed "the handwork in the actuary's craft"; Warwick, "Laboratory of Theory", pp. 329–331.

continue working hard in order to reinforce his claim to compensation. In January 1785 the Committee members relented and agreed to grant the "mad clerk" a gift of four Pistoles, the equivalent of 11 Rtl. It was minuted that this should not constitute a precedent.[57]

SERVICE OR LABOUR? THE HAZARDS OF INFORMATION WORK

A comparison of Rath's gratuity with the fee of 40 Rtl that Dies was paid in 1782 for his free-lance calculation work for the Calenberg suggests the differentials in earning-power associated with different degrees of access to privileged information and skill in its management (or calculation).[58] But while none of these men was a master, all were more than operatives. The pattern of their work, the skills it required and the schooling it presupposed, the respect to which they aspired and which was accorded them, all bear the familiar marks of middle-class employment. Even the financial insecurity they suffered and their dependence on patronage, mutual arrangements and shifts were not different in kind from the terms on which officers of civil and municipal administration were employed in the German states in the century before the legal regularization of the civil service. In what sense can we speak of labour in connection with this group of workers? Eisendecker began his letter of 1783 with a formula that was also a statement about the nature of his work: "Your honours most graciously and indulgently allow me to set down for a few moments the pen which my service bids me wield and occupy myself with the drafting of the present memorial." Eisendecker used the term "service" (*Dienst*) self-consciously here, and meant by it those things which distinguished the work that he (and Dies and Rath and others like them) did from that of the common labourer or tradesman. But at the same time the formula visualizes his work as (literally) manual labour, in the same way as Dies's use of the phrase "under my hand" (*unter meinen Händen*) draws attention to the physical process by which the "documentation under so many different heads" was produced. Maria Rath, similarly, referred to the copyists her husband had had to employ as "helpful hands". Eisendecker's formulation foregrounds the paradox in all this correspondence: his letter was no less a product of the pen than the hundreds of pages of tables and memoranda and correspondence that constituted his "service". Similarly, Rath could only effect his claim to compensation for his services as a scribe by "threatening" to do more writing, drawing up a catalogue of all the documentation he had produced for the Calenberg. But Eisendecker's

57. Correspondence between Maria Rath and Treasury Committee and minutes of meetings of the Treasury Committee, March 1784–January 1785, HStAHann, Dep. 7B, vol. 371, pp. 293–298.
58. Minutes of Treasury Committee meeting, 15 October 1782, HStAHann, Dep. 7B, vol. 371, p. 147.

imagery bespeaks an awareness of the distinction between work done at the behest of others and that done "on one's own account", and thus helps us to see these middle-class occupations as labour.

The self-representations of these men also reveal that it was not only their physical powers and skill – their stamina and ability to write – that they placed at the disposal of their employers. The work they did required skills of intellect and argument in which considerable self-esteem was invested, since they were responsible not only for communicating but also for generating and managing information; accuracy was at a premium, the products of their labour subject to scrutiny by critical eyes as well as to the test of experience, and getting it wrong could cost them their employment and their reputations. The duty of confidentiality associated with handling sensitive data laid a permanent constraint on their speech and action. It is not surprising, then, that while only Rath actually suffered a breakdown, all the correspondence makes reference to states of mind, to mental as well as physical health. The German terms which Dies used to convey his "embarrassments, worry and strife" – *Bedrängnisse, Sorgen, Gram* – implied constraint and mental conflict. Eisendecker characterized the distraint on his salary and his unrecompensed subsidy to Dies as things that had "uncommonly discouraged" him over the years.

Dies's paralysis of the right arm and Rath's nervous breakdown reveal the combination of physical, mental, and emotional demands made on this generation of clerical workers in the acute form of occupational disease. The medical literature on occupational hazards which circulated through-out Europe provides one kind of measure of the extent to which activity of this kind was identified by contemporaries as work. While the conditions reported by Dies and Rath find an echo in this literature from an early date, the perception of clerical workers as having a distinct occupational profile defined by a labour process was uneven before the nineteenth century. In the 1713 supplement to his *De morbis artificum* of 1700, the first modern writer on occupational diseases, Bernardino Ramazzini, devoted a section to the diseases of scribes and secretaries – in spite of his view that the introduction of printing must have reduced the demand for their services. (The first edition included a section on the diseases of academics and scholars, but his publisher clearly thought something more specific was needed.) He described the pathogenic features of these occupations as their sedentary character,[59] the necessity of constantly carrying out the same motion with the writing hand, and the need for mental concentration "lest their writing be spoilt by errors or they cause their employers loss through

---

59. In spite of evidence that writing desks at which the writer stood were in use in the early modern period, all the eighteenth-century literature on clerical workers I have seen presumes that they worked sitting down. See also Winfried Hansmann, *Kontor und Kaufmann in alter Zeit* (Düsseldorf, 1962), pp. 78–85 (with contemporary images).

errors of arithmetic". As an example of the physical hazards of the job, Ramazzini provided a description of a case of paralysis of the hand and arm which proved incurable. To the mental strains arising from the need for accuracy, Ramazzini added the stress suffered by those men who were secretaries to "princes", and had to contend with the inscrutability of the great and the ambiguities of diplomatic discourse.[60] The editions of Ramazzini that circulated in translation later in the century, and works on occupational disease that continued to draw heavily on his work, did not all include the section on scribes and secretaries. A 1746 English edition entirely deleted the references to courtly employment (not surprisingly), and telescoped the sources of mental stress. A sentence inserted by the translator collapsed clerical work back into a broad category of intellectual activity: "These misfortunes are principally incident to Philosophers, Arithmeticians, Merchants Clerks, and Secretaries, whose minds are often perplex'd with a Multitude of Letters, and the variety of the Subjects on which they write." Similarly Buchan's popular *Domestic Medicine* contained a section on the afflictions of "the studious", but had nothing to say about those who wrote for pay. The supplement was not included in the 1718 German translation of Ramazzini, and the editor of a 1780 German edition was more interested in the diseases of manual workers like the weavers and stocking-knitters who attended his practice.[61]

The recognition of clerical work as a form of labour in terms of a specific combination of muscular and neuropsychological pathologies occurred only in the 1830s. The editions of Ramazzini published in the 1820s displayed a new interest in clerical workers, updating Ramazzini's categories to include "notaries, lawyers, and employees in public administration" as well as "secretaries, clerks, commercial employees,

60. Bernardino Ramazzini, *Diatribae de morbis artificum supplementum* (1713), in B. Ramazzini, *Opera Medica*, 2 vols (Leipzig, 1828), p. 192. It has been remarked that the Supplement is more circumstantial in its treatment of specific trades than the first edition, and in particular lacks the element of social satire that characterizes the treatment of groups like academics among "artificers"; Stefan Goldmann, "Zur Ständesatire in Bernardino Ramazzinis 'De Morbis Artificum Diatriba'", *Sudhoffs Archiv*, 74 (1990), pp. 1–21; Axel Gils, *Bernardino Ramazzini (1633–1714). Leben und Werk, unter besonderer Berücksichtigung der Schrift "Über die Krankheiten der Künstler und Handwerker"* (Göttingen, 1994), pp. 83–84.
61. *A Dissertation on Endemial Diseases, or those Disorders which Arise from Particular Climates, Situations and Methods of Living; together with a Treatise on the Diseases of Tradesmen* (London, 1746), pp. 400–401; William Buchan, *Domestic Medicine: Or a Treatise on the Prevention and Cure of Diseases*, 6th edn (London, 1779), pp. 57–65; *Bernhardi Rammazini Untersuchung von denen Kranckheiten der Künstler und Handwercker* (Leipzig, 1718); *Bernhard Ramazzini's [...] Abhandlung von den Krankheiten der Künstler und Handwerker, neu bearbeitet und vermehret von Dr Johann Christian Gottlieb Ackermann* (Stendal, 1780). Cf. *Essai sur les maladies des artisans, traduit du Latin de Ramazzini, avec des notes et des additions, par M. de Fourcroy* (Paris, 1777).

scribes and copyists".[62] But in the 1830s writers began to provide their own specific and circumstantial accounts of the conditions under which clerks, bookkeepers and accountants worked.[63] At the same time, physicians began to observe for themselves and to report on examples of cramp and paralysis of the hand and arm of the kind described by Ramazzini (and which Dies seems to have suffered). This syndrome now entered into the English medical literature under the name "scrivener's palsy", a phrase which firmly attached the disease to the occupation, and later simply "writer's cramp" (in German *Schreibekrampf*). Charles Bell is credited with the first published report on the syndrome, in a brief note of 1830. It seems clear, though, that its "discovery" occurred more or less simultaneously in Britain, France, and Germany.[64] While some observers regarded the introduction of steel-nib pens as a predisposing factor, the common aetiology was identified in the volume and intensity of the work, and also in its alienated character; academics and authors did not present with these symptoms. By the same token, cramp seemed in many cases to include an element of psychic resistance to the specific task, with the affected limb still being usable for leisure activities. By the 1890s, similar symptoms were being noted in telegraphers, the latest generation of information workers to be affected by changes in the conditions of work – this time unequivocally related to new communication technologies. But as late at 1897 Herbert Spencer would invoke the image of the clerk "who, daily writing for hours after his fingers are painfully cramped, is attacked with 'scrivener's palsy', and, unable to write at all, sinks with aged parents into poverty" as a universally recognisable example of the perils of "inadequate egoism".[65]

62. Philippe Patissier, *Traité des maladies des artisans et de celles qui résultent de diverses professions, d'après Ramazzini* (Paris, 1822); Julius H.G. Schlegel, *Die Krankheiten der Künstler und Handwerker und die Mittel sich von denselben zu schützen* (Ilmenau, 1823) (an annotated translation of Patissier's edition).
63. E.g. C. Turner Thackrah, *The Effects of Arts, Trades and Professions and of Civic States and Habits of Living on Health and Longevity*, 2nd edn (London [etc.], 1832), p. 176.
64. Charles Bell, *The Nervous System of the Human Body* (London, 1844), pp. 429f (1st edn 1830); cf. *Karl Bell's physiologische und pathologische Untersuchungen des Nervensystems*. Moritz Heinrich Romberg (transl.) (Berlin, 1832), p. 362. The earliest German account, by Brück, dates from 1831, and a continuous and intensive exchange of views in the German medical press set in in 1835; A.C.L. Halfort, *Entstehung, Verlauf und Behandlung der Krankheiten der Künstler und Gewerbetreibenden* (Berlin, 1845), pp. 533–541; K.E. Hasse, *Handbuch der speciellen Pathologie und Therapie. 4. Band, 1. Abteilung: Krankheiten des Nervenapparates* (Erlangen, 1855), pp. 142–148; communications by Heyfelder, Albers, and Siebold in *Medicinische Zeitung von dem Verein für Heilkunde in Preussen*, 4 (1835), pp. 5, 37–38, 82–83. For surveys of an extremely complex literature, see J. Quintner, "The RSI Syndrome in Historical Perspective", *International Disability Studies*, 13 (1991), pp. 99–104; Allard E. Dembe, "The Changing Nature of Office Work: Effects on Repetitive Strain Injury", *Occupational Medicine: State of the Art Reviews*, 14 (1999), pp. 61–72.
65. Herbert Spencer, *The Principles of Ethics* (London, 1892–1893), p. 195.

CONCLUSION

Having noted that the expansion of clerical work in information management predates its "discovery", what can we conclude? Nineteenth-century observers rarely failed to note that writer's cramp was an affliction mainly of men – because the work that brought it on was men's work. Academic and medical interest has recently been focused on nineteenth-century discussions in the light of our own "epidemic" of repetitive strain injury – a typical occupational disease of those who work with information technology, and now mainly women.[66] The story of information (clerical and communications) work since the late nineteenth century is sometimes written as a story of proletarianization, and at the same time a story of the way in which a gendered division of labour reproduces itself with each successive technological advance. By contrast, the eighteenth century seems to be period of relatively little change, but (granted the paucity of the data) it seems possible to identify not only shifts in the volume and character of information-related work but also emerging particularities in the conditions of service that attached to it. A close look at those features that were not new or particular to information work can also make us attentive to the areas of change to come which implied increasing specialization and division of labour in the work of men like Dies. The move towards fixed and regular salaries in the late eighteenth century has already been noted. At a quite different level, advice literature for men of the clerical classes in Germany seems to have undergone a degree of specialization at the same time, with compendia that covered everything from morality and personal habits to the drafting of wills replaced by distinct genres, one offering general advice on conduct and manners, and another guidance on current problems and practices in specific occupations.[67] This parallels the beginnings of formal schooling in commercial and low-level administrative skills as a form of qualification for men without access to university training.[68] The British case suggests

---

66. Thus Leonard F. Peltier's comment in his introduction to a reprint of Samuel Solly's 1864 lecture "On Scrivener's Palsy, or the Paralysis of Writers": "Solly's description of a repetitive strain injury in male secretaries in 1864 has many similarities with the types of repetitive strain injuries seen in female secretaries laboring over their computer keyboards 130 years later"; *Clinical Orthopaedics and Related Research*, 352 (1998), pp. 4–9.

67. The classic examples of the former are Carl Friedrich Bahrdt, *Handbuch der Moral für den Bürgerstand* (Halle, 1789); Adolf von Knigge, *Über den Umgang mit Menschen* (Hanover, 1788). An example of the latter: *Magazin gemeinnütziger Aufsätze für Wirtembergische Schreiber* (Stuttgart, 1797). A promising project analysing the surviving corpus of early modern business handbooks has yet to cover the eighteenth century: Jochen Hoock, Pierre Jeannin *et al.* (eds), *Ars Mercatoria. Handbücher und Traktate für den Gebrauch des Kaufmanns, 1470–1820*, 6 vols projected, 3 published to date (Paderborn, 1991–2001).

68. See the texts reprinted in Klaus Friedrich Pott (ed.), *Über kaufmännische Erziehung* (Rinteln, 1977).

that the early nineteenth century would witness a complex dialectic of professionalization and tendential (though incomplete) proletarianization as different aspects of what in Dies's case had been a single workload – clerical, computational, "scientific", and public relations work – began to separate out. In the work of actuaries (which is more or less what Dies and Eisendecker were), the tension between science and commerce became acute and sought resolution in a process of professionalization.[69] The demand for accuracy which grew with the possibilities of achieving a universal standard through the use of technical instruments progressively lessened the scope for discretion on the part of civil servants like excise officers, subjecting their work to new kinds and degrees of discipline.[70] It was not any direct application of new mechanical technologies, though, that made for the "discovery" of clerical work as a problem area in the 1830s; mechanical calculators and typewriters in their time were introduced as solutions to the stresses of low-tech clerical work. But neither can that discovery be seen as a simple reflex of a sudden increase in numbers.[71] It seems rather to reflect a dialectic between the presence of an occupational group which had been growing for a century or more, and an awareness of the possibilities of both mechanical and managerial "solutions", which depended on the experience of fully-realized machine production and industrial forms of labour discipline.

69. Timothy W. Alborn, "A Calculating Profession: Victorian Actuaries Among the Statisticians", *Science in Context*, 7 (1994), pp. 433–468; Theodore M. Porter, "Precision and Trust: Early Victorian Actuaries and the Politics of Calculation", in Wise (ed.), *The Values of Precision*, pp. 173–197.

70. William J. Ashworth, "'Between the Trader and the Public': British Alcohol Standards and the Proof of Good Governance", *Technology and Culture*, 42 (2001), pp. 27–50.

71. Gregory Anderson dates an acceleration of growth the number of clerical workers in Britain only from the 1850s: *Victorian Clerks* (Manchester, 1976), p. 10.

IRSH 48 (2003), Supplement, pp. 45–71 DOI: 10.1017/S0020859003001263
© 2003 Internationaal Instituut voor Sociale Geschiedenis

India's First Virtual Community and the Telegraph General Strike of 1908*

DEEP KANTA LAHIRI CHOUDHURY

The telegraph strike of 1908 occurred at many nodes of the telegraph system in British India and Burma, paralysing governance and business. In this paper, I suggest that the strike was a symptom of the systemic crisis in world telegraphy faced with technological change and competition. I introduce the category of transregional economic general strike as a tool to analyse strikes in the communication sectors. The strike demonstrated the ability of one of the earliest virtual communities in India to combine and organize worker protest. This multistage strike momentarily transcended the specific, and usually rigid, distinctions of race, class, and ethnicity through the production of community-at-a-distance. The strike occurred simultaneously among different sections of workers in Rangoon, Moulmein, Calcutta, Allahabad, Agra, Bombay, Madras, Lahore, and Karachi, to name just a few of the places involved. Both telegraph signallers as well as the subordinate staff went on strike. By concentrating on the relationship between technological change and labour, the paper demonstrates how workers across this part of the British Empire were capable of charting a general agenda in the first decade of the twentieth century, using technology to combine and combat technological rationalization.

Previous historiography on Indian labour either subsumed the telegraph strike of 1908 within the nationalist narrative of political unrest under the *swadeshi* and boycott[1] movement, or ignored strikes in the communications sector by various classes of workers.[2] Studies began from the 1880s and characterized the period 1880–1919 as the "prehistory" of labour mobilization in India and as the period of the emergence of "community

---

* I am grateful to the editors for their comments and suggestions. This paper is a part of the chapter on the strike in my Ph.D thesis, completed under the supervision of C.A. Bayly, University of Cambridge.

1. *Swadesh* means one's own country. The *swadeshi* and boycott movement in India 1905–1912, echoed the boycott of foreign goods in China and Ireland, and envisaged the promotion of indigenous industry by the promotion of *swadeshi* enterprise.

2. Work has been done on the railways, for example by I.J. Kerr, who looks at the labour employed in constructing the railways: *Building the Railways of the Raj 1850–1900* (Delhi [etc.], 1997).

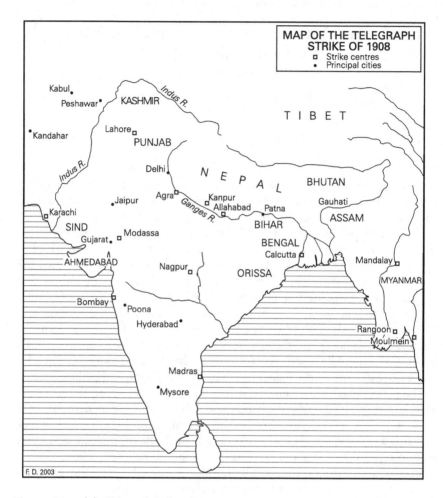

Figure 1. Map of the Telegraph Strike of 1908

consciousness" within Indian labour.[3] This labour historiography, reminiscent of the Wisconsin School,[4] studied working-class formation
without considering the kinds of opposition shaping their experience.
The study of relatively underdeveloped agro-economic sectors, and the

3. For example, G.K. Sharma, *Labour Movement in India* (Delhi, 1971); P. Saha, *Bangla Sramik Andoloner Itihas* (Calcutta, 1972); S. Sarkar, *The Swadeshi Movement in Bengal 1903–1908* (Delhi, 1973). The argument regarding community-consciousness, as opposed to class-consciousness, was made by D. Chakrabarty, "Communal Riots and Labour: Bengal's Jute Mill-Hands in the 1890s", *Past and Present*, 91 (1981), pp. 140–169. For a critique, see Subho Basu, "Strikes and 'Communal' Riots in Calcutta in the 1890s", *Modern Asian Studies*, 32 (1998), pp. 949–983.
4. C. Craypo, "Introduction", *Labour Studies Journal*, 3 (1979) (special issue: *The Impact on Labour of Changing Corporate Structure and Technology*), pp. 195–200, 196.

concentration on particular localities led to an argument about the peculiarity and community consciousness of Indian labour: labour in these sectors reflected the colonial forms of industry in which they were situated. This paper, by studying protest in one of the core sectors of industrial communication technology, questions this topology. Class solidarities in the telegraph strike were formed directly through the communication system, in contrast with the more inchoate, mediated, and nationalized identities theorized in the work of Marx and Benedict Anderson.[5] This research suggests that community and race identities were not inherent but hardened through the experience of working-class action and the different ways in which the colonial state responded to it.[6]

In the United States, work concentrated on telegraphy's impact on economic and organizational aspects, especially business history. Accounts from Blondheim to Lubrano celebrated the emerging national unity brought about by the telegraph,[7] while others noticed the conflict between democratic values and centralizing tendencies.[8] Though rightly celebrating the nation-building aspects of the telegraph, some of the work has relatively neglected the points of conflict and difference. Authors used telegraph workers to engage with labour historiography, bureaucratization, and unionization.[9] Recent work has engaged with telegraph workers not as illustrators of labour union history but discussed them in light of their position within the industry and communication networks.[10] However, while accepting the notion of successive and competing communication technologies as technologically deterministic, the cooperation between railways, telephone, and telegraphs can be exaggerated. There was indeed considerable overlap, especially in terms of personnel, but there was also intense competition: the issue was not one of physical succession but that of hegemony. Though enthusiastic about the telegraph transforming communication in the United States and serving to "centralize, even

5. Karl Marx, "The Future Results of British Rule in India", *New York Daily Tribune*, 8 August 1853, in Marx and Engels, *Collected Works*, vol. 12, p. 217; Benedict Anderson, *Imagined Communities: An Inquiry into the Origins of Nations* (London, 1991, rev. edn).

6. Cf. R. Chandavarkar, *The Origins of Industrial Capitalism in India: Business Strategies and the Working Classes in Bombay, 1900–1940* (Cambridge, 1994).

7. K.G. Garbade and W.L. Silber, "Technology, Communication and Performance of Financial Markets 1840–1975", *The Journal of Finance*, 33 (1978), pp. 819–832; Annteresa Lubrano, *The Telegraph: How Technology Innovation Caused Social Change* (New York [etc.], 1997).

8. L.G. Lindley, *The Impact of Telegraph on Contract Law* (New York and London, 1990); R.B. DuBoff, "The Telegraph and the Structure of Markets in the United States, 1845–1890", *Research in Economic History*, 8 (1983), pp. 253–277.

9. See, for Britain, A. Clinton, *Post Office Workers: A Trade Union and Social History* (London, 1984); C.R. Perry, *The Victorian Post Office: The Growth of a Bureaucracy* (London, 1992); Edwin Gabler, *The American Telegrapher: A Social History, 1860–1900* (New Brunswick, NJ [etc.], 1988).

10. Gregory J. Downey, *Telegraph Messenger Boys: Labor, Technology, and Geography, 1850–1950* (New York [etc.], 2002).

nationalize, information", energizing the entire nation with one idea and one feeling, Blondheim showed how the extension of information monopoly and centralization, in the short term, exaggerated difference and dissension. While the Western Union and the Associated Press emerged as the twin pillars of information circulation in the United States, the nation engaged in bitter civil strife.[11] He noted that "Americans had no inkling that an American Reuter existed", and were unaware of the monopolies over information transmission, distribution, and circulation.[12] This paper qualifies the linearity inherent in the celebration of the benefits of technological progress to point out the fragility of technology and the identities forged through it.

THE IMPORTANCE OF INDIA IN THE WORLD TELEGRAPH NETWORK

Over the period 1860 to 1900, the Indian Empire emerged as a crucial strategic element in the telegraph network of the world. The British Indian Empire included present-day Myanmar, Sri Lanka, Bangladesh, Pakistan, and parts of Iran (Persia), and Afghanistan. It also included the broader sphere of British Indian "informal empire" in the Persian Gulf, southern Arabia, the Indian Ocean, and the Bay of Bengal. By 1875, India was the main overland link between the West, and both the Far East and Australasia. The private corporate giant, the Eastern Cable Company, was vulnerable in India because it did not control the landlines from Bombay to Madras, from which its near-monopoly stretched to Penang and Australasia. The Indian Telegraph Department controlled this relatively short connection while it ran the lines through the breadth of India from Karachi to Rangoon. After Karachi, the Indo-European Telegraph Department of the government of India managed the lines to Tehran.

Like the Western Union and Associated Press monopolies in the US, Reuters had a national and international news monopoly that combined with the Eastern Group of submarine companies, which controlled most of the eastern traffic in the British Empire. Though the Indian Telegraph Department controlled the overland link between Bombay and Madras, it had little say in the distribution of traffic from London to the East.[13]

---

11. Menahem Blondheim, *News over the Wires: The Telegraph and the Flow of Public Information in America, 1844–1897* (Cambridge, MA [etc.], 1994), p. 192.
12. *Ibid.*, p. 195.
13. Government of India [hereafter GoI], Public Works Department [hereafter PWD], Civil Works Telegraph [hereafter CWT] (A) Proceedings, May 1875, nos 15–17. Further correspondence regarding the proposed extension of telegraphic communication to the Andamans, no. 16, from Major J.U. Bateman-Champain, Director, Indo-European Telegraph Department [hereafter IETD], no. 440, 8 December 1874; National Archives of India, Delhi [hereafter NAI].

Indian telegraph policy was dominated by the notion that no reduction in the rates charged on internal traffic would be enough to generate an increase in volume sufficient to justify the initial loss of revenue for the department. As a result, rates within India froze at a comparatively prohibitive rate for the period 1865–1885.[14] In contrast, the transit rate to and from Europe continued to reduce during this time. The pattern of indigenous usage emerges from the great distances telegrams covered in India. In Europe telegrams often travelled between neighbouring towns. This was not true of India, where the bulk of the messages travelled between the greater trading centres, and between the producing districts of the interior and the seaboard.[15]

Most of the messages sent were on commercial business. The majority of Indians could not afford private telegrams and the arrival of one was perceived as calamitous, usually bringing tragic news. Indian business used the telegraph selectively, depending on whether the message had anything to do with international trade and prices. The government, media, and European-capital-dominated international business were the biggest users of the telegraph. For example, the Indian Telegraph Department handled 10,382 highly subsidized press messages that paid revenue of only Rs 40,553 during 1882–1883.[16] In short, Indian revenues subsidized international business and media telegrams.[17]

The inexorable decline in rates affected both international and internal systems, especially after 1885, low rates becoming the norm after the Imperial Pacific Cable commenced operations in 1902.[18] By 1910, there were a total 11 million inland telegraphic messages.[19] After 1884, the decline of rates across telegraph systems in order to survive emerging competition externally, from the telephone and wireless, and internally, to combat state and cable competition, allowed expansion in indigenous communication. Greater national economic and political cohesion emerged in India after reduction of the rates charged for telegrams, especially press telegrams, within the country after 1904.

There were two important concerns of the government of India

---

14. GOI, PWD, CWT(A) Proceedings, November 1884, nos 5–9, no. 5, from Colonel J.U. Bateman-Champain RE, Director General [hereafter DG], IETD, to Secretary, GOI, PWD, no. 546, 30 July 1884; NAI.

15. *Administrative Report of the Indian Telegraph Department, 1886–1887* (Simla, 1888), p. 10; National Library, Calcutta [hereafter NL].

16. *Annual Report of the Telegraph Department, 1882–1883*, p. 9; NL.

17. Cf. D.K. Lahiri Choudhury, "A Social and Political History of the Telegraphs in the Indian Empire, c. 1850–1920", (unpublished Ph.D. dissertation, University of Cambridge, 2002).

18. Hugh Barty-King, *Girdle Round the Earth: The Story of Cable and Wireless and Its Predecessors to Mark the Group's Jubilee 1929–1979* (London, 1979), pp. 138, 141.

19. Hardinge Papers 117, Correspondence with the Secretary of State for India, 1911, no. 36, from Lord Hardinge, Viceroy, to the acting Secretary of State for India, Viscount Morley, Simla, with enclosures, 11 May 1911; Cambridge University Library [hereafter CUL].

regarding information: there was a demand for information as well as a
need to contain information. One of the main concerns of the government
was to contain information and prevent media access to sensitive
documents. The India Office and the government of India were under
scrutiny by the Liberal government in Britain. This meant that the
government of India had to exercise extra caution in its acts dealing with
Indians and protect itself from charges of oriental despotism. Lord
Curzon, as Viceroy, had initiated a series of reforms, and imported
experts and appointed committees to implement them. This meant that the
government was under scrutiny internally in India, and the public and the
media waited to learn what the reports said. Finally, the Russo-Japanese
War had increased the British government's fears of a pan-Asiatic revival
and penetration and competition in India from Japan. The government
threatened officials with penal proceedings for passing on secret information. The government also checked communications and association
among its employees through the Official Secrets Act of March 1904.
Collective bargaining by government employees was prohibited. The
international climate of workers' movements, unionization, and association among various classes of workers at this time contributed to the
concerns of the government.

The government of India, shortly after the passing of the Official Secrets
Act, cut its rates on international and national telegrams as well as the rates
charged on international press telegrams. First, it needed to increase
information flows to maintain its competitiveness in the international
telegraph network dominated by the cable companies. The government
wanted to increase revenue by cutting rates to increase the volume of
business and square its rates with the falling cost of the individual telegram
because of growing automation within the telegraph industry. Secondly, it
was an attempt by the government to discover the currents of unrest that
were suspected of flowing beneath the surface of indigenous society.
Printing was encouraged and the cost of registration of newspapers
decreased.

After 1904 a number of politically radical newspapers were published in
different parts of Bengal, Maharashtra, and the Punjab. *Charumihir*,
published in what was now, after Partition, called Eastern Bengal and
Assam, was a typical paper that condensed Calcutta and local happenings,
employed correspondents, and enjoyed a rapidly growing regional readership. These papers, using the opportunities given by cheaper information
transmission, addressed local news and events, momentarily breaking the
international and national information stranglehold of Reuters. A mix of
government policy, itinerant preachers, revolutionary and extremist
propaganda, famine, disease, and discontent were bringing together
different strands and networks of discontent. These waves were occurring
in a situation of famine in eastern India and the plague in western India,

together with a sharp rise in the price index and in the general cost of living.[20] The Durbar celebrations held by Lord Curzon commemorated, as a side event, the fiftieth anniversary of the victory of the British in the mutiny and uprisings of 1857. This propaganda was mirrored in the countryside beyond the control of the government where a similarly celebratory rhetoric resurrected the spectre of 1857. The government fell victim to these whisperings as much as it had helped generate them by its commemorations. Astrologers, revolutionaries, and government officials were now working on a common schedule in anticipation of an uprising around 1907–1908.

THE TELEGRAPH AND THE STANDARDIZATION OF TIME

Recent research on the telegraph in the US noted that telegraphy's "commercial success demonstrated that the economic value of a message depended not only on its content, point of origination, and point of destination, but also on the expected mean and variance of transmission time".[21] In P.G. Wodehouse novels telegrams play a central role, symbolizing the speed of modern communications and the consequent rapidity of alarums and incursions:

> *Bertie*: When you have brought the tea you had better go out and send him a telegram, telling him to come up by the next train.
> *Jeeves*: I have already done so, sir. I took the liberty of writing the message and dispatching it by the lift attendant.
> *Bertie*: By Jove, you think of everything Jeeves!
> *Jeeves*: Thank you, sir. A little buttered toast with the tea? [...]
> *Rocky*: [the recipient of the telegram] [...] when your telegram arrived I was just lying down for a quiet pipe, with a sense of absolute peace stealing over me. I had to get dressed and sprint two miles to catch the train.[22]

The telegraph impacted upon and changed lives in both tangible and intangible ways. Business transacted over vast distances through the telegraph needed centralized and standardized time instead of the prevailing freedom of local times. Though much has been written on what constitutes time and its meaning in sociology, anthropology, and geography, the actual historical minutae of the construction of time have been relatively neglected.

Early Indian texts explaining the telegraph lapsed into discussions of Western versus Eastern methods of reckoning time. Kalidas Maitra, in the

---

20. Sunanda Sen, *Colonies and Empire: India 1890–1914* (London, 1992), Table 3.4: Council Bills and Telegraphic Transfers 1890–1913, p. 80.
21. A.J. Field, "The Magnetic Telegraph, Price and Quantity Data, and the New Management of Capital", *The Journal of Economic History*, 52 (1992), pp. 401–413, 403.
22. Sir Pelham Grenville Wodehouse, *Carry on, Jeeves* (Harmondsworth, 1999, 1st edn 1925), pp. 104–105, 109.

first book in Bengali on telegraphy, gave elaborate conversions between *Puranic* or classical Indian time reckoning and Western time.[23] Switching to Madras Standard Time in 1861 implemented this early consciousness of the importance of the telegraph to a new conception of time. The Indian Telegraph Department switched to a continuous timescale, that is, calculating time not in terms of divisions of twelve but in terms of twenty-four.[24] The increasing unification of the first electronic network had an immediate and fundamental urgent impact:[25] at midnight on 1 July 1905 all telegraph clocks in India were synchronized. Greenwich Standard Time was introduced in India and Burma.[26]

In the reports from the local governments several notes of caution were sounded. MacLagan noted

> [...] the apparent readiness of Calcutta but not of Bombay and Karachi to adopt the five and a half hour's standard [from Greenwich Mean Time] for local time [...] it appears that if the Standard Time is adopted in Bombay, Calcutta and Karachi, it will for all practical purposes be universal in India.

He suggested a vigorous campaign by the government through the introduction of Standard Time in post offices, schools, government offices, and the firing of midday guns.[27] Denzil Ibbetson disagreed in his note and warned that any "appearance of trying to force the hand of the nonofficial community will do more harm than good". He pointed out that it was the Lieutenant Governor Sir John Fergusson's attempt to "hustle" the Bombay people by introducing Madras time in all government institutions that led to the failure of the experiment, and that most of the private sector and banking had kept to the local time.[28]

The city of Karachi managed to drum up public support from its local elites[29] but the Bombay business community presented a different case. The government of Bombay warned that though the "bulk of opinion" supported the replacement of Madras Time with Standard Time on

23. Kalidas Maitra, *Electric Telegraph Ba Taritbartabaha Prakaran* (Srirampur, 1855), pp. 150–153.

24. *Report of the Telegraph Department, 1860–1861*, Appendix L, General Branch Circular no. 43, from Major C. Douglas, 6 September 1861. Extract from the periodical *Once a Week* for March 1861, p. 273; NL.

25. Cf. Leonard Waldo, "The Distribution of Time", *Science*, 1: 23 (4 December 1880), pp. 277–280.

26. Department of Commerce and Industry [hereafter C & I], Telegraph (A), August 1905, nos 20–25, Adoption of the Standard Time in India and Burma with effect from 1st July 1905; NAI.

27. Department of Agriculture and Revenue (Revenue), Meteorology (A) Notes, June 1905, nos 6–35; note by E.D. Maclagan 21 January 1905; NAI.

28. *Ibid*; note by Denzil Ibbetson, 22 January 1905; NAI.

29. *Ibid.*; Proceedings no. 30; from the government of Bombay, no.135P, 26 June 1905; the Port Trust and the municipality of Karachi adopted resolutions in favour of the adoption of the Standard Time; NAI.

railways and telegraphs, in the city of Bombay and in Karachi there was "a strong preference for Local Time".[30] Protests started among workers, especially telegraph workers and postal deliverers who were first to be hit, along with the railway workers. However, railways were comparatively less affected, with an approximately eight-minute adjustment from their previous Madras Time schedule. The *Bombay Samachar* wrote in an editorial entitled "The unpopularity of the Standard Time with the masses" that the "government will earn the blessings of the native population by restoring to the City its old time".[31] The postal delivery establishment in Karachi and Sindh complained in the press and through strike actions that the new railway schedules had forced them to do three deliveries a day when they had previously done two. "Owing to the change in the Railway Time-table [...] Posts have to be delivered thrice in stead of twice, yet there is no increase in the staff."[32] Sporadic strikes began to break out in the public sector and in the mills. Bombay telegraph delivery staff went on strike to protest against longer delivery schedules, as well as to demand a special allowance to compensate them for the increases in price of basic necessities and the general cost of living in that city.

REFORMS IN THE INDIAN TELEGRAPH DEPARTMENT

In India the telegraph consisted of two broad branches: military and civil. The latter was further divided into the Telegraph Department, railway telegraph branches (increasingly managed by the Telegraph Department), and, in some areas, telegraph signallers attached to the Post Office. The Indian Telegraph Department also managed the the Indo-European Telegraph Department. This handled telegraph lines in southern Persia and Afghanistan, and was almost exclusively European. The Military Field Telegraph was established during 1857 and continued as an integral element in British campaigns. Its signallers, usually British and European, were spread over the many military cantonments in India. Eurasians dominated in the staff of postal and railway signallers. Because the Indian Telegraph Department had been taking over these departments since 1874, the few that remained as reserves were not really important until the strike. The Railway Mail Service had a significant number of Indian employees. The delivery and clerical staffs were a heterogeneous group including Eurasian and Indian Christian young adults from orphanages. It also

---

30. *Ibid.*; Proceedings no. 8; from the government of Bombay, no. 7148, 29 December 1904; NAI.

31. *Bombay Samachar*, 5 February 1907; *Mukhbir-i-Islam*, 4 Febrary 1907; *Akbar-e-Saudagar*, 5 February 1907; Report on Native Newspapers/Press [hereafter RNN/P], Bombay Presidency, no. 5 for the week ending 7 February 1907; Maharashtra State Archives [hereafter MSA].

32. *Phoenix*, 16 February 1907: RNN, Bombay, no. 7 for the week ending 16 February 1907; MSA.

included a number of men from Bihar and Uttar Pradesh. Peons, who delivered messages, and clerks, who recorded, dispatched, and kept records and accounts, tended to be Bengalis and men from Madras, Pune, and Bombay.

Finally, the Indian Telegraph General Signalling establishment was mostly Eurasian and European in composition. A subsidiary local service existed and had more Indians on the rolls but they were not transferable. Open examinations were held at centres like Madras, Bombay, and Calcutta for recruitment of Indians into the Telegraph Local Service, who had little prospect of promotion to the senior grades. The Rourki Engineering College, for example, was important in training and educating Indians. This local service was increasingly made redundant while the general service was expanded. The general service departments were increasingly exclusive racial reserves.

There were two broad categories of workers that withdrew labour during the telegraph strike. There were the subordinate sections of clerks and peons, usually Indians. The delivery establishment had a preponderance of adult Indian male temporary employees, who sometimes had been in employment for over twenty years. They received very little wage increases, perks, pensions, or medical facilities, and because they were on a temporary or daily register their holidays were practically nonexistent. The clerks and peons were mostly Indian and Christian Indians. There were the signallers, of which 75 per cent were European and Eurasian in 1908.[33] The haphazard Europeanization of the uncovenanted civil service in the 1860s had serious consequences for the future. The rapid recruitment of telegraph staff in Britain between 1866 and 1871 meant that between 1903 and 1907 there would be almost forty retirements at a senior level and blocks in promotion plagued the telegraph establishment from the 1880s.

To reconstruct the immediate and the general context of the Telegraph Strike of 1908, conditions specific to the Indian Telegraph Department and the changing structure of technology and politics within which it was situated need elaboration. A brief note was circulated between the highest levels of the Telegraph Department and the government of India in 1904. It was a prelude to the more public Telegraph Committee of 1906, and envisioned a drastic reduction in the staff of the Telegraph Department to improve efficiency, cut down on subordinate establishment costs, and allow for increased automation. The report reflected the need of the Telegraph Department to be competitive with the cable companies and maintain parity in rates. The size and the cost of the establishment were

---

33. However, such distinctions cannot be rigidly maintained for the course of the strike. For example, the Bengali signallers in the Calcutta Telegraph Office did not openly join the strike but the boy peons, often Eurasian, joined the strike of the peons and clerks.

not proving viable. This combined with the need to keep increasing the number of users by cutting rates. The report proposed that an additional 20 per cent be added to the strength of the general service of the signalling branch through selection from within the service, and that they would receive a higher rate of pay. The conditions of general service were formulated as follows: (1) staff must be European and Eurasian; (2) they must be qualified in code and figure tests; (3) be liable for service in any circle; and (4) reversal to local service was possible and permissible at any time but would entail lower pay and fewer facilities.[34] The authors of the scheme designed an "overall reduction in establishment through new standards of work". However, they warned the government that it would take a "considerable number of years before the disappearance of the existing signallers is effected".[35] As an immediate recruitment and retention measure they proposed that in addition to pay, "all European and Eurasian signallers, who compose 75 per cent of the total establishment [the total being 2,279 in British India and Burma in 1904], be granted free quarters or allowance in lieu".[36] The "decentralization plan" would then lead to a saving in the clerical establishment that would reduce the budget cost to Rs 3,249, a saving of Rs 1,412. Over time more than a few livelihoods, especially in the subordinate sections, were to be lost.[37]

As a consequence of this plan, and of fears about their future, signallers and clerks began to combine towards a union. The Telegraph Association began to be organized and the movement for a subordinate relief fund was started. Within a few months of this, a further aggravating factor appeared. Alfred Newlands, the Traffic Manager brought from Britain to reform the Indian Telegraph Department, submitted his proposal for a series of reforms that would fundamentally change the department. There was already resentment in the department over the appointment of an outsider to reform the Indian Telegraph Department. Along with technical changes and increased efficiency tests, he also proposed twenty to twenty-four hours of work every thirty-two hours[38] and eight- to eleven-hour night shifts. It should be remembered that the signallers worked nights and weekends and got leave infrequently. However, it would also appear that the strikes arose out of ignorance of the aims of the Department, and the Director General subsequently publicly clarified that the eventual average

34. GoI, Department of C & I, *Scheme for the Reorganization of the Indian Telegraph Department*, J.H. LeMaistre, Officiating Under Secretary, Government of India, and I.C. Thomas, Superintendent of the Telegraph, and personal assistant to the Director General, Indian Telegraph Department, p. 12; Simla: government publication, 1904; NAI.
35. *Ibid.*, p. 29; NAI.
36. *Ibid.*, p. 14; NAI.
37. *Ibid.*, pp. 10–11, 22; NAI.
38. [Confidential], *Reorganisation of the System of Work in the Telegraph Department* (Simla, 1908), p. 5, from the General Secretary, Telegraph Association, to Private Secretary to the Viceroy, Simla, 6 April 1908; Minto Papers, National Library of Scotland, Edinburgh [hereafter NLS].

working hours would be eight hours every day of the week and a reduction of night work from eleven hours to eight.[39] Sporadic strikes also began to break out in the public sector and in the mills.

The Telegraph Committee's Report, which was submitted in 1907, had some disturbing proposals. During its deliberations it received as many as eighty-seven joint petitions from the subordinate ranks of the establishment. To summarize the issues, clerks and peons wanted the same status as signallers with openings for induction into the signalling establishment. They demanded a provident fund and pension, along with a proposal for the formation of an all-India association for welfare and recreation. Better medical facilities and allowances for rises in the cost of living were included in their list of demands. They also protested against the prevailing system of financial penalties for mistakes and frequent transfers over long distances. Finally, revision in the scales of pay, promotion, and the department's policy on temporary employment, were key issues. Apparently the department had been using casual labour, and a clerk or peon could be classed as temporary for as long as fifteen or twenty years with no prospect of getting a pension or benefits.[40] Nearly all the demands were refused. Attempts were made to amalgamate the post and telegraph departments and substantial reductions in the clerical and delivering establishment were proposed.[41]

The Telegraph Committee proposed to freeze recruitment and induct women, military signallers, and Eurasian and European youths from the orphanages and mission schools in India. They also quite frankly recorded their reservations against "smart" men from Calcutta, Bombay, and Madras. These standard pools of successful examination recruits were to be replaced by women and young recruits from the orphanages. The argument against the Bengali, "Bombayite" and "Madrasi" was that they might not be physically in shape for the task of touring and inspecting offices. Arbitrary fines, penal transfers, and temporary, unpensioned, and insecure employment were genuine grievances and had been admitted by the Telegraph Committee which wrote, "Not only is the organisation of the signalling establishment defective but the existing rates of pay are [...] inadequate." The Committee recorded that between May and October of 1906 alone as much as 18.5 per cent of the signalling establishment was transferred, often for very long distances. It stated that this percentage of transfer "practically amounts to the transfer of the whole staff of every office in three years".[42]

39. *Ibid.*, p. 25, from T.D. Berrington, Director General, Telegraph Department, to the Secretary, Department of Commerce and Industry, Kanpur, 10 April 1908; NLS.
40. *Report of the Telegraph Committee, 1906–1907*, Appendix, Calcutta: Superintendent, Government Printing, 1907, pp. 86–90 [hereafter *Telegraph Report*]; CUL.
41. *Ibid.*, Summary of the recommendations of the Committee; CUL.
42. *Ibid.*

PREPARATIONS FOR THE STRIKE

The telegraph workers' movement started with fresh impetus in November 1907 as rumours about the impending submission of the Committee's report began to circulate. Most of the establishment suspected the report to be unfavourable. It was reported in the press that "messages were exchanged between the signallers in all the main offices in India and a general assent was obtained from to concerted action [...] great excitement at Bombay, Calcutta, Karachi, Madras, Rangoon, Gauhati, Allahabad and other offices".[43] So it was a process by which anonymous individuals tapping the telegraph keys became individual identities in order to coordinate and communicate between each other. The telegraph workers had to engineer a crisis of sufficient dimension to escape victimization and to underline their irreplaceability to the state and business. The volume of messages between telegraphers was growing and a different network and virtual community with its own politics and codes functioned within the telegraph network. Rangoon was one of the main coordination centres for the movement. The Director, Criminal Intelligence, reported to the government on the agitation amongst the subordinate staff and activity of the representatives of the Telegraph Memorial Committee at Rangoon in December 1907.

Henry Barton took the initiative for telegraph unionization in the autumn of 1907. Barton was a senior employee having served twenty-six years in the service. Later, in the report to the Viceroy on Barton, the Director General of the Telegraphs explained Barton's motives away as pique at a missed promotion. During the same month Henry Barton was addressing telegrams on behalf of the Telegraph Association.[44] These telegrams requested a reply to the general memorial and listed their grievances, which included protest against overtime. Above all they demanded the early publication of the Telegraph Committee's Report submitted in December 1907. From the start Barton was a problem for the government. He had none of the discretion essential in government service. In December 1907 or January 1908, Newlands met Barton in Burma while on tour as Traffic Manager. Barton brought along the local representative of the Telegraph Association to this meeting, who was on the staff of the *Rangoon Times*. The details of the interview were published in both the *Telegraph Recorder* and the *Rangoon Times*. A lecture delivered before the staffs by Newlands was similarly cited in detail in the same week in these publications.

The Director General, in his note to the government, saw this as a clear

---

43. *The Panjabee*, 7 December 1907, Centre for South Asian Studies, Cambridge [hereafter CSAS].

44. Department of C & I, Telegraph Estab. (A), December 1907, nos 1–15; NAI.

breach of official etiquette if not actually of the Official Secrets Act. He
held that Barton "was mainly responsible for the appearance of the
communications". Moreover, Barton in his February 1908 address in
Calcutta, "in contravention of the special orders, [...] read out a official
communication which I had issued to the staff, and which was in
consequence published next morning in the local papers". The government
noted that he "did good work" in upper Burma, but this did not entitle him
to any consideration in the eyes of the Telegraph Department. The
Director General posted him from Rangoon to Berhampur. It was not a
central location and Barton refused to go to Berhampur. Instead, he asked
for a posting either in Rangoon or in Calcutta. Upon his request being
turned down, Barton resigned in January 1908 and proceeded on a

> [...] tour of the principal telegraph centres in India and delivered inflammatory
> speeches to the men. Owing to the fact that he possesses undoubted ability above
> the average of the ordinary signaller, and to the gift of delivering addresses, he
> has had great influence over almost the entire signalling staff.[45]

Henry Barton, as Secretary to the Telegraph Association, began to publish
the *Telegraph Recorder* from Rangoon in January 1908.[46] It is perhaps this
early revolt against arbitrary transfers that allowed the movement to gain
in coherence and organization.

The flows and eddies in information supplies crucially determined the
chronology of events. The government declined to publish the Report. The
Times of India complained, "although the Committee's report was
delivered at Simla a year ago, the public know nothing of it".[47] In
February 1908 the entire staff sent identical memorials to the Viceroy. The
government in reply stated that it adhered to its decision "not to publish
the report of the Telegraph Committee until they have submitted their
recommendations to the Secretary of State and his orders obtained there on
[...]. Regarding the questions raised (by the petitioning workers) [...] the
Government are at present unable to hold out any hope".[48] The
government of India was extremely sensitive to the press and had to be
very aware of the language of its official publications, especially in the
context of the growing heat generated in the British parliament on Indian
affairs. The Telegraph Committee's report could not be published in the
form it was submitted. The telegraph employees of Allahabad met on the

45. *Ibid.*, no. 4, from the Director General, Telegraphs, to the Private Secretary to the Viceroy,
no. 29-T, 29 April 1908; NAI.
46. Sharma, *Labour Movement in India*, pp. 65–66.
47. *Times of India*, Bombay, 20 February 1908: letter to the Editor; MSA.
48. *Amrita Bazar Patrika*, 18 January 1908, p. 5, NL; also *Times of India*, Bombay, 20 February
1908; MSA.

19 January 1908 to agree to join the Subordinate Relief Fund, and significantly, "promising to enlist all absentees in the same cause".[49]

The government of India was shocked at the sheer volume of messages that it was inundated with: 116 identical memorials were sent to the Viceroy on one day from the signal room clerks in the Bombay Division alone.[50] Many sections among the clerks, signallers, and peons coordinated to achieve this effect. Waves of petition followed with growing concentrations from December 1907 up to February 1908.[51] In January the entire signalling staff of India and Burma sent in almost identical petitions to the Viceroy.[52] The government was also surprised by the fact that the petitions poured in from different parts of the system. Nagpur, Bombay, and Karachi clerks experimentally coordinated to be received on the same day. Nagpur sent its petitions on the 8 February,[53] as did Karachi,[54] while Bombay had sent its petitions two days earlier on the 6 February.[55] An infuriated Director General lashed out in his report to the government at the problem of "surplusage of temporary clerks", and commented on the identical nature of the submissions, that the "*generality of the prayers made are such as to court refusal*" [italics mine].[56] The Director General pointed out, "as a rule they [the clerks] are not up to the required standard of education, and it is most undesirable that a clerical post should ever get to be looked upon as a stepping stone to the Signalling Establishment".[57]

THE STRIKE OF THE PEONS

On the night of Thursday 27 February 1908, the delivery peons of the Telegraph Department struck work. There had being growing discontent as new methods of delivery and attendance were introduced over December and January. Barton, General Secretary of the Indian Telegraph Association, asked for public sympathy and support from the press.[58] He urged the workers to adopt constitutional means of action.[59] By Saturday

49. *Amrita Bazar Patrika*, 22 January 1908, p. 9; NL.

50. Department of C & I, Telegraph Estab. (A), nos 7–10, February 1907; NAI.

51. *Ibid.*, nos 1–15, December 1907; NAI.

52. *Ibid.*, nos 27–29, January 1908; forwarded with report from the Director General; NAI.

53. *Ibid.*, nos 7–10, February 1908, no. 8, from Nagpur; NAI.

54. *Ibid.*, no. 9, from Karachi; NAI.

55. *Ibid.*, no. 7, from Bombay; NAI.

56. *Ibid.*, nos 18–20, January 1907; NAI.

57. *Ibid.*, no. 18, from Sir Sydney Hutchinson, Director General of Telegraphs to the Secretary, Government of India, Department of Commerce and Industry, 15 December 1906; NAI.

58. *Times of India*, 21 February 1908; MSA.

59. *Amrita Bazar Patrika*, 28 February 1908, p. 5; NL.

the entire system of delivery in Calcutta appeared threatened. Initially 173 permanent and 193 temporary men went on strike. Their numbers swelled and almost 400 men were involved. The striking workers met at the Calcutta maidan, beneath the Ochterlony monument, and held a meeting adopting resolutions. This echoed the methods adopted by political parties across the spectrum. It was as much a protest action as it was a publicity stunt; the striking workers chose one of the oldest and most familiar locations for political speeches and meetings. They demanded the same wages as the Bombay staff, better hours and conditions of work, winter clothing, *batta* [cost of living allowance], and promotion according to seniority regardless of temporary or permanent positions, and, most provocatively, the reinstatement of the two peons dismissed from service as the ringleaders of the 1907 strike in Bombay.[60] As mentioned before, the Bombay post and telegraph delivery establishment had struck work over the new delivery schedules and their demand for an allowance to meet the sharp rise in the general cost of living in that city.

That there were wider issues and feelings involved is shown by the fact that by Monday 2 March, the boy peons at the Calcutta Central Telegraph Office, numbering about 100, joined the strike. These were probably Eurasian and Indian Christian orphans aged between sixteen and eighteen.[61] Madras telegraph peons, numbering around sixty, went on strike on 4 March.[62] Telegraph Delivery peons in Bombay followed suit on the 29 March in spite of the concessions they already enjoyed because of the strike in 1907.[63] These latter two were largely Indian. The Post Office clerks sent a petition threatening to join the strike.[64] The postal workers in Modassa, Ahmedabad, joined in the movement.[65] The same day, the clerks at the Accountant General's Office threatened to strike work.[66] Everywhere around them there were workers striking: in mills in Tuticorin, 2,000 men in the marine dockyard in Khidirpur in Calcutta, in jute mills in Chandernagar, 6,000 workers at the railway workshop at Parel in Bombay. The Railway Mail Service was dismantling the railway and mail schedules. Letters were written to the press against the actions of the Inspector General, Railway Mail Service.[67] The labourers employed to look after the

60. *Ibid.*, 29 February 1908, p. 7; NL.
61. *Ibid.*, 2 March 1908, p. 4; NL.
62. *Ibid.*, 6 March 1908, p. 8; NL.
63. Department of C & I, Telegraph Estab. (A), nos 3–8; administrative report of the Indian Telegraph Department for 1907–1908 with notes; *Gujarati*, 5 April 1908; NAI.
64. *Amrita Bazar Patrika*, 13 March 1908, p. 6; NL.
65. *Mahi Kantha Gazette*, 8 March 1908; *RNP*, Bombay, no. 11, for the week ending 14 March 1908; MSA.
66. *Amrita Bazar Patrika*, 5 March 1908, p. 6; NL.
67. *Ibid.*, 25 February 1908, p. 7; NL.

overhead lines in the Calcutta Tramway Company struck work; they were dismissed overnight.[68] In short, in 1907–1908 many of the branches of the administration seemed to be on the verge of open revolt. The strikes ended suddenly: the boy peons and the delivery peons and clerks were summarily sacked,[69] and the 10th Jat regiment was deployed for the delivery of messages until a new establishment was employed.[70] Peons were brought in from Jullunder and Delhi.[71] The striking workers showed precocity in their demands, organization, and solidarity in different parts of the country. Their method and strategies were mature. They sent a petition to the Commissioner of Police requesting him to intercede with the Director General and the Superintendent of the Telegraph Department on their behalf or accept their resignations. Here they stressed the loyal and peaceful nature of their rally. They "wished to hand over their badges and uniforms to the Commissioner of Police and requested him to get their dues from the Department".[72]

The peons showed both organization and courage. The workers combined in Calcutta, Bombay, Karachi, and Madras to go on strike on both general and specific demands. The majority of these were Indian workers. Their willingness to sacrifice their jobs showed increasing politicization in their ranks. Ultimately they were replaceable, yet with the help of the media and possibly interoffice communication through some of the signalling staff, they combined across centres to provide the spark for the signallers' strike. The number of strikes breaking out demonstrates sympathy existing horizontally and vertically across different types of administrative labour. These were the delivering and maintenance sections crucial to the functioning of state administration, communication, and business, yet they were at the fringes of the city spatially and socially, and acted simultaneously with other wage labour such as millhands. In the case of these wageworkers the media played a crucial role by reporting workers' actions in different centres, facilitating sympathy strikes. However, within each centre the worker also stood united with wageworkers in other industrial sectors. Significantly, the signallers sympathized with them, and it is this gesture of sacrifice and valour without any hope of success that possibly goaded the salaried workers to strike.

68. *Times of India*, 29 February 1908; MSA.
69. *Amrita Bazar Patrika*, 2 March 1908; NL.
70. Department of C & I, Telegraph Estab. (A), nos 3–8; administrative report of the Indian Telegraph Department for 1907–1908 with notes, p 4; NAI.
71. *Ibid.*, no. 20; demi-official from G. Rainy, Under Secretary, Government of India, to T.D. Berrington, Director General, Telegraphs, Tel. no. 2522, 9 March 1908; NAI.
72. *Amrita Bazar Patrika*, 6 March 1908, p. 8; NL.

THE STRIKE OF THE SIGNALLERS: "PASSIVE RESISTANCE"

A month after the strike of the peons was broken, Alfred Newland, the Traffic Manager imported from Britain, launched a scheme of work shifts for signallers, which was implemented in all offices on 3 April 1908. *The Statesman* reported a heavy accumulation of messages in Burma, while the *Bandemataram* discussed the warning issued by Director General Berrington which pointed out that the rate of sending was being purposely and wilfully slowed down and "faults on wires and apparatus are also abnormally high". It was reported that "large numbers of men in Rangoon and Mandalay had reported sick".[73] Throughout March the government had been occupied with the dismissal and re-employment of the delivery establishment at some of the vital centres of commerce and communication. The last batch of dismissed Bombay peons handed in their uniforms and collected their dues on 6 April.[74]

By 8 April 1908 the system was in the throes of the second crisis. The main wires were fused and rendered dysfunctional. Either engineering electrical faults or persons literally fusing the wires did this. On 6 April, fifteen trunk lines went out of order in Calcutta. Bombay had huge accumulations of messages, and two lines between Bombay and Madras were handed over to operators of the Eastern Cable Company, almost exclusively British and trained at Porthcurno. These operators showed that the lines were working and demonstrated that the signallers in the rest of India were "slacking off". The Calcutta office staff insisted that it was Rangoon and Bombay that held them up; Rangoon was commonly believed to be the source of the trouble.[75] It was reported that Madras was coping but Bombay, Calcutta, Rangoon, Agra, and Karachi were "affected". Lahore soon joined their ranks.[76]

The *Empire* thundered, "the operators are fooling [...]. They waste their time in keeping the offices informed of the accumulation of messages, discussing the situation and sending wires at different centres giving accounts of the Press attitude."[77] The *Rast Goftar* joined in the criticism.[78] Tilak's *Kesari* wrote that while the "signallers who have gone on strike are mostly Eurasian and European [...] they have our sympathy. It is a little curious, however, that strikes undertaken by white employees are always successful, while those organized by native subordinates fall through."[79]

73. *Bandemataram*, 6 April 1908; NL.
74. *Ibid.*, 7 April 1908; NL.
75. *Ibid.*, 8 April 1908; NL.
76. *Ibid.*, 9 April 1908; NL.
77. Reprinted; *Ibid.*, 8 April 1908; NL.
78. *Rast Goftar*, 19 April 1908; RNP, Bombay, no. 16, for the week ending 18 April 1908; MSA.
79. *Ibid.*, *Kesari*, 14 April 1908; MSA.

Another main wire was found fused in the Calcutta office by noon on 10 April. By now 8,000 messages were delayed and the figure was growing. The Director General issued a fresh circular, reminding the staff of the circular of 22 February and demanding "loyalty and good sense". Superintendents of Rangoon, Calcutta, Bombay, Agra, Lahore, Karachi, and other offices facing similar problems were given the power to dismiss arbitrarily up to 10 per cent of the signalling staff.

As early as February, the Bengal Chamber of Commerce had warned the government, referring to the discontent in the subordinate ranks and had suggested "an enquiry into their [the workers'] alleged grievances with a view to avert a strike and the consequent disorganization of public business".[80] Officials thought this blatant impertinence on the part of the Chamber. In his note on the letter, G. Rainy wrote that the Chamber's suggestion was "quite unreasonable and unintelligent [...] they are not in a position to advise Government. Their action can only be described as most unfortunate and tending directly to the encouragement of insubordination amongst the men."[81] The Viceroy, Lord Minto, commented that "the Chamber of Commerce letter was most ill-judged and unjustifiable".[82]

In its reply to the Chamber's letter, the government stated that the difficulties were being removed by (1) introducing reforms of a radical nature in the working of the Department, and (2) improving conditions of service of the subordinate staff. The government also categorically stated that it did not apprehend a general strike of the signallers.[83] The Marwari Chamber of Commerce received a much more terse reply to its letter of 10 March.[84] The Chamber had complained of the "Indian merchants and traders who have suffered and are still suffering considerable loss and inconvenience through the phenomenal delay because of the strike of the delivery peons".[85] The Anglo-Indian papers pointed out that "Trade and commerce everywhere throughout India is in a state of paralysis, and our happy-go-lucky Viceroy is away enjoying himself shooting tigers, apparently not caring a tuppenny damn whether the commerce of India goes to the devil or not."[86]

The Bengal Chamber of Commerce appealed to the Viceroy on 7 April

80. Department of C & I, Telegraph Estab. (A), March 1908, nos 18–25, no. 18; from the Secretary, Bengal Chamber of Commerce, no. 296, 26 February 1908; NAI.

81. *Ibid.*, March 1908, no.19; note by G. Rainy, 3 March 1908; NAI.

82. *Ibid.*, March 1908, no. 19; notes by Harvey and Minto, 7 March 1908; NAI.

83. *Ibid.*, March 1908, no. 20; to the Secretary, Bengal Chamber of Commerce, no. 2544–59, 10 March 1908; NAI.

84. *Ibid.*, March 1908, no. 23; to the Secretary, Marwari Chamber of Commerce, no. 3208–59, 26 March 1908; NAI.

85. *Ibid.*, from Secretary, Marwari Chamber of Commerce, no. 59, 26 March 1908; NAI.

86. *Oriental Review*, RNP Bombay, for the week ending 15 April 1908, reprinted from Max's column in the *Capital*; MSA.

to appoint a Conciliation Board as had been done in the case of the railway strike in 1906–1907. This strike had paralysed transport and commerce but, with strong lobbying from the Bengal Chamber of Commerce, it had a relatively quick solution. The Viceroy's Personal Secretary telegraphed a reply that refused viceregal intervention and was a tirade against the staff who have "chosen to deliberately block the introduction of the new hours of duty by delaying messages and absenting themselves from duty".[87] The workers used what they and the government called the strategy of "passive resistance": slowing down of work speed, engineering faults, and collective absence at work through medical certificates and other forms of legal leave, leading to accumulation of messages on most of the major Indian lines. Pile-ups meant delays, not immediate disruption. Delay meant that the unified world time and the emerging global market were in jeopardy. The primary difficulty faced by the administration was the fact that, this being a system of electronic communication, it was more concerned with transmission and motion than with posts and stations. The workers could delay the system considerably yet blame the next station and it was difficult in an emergency to pinpoint the exact source of the accumulating information snowball; delay, in this case, was cumulative. This element of surprise was removed when the workers went public with their demands. The realization of this strategy dawned on the government slowly as it became aware that there were too many accidental breakdowns, absences and pile-ups to be a coincidence.

Henry Barton, Secretary to the as yet unrecognized Telegraph Association, addressed a large meeting in Rangoon towards the end of April 1908. The Director General of the Indian Telegraphs issued a threatening circular in response that the *Rangoon Times* called an "egregious blunder". The Director General's circular prohibited the further use of the workers' club premises for meetings, threatened dire punishment for attendance "where such language was used", and warned the signalling staff that "unauthorized publication of information obtained officially" would render them liable to prosecution.[88] This was reported by the local press along with the government's refusal to countenance a provident fund for the subordinates, arguing that it was too close a copy of the privileges of the superior establishment.[89] A number of letters began to appear in newspapers complaining of the plight of the clerks, signallers, and delivery service, and citing unhappy work conditions as the reason for

---

87. *Ibid.*, 12 April 1908; MSA.
88. Department of C & I, Telegraph Estab. (A), no. 4; from the Director General, Telegraphs, forwarding with his remarks the memorial addressed by Henry Barton, late Telegraph Master, no. 29-T, 29 April 1908; NAI.
89. *Amrita Bazar Patrika*, 21 February 1908, p. 9; NL.

the prevailing mismanagement.[90] The Bengal Chamber of Commerce and the Calcutta Trades Association voiced criticism and concern.[91] The Director General of the Telegraph, T.D. Berrington, agreed to meet the representatives of the Chamber of Commerce in secret; "the Director General stipulates that no reporters are to be present and that no report of the meeting will be published in the newspapers". The negotiations were conducted over the telephone.[92] As soon as the government's reply reached the staff through the Chamber of Commerce, Rangoon declared the strike. Discontent was reported among the signallers in Chittagong.[93] The *Statesman* reprinted a telegram from Barton announcing the strike in protest against the summary dismissals from the staff at Rangoon.[94] The Director General summoned Barton from Rangoon to Calcutta. Upon his landing, Barton addressed a large gathering at the Town Hall.

STRIKE AND PANIC

The signallers went on strike in shifts so as not to lose out on their day's pay. The signal "Diabolic 15" was flashed to all the offices. It meant "general strike at 3 pm". A detailed description of the strike in Calcutta is available in the *Bandemataram*. The first batch struck in Calcutta at three in the afternoon. "The new watch and the old watch gathered on the steps and beckoned those inside to come out by waving sticks, hats and handkerchiefs. Two Eurasian youths, no doubt in their excitement, yelled the fatal word 'strike'."[95] In Bombay they began at 2 pm. Agra joined at 4. Kanpur and Allahabad were rumoured to be ready to strike at 5 in the evening. In fact, Allahabad joined the following day. In Bombay, twenty-five signallers were served with notices of summary dismissal. The notices were dated 8 April 1908. In short, there seemed a genuine possibility of a "general strike by the signallers throughout the country".[96] Asked by the *Bandemataram* reporter whether the strike would be "universal", a spokesman for the strikers said that some of the senior men, while in complete sympathy, would not join the strike and that these men would be of use in keeping open communication between the different centres. He

90. e.g. *Ibid.*, 25 February 1908, p. 7, letter to the editor from a Railway Mail Service sorter; *ibid.*, 27 February 1908, p. 10, letter to the editor accusing the Inspector General of degrading behaviour, arbitrary fines, and penal transfers of subordinates for trivial offences, from a "sufferer"; NL.
91. *Times of India*, 3 March 1908; MSA.
92. Department of C & I, Telegraph Estab. (A), no. 20; demi-official from G. Rainy, Under Secretary, Government of India, to T.D. Berrington, Director General Telegraphs, tel. no. 2522, 9 March 1908; NAI.
93. *Bandemataram*, 13 April 1908; NL.
94. *The Statesman*, Calcutta, 12 April 1908; NL.
95. *Bandemataram*, 13 April 1908; NL.
96. *Times of India*, 3 March 1908: memorial by the Bombay Chamber of Commerce; MSA.

added that the 60 Bengali signallers, out of a total of 240 in Calcutta, would not "by any chance go on strike".[97] By December 1907 reports had circulated in the press regarding discontent among Indian signallers who were discouraged to enter "general service" with its better pay and prospects. It was alleged that the "department was closing its doors to Indians".[98] In the meanwhile, they could help keep communications open.

Large batches of postal signallers and military telegraphers were deployed to replace the striking workers. Burma was particularly hard hit because it had very few postal and military reserves. The main line often could not be operated. Another crucial problem was the new high-speed "Baudot" signalling instruments recently introduced on the main routes and in the main centres. The substitute signallers, so technologically out of touch that some of them had not tapped a key in the past three years, were rarely found to possess any working knowledge of the sophisticated Baudot.[99] Thus, replacement of the strikers by sufficient numbers of efficient workers proved impossible. The Superintendent of the Agra office was removed; he had panicked and contacted the Deputy Super-intendent of Police, who reported that,

> The unrest among the telegraph clerks has extended to Agra, which is the biggest telegraph office after the three great centres of Calcutta, Madras and Bombay [...]. However, Mr Morgan [Superintendent, Telegraphs] was unnecessarily alarmed. [...] *I send this by letter, and have not wired, as it is not desirable to attract more attention to the matter than is absolutely necessary and which would be the case if I sent long cypher wires under the present circumstances through the local telegraph offices* [emphasis mine] [...]. The attitude taken up is obviously one of passive resistance and has taken the form of getting "sick" [...] at present the strike is not apparent to anybody unconnected with the with the Department.

He went on to add that Morgan had "panicked".[100] The quandary of the government in having to avoid its main means of communication multiplied its feeling of panic and vulnerability.

The Telegraph Department resorted to the omission of the date of despatch from the telegrams so that receivers could not be sure of the time and date of despatch. This compounded the confusion. The *Indu Prakash* wrote in its columns,

> [...] we have before us a telegraphic press message, which bears neither the date of despatch nor the timing. While we can suppose that hours and minutes have been

97. *Bandemataram*, 13 April 1908; NL.

98. *The Panjabee*, Lahore, 11 December 1908; RNP, Punjab; Seeley Library, Cambridge [hereafter SL].

99. Department of C & I, Telegraph Establishment (A), December 1908, nos 1–3, Orders of the government of India on the memorials addressed to the Viceroy by the signalling staff; NAI.

100. *Ibid.*, August 1908, no. 5; extract from the fortnightly report, commissioner, Agra, 7 April 1908; NAI.

ignored in the hurry and confusion obtaining at present, it is difficult to ascertain why there is no room for the *date* of the message [...]. And in all business matters a good deal depends on knowing the date.[101]

The *Sind Gazette* added,

> To all appearances there is a complete breakdown in the telegraph service between Calcutta and Karachi and a partial breakdown between Bombay and Karachi. Telegrams are filtering through slowly and, in the absence of any date of despatch, it is impossible to say whether the messages were despatched on the day of receipt or on the previous day or a week before that.[102]

Similarly, "at all the main centres efforts are being made to show a clean slate [...] sub-offices are being shut down and men are being drafted in post-haste from the *mofussil*".[103] The disappearance of date and time of despatch from telegrams seemed to threaten the very basis of the need for rapid communication. Marwari merchants were complaining bitterly at the delay in the opium despatches. The government of India was forced to issue a notice in the government *Telegraph Gazette* refusing to accept ordinary and deferred telegrams at their telegraph offices until further notice. Telegraph offices were accepting only the very urgent ones at double the price.

Henry Barton was once again summoned to Calcutta from Rangoon. W.L. Harvey, Secretary, Department of Commerce and Industry, wanted officially to meet Barton, Secretary to the Indian Telegraph Association. This was the political breakthrough that the strikes had aimed for. Barton met Harvey as the representative of an officially recognized organization and "an amicable resolution was expected".[104] The government of India announced an approximately 20 per cent rise in pay for the subordinate grade staff.[105] The official strike ended twelve days after it had started. Speaking to the Rangoon Telegraph Association in 1909, Barton described the "history and spread of the Association during the past eighteen months" and advocated as their motto "Definite Forwardness".[106] On 22 April 1908 wires were sent to all the centres in Burma and India announcing the return to work. Barton expressed his gratitude for the support of the press and the Chambers of Commerce.[107]

101. *Indu Prakash*, Bombay, 7 April 1908, Eng. cols; RNP Bombay, no. 15 for the week ending 11 April 1908; MSA.

102. *Sind Gazette*, 3 April 1908; RNP Bombay, no. 15; MSA.

103. *Sanj Vartaman*, 16 April 1908; RNP, Bombay, no. 16 for the week ending 18 April 1908; MSA.

104. *Bandemataram*, 19 April 1908; NL.

105. Department of C & I, [Confidential] *Reorganisation of the System of Work*, p. 29, from the Secretary of State to the Viceroy, 13 April 1908; NL.

106. *Amrita Bazar Patrika*, 4 June 1909, p. 4; NL.

107. *Bandemataram*, 22 April 1908; NL.

CONCLUSION

The workers had struck work over the government's refusal to publish the Telegraph Report. An obsessively secret bureaucracy generated its own scares and panics with an over anxious surveillance and policing. A strike at the centre of the communication system increased its sense of panic. The government could not communicate while the system to do so was in revolt. This was the second mutiny so anxiously looked for by the government yet completely surprising and paralysing when it happened. The telegraph strike over the summer of 1908 reveals that there was a perception of unity, as the workers withdrew labour at around the same time in different centres. The strike was not a Luddite, millenarian, or communitarian uprising but one that was integrally linked to the world economy and technological change. It involved European, Eurasian, and "up-country" men, Bengali clerks, and maintenance staff. Traditional means of ethnic, racial, and caste enumeration are possibly inadequate to describe the workers involved. The victory of the signallers had as its underbelly the sharp polarization between Indian, Eurasian, and European workers. It was the direct experience of state repression and representational politics of the time that led to the subsequent hardening of community identities among the workers. The Eurasian and European signallers were re-employed if they agreed to try out the new working system and hours. Though many requests were made to re-employ the dismissed peons they were not taken back.[108]

The experience of 1908 and after showed how a high degree of organization and mutual sympathy could crumble without a platform. The Telegraph Association was both a symbol and a platform for the unity of signallers, and in this the Chambers of Commerce helped them. The peons and clerks had no similar organization that could give coherence to a sustained campaign. However, these experiences allowed the political process and the system of government to be understood. In contrast, the European and Eurasian workers had to be unequivocal about their patriotism and loyalty to the Empire and government and promise not to strike. Henry Barton, as Secretary of the Telegraph Association, publicly protested that the "movement was free from anything approaching insubordination or disloyalty".[110] In the end it was both a failure of representation and an inability to avoid unionization that led to the abandonment of broader political ambitions and the crossclass cooperation of the strike. The emergence of community and racial identity in the process of working-class unionization reflected on a smaller scale the partial democracy, the form of political or rights representation, and the communal award system soon to be introduced at an all-India level.

108. *Ibid.*, 24 April 1908; NL.
109. *Times of India*, 18 March 1908; MSA.

Henry Barton was imprisoned as a pre-emptive measure by the government under the Defence of India Act passed after the outbreak of World War I. The government was not prepared to risk jeopardizing its main communications. After the War, the Telegraph Committee of 1920–1921 was formed to look into the petition sent by Barton, once more General Secretary of the Indian Telegraph Association after his release from prison. This was after a large revision in pay scales and organization had been implemented in 1919. The revisions came from the proposals of two different committees: the first looking into the affairs of the Post Office and the other into the Telegraph Department. The government's anxiety to address workers' issues and concerns contrasted vividly with the attitude of the state slightly more than a decade ago. The Committee's

> [...] anxiety was to arrive at a decision which should satisfy reasonable men [...]. The Government has already incurred an additional expenditure of nearly 32 lakhs per annum since November 1919 over this [Telegraph] Branch and another 130 lakhs per annum on the Postal Branch. These proposals are likely to make a substantial addition. It is now up to the men to combine to respond loyally to this generous treatment.[110]

While greater articulation and confidence can be seen in the demands of the workers, there was a growing tendency to encourage factional representation. Thus, telegraph signallers, inspecting staff, and clerks were invited to petition separately.[111] The state's interest in dealing with factions and fragments was clear, and at one point Barton's petition argued against the divisive policy adopted by the government which was dealing with about 100 senior temporary clerks on a piecemeal, individual basis. The issue was the transfer of slightly over half into permanent positions but again dividing them by giving some a time-scale salary while others got fixed increases.[112] Yet the workers too showed increasing factionalism and Barton, sitting with government nominees on the Committee, held forth against the "outsiders" and women who were employed at the cost of permanent staff, especially on telephone duty.[113]

The transregional economic general strike of 1908 in India was remarkable because of the workers' ability to use the telegraph to coordinate and organize. Flooding the government with petitions from different centres and in huge quantities demonstrated the new weapons forged by the workers, with a consciousness of themselves as a larger entity beyond the immediate neighbourhood or region. The government's inability to deal with this shows how startling were the methods forged by the first virtual community through and because of the telegraph, that held

---

110. *Report of the Telegraph Committee, 1920–1921*, Simla, 1921, p.13; NL.
111. *Ibid.*, Annexure; NL.
112. *Ibid.*, pp. 5–7; NL.
113. *Ibid.*, p. 17; NL.

the attention of business, state, and media simultaneously. An industry-wide strike was achieved involving vertical as well as lateral cooperation, and the telegraph and media were used to organize strikes at the same time in different centres. The study of general strikes in India in the social and political sense has led to a concentration on the spaces and associations of mobilization that included teahouses, messes, native place and caste associations, and the *mohalla* or neighbourhood.[114] However, these networks were not primary or crucial in the case of the telegraph strike; combining across regions and cities meant the neighbourhood had little significance. The emergence of community and racial identity in the process of working-class unionization thereafter reflected upon a smaller scale the partial democracy and communal award system seen at all-India level. Increasing factional representation yet growing horizontal coordination after 1908 contrasts with the case of monopoly capital, which saw large centralized unions in the US.[115]

Alongside the specific demands of the workers, there were more universal and general demands, echoing labour movements across the world. The universal standardization of time and the changes proposed in work-hours reflected an international concern of information labour. In 1907, the telegraph workers struck work in the USA. The Indian press reported in August 1907 that there was a "great strike of telegraphists [...] over 1600 operators in Chicago, sympathetic strikes in Denver, Colorado, and Salt Lake City [...]. The telegraphists strike has spread to 50 cities in the western and southern States."[116] It was reported that Toronto and Montreal had joined in the strike and that "communication has stopped throughout the USA except by telephone".[117] In the US, perhaps more so than in India, the strike of 1907 was successful in scale but tragic in consequence. After 1907, messenger boys were absorbed in general unions and made irrelevant in the media,[118] and signallers were rapidly replaced by automation and women; neither could maintain their positions within the industry.[119]

Downey's argument about the agency of telegraph delivery boys is borne out in the Indian strike: in India, peons, clerks, and delivery staff were the catalysts that precipitated the signaller strikes. This does not

114. Bryna Goodman, *City and Nation: Regional Networks and Identities in Shanghai 1833–1937* (Berkeley, CA, 1989); R. Chandavarkar, *The Origins of Industrial Capitalism in India: Business Strategies and the Working Classes in Bombay, 1900–1940* (Cambridge, 1994).
115. Cf. C. Craypo, "The Impact of Changing Corporate Structure and Technology on Telegraph Labor, 1870–1978", in *idem* (ed.), *Labor Studies Journal*, pp. 283–304.
116. *Amrita Bazar Patrika*, 14 August 1907; NAI.
117. *Ibid.*, 17 August 1907; NAI.
118. Downey, *Telegraph Messenger Boys*, pp. 173–174, 177.
119. Craypo, "Impact of Changing Corporate Structure and Technology on Telegraph Labor", pp. 294–295.

mean that they were successful; the signallers because of their organization were able to historicize their action and get their own union. The peons and clerks, mainly Indian, achieved this in the 1920s through, in part, the leadership of union leaders like Tarapada Mukherjee. Thus, even though the delivery boys, peons, and clerks were the agents/catalysts of the strike, they did not have the agency to realize their political objectives. Ironically, unionization allowed workers to articulate a history and process though sacrificing spontaneity and broader working-class unity. The unionization that occurred under the patronage of the middle class, for example on the railways in India, was Masonic.[120] In the Indian case, the delivery and clerical staff were heterogeneous and perhaps did not have the same iconic connotations that they had in the US. The majority was Indian, male, mainly adult, and usually temporary. Though in places like Calcutta and Bombay young boys were employed, they did not constitute a majority or significant agency. In India, subordinate unionization across different communication industries was realized after the first two decades of the twentieth century. The suggestion that the messenger boys were enmeshed with the survival of the industry in the US is provocative:[121] perhaps the associations of the mass of subordinate delivery workers and various grades of signalling staff in India after 1920 and the telegraph as a government-run public utility contributed to the telegraph being a living reality in India.

120. This possibly happened in the US telegraph unionization of the 1880s; cf. Gabler, *The American Telegrapher*, p. 188.
121. Downey, *Telegraph Messenger Boys*, p. 202.

IRSH 48 (2003), Supplement, pp. 73–95 DOI: 10.1017/S0020859003001275
© 2003 Internationaal Instituut voor Sociale Geschiedenis

Perpetually Laborious: Computing Electric Power Transmission Before The Electronic Computer

ARISTOTLE TYMPAS

INTRODUCTION

Placing Thomas Edison at the beginning of a history on electric power transmission hardly needs justification. Thomas Edison's abundant supply of pictures of himself as an inventive genius – and America's pressing demand for a myth of an ingenious inventor – combined to bestow a "Eureka" moment upon Edison's pioneering Pearl Street (New York) Station electric lighting network. But the history of the laborious computations that took place at Menlo Park and the division-of-computing labor of which Edison took advantage suggests a different view of inventive genius. The story of the computational pyramid formed by the labors of Francis R. Upton, Charles L. Clarke, and Samuel D. Mott (1879–1880) can be reconstructed from the existing literature.[1] In his reminiscences from Menlo Park, Edison's employee, Francis Jehl, detailed how Edison thought of constructing a miniaturized network to be used as a computer of the actual network. Knowing that constructing, maintaining, and using the miniature network required a considerable amount of skilled labor, Edison decided to hire an employee for it, Dr Herman Claudius. Edison enthusiastically welcomed Claudius to perform a type of computing work "requiring nerve and super abundance of patience and knowledge". Jehl remembered that the labor of constructing a miniature network of conductors, "all in proportion, to show Mr Edison what he would have to install in New York City in connection with the Pearl Street Station" was "gigantic".[2] Following the pattern of the Pearl Street Station electric lighting network, several similar networks were built in the early 1880s. In response, Edison's labor pyramid was enlarged by giving Claudius an assistant, Hermann Lemp, who performed the monotonous task of constructing the new miniature networks, which Edison needed for

---

1. See Robert D. Friedel and Paul Israel, *Edison's Electric Light: Biography of an Invention* (New Brunswick, NJ, 1986), pp. 120 and 124. See also, Paul Israel, *Edison: A Life of Invention* (New York, 1998), p. 179, Friedel and Israel, *Edison's Electric Light: Biography of an Invention*, pp. 36 and 148, and Francis Jehl, *Menlo Park Reminiscences* (Dearborn, MI, 1939), pp. 729–731.
2. See Jehl, *Menlo Park Reminiscences*, pp. 545–546.

computation. Inconvenient as it might be for those who assume that technological change is the product of inventive genius, electrification was, from the beginning, laboriously computed; it was not, like Athena, a deity that leapt from a godly head.[3]

Taking the history of computing electric transmission after Edison as my reference, I shall argue in this paper that the computing work required for the reproduction of the capitalist mode of production was expropriated from human labor – labor defined by the understudied work of men and women computing workers, usually referred to as "computers" or "computors". As a student of the history of computing for the period before the so-called Information Revolution – which, supposedly, was instigated after the 1940s by the electronic computer – I was surprised by the uniformity in which pre-40s authors refer to their own technical civilization as one that depended on computing. Furthermore, I was struck by the frequency of technical authors who referred to computing as "labor". This article provides the labor historian with a representative sample of the innumerable, yet understudied, pre-1940s references to the act of computing as an act of labor. But, more importantly, in thinking about how to interpret those references, instead of simply presenting a list of laborers whose role has been neglected, this article considers the mechanism by which the act of neglecting such a large and skillful population of laborers became possible.

Regarding the history of computing electric power transmission before the 1940s, most of the hundreds of articles that I considered start by introducing the reader to a crisis of computing laborers. Yet, in this pre-computing era, these very laborers employed an extensive variety of computing tools and machines! These apparatuses ranged from ubiquitous tools, such as the inexpensive and humble "slide rule", to uncommon state-of-the-art industrial and academic laboratory computing machines like the sizable "network analyzers" and its immediate ancestors, "artificial lines" and "calculating boards".

Like the miniature network that Edison hired Claudius to construct, artificial lines, calculating boards, and network analyzers – for simplicity I refer to them as analyzers – were laboratory models of the networks to be computed. Unlike many mechanical models devised and used during the same period also for the purpose of computing the transmission of electric power, the analyzers were electrical artifacts. The first calculating board of 1916 was a common wooden table upon which a set of electrical elements representing resistance was mounted. Adding electrical elements representing reactance and capacitance, and increasing the number of electrical

---

3. For America demanding the myth of an inventive genius and for Edison supplying it, see Wyn Wachhorst, *Thomas Alva Edison: An American Myth* (Cambridge, MA, 1981), and Charles Bazerman, *The Languages of Edison's Light* (Cambridge, MA, 1999), respectively.

elements and their interconnections as a whole, resulted in the rapid evolution of the calculating board to a room-sized artifact like the first 1929 network analyzer. Mounted on tables or library shelves, the artificial line of the late 1910s and the early 1920s provided a better computing analogy than did a calculating board, but at the cost of being more demanding in terms of the skill and the amount of labor needed to construct and maintain it. Thus, the network analyzer can be interpreted as an enlarged calculating board or as a combination of artificial lines (to make the transition from computing lines to computing networks of lines possible).

In the transition from calculating boards and artificial lines to network analyzers, analyzers were devised into subsections while peripheral components were also added to assist in the subdivision of the labor involved. Moving to the 1940s, we find pictures of a stark contrast: men sitting at control desks that were separated from the analyzer computing units that they monitored, but women standing directly before the network analyzer computing units that they set up. These pictures of the electrical analyzers predate the nearly identical pictures of the gendered division-of-computing labor that accompanied the introduction of the first, equally large electronic computers of the 1940s (see below). Revealing also is a sketch from 1944 that accompanied a *Westinghouse Engineer* editorial, which featured a man sitting at a control desk in a room made cramped by a network analyzer while boys were rushing around with the data and results.[4]

Within this article, I focus only upon the introduction of new varieties of analyzers because each new wave of these artifacts was ideologized and mythologized by the engineering professionals of that period. On each occasion, these professionals testified that the latest analyzer provided evidence of the ultimate revolution in computing technology. Here, Marxist theory can offer brevity while remaining analytically precise: of all technologies for computing electric power transmission, the one involving analyzers exemplified the highest ratio of constant to variable capital (dead to living labor, machines to humans). It follows that these moments can illustrate both the permanent technical revolution in computing and the perpetual labor crisis of computing that accompanied it.[5] I shall argue that each subsequent wave of analyzers failed to mechanize computing and thereby permanently eliminate the computing labor crisis. As a result, we find within the same technical literature that enthusiastically welcomed

4. "*Network Calculator* [...] Mathematician Par Excellence", *Westinghouse Engineer*, 4 (July 1944), front cover.
5. For the concepts of constant and variable capital, see Karl Marx, *Capital*, vol. 1, (London, 1990). For a Marxist class analysis that I found useful in thinking about the laborers involved in computing electric power transmission, see Nicos Poulantzas, *Classes in Contemporary Capitalism* (London, 1975).

each new wave of analyzers as providing the definite solution, the surprising revelation that the preceding wave of analyzers had all but solved this crisis. Certainly, each new wave of analyzers provided a momentary solution to the crisis. Given, however, the dynamic (expansive) reproduction of the capitalist mode of production, the spontaneous mechanization of the computing of one network was instantaneously turned into the basis for the construction of another, more complex network, which, in turn, immediately turned the previous wave of analyzers into something obsolete. In this dynamic, as new networks (of canals, roads, rails, electrical and electronic lines of energy and communication, etc.) brought about new computers and new computers brought about new networks, the dependence on computing labor remained intact.

The aforementioned 1944 *Westinghouse Engineer* editorial heralded the replacement of calculating machines by network analyzers as the event that saved the field from a computing labor crisis. The editor informed his readership that when the plans for the electrification of the Virginia railroad were being drawn up in the mid-1920s,

> [...] two crews of three men each worked several months with a battery of adding machines making the necessary calculations [...] for the almost endless combinations of circuits and loads. Each team would work furiously for a couple of weeks and then spend the next week or so checking the results of the other team.

For the *Westinghouse Engineer* columnist, this was "a monumental task and utterly hopeless" and, as a result, "[e]lectrical systems threatened to become a Frankenstein out of [c]ontrol".[6] In the history of electric power transmission, computing revolutions came and went with an impressive frequency. Given that moments of explicit celebration of new machines are also moments of implicit disappointment in the old ones, I find that the study of these moments offers a privileged instance for making invisible human labor visible.

This contention also raises an important historiographical point. In the previous example, the network analyzer, considered by contemporary scholars to be an exemplar of an analog computer, came as a savior of the calculating machine (in this case an adding machine), now considered an exemplar of a digital computer. The *Westinghouse Engineer* editorial suggests that an essentialist demarcation between a technically superior (digital-mental) and a technically inferior (analog-material) computing technique is unfounded. Moments of shift in the emphasis from (digital) calculating machines to (analog) analyzers have been moments when the computing labor crisis became apparent. We know little about these moments because the post-40s demarcation between the analog and the

---

6. "*Network Calculator* [...] Mathematician Par Excellence".

digital was *a posteriori* projected to the pre-40s history of computing. As a result, analyzers are now historiographically devalued, despite their importance during their period of use. Accordingly, the computing labor crisis that marks the history of using them has yet to receive the attention that it deserves.[7]

In a few pioneering accounts of the place of human computers, the invisibility of labor is usually attributed to ceremonial introductions of computing machinery.[8] Granting the reality of this omission, it only tells us half of the story. One example may illustrate my point. In her otherwise suggestive study of the important group of women computors who worked for the ENIAC – the pioneer electronic computer of the 1940s –

---

7. For an elaboration, see Aristotle Tympas, "The Computor and the Analyst: Computing and Power, 1870s–1960s" (unpublished Ph.D. thesis, Georgia Institute of Technology, 2001).

8. See Jennifer Light, "When Computers Were Women", *Technology and Culture*, 40 (1999), pp. 455–483. A history indicative of the unbroken line of computors working with what we now call digital machines before, but also after the ENIAC, and the associated enlargement of the capitalist division-of-computing labor can be reconstructed by reading together the following references (in order of the chronology covered: Lorraine Daston, "Enlightenment Calculations", *Critical Inquiry*, 21 (1994), pp. 182–202; I. Gratan-Guinness, "Work for the Hairdressers: The Production of de Prony's Logarithmic and Trigonometric Tables", *Annals of the History of Computing*, 12:3 (1990), pp. 177–185; Andrew Warwick, "The Laboratory of Theory or What's Exact About the Exact Sciences?", in M. Norton Wise (ed.), *The Values of Precision* (Princeton, NJ, 1994), pp. 311–351; Mary Croarken and Martin Campbell-Kelly, "Beautiful Numbers: The Rise and Decline of the British Association Mathematical Tables Committee, 1871–1965", *IEEE Annals of the History of Computing*, 22:4 (2000), pp. 44–61; Margaret W. Rossiter, "'Women's Work' in Science, 1880–1910", *Isis*, 258 (1980), pp. 381–398; Peggy Aldrich Kidwell, "American Scientists and Calculating Machines: From Novelty to Commonplace", *Annals of the History of Computing*, 12:1 (1990), pp. 31–40; Mary Croarker, *Early Scientific Computing in Britain*, (Oxford, 1990); Paul Ceruzzi, "When Computers Were Human", *Annals of the History of Computing*, 13:1 (1991), pp. 237–244; David Alan Grier, "Gertrude Blanch of the Mathematical Tables Project", *IEEE Annals of the History of Computing*, 19:4 (1997), pp. 18–27; idem, "The Math Tables Project of the Work Project Administration: The Reluctant Start of the Computing Era", *IEEE Annals of the History of Computing*, 20:3 (1998), pp. 33–49; idem, "Ida Rhodes and the Dreams of a Human Computer", *IEEE Annals of the History of Computing*, 22:1 (2000), pp. 82–85; and Harry Polachek, "History of the Journal 'Mathematical Tables and For Other Aids to Computation', 1959–1965", *IEEE Annals of the History of Computing*, 17:3 (1995), pp. 67–74. For an example of the survival of women computors in the post-ENIAC era, see Denise Gurer, "Pioneering Women in Computer Science", *Communications of the ACM*, 38:1 (1995), pp. 45–54. For a group of male-only computors, see Jan van den Ende, "Tidal Calculations in the Netherlands, 1920–1960", *IEEE Annals of the History of Computing*, 14:3 (1992), pp. 23–33. The role of computors is generally missing from most of the available studies on the history of calculating and punched-card machines. However, some of these studies contain pictures of rooms full of working computors. For a sample of this suggestive visual record written by a professional historian, see pictures in James Cortada, *IBM, NCR, Burroughs, and Remington Rand and the Industry They Created, 1865–1956* (Princeton, NJ, 1993). For an example from a corporation that published its own history, see pictures in Edwin Darby, *It All Adds Up: The Growth of the Victor Comptometer Corporation* (Chicago, IL, 1968). For an introduction to precapitalist computors and calculators, see Arno Borst, *The Ordering of Time: From the Ancient Computus to the Modern Computer* (Chicago, IL, 1993).

Jennifer Light argues that the tasks these women performed was only programming. In doing so, Light risks severing the mental from the manual, regarding the labor the ENIAC women actually conducted. While she succeeds in inviting our attention to their unappreciated mental skill, she reproduces standard historiographical distinctions concerning the unjustifiable devaluation of the skillful manual labor when these women set switches and plugged cables.[9] In diminishing the computor's rung in the labor hierarchy, there was a relative increase in the ratio of manual to mental computing skills. Yet skill as a whole became all but unnecessary. As I understand it, we need a re-evaluation of the manual skills involved, not simply a re-evaluation of mental skills. Without such re-evaluation, the (largely) manual skills possessed by the lower computors will remain overlooked.

This historiographical strategy seems especially appropriate when the considerable differences within the ranks of computors are taken into account.[10] True, the exceptional mental-digital skills of the few top women computors were historically and (are) historiographically unappreciated. But even more unappreciated were the less digital but equally indispensable material-analog skills of many subclasses of women computors populating the pyramid of computors below them. And another facet remains disguised – history neglects the material-analog side of the skills possessed by the top women computors at ENIAC (i.e. references to their work in programming erases the significance of the actual plugging and switching over analyzing). Worse, we know practically nothing of the computing labor of a great mass of men possessing computing skills because the computing machines with which they worked are rendered historically unimportant on the grounds that their *a posteriori* designation belongs to an inferior technical class – analog computers.

Extending the previous statement, the computor could be even a male electrical engineer as long as his work could be ideologically devalued beside the work of someone else – an "analyst" – placed above him in the pyramid of the division of labor. Hence, I understand the difference between an "analyst" and a "computor" to be relative, not absolute. What I find is a hegemony of an ideology that presented this relative difference as absolute, thereby preventing laborers from developing a shared identity to resist the devaluation of their labor power in a more effective manner.[11] For an introduction to the ideal extremes of the analyst-computor

9. See Light, "When Computers Were Women", p. 477.

10. The best testimony of the variance within computors that I know of is contained in the memorandum on the work of computors at a military facility. See Ceruzzi, "When Computers Were Human", especially the section on the subclasses of computors and the significant difference in their salaries.

11. On the mechanism of presenting relative work differences as absolute, and on how crucial it is for the capitalist mode of production, see Poulantzas, *Classes in Contemporary Capitalism*.

distinction, I quote from Vannevar Bush's influential textbook on electrical engineering mathematics: "It is entirely possible for a computer to perform the algebraic work necessary for the symbolic solution of alternating current networks in the steady state without any grasp of the philosophy of the symbolic treatment or of the mathematics or differential equations on which it is based." "It is entirely possible", added Bush, "to utilize the operational method on specific problems without the slightest idea of why and when it does or does not work. This, however, is computation and not analysis."[12]

Computing labor ranged from the labor to construct the machines to the labor to maintain them. In addition, before the labor to use the machine came the labor to educate and become educated on how to use it. This included not only education on the computing method to be selected, but also how to use this method in conjunction with the machine. To this accounting one may add the labor to link the producer of a computing machine to the user of a computing machine, a labor of intermediary individuals, or later on, of groups of individuals forming certain institutions.[13]

The history of those laboring with electric lighting and power transmission is representative of a broader tradition of computing labor. First, computing the transmission of electric lighting and power was part of a broader whole, which included the labor to compute the electric transmission of communication messages. Second, the engineering side of electric power transmission computations was related to the business part of computing (the computing taking place in the accounting department of an electric power manufacturer was, for example, linked to all aspects of electrification-related computations, including the engineering ones).[14]

---

12. Vannevar Bush, *Operational Circuit Analysis* (New York, 1929), p. iii. In addition to many good articles on aspects of Bush's work, there is a book-length biography of him; see Pascal Zachary, *Endless Frontier: Vannevar Bush, Engineer of the American Century* (New York, 1997).

13. The importance of the labors of intermediary agents is increasingly acknowledged in the historical literature. Their long list should include salesmen and those who trained them, important in the computing field from early on (see Cortada, *IBM, NCR, Burroughs, and Remington Rand*); consultants and members of other professional or volunteering groups, scientific and other (see Atsushi Akera, "Calculating a Natural World; Scientists, Engineers, and Computers in the United States" (unpublished Ph.D. thesis, University of Pennsylvania, 1998), whose knowledge ranged from system analysis (see Thomas Haigh, "Inventing Information Systems: The Systems Men and the Computer, 1950–1968", *Business History Review*, 75 (2001), pp. 15–61) to machine interconnection (see Onno de Wit, Jan van den Ende, Johan Schot, and Ellen van Oost, "Innovation Junctions: Office Technologies in the Netherlands, 1880–1980", *Technology and Culture*, 43 (2002), pp. 50–72.)

14. In the accounting departments of electric utilities and manufacturers the use of standard calculating and punched machinery, and an associated emphasis on a more developed capitalist division-of-labor was much more customary than in the engineering departments; see Tympas, "The Computor and the Analyst", ch. 6.

Third, the computation of the electrical phenomena of electric power transmission was developed in parallel with the computation of the mechanical phenomena of electric power transmission. For example, computing the electric stability of the current running through lines would have been meaningless without having computed the mechanical stability of the transmission towers upon which these lines hung. Fourth, the development of the "off-line" computing history that I introduce in the following pages interacted with an "on-line" computing tradition that stands at the core of what is referred to as regulation, control, and automation. In reality, the development of on- and off-line computing interacted.[15] Fifth, the history of computing power transmission took place in several related directions. For example, computing the transmission of power for civilian purposes interacted with its military analogs, namely computing the transmission of power for military purposes, which was a key component of what is known as external ballistics or "fire-control" computing. When comparing the historiography of military fire control and civilian electric power transmission, once can surmise that the individuals and the institutions involved are the same.[16] Finally, the development of computations in technical environments interacted with the development of computations in scientific environments. For example, the network analyzer, which was devised for computing electric power networks, ended up being used in many scientific contexts. The experience gained through such uses fed back into the development of the network analyzer. I focus on a technical rather than a scientific computing environment because the historiography of technical computations is the

15. For an introduction to the invisibility of human labor in the history and historiography of the technology of on-line computing through negative feedback, the core of the ideology of self-regulation (self-control, automation), see Aristotle Tympas, "An Artificial Line, or Technology as Spectrology", *Antenna: Newsletter of the Mercurians, in the Society for the History of Technology*, 13 (2000), pp. 4–5, and 10. In the *Antenna* article, the artificial line is discussed through its use as an on-line computer, i.e. as a regulator, whereas in this one I focus on its off-line use as a computer. Reading David Mindell's recent history of electronic negative feedback amplification from the perspective of labor history suggests that underneath an elusive drive for automation laid a world of intensive and extensive engineering labor. See David Mindell, "Opening Black's Box: Rethinking Feedback's Myth of Origin", *Technology and Culture*, 41 (2000), pp. 405–434.
16. Read from the perspective of labor history, the rich historiography of fire-control computing points to another ocean of human labor, ranging, for example, from the computing labor of thousands of groups of soldiers and sailors who were skillfully using an anti-aircraft gun director by tracing the movements of an invading bomber, to the computing labor of the bombardiers who used computing bombsights. A uniform problem of the existing literature is that the emphasis is placed on the technical parameters of fire-control machines at the cost of providing us with knowledge of the skill required to use them. For a sample of the labor required to construct, use, and maintain bombsights such as the one used to drop the first atomic bomb, see Stephen L. McFarland, *America's Pursuit of Precision Bombing, 1910–1945* (Washington DC, 1995).

more understudied of the two. Taken together, the interactions mentioned in this paragraph indicate that the history of laboring with electric power transmission can offer us a privileged insight to the role of human labor in the history of a broader whole of complex computational processes.

"FRANKENSTEINS OUT OF CONTROL": A PERMANENT CRISIS OF COMPUTING LABOR

The step-up in computing complexity involved in the transformation from Edison's direct-current short-distance distribution to alternating-current long-distance transmission was considerable. As longer transmission schemes were tried and, accordingly, as transmission by alternating current and higher voltage were chosen, the labor of calculation was dramatically increased. "Engineers", wrote Jonathan Loki in his 1932 biography of Charles Steinmetz, "as yet were almost completely in the dark about how to calculate its values under practical conditions", and "they had to use the old faithful cut-and-try". "This", explained Loki, "was the dragon which Steinmetz undertook to tame".[17] For Leonard Reich, Steinmetz's Calculating Department was the "most important" research organization at General Electric during the 1890s.[18] However, a mere decade later, calculation was already too big a task for one department because of the frantic increase of the distance of alternating current transmission, and the Calculating Department could not catch up with the aggressive demand. Steinmetz's Calculating Department was dismantled and calculation became a distinct function within each department.[19]

Moving from the 1880s (Edison) and the 1890s (Steinmetz) to the 1900s, proposals for laying and interconnecting lengthy sections of electric lines into complex networks gathered speed. Engineers hastily sought to solve the ensuing computing labor crisis, and, in order to do so, devised more elaborate computing models of the networks to be build. The "artificial lines" and the "calculating boards" were typical examples of such models of the years between the 1900s and the 1920s.

Considerable labor was required to design, construct, and operate the artificial line. In his 1911 description of Union College's smooth artificial line, J.H. Cunningham described in detail the work required during each phase. In some instances, the mismatch between design and construction appeared quite mysterious. "A great amount of trouble", reported Cunningham at a 1911 AIEE conference, "has been caused by the breaking

17. See Jonathan Norton Leonard, *Loki: The Life of Charles Proteus Steinmetz* (New York, 1932), p. 131.
18. Leonard Reich, *The Making of American Industrial Research: Science and Business at GE and Bell, 1876–1926* (Cambridge [etc.], 1985), p. 58.
19. Ronald Kline, *Steinmetz: Engineer and Socialist* (Baltimore, MD, 1992), Part 2.

of tubes. After being completed and placed on the racks they would crack with no apparent cause." The solution to this problem inspired an extended research program on computing coils at MIT in the early 1920s.[20] Constructing an artificial line was so laborious that in many cases it required years. And the methods were never fail-safe; for example, the Harvard artificial line required many experimental trials before permanent installation. The engineers developing the University of Washington's artificial line resisted presenting their line at an AIEE conference until they tinkered with it for three years. Once the original designer left the company, the Telluride Power Company invested many additional years to complete their project. In 1923 Dellenbaugh presented MIT's artificial line, yet they had begun their construction as early as 1920.[21] Maintenance and operation were also affected by unpredictable instabilities. For example, in 1912 Arthur Kennelly and H. Tabossi reported that changes in temperature could produce serious disturbances. Inferring from the case of the broken Union College line coils, skill proved necessary even for mounting an artificial line. Mounting Harvard's line was not problem-free either. Evidently, details could make considerable difference – such as first carefully mounting the line's coils on a shelf and then arranging them vertically so that they were alternately perpendicular to one another because laying them so could minimize the unwanted action from mutual induction.[22]

Problems of this kind are what Dugald Jackson, the director of MIT's Electrical Engineering Department, had in mind when he referred to the history of the artificial power line as a "struggle".[23] Kennelly, the world's expert on the artificial power line, unceasingly emphasized the need to focus attention while laboring with seemingly unimportant details. In his textbook, he cautioned about the difference that improper plugging could make. Considering that some units would deviate considerably from the

20. See J.H. Cunningham, "Design, Construction, and Test of an Artificial Transmission Line", *AIEE Transactions*, 30 (1911), pp. 245–256, 251; and F.S. Dellenbaugh, "Artificial Lines with Distributed Constants", *AIEE Transactions*, 42 (1923), pp. 803–823.
21. See Arthur E. Kennelly and H. Tabossi, "Artificial Power-Transmission Line", *Electrical World*, 59:7 (17 February 1912), pp. 359–361, 359; Edward C. Magnusson and S.R. Burbank, "An Artificial Line with Adjustable Line Constants", *AIEE Transactions*, 35 (1916), pp. 1137–1153, 1138; George H. Gray, "Design Constructions and Tests of an Artificial Power Transmission Line for the Telluride Power Company of Provo, Utah", *AIEE Transactions*, 36 (1917), pp. 789–831, 791–792; and Dellenbaugh, "Artificial Lines with Distributed Constants".
22. Kennelly and Tabossi, "Artificial Power-Transmission Line", pp. 359–361.
23. Dellenbaugh, "Artificial Lines with Distributed Constants", p. 821. On Jackson and the MIT-General Electric partnership, see Bernard W. Carlson, "Academic Entrepreneurship and Engineering Education: Dugald C. Jackson and the MIT-GE Cooperative Engineering Course, 1907–1932", *Technology and Culture*, 29 (1988), pp. 536–567; and Karl L. Wildes and Nilo A. Lindgren, *A Century of Electrical Engineering and Computer Science at MIT, 1882–1982* (Cambridge, MA, 1985).

designed average, he suggested that it was better to place them away from the generator-end of the line because it was "very disconcerting to observers and computers to find certain sections far off the average".

In his 1925 *Bell Laboratories Record* article, Hoernel included a photo of two young men, Breivogel and Northrup, plugging an artificial communication line. They performed a job similar to what women computors would do in the 1940s when arranging ENIAC.[24] Underpaid electrical engineering undergraduates performed tasks such as winding coils, graduate and research assistants constructed the remainder and conducted a few experiments, while research directors made most experiments and designed nearly all the apparatus. For example, in the spring of 1910, Becker and Grover – two seniors in Union College's Department of Electrical Engineering – constructed 150 tubes. One could surmise that when the tubes broke, that engineers could demand better products. More than ten years later, L. Becker worked as a research assistant at MIT and supervised making coils with distributed constants. In the 1920s, M. Gardner and E. Arnold, two research assistants, carried out the first MIT tests with the artificial lines. Frederick Dellenbaugh, Jr, Director of MIT's Electrical Engineering Research Division, created the design for the single-phase line, while many extensive tests were carried out by his graduate students, Scott, Van Ness, and Jackson, who were supervised by Jones, another research assistant. Coffin and Buckner documented the design of the three-phase artificial line in their MIT graduate thesis and groups of graduate students later performed the test work.[25]

Upon experiencing the workings of computing pyramids, most students of electrical engineering later sought to reproduce them to their advantage. From 1900 to 1910, Kennelly and his dissertation advisee, Vannevar Bush, offer the classic example of a "top analyst". Another of Kennelly's graduate students from the 1910s, Edith Clarke, also offers the classic example of an electrical engineer who struggled to enter the electrical engineering computing pyramid from below, i.e. from the ranks of the computors. Sexism contributed considerably to an essentialist demarcation between analysts and computors. The fortunes of a female electrical engineer, Clarke – who had the same age, intelligence, and desire to learn as did her counterpart Bush – can help us to understand how such demarcation could be created.

In his 1919 letter to Steinmetz, Dugald Jackson recommended Clarke as an expert in power transmission analysis:

24. For Kennelly, see Arthur E. Kennelly, *Electric Lines and Nets: Their Theory and Electrical Behavior* (New York, 1925), pp. 220–221. On plugging the ENIAC, see Light, "When Computers Were Women".
25. See Cunningham, "Design, Construction, and Test of an Artificial Transmission Line", p. 249, and Dellenbaugh, "Artificial Lines with Distributed Constants", p. 805.

Dr Kennelly tells me that Miss Clarke has been an uncommonly competent student in Mathematics and allied branches, and that she has done excellent research in connection with the characteristics of power transmission as represented by our artificial transmission lines. She is proposing to communicate with you for the purpose of seeing whether there may not be a need for such a mind as hers in connection with your work.[26]

Regardless, the best that Clarke could do upon completing her 1919 thesis, entitled "Behavior of a Lumpy Artificial Line as the Frequency is Indefinitely Increased", was to upgrade her status to "computor". The relationship between alternating current frequency and computing accuracy was the thorniest issue during the 1910s. Unless we turn to the ideology that perpetuated women's inferiority, which contributed to the division-of-labor pyramidization, we cannot explain why Edith Clarke could not find any job as an electrical engineer. Yet, Clarke's career was, as the knowledgeable James Brittain commented, "remarkable". In 1918, Clarke was the first woman to earn an electrical engineering degree from MIT and was awarded her MS in 1919. Although she obtained these degrees, Clarke fought a battle to move, first, from computor to the rank of the electrical engineer, and, subsequently, to move from engineer to the superior rank of the analysts.[27] Clarke contributed substantially to electrification computing technology. Evidently, her exposure to artificial line-related computing began well before earning her MS. After her first year as an engineering undergraduate in 1911 at the age of 28, George Campbell, who had computed the principle of the loading coil by using an artificial line, hired her for the summer as a computer assistant.[28] For most of that decade, Clarke worked as a computor in crash projects devoted to computing the long distance transmission of communication. The division of labor between analysts like Campbell and computors like Clarke – and among the various computors like Clarke and her colleagues – confirms what we know about other, non-engineering computing projects that employed computors in both governmental and private contexts, scientific or otherwise. In all these cases, we find a division-of-computing labor

26. For Dellenbaugh and Bush, see Karl L. Wildes and Nilo A. Lindgren, *A Century of Electrical Engineering and Computer Science at MIT, 1882–1982* (Cambridge, MA, 1985), p. 68. For Jackson's letter see Edith Clarke's file at the General Electric Archives (Schenectady, New York).
27. See Edith Clarke, "Behavior of a Lumpy Artificial Line as the Frequency is Indefinitely Increased", (unpublished manuscript, Massachusetts Institute of Technology, 1919); James E. Brittain, "From Computor to Electrical Engineer: The Remarkable Career of Edith Clarke", *IEEE Transactions on Education*, E–28:4 (1985), pp. 184–189; and Edward L. Owen, "Edith Clarke: Pioneer Woman Engineer", *IEEE Industry Applications Magazine*, 1:3 (1995), pp. 40–43.
28. On how Campbell employed the artificial line, see James E. Brittain, "The Introduction of the Loading Coil: George A. Campbell and Michael I. Pupin", *Technology and Culture*, 11 (1970), pp. 36–57.

pyramid, with the women computors remaining invisible even though they may have possessed a college education. After a period of unemployment following her graduation from MIT, Clarke herself organized and managed one such computing pyramid at General Electric from 1919 to 1921.[29]

We know the names of some computors like Clarke and the mathematician Gertrude Blanch because there was something remarkable in both women that had nothing to do with their work as computors. Like Clarke, Blanch started as a top computor to become a top analyst. Had she not become an analyst, Clarke might have also been unknown. For more examples of women computors who worked to produce engineering computations in general and electric power transmission in particular, i.e. for computors who remain historiographically invisible, one would have to pay attention, literally, to the footnotes of computing treatises authorized by male analysts. A footnote in one of Kennelly's handbooks on electrical engineering computations in the 1910s offers a representative example. Kennelly wrote this handbook series to present computations based on artificial lines. They included a book with computing equations (applications of hyperbolic functions to electrical engineering), a book with computing tables (tables of complex hyperbolic and circular functions), a book with computing graphs (chart *Atlas* of complex hyperbolic and circular functions), and a book on the theory, mode of construction, and uses of artificial lines. In the 1914 preface to the first edition of his handbook on electrical engineering computing tables, Kennelly proudly stated that to solve the same electrical engineering computing problem, "to a like degree of precision without aid from these functions, and by older methods, would probably occupy hours of labor and cover several sheets of computing-paper".[30]

Valuable computing labor could be saved by using Kennelly's tables. But vast computing labor had been appropriated to produce these handbooks in the first place. In an explanatory appendix, Kennelly confessed that the steps between computations were larger than he originally intended because his applications for financial assistance were unsuccessful. Without financial assistance, Kennelly's computational

29. For Clarke's talk, see Edith Clarke, "Trends in Power System Analysis", *Midwest Power Conference Proceedings*, 7 (1944), pp. 172–180. For her work as a computor and as a manager of computors, see Brittain, "From Computor to Electrical Engineer: The Remarkable Career of Edith Clarke", and Owen, "Edith Clarke: Pioneer Woman Engineer".
30. Arthur E. Kennelly, *The Application of Hyperbolic Functions to Electrical Engineering Problems* (New York, 1925) (first edited in 1912 and re-edited in 1919); idem, *Tables of Complex Hyperbolic and Circular Functions* (Cambridge, MA, 1914), idem, *Chart Atlas of Complex Hyperbolic and Circular Functions* (Cambridge, MA, 1914), and idem, *Electric Lines and Nets: Their Theory and Electrical Behavior*. For the quoted passage see, idem, *Tables of Complex Hyperbolic and Circular Functions*, Preface.

project was enormous; for example, to control against errors, all computing of the tables were computed twice by using two different formulas of the computing equation. All the tables were subsequently reduced to graphic form in the book with the computing charts – which Kennelly called the *Atlas* – by marking off each entry of the tables on its proper chart with a sharp needle. Then a ruling pen was drawn through the successive punctures. The graphs (charts) of Kennelly's *Atlas* of electrical engineering were not a passive picture of the tables, because in the process of drawing errors were discovered and rectified. Thus, computing tables were computed three times before they were set in type. After this, the tables were proofread three times again. As Kennelly explained, if the two initial computations differed, "the steps of the computation were gone over afresh".[31] Who provided the devaluated labor power required for this project, given that money was scarce? We cannot learn the answer to this question by reading Kennelly's preface, in which he mentions some of his fellow electrical engineering analysts who exercised an indirect influence on his computing project. To learn who exercised the direct influence we would have to stumble luckily across the appendix footnote on page 209. There, in small letters, Kennelly wrote that he "desired to express his acknowledgment" to four women computors for "the care and painstaking efforts of his assistants engaged in computation, namely Miss Ethel Smith, A.B. Radcliffe, 1911, Miss A.F. Daniell, A.B. Radcliffe, 1911, Miss Mary M. Devlin, A.B. Radcliffe, 1912, and Miss Hope M. Hearn, A.B. Radcliffe, 1912".[32] If Edith Clarke's case points to the internal limit within the electrical engineering computing pyramid, their cases point to the external limit of this pyramid. In other words, since they lack a meaningful history, we can only elaborate on Clarke's exceptional case.

The computational project that Kennelly completed in the 1910s, with the publication of his series of handbooks, actually started much earlier. The first mention of the potential use of artificial lines in the context of power transmission goes back to 1895. We get an idea of how much computing labor would eventually be stored in Kennelly's computing handbooks by considering how impressed the 1895 discussants were who noted the vast work required to produce a single computing graph. One of the discussants, the physicist Arthur G. Webster, began his comments by acknowledging that computing required much labor:

> Not being an engineer myself, and not knowing engineers as well as I wish I did, I had supposed that an engineer was an extremely busy man and that he was mostly occupied in doing practical things which brought him in a certain amount of very pleasant returns which are not open to people in my position. But I came to the conclusion that there are engineers who delight in doing other things, who

31. Kennelly, *Tables of Complex Hyperbolic and Circular Functions*, p. 102.
32. *Ibid.*

are willing to do arithmetic, which I may say for myself I find a terrible grind. If I have been fortunate enough to get certain experimental results and put them down in my notebook, when it comes to working the calculations over, I should prefer to send them several hundreds miles rather than do it myself. But I have come to the conclusion that business is probably a little slack in Philadelphia. I have always had the impression that there were more hours in the day in Philadelphia than in New York. But I see that there must be many more days in the week, and if I might take the liberty I should be glad to ask Mr Kennelly privately how long it took him to draw that diagram. I was extremely interested in that part.[33]

In his reply, Kennelly proudly shared the story of the machine that he imported in order to plot Plate 1: "In order to draw that diagram", explained Kennelly, "we had to send to Europe for a machine. We could not find anywhere in this country a machine which would draw the lines accurately enough." Yet, the machine could not draw the lines by itself. A human was needed to guide it. Kennelly, however, mentioned nothing in public about the computing labor required to produce Plate 1. The computing labor story was indeed to be discussed "privately".[34]

Kennelly argued that:

[...] it may be said that hyperbolic functions [...] have risen from the state of theory [...] to a stage of practical utility; because problems which would take hours of labor to solve by other methods, may be solved in a few minutes by the use of the hyperbolic tables and curve sheets.

He appraised his computing artifacts by portraying them as "a practical engineering tool of great swiftness and power". For comparison, as was customary, he contrasted his computing technology to computing by a slide rule. The savings in living labor seemed impressive: "In fact, with the atlas [containing the computing graphs] open at the proper chart, any complex hyperbolic function can be read off within a few seconds of time, ordinarily, to at least such a degree of precision as is offered by a good 25-centimeter slide rule."[35] However, Kennelly's comparison failed to note a whole series of parameters (e.g. portability of the slide rule, specificity of slide-rule scales to concrete computing works, and, above all, price, which could determine who would be the owner of the means of computing production) that persuaded electrical engineers to prefer a slide rule to everything else. This preference held for many subsequent years. An incredible variety of slide rules, including those that calculated electric power transmission, would remain for years the most popular computing

---

33. Edwin Houston and Arthur Kennelly, "Resonance in Alternating Current Lines", *AIEE Transactions*, 12 (1895), pp. 133–169, 160–161.
34. *Ibid.*, p. 168.
35. Kennelly, *Application of Hyperbolic Functions to Electrical Engineering Problems*, p. vii.

artifact, and the tools always provided the standard reference of computing comparisons.[36]

In presenting Westinghouse's first calculating board, W. Woodward explained that it was constructed for cases "when calculations are very lengthy and in a few cases practically impossible".[37] The mechanical method of computing with a calculating board is "convenient", clarified R. Evans in an attached 1919 *Electric Journal* article, but "the initial cost" and its unavailability demanded that progress in new mathematical-analytical methods was also necessary.[38] Evans kept returning to advances within analytical methods "to reduce the labor of calculations" when the board was not available,[39] while others kept improving the calculating board since "analytical solutions are laborious".[40] Only ten years after the introduction of the first calculating board to remedy these laborious calculations, the Westinghouse engineers introduced another calculating board, an alternating current variety, as a device that "would reduce to a minimum the tedious mathematical calculations now involved".[41] The story was identical for the General Electric electrical engineers. After introducing their first calculating board in 1916 as a solution to computing "complexity",[42] and after justifying a series of modifications as solutions to the fact that "the mathematical methods were very laborious and often impossible of application",[43] they and their MIT partners would, by 1925, find that "the size and complexity of present-day power systems have increased to the point where the prediction of the behavior of the system by analytical methods is more and more difficult" and the calculating table is "too inaccurate".[44] By 1930, they were prepared to introduce their own alternating current calculating board – baptized the "network analyzer" and ceremoniously presented at MIT to emphasize how revolutionary a machine it was. It too was offered as the solution to "lengthy and usually impracticable mathematical calculations".[45]

36. See Tympas, "The Computor and the Analyst", ch. 7.
37. W.R. Woodward, "Calculating Short-Circuit Currents in Electric Networks: Testing with Miniature Networks", *Electric Journal*, 16 (1919), pp. 344–349, 345.
38. Robert D. Evans, "Analytical Solutions", *Electric Journal*, 16 (1919), pp. 345–349, 346.
39. *Idem*, "Analytical Solution of Networks", *Electric Journal*, 21 (1924), pp. 149–154, 150.
40. I.T. Monseth and R. De Camp, "Short-Circuit Calculating Tables: Of the Variable Resistor Unit, Direct Current Type", *Electric Journal*, 23 (1926), pp. 299–305, 299.
41. H.A. Travers and W.W. Parker, " An Alternating Current Calculating Board", *Electric Journal*, 27 (1930), pp. 266–270, 266.
42. Anon., "A Device for Calculating Currents in Complex Networks of Lines", *General Electric Review*, 19 (October 1916), pp. 901–902, 901.
43. W.W. Lewis, "Calculation of Short-Circuit Currents in Alternating-Current Systems", *General Electric Review*, 22 (February 1919), pp. 140–145, 140.
44. H.H. Spencer and H.L. Hazen, "Artificial Representation of Power Systems", *AIEE Transactions*, 64 (1945), pp. 72–79, 72.
45. H.I. Hazen, O.R. Schuring, and M.F. Gardner, "The MIT Newtork Analyzer", *AIEE Transactions*, 48 (1929), pp. 1102–1114, 1102.

In 1935, those at Commonwealth Edison reported "savings approximately eight times is installed costs in two years of operation".[46] In his sales pitch, General Electric's Robert Treat claimed that "by using this specialized algebra machine the saving in labor is so great that many problems may now be solved fairly rapidly which would not be undertaken at all without it".[47] Several variations were introduced throughout the 1930s, all as a response to the evidently persistent need for "longhand methods", which were "generally laborious – frequently, sufficiently laborious to greatly curtail the scope of the study and at times to prevent the study being made altogether".[48] Amidst the Great Depression that offered an abundant supply of labor, the computing labor crisis persisted. General Electric's R. Slinger introduced another network analyzer variant because "longhand calculations requires an infinite amount of patience and an almost prohibitive amount of time".[49] Reports on improvements made it into the late 1940s and beyond.[50] A balanced and inclusive account of the impressively long list of uses for calculating boards and network analyzers was offered by General Electric's H. Peterson and C. Concordia immediately after the war: "[w]ithout the use of these modern devices", they remarked in 1945, "many investigations would not be undertaken simply because the amount of work and time required to arrive at satisfactory quantitative conclusions would be prohibitive".[51]

The same finding was reported with flourish during the same year in an article in the *General Electric Monogram*, entitled "Beyond Human Calculation":

> In one of the General Office buildings in Schenectady there is a door that might well be marked "through this portal pass power company representatives from all over the world": The door is labeled simply "A–C Network Analyzer". This means little or nothing to the average passer by; but to power company men it means the solution of problems too difficult for human calculation, and the savings of many thousand dollars.

This "modern electrical brain" was presented as an "infallible arbiter" that "in a few hours can perform calculations that ordinarily require weeks or months". According to the *General Electric Monogram* article, more than

46. T.G. Leclair, "Board Earns Eight Times Its Cost", *Electrical World*, (23 November 1945), pp. 28–29, 28.
47. Robert Treat, "Critical Analysis of System Operation Improves Service and Saves Money", *General Electric Review*, 41 (July 1938), pp. 306–311, 307.
48. H.P. Kuehni and R.G. Lorraine, "A New A–C Network Analyzer", *AIEE Transactions*, 57 (1938), pp. 67–73, 67.
49. R.N. Slinger, "Network Analyzer Points", *Electrical World*, (16 July 1938), pp. 30–32, 30.
50. W.A. Morgan, F.S. Rothe, and J.J. Winsness, "An Improved A–C Network Analyzer", *AIEE Transactions*, 68 (1949), pp. 891–897.
51. H.A. Peterson and C. Concordia, "Analyzers [...] For Use in Engineering and Scientific Problems", *General Electric Review*, 48 (September 1945), pp. 29–35, 29.

Figure 1. Electrical engineers renting and using a network analyzer in the early 1940s. A General Electric 480-cycle A–C network analyzer set-up for the Virginia Public Service Co. in March 1941.
General Electric Archives (Schenectady, New York), Filing no. 170D, 8851; used by permission

100 companies and industrial power companies and concerns had rented it to carry out more than 300 hundred investigations. In its 7-year tenure at the Central Station Engineering Division, the network analyzer had become "a proving ground for engineers' ideas".[52]

The fate of the network analyzer was not, however, different from that of the machines already considered above. On a more cautious note than that of the promotional *Westinghouse Engineer* (1944) and *General Electric Monogram* (1945) editorials, which ideologized the network analyzer as the ultimate "brain", an *Electrical World* editor warned (1946) that it was "no substitute for brains and must be operated by engineers who can recognize a problem, plan, analyze and carry through its investigation".[53] John Casazza's memoirs, offered on the occasion to protest the transition from the network analyzer to the electronic computer, suggest that computing with the network analyzer was not "beyond human calculation", in fact the opposite is true. "The skill of the person doing the network analyzer analysis", argued the veteran electrical engineer, "was enhanced considerably" by "short-cut methods". He

52. "Beyond Human Calculation", *General Electric Monogram*, 22:1 (1945), p. 25.
53. Braymer, "Today's Network Calculators Will Plan Tomorrow's Systems", p. 52.

added, "along with the development of this skill came a better fundamental understanding of how the network operated". This understanding for Casazza was akin to "surgical skills", having to do with "ability to go into a network and search only the specific answer needed". Although disagreeing with what he perceived to be a substitution of digital "speed for brains", Casazza clarified that computing with the network analyzer, a machine promoted as the "brain", the brains were actually human.[54]

The ongoing interconnection of regional networks into inter-regional pools, national and international, was creating a computing complexity that exacerbated the pressure for advance towards the digital direction. In the mid-1940s, paralleling the plans for establishing numerous network analyzer laboratories, the electrical engineering community kept an open eye for alternatives. The analyzers, informed Philip Jennings and George Quinan, engineers at the Puget Sound Power and Light Company, "have afforded welcomed relief from tedious calculations", but since they were not located conveniently, power engineers still had to use "longhand methods". Their method involved a "large amount of labor" – labor that could be, hopefully, mechanized by the use of digital electromechanical machinery (punched-card machines).[55] L. Dustant, an engineer at the Federal Power Commission, ran tests on how to replace the network analyzer with calculating machines and punched-card machinery.[56] Electrical engineers needed not merely the mechanization of the old techniques of hand calculation, but development of new techniques. A decade later the complaints became loud and clear. "With the expansion and increase in complexity of power systems throughout the country", wrote D. Johnson and J. Ward of the University of Washington and Purdue University respectively, "a more accurate and less time-consuming means of determining the transient stability characteristics of power networks is required". The network analyzer, which they were now calling an "analog computer", was introduced by the two engineers as an exemplar of the past – the "immediate past", but, nevertheless, the past.[57]

It was only on the condition of existing precalculation that the digital was advantageous. In the absence of such precalculation, engineers like Bonneville's Rodney Brown and William Tinney stopped short at simply outlining the requirements for the successful introduction of the digital.[58]

54. John A. Casazza, *The Development of Electric Power Transmission* (New York, 1993), p. 78.

55. Philip D. Jennings and George E. Quinan, "The Use of Business Machines in Determining the Distribution of Load and Reactive Components in Power Line Network", *AIEE Transactions*, 65 (1946), pp. 1045–1046, 1045.

56. L.A. Dunstan, "Machine Computation of Power Network Performance", *AIEE Transactions*, 66 (1947), pp. 610–624, 610.

57. J. B. Johnson and J. B. Ward, "The Solution of Power System Stability Problems by Means of Digital Computers", *AIEE Transactions*, 76 (1957), pp. 1321–1329.

58. Rodney J. Brown and William F. Tinney, "Digital Solutions for Large Power Networks", *AIEE Transactions*, 76 (1957), pp. 347–355, 347.

Even if we assume that appropriate digital hardware was available at competitive cost, producing the software to run on such a machine was definitely emerging as a key issue. The first programs for computing electric power transmission addressed the needs inadequately. Westinghouse's Long, Byerly, and Rindt, welcomed the "tremendous power of large-scale digital computers" only to admit that their use could only be partial due to the lack of appropriate programs to run them.[59] As late as in 1963, in discussions of the first digital computer programs for computing the complex problems like the stability of electric power transmission, engineers acknowledged that there was still a "serious limitation" in the field.[60] In his 1957 introduction to using digital computers for the easier short-circuit calculations, M. Lantz, who was with the Bonneville Power Administration, clearly stated that the advantages of the digital – speed, accuracy, and the ability to be operated without highly trained professional personnel" – rested in necessary "pre-calculation".[61]

The best way to relate how much and what kind of labor was involved in the shift from analog hardware (analyzer) to digital software of the computer is to study the panel papers on these artifacts within the volumes of the *Proceedings of the American Power Conference* during the 1950s and 1960s. By way of introducing to the continuity between working with the old analog network analyzer and the new digital computer, I refer to what several General Electric's network analyzer old-timers had to report about "training electric utility engineers in the application of digital computers". For G. Carter, C. Concordia, and F. Maginnis, who had experimented with early digital computers in 1946,

> [...] the engineer must have had some actual experience in problem reduction, flow diagramming, programming, and checking out if he is to be in good position not only to recognize the possible applications but also to distinguish between those that are really worthwhile and those that are not yet economically feasible.

"Without such training", they explained, "there has been a tendency to go to the extremes of thinking that either all or none of his problems were suitable computer applications".[62] To provide such training, they started a digital computer course at General Electric, which, by 1963 had graduated over 100 engineers.[63] The passage to the digital was all but effortless.

59. R.W. Long, R.T. Byerly, and L.J. Rindt, "Digital Computer Programs in Electric Utilities", *Electrical Engineering*, (September 1959), pp. 912–916, 912.
60. A.J. McElroy and R.M. Porter, "Digital Computer Calculation of Transients in Electric Networks", *AIEE Transactions*, 82 (1963), pp. 88–96, 95–96.
61. M.J. Lantz, "The Digital Computer and Power System Short-Circuit Calculations", *Electrical Engineering*, (November 1957), pp. 981–983, 981.
62. G.K. Carter, C. Concordia, and F.J. Maginnis, "Training Electric Utility Engineers in the Application of Digital Computers", *Proceedings of the American Power Conference*, 25 (1963), pp. 834–847, 835–836.
63. *Ibid.*, p. 837.

Engineers considering converting to the digital computer would have to labor hard, since the course was intensive.[64]

In 1959, Westinghouse engineers reported a service through its analytical department, which was organized around paying for the use of an electronic computer in the same manner that the use of the network analyzer.[65] Their problem in developing such a service suggests that the change in the technical vocabulary has left the process of the dynamic reproduction of the computing labor crisis intact. "The necessary work", admitted the Westinghouse engineers, "in preparing for a program release could delay the actual release by many months from the time when the program would be available for use on a service bureau basis."[66] In this case, I interpret one typical early instance of the computing labor crisis known as the "software crisis". The software crisis surfaced when one more machine – the computer introduced in the 1940s – soon turned out to be more of the same. By the late 1950s, a decade after the emergence of the analog-digital demarcation, digital won the battle. Yet, by then the software–hardware split had emerged, and along with it, the associated "software crisis", which is a computing labor crisis that has marked the history of computing since then.[67]

CONCLUSION

The most celebrated attempt at constructing a calculating machine during early industrial capitalism was that of Charles Babbage. Despite several studies that insightfully relate Babbage's calculating machines to his views on capitalist industry, it has to date escaped attention that there are actually computors in Babbage's scheme. Babbage called them "attendants", and, as the term implies, he thought of them as exercising no influence in the computing process.[68] As is well known, Babbage failed to have such a machine constructed. The first commercially available calculating machine of industrial capitalism, the Thomas de Colmar Arithmometer, was similar in principle to one of the infamous first calculating machines of merchant capitalism, that of G.W. Leibnitz. Leibnitz introduced his machine by arguing that "it is unworthy of excellent men to lose hours like slaves in the labor of calculation, which could safely relegated to anyone else if the

---

64. For a brief historical overview on the introduction of digital computers to the context of computing electric power networks, see Glenn W. Stagg and Ahmed H. El-Abiad, *Computer Methods in Power System Analysis* (New York, 1968), pp. 1–2.
65. Long, Byerly, and Rindt, "Digital Computer Programs in Electric Utilities", p. 916.
66. *Ibid.*
67. For an introduction to the history of the software crisis, see Paul Ceruzzi, *A History of Modern Computing* (Cambridge, 1998).
68. On Babbage's attendants, see Charles Babbage, *The Exposition of 1851: Views of Industry, The Science and the Government of England* (London, 1851), p. 169.

machine were used".[69] This indicates that from before the beginning, the calculating machine existed as a split between "excellent men" and a "slave", who could be "anyone else". As, however, there are no slaves in capitalism, those to populate the lower places in the hierarchy of computing with such machines were searched in the ranks of devaluated free workers.[70] These free workers could be women computors like the ones mentioned above, victims of the hegemony of an ideology that blended successfully the time-honored ideology of sexism with that of technological determinism.

The fact that one can find so many references to the computing labor crisis suggests that there were many computing laborers involved in the history of pre-40s computing. Labor historians might choose to place emphasis on political struggles in which these workers become involved – struggles of a classic political form (e.g. unions) or struggles exemplifying other forms of political resistance and organization (struggles more passive than unionism, but, at times, even more effective, e.g. careless use of sensitive computing machinery). Seeking to reach common ground with labor history after starting from history of technology, I suggest a less standard approach. In addition to retrieving as many as possible of those technicians that were consciously hidden by the (visible) writings of their masters,[71] I propose that we interpret the role of technicians by what their masters unconsciously wrote in their most visible writings. Accordingly, in the pages above, I have relied extensively on what top-ranking electrical

69. Leibnitz quoted in David Eugene Smith, *A Source Book in Mathematics* (New York, 1929), pp. 180–181.

70. From the rich literature on the blend of technological determinism and sexism, I find useful Katherine Stubbs's account of the technocratic rhetoric that aimed both at mechanizing work and, at introducing women as physiologically suitable for it, on the grounds of them being naturally tolerant to repetitive-monotonous jobs requiring manual dexterity. Stubbs refers to industrial female work in general, but what she finds seems appropriate for introducing to the general context of the labor of the lowest-ranking human computors (the majority of whom were women), whose work was uniformly considered to be the *par excellence* province of manual dexterity, tolerance to monotony, and undemanding intellectually; Katherine Stubbs, "Mechanizing the Female: Discourse and Control in the Industrial Economy", *Differences*, 7 (1995), pp. 141–163. For a introduction to how women's intellect was, from the commencement of modern capitalism, ideologized as suitable to such tasks, see Lorraine Daston, "The Naturalized Female Intellect", *Science in Context*, 5 (1992), pp. 209–235. In her study of Gaspar De Prony's division-of-computing-labor scheme, Daston focuses specifically on the effects of this ideology in the compound attempts at mechanizing calculation while devaluating it as unworthy intellectually. Daston's references to nineteenth-century bureaucratic projects of calculation that were inspired by De Prony's scheme – works that included the employment of women computors – conveniently sets the stage for the literature on women computors in subsequent contexts. See Daston, "Enlightenment Calculations".

71. For an original argument about the consciously hidden "invisible technicians", see Steven Shapin, *A Social History of Truth: Civility and Science in Seventeenth-Century England* (Chicago, IL, 1995).

engineers had to say about the computing labor crisis within electric power transmission on the occasion of introducing new analyzers.

In studying the repeated attempts at mechanizing "electrical computations", I find evidence of the prevalence of a mode of producing computations marked by the restless introduction of computing machines – each of which introduced with much clamor as, supposedly, to bring about an end to human labor – before it was silently withdrawn to make room for the perennially cacophonous introduction of a subsequent device. I would suggest that we give serious attention to the hypothesis that the information revolution (of which the computing revolution is a core component) is integral to capitalism as a whole. Specifically, I suggest that the popular divide between an industrial and an information revolution (and the associated assumption for a passage to a post-capitalist order) is perhaps untenable: the industrial revolution was, from the beginning, an information revolution.[72]

72. For an introduction to the broader historiography of the information revolution that is sensitive to the continuity beyond the analog-digital demarcation see Greg Downey, "Virtual Webs, Physical Technologies, and Hidden Workers: The Spaces of Labor in Information Internetworks", *Technology and Culture*, 42 (2001), pp. 209–235.

IRSH 48 (2003), Supplement, pp. 97–122 DOI: 10.1017/S0020859003001287
© 2003 Internationaal Instituut voor Sociale Geschiedenis

Breaking the Buffalo: The Transformation of Stevedoring Work in Durban Between 1970 and 1990[*]

BERNARD DUBBELD

The appropriation of living labour by capital is directly expressed in machinery. It is a scientifically based analysis, together with the application of mechanical laws that enables the machine to carry out the work formerly done by the worker himself [...] hence we have the struggle of the worker against machinery. What used to be the activity of the living worker has become that of the machine.[1]

Karl Marx

The contemporary maritime world offers little in the way of reassurance and nostalgic anthropomorphism, but surrenders instead to the serial discipline of the box. The cargo container, an American innovation of the mid-1950s, transforms the space and time of port cities and makes the globalization of manufacturing possible. The container is the very coffin of remote labor power, bearing the hidden evidence of exploitation in the far reaches of the world.[2]

Alan Sekula, "Freeway to China"

INTRODUCTION

In Durban, South Africa, stevedoring workers were the most physically powerful workers of all, and were known as *onyathi* in Zulu, or buffalo, which aptly described the physical and collective nature of their work. Throughout the century, the stevedoring industry was especially labour-intensive, necessitating teams of workers. As in most industries in South Africa, African workers built and maintained the docks. These buffalo developed the linkage that made Durban a thriving city and sustained the apartheid economy. Yet today the buffalo are all but gone, replaced by onboard warehouses known as containers. Machines have replaced the men once so integral to the survival of the city.

This paper presents an account of the transformation of work in Durban harbour between 1970 and 1990. At the most basic level, I discuss the

---

[*] I wish to thank Keith Breckenridge, Stephen Sparks, Fiona Ross, Jean Comaroff, Benjamin Dawson, and Mark Geraghty for comments and suggestions. Any errors however, are the sole responsibility of the author.
1. Karl Marx, *The Grundrisse*, David McLellan (ed. and trans.) (New York, 1971), p. 140.
2. Alan Sekula, "Freeway to China", in Jean and John Comaroff (eds), *Millennial Capitalism and the Culture of Neoliberalism* (Durham, NC, 2001), p. 147.

development and the impact of containerization in a local context, and attempt to engage with the responses of the stevedores, whose working conditions and lives were dramatically shaped by this technological innovation. Through a presentation of variety of sources, I attempt to come to grips with the complex relationship between global technological change and a particular local context: working in South Africa during the late apartheid period.

In this paper, exploring the tensions between global innovation in a particular industry and local conditions provides a framework for a deeper theoretical engagement. At the heart of this engagement is an investigation of the extent to which technological change simply homogenizes societies, and a discussion of the importance of understanding both local political conditions and historical legacy. What is also at stake is how the "information economy" is to be understood and interpreted.[3] Whilst I will focus on the occupational and economic changes that occurred in Durban, I will not assume that this narrative represents all workers' experience of this economy. It is precisely in the particular industry and in the particular political space that the stevedores in Durban worked that informs my analysis of the transformation of work in South Africa.

An ancillary problem revolves around the nature of work in South Africa and the possibilities of considering whether a different scenario, other than the predicament that stevedores currently face, could have been possible. As my introductory paragraph hinted, stevedores in Durban were, by the early 1990s, predominately casual or flexible workers without any job security. The key actors in this problem are thus the trade unions in the stevedoring industry, and their positions and decisions vis-à-vis other trade unions in South Africa and throughout the world.

Allied to all these considerations is a discussion of the manner in which we characterize the position of the Durban stevedores today. A core argument of this paper is that, while these workers have suffered an entirely different fate to their European counterparts in the same industry, they do share the fate of many industrial workers throughout the world. Here I will engage Pierre Bourdieu's recent work, and suggest that the stevedores of Durban are in an important sense typical workers of the postindustrial, neoliberal, or information age. Yet this comparison also has its limits, which I will discuss below.

Given that these concerns are central to this paper, it is necessary to

3. Frank Webster argues that the definitions of the "information society" are as a whole vague and incoherent, and that in examining different evidence, theorists disagree about whether it represents rupture or continuity. See Frank Webster, *Theories of the Information Society* (London, 1995), pp. 4–6, 29. In this paper, I will privilege those theorists of the information age that I consider relevant to the discussion of the transformation in Durban. The point here is not to provide a new theory of the information society, but rather to understand how these global changes were dealt with in the local arena.

emphasize that I have not been comprehensive in treating the precise mechanisms of apartheid control, which are fundamental to understanding the specifics of the transformation I describe. I have also not discussed the historiography of the relationship between work and culture in South Africa. I have dealt with these in other places.[4] However, before proceeding with the main narrative, I will present an brief analysis of the shipping industry and containerization which informs many of the terms of my subsequent discussion.

DOCK WORK, THE SHIPPING INDUSTRY, AND TECHNOLOGICAL TRANSFORMATION

Throughout the twentieth century and before, there was a constant drive to improve the pace and efficiency of the stevedoring operation, and thus technological change occurred frequently in this industry.[5] Yet unitization (of which containerization was the most significant manifestation) was the most dramatic change in the industry in at least sixty years, in the sense that it reordered the entire operation of work on the docks. Before containerization, commodities were stored in the hold of ships in a variety of boxes, crates, and packages of different sizes. The primary function of stevedoring workers (or "longshoremen" as they are known in the United States) was to load and offload goods from ships to shore. A stevedoring gang, made up of between eight and sixteen workers, coordinated this process amongst themselves. In the early twentieth century, nets were used to secure goods in the hold by some members of the gang, while others operated simple cranes. These cranes were later replaced by mechanical winches. Goods were then placed onto trucks, or alternatively stored in warehouses.

Work-gangs were not only at the heart of the work operation, they were groups where intense solidarities developed. Workers would normally remain in the same gang for a considerable period of time. As a social group, the members of the gang protected one another, protested together, and often used the gang as a mechanism for the theft of a limited amount of goods.

The idea of containerization was pioneered in the mid-1950s by a US truck owner, Malcolm MacLean, who became frustrated at the long

---

4. Bernard Dubbeld, "Labour Management and Technological Change: Stevedoring in Durban, 1959–1990", (M.A. dissertation, University of Natal, South Africa, 2002). It is also worth mentioning that the thesis contains wider accounts of the role of ethnicity on the docks, and the politics of production within the workplace.

5. Peter Linebaugh's discussion of the development of the panopticon in the London docks is a good example of such technological innovation developed to ensure more efficient labour control. See Peter Linebaugh, *The London Hanged: Crime and Civil Society in the Eighteenth Century* (Cambridge, 1992), pp. 371–401.

turnaround time that trucks spent waiting for cargo and developed the idea of a standardized box which could carry different kinds of cargo. Initially operating between a few ports in the United States, this technological change was to spread to the world's harbours during the following thirty years. What containerization essentially became was a mechanism not only to speed up turnaround time, but also one that prevented theft and pilferage. Containerization was part of a broader process of unitization that standardized cargo into 20- and 40-ton units that could be carried on the decks on ships rather than in the holds, and be quickly transferred from ships to trucks and trains. A good example of the type of ship that developed as a result of containerization was the roll-on roll-off vessel that required almost no physical labour to unload. Not incidentally, the revolution in the telecommunications sphere and the development of information technology facilitated even greater efficiency in container transport.

Containerization had huge implications for stevedoring. No longer would large gangs of workers be required to coordinate intricate loading and unloading operations. Furthermore, the inevitable idle time that existed when stevedores were not actually unloading was substantially curtailed. While some dock work is still available in harbours (approximately just over half of Durban's total cargo was containerized by the early 1990s), stevedores are substantially less important for harbour operations.

Besides the actual ports themselves, international shipping lines are important actors in maritime transport. Before the 1960s, shipping lines had very close ties with local stevedoring companies. These links ensured that their liners would be serviced as fast as possible. In South Africa, for instance, the Union Castle line owned African Associated Stevedores, a major stevedoring operator in Durban.[6] During this period, shipping lines were more or less bound to traditional ports of call and well established markets. As in local companies, an international tradition of dockworker militancy and a high level of unionization meant that their turnaround times were often severely affected. In addition, time losses due to the limits of human endeavour and the regularity of pilferage and theft severely hampered their operations. By the mid 1960s, Frank Broeze noted that liner shipping faced a massive financial crisis, unable to sustain turnaround times and severely affected by both worker militancy and theft.[7]

Broeze suggests that containerization saved liner shipping, but also

6. Mike Morris, "Stevedoring and the General Workers' Union, Part 1", *South African Labour Bulletin*, 11 (1986), p. 90–114, 91.
7. Frank Broeze, "Containerization and the Globalization of Liner Shipping", in David J. Starkey and Gelina Harlaftis (eds), *Global Markets: The Internationalization of the Sea Transport Industries Since 1850*, special issue of *Research In Maritime History*, 14 (1998), pp. 1–24, 2.

fundamentally changed it. Since the mid-1960s, following on from high-powered take-overs and mergers between companies, shipping lines have become part of the global service economy. The industry has "de-nationalized" entirely by breaking links with traditional "home" ports and countries and sometimes moving into ownership, of or partnership with, rail and road companies.[8] But this is not to say that containerization occurred uniformly in every port around the world. Worker-controlled unions, and to an extent state initiatives (such as the Devlin Report in London), shaped the specific form of changes that containerization would bring to the dock labour force. In this context we now turn to Durban, before the containerization which would arrive at the port in 1977 when the container terminal was completed.

STEVEDORING WORK IN DURBAN

Durban was established as a harbour in the nineteenth century and became the dominant port in South Africa in the early twentieth century. Primarily, this was a result of its relative proximity to the gold fields on the Witswatersrand and to the sugar-cane fields of Natal. By 1955, Durban was handling approximately 48 per cent of the country's total cargo.[9] From the late nineteenth century, there was a constant demand for labour in the port to cater for the increasing amounts of cargo in the harbour.[10]

Until the end of the 1950s, the port relied almost exclusively on casual labour. This was not merely a peculiarity of Durban harbour – Stephen Hill has shown that in London dockyard employers refused to de-casualize workers until the late 1960s – but it was not common in other industries in South Africa.[11] Owing to influx-control regulations, it was unusual for African casual workers to be permitted in the city during the 1920s and 1930s. The majority of African workers were migrants, residing only in the city for the duration of their contracts. Yet stevedoring employers argued, like their London counterparts, that in as unpredictable an industry as stevedoring – where the demands of work could vary enormously on a daily basis – they could not employ a fixed workforce.

The unique position of stevedores meant that, despite their status as casual workers, they enjoyed a fair degree of permanence in the city, and by the 1940s the casual stevedores working in Durban numbered in excess

---

8. *Ibid.*, p. 24.
9. Trevor Jones, *The Port of Durban and the Durban Metropolitan Economy*, Research Monograph, Economic Research Unit, University of Natal (Durban, 1997), p. 14.
10. David Hemson, "Class Consciousness and Migrant Workers: The Dock Workers of Durban", (unpublished Ph.D. thesis, University of Warwick, 1979), p. 35. According to Jeff Guy, rebellion against the colonial state in Natal was often punished by forced labour in Durban harbour.
11. Stephen Hill, *The Dockers: Class and Tradition in London* (London, 1976). p. 15.

of 3,000. In an important way this set them apart from other industrial workers in South Africa. Casual workers found themselves in a paradoxical position. While they were not guaranteed any work, there was a constant demand for workers, and stevedores could literally move between different stevedoring companies in search of the best wage on any particular day. They were also surprisingly well organized and recognized their permanence in the city. During a strike, stevedores claimed Durban as their home when told "to go home to rural areas" by white officials.[12] David Hemson notes that casual dockworkers had a long history of struggles to improve wages and working conditions, and engaged in wider political and economic struggles.[13] A 1956 report on the conditions of stevedoring workers by Sergeant Mentz of the Central Native Labour Board noted that workers were able to embark on strikes and go-slows on the issues of wages and work categorization.[14] Other authors emphasized the relative freedom that casual workers enjoyed, in being able to determine when and where they worked. Of course, it must be noted that these casuals existed at a time when work was in abundance and workers were in short supply.[15]

As in many countries throughout the world, the war economy of the 1940s resulted in many structural changes in the labour market in South Africa. In general, state officials turned a blind eye towards influx-control legislation and allowed African workers into the city to replace men who had gone to war, and to meet the increased demands of production. After the war, however, the ruling United Party did not reimpose influx control, and many African workers began to live permanently in cities throughout the country. Yet this was short-lived; the National Party swept to power on the apartheid ticket – largely by appealing to the fears of the white electorate that Africans posed both a moral and economic threat to their security. A basic cornerstone of early apartheid policy was the need to reverse urbanization and control African entry into the cities even more tightly than before. The 1950s saw sustained effort by the National Party government to enforce this promise by the promulgation of the Population Registration Act (1950), the Abolition of Passes and Co-ordination of

---

12. David Hemson. "Dock Workers, Labour Circulation and Class Struggles in Durban, 1940–1959", *Journal of Southern African Studies*, 4 (1977), pp. 88–124, 93.
13. *Ibid.*, pp. 91–92.
14. South African National Archive Depot (SAB), ARB 3317 1196/5/4/1, vol. 1, Sgd. S Mentz, Central Native Labour Board, "Report on Conditions of Employment of Stevedoring Workers".
15. For interesting reading on this form of casual work in South Africa and elsewhere, see Patrick Harries, *Work, Culture, Identity: Migrant Labourers in Mozambique and South Africa c. 1860–1910* (Portsmouth, NH [etc.], 1994); Keletso Atkins, *The Moon is Dead! Give Us Our Money! The Cultural Origins of an African Work Ethic in Natal, South Africa, 1843–1900* (Portsmouth, NH, 1993); Frederick Cooper, *On the African Waterfront: Urban Disorder and Transformation of Work in Colonial Mombasa* (London, 1982), pp. 37–41.

Documents Act (1952) and the establishment of the Bewysburo to administer passes and regulate influx control.[16]

The implementation of these new apartheid policies in the harbour was met with resistance by stevedoring employers. For almost a decade, the stevedoring industry in Durban remained as a unique space in the city for casual workers. Yet, the evident militancy of workers was a cause of increasing concern for employers and finally, following a strike by 1,400 workers in February 1959, and under tremendous state pressure, employers agreed to reform the labour system in the docks.[17] The five major stevedoring companies met government officials over the following month, and by the beginning of April 1959 had refashioned the conditions under which stevedoring workers were to be employed in Durban. The companies decided that a central system of labour should be introduced, requiring workers to be recruited on a weekly basis, reside in company compounds and be signed on to work when necessary.[18] Weekly labour agreements soon became ten-month contracts of employment, approved by traditional leaders in African areas (mostly in Zululand) and by representatives of the Department of Native Affairs. The central system controlling the recruitment and administration of all African labour in Durban was known as the Durban Stevedoring Labour Supply Company.

The development of the Labour Supply Company fitted in with general apartheid labour policy, and was known as the Labour Bureaux system. Under this system, codified by the 1964 Bantu Labour Act, in order for Africans to work in cities, they had to register as work-seekers with traditional authorities in designated tribal areas. Only through a certain kind of patronage with local chiefs could Africans ever hope to work in the cities. This apartheid policy aimed to create areas and places of work according to a nineteenth-century European conception of inherent tribal and cultural difference. As David Hemson notes, "What the national network of labour bureaux sought to achieve in relation to thousands of companies, the Labour Supply Company worked out in relation to the stevedoring companies."[19] The key functions of the Labour Supply Company were to control recruitment, to remake authority, and to regulate and administer work itself. African casual stevedores, for so long a feature of Durban harbour, disappeared.

But the maintenance of this centralized system of control required a great deal of money. The administration of the Labour Supply Company

16. Two notable pieces detailing this process are Deborah Posel, *The Making of Apartheid, 1948–1961* (Oxford, 1991), and Keith Breckenridge, "From Hubris to Chaos: The Makings of the Bewysburo and the End of Documentary Government", (n.p., May 2002).

17. SAB ARB 1229 1042/15/1959; Strachan, P. (Divisional Inspector Labour: Natal), "Notes of a Meeting Held at 150a Point Road, Durban on 25 February 1959".

18. SAB MAR vol. 81, file A2/44; Memorandum by Department of Labour, 16 May 1959.

19. Hemson, "Class Consciousness and Migrant Workers", p. 388.

was costly, not only in employing bureaucrats but also in maintaining a certain guarantee of wages for workers. Despite difficult power relations, workers thrived on the security of a fixed wage and the bonus of lots of overtime work during the economic boom period of the 1960s.[20] Contrary to the state's belief that the intricate measures of power and authority present in the Labour Supply Company, based on "cultural" practices, were responsible for relative industrial tranquility, what maintained stability within the Company was the relatively good wage levels, which were high even in comparison to some other forms of work available to Africans in cities. And despite the celebration of the Company as a model of labour control by the state during the 1960s,[21] it would be the period following 1968 and the slowdown of the South African economy that would prove a real test. After this, and especially after 1970, it would be increasingly difficult for the Labour Supply Company to survive.

THE CRISIS IN PRODUCTION AND THE MOVE TOWARDS CONTAINERIZATION

The boom in cargo-handling in docks slowed down after 1966, and by 1970 the level was as low as at the beginning of the decade.[22] Because there was less work available, the stevedores suddenly found themselves earning less. In addition to this, the final wage determination of 1969 based its recommendations on 1966 figures of average earnings, grossly over-estimating the actual wages of the workers.[23] A combination of this overall economic decline and the refusal of stevedoring companies and the state to recognize the real decline in stevedoring wages led to a strike on 4 April 1969 by almost 2,000 stevedoring workers. The method for dealing with the strike was immediate and left little doubt of the state's commitment to urban order. More than 1,000 workers were dismissed and sent back to perceived "homes" in rural areas.[24] The strike was the first major one in over ten years and, at the very least, showed the workers' determination to be paid properly.

In the aftermath of the strike, the Department of Native Affairs, in conjunction with the Labour Supply Company, set up new and stricter controls of recruitment. By 1972, the emphasis of recruitment had shifted to predominately traditionally Zulu areas such as Nongoma and

20. *Ibid.*, p. 526.
21. SAB BAO 2401, file 31/3/336; letter from P.J. Kemp (General Manager) to Dr P. van Rensburg (Dept of Bantu Administration and Development), 22 April 1966.
22. Statistical Year Book 1976, quoted in Hemson, "Class Consciousness and Migrant Workers", p. 512.
23. *Ibid.*, pp. 516–517.
24. *Natal Mercury*, 7 April 1969, "Half Durban's Dockworkers Set Off Home".

Mahlabatini, and away from Pondo areas such as Mount Ayliff.[25] While labour recruitment had always favoured a Zulu labour force, the move entrenched this supply of migrants from areas that were known for being conservative and having especially strong links with the Department of Native Affairs.

The strike was viewed more ambiguously by stevedoring companies. It led to a bottleneck of ships in the harbour, and many of the companies supported the call to reinstate many of the dismissed workers. But there were more serious long-term implications. Because the government viewed stevedores as unskilled, it was possible to simply replace strikers with more "disciplined" workers. Yet many of those dismissed workers had gained skills while working during the boom of the 1960s. There was a dramatic increase in the incidence of injury to dockworkers through accident in 1970.[26] This was undoubtedly due to the recruitment of a whole set of new workers who were expected to work as productively as those of the 1960s. The productivity of stevedores underwent a sharp decline in the early 1970s, causing major port delays.[27]

As I suggested earlier, an intimate relationship existed between South African stevedoring companies and international shipping lines. Towards the end of the 1960s, goods began to be carried in containers, and many predicted that it would make the stevedoring industry substantially less important in ports world-wide. The shipping lines were aware of the coming technological changes, and demanded a change in method of payment from a cost-plus-rate standard contract to an all-in-rate structure, irrespective of the cargo handled.[28] This change meant two things: firstly, the cost-plus-rate structure was based on set amounts, depending on what kind of cargoes were handled, and made allowance for more difficult cargoes for stevedores; secondly, breaking the standard contract allowed for stevedoring companies to set their own rates. This meant that the companies continually undercut each other, and shipping lines always chose the cheapest option. Independent operators (outside the Labour Supply Company) employed casual labour, despite government regulations, and actively competed to provide better rates for the shipping lines. This caused vigorous protest from the local Bantu Administration Board.[29]

Competition and undercutting went on for about five years, and by 1976 the major shipping lines had pulled out of stevedoring altogether, either

25. Interview with Dreyer by David Hemson, quoted in *idem*, "Class Consciousness and Migrant Workers", p. 581.
26. *Ibid.*, p. 534.
27. *Natal Mercury*, 23 January 1970, "Mechanisation the Answer to Port Delays, Say Agents".
28. Morris, "Stevedoring and the General Workers Union, part 1", pp. 91–92.
29. Durban Repository Archives, PNAB 2/3/7/1 (sub committee of Labour and Transport); "Minutes of a Meeting Addressing the Labour Problems in the Point on Harbour Areas", 20 November 1974.

disappearing or transporting new containerized cargo.[30] The first five years of the 1970s were critical, because they represented a change in the dominant form of cargo transportation internationally from break-bulk to containers. Captain Gordon Stockley, whose involvement in stevedoring in South Africa stretched for twenty years (1974–1994), and who became a prominent actor in the liberalizing of labour relations in the stevedoring industry during the 1980s, explains what the tactics of the shipping lines were:

> What these guys in the shipping industry knew about was the effects of containerisation. This made me a little bitter, because they knew what was going to happen to the labour and that we would have a massive problem, but they weren't too interested in helping or showing us the direction to go. They just ripped the guts out of it to get better profits and to hell with the future of the industry.[31]

Given these near impossible conditions of operations, stevedoring companies had to decide the best way forward. The previous five years of bitter competition had not done any of the companies much good, and it was clearly impossible to continue in this manner. In 1976, the twelve stevedoring companies operating in Durban, including many of the old companies previously owned by shipping lines, either merged into four main companies or dissolved entirely. At the end of the 1970s, the four main companies operating in Durban were South African Stevedoring Services Company (SASSCO), Aero Marine, Rennies, and Grindrods. The dominant company was SASSCO, occupying 60 per cent of the market.[32]

The exploitation of the stevedoring market and merger of stevedoring companies was perhaps the first tangible effect of containerization. The second was on the labour front. As companies merged, and the stevedoring trade became increasingly difficult to make profitable, remaining companies looked at ways of cutting costs. In the late 1970s SASSCO, as the dominant stevedoring company, found that it was investing the most in the Labour Supply Company and not getting any real material benefits from doing so. Furthermore, smaller companies were using the large labour pool of the Labour Supply Company whenever they needed it, which caused SASSCO to feel as if it was providing the labour for these smaller companies. SASSCO also felt that it was important to give workers a company identity and bring workers closer to management.[33] The traditional hierarchies maintained in the Labour Supply Company were

---

30. Morris, "Stevedoring and the General Workers Union, part 1", pp. 92–93.
31. Interview by the author: Captain Gordon Stockley, 25 June 2001. Captain Stockley had been involved with the Union Castle line in the 1960s and came to stevedoring in Durban in 1973. He was the Operations Manager of South African Stevedores until his retirement in 1994.
32. Morris, "Stevedoring and the General Workers' Union, part 1", p. 95.
33. Interview with Captain Gordon Stockley, 25 June 2001.

expensive, and for a SASSCO management far more interested in surviving as a stevedoring company than maintaining apartheid, the decision to withdraw from the Labour Supply Company proved quite simple. In 1979, the Labour Supply Company was wound up without any real protest, in contrast to its difficult and contested beginnings.

THE DECLINING INFLUENCE OF THE STATE AND THE RISE OF TRADE UNIONS

It was not coincidental that the Labour Supply Company disappeared without a struggle. Instead it reflected the growing crisis in apartheid administration. The economic prosperity of South Africa during the 1960s was not sustained in the 1970s. After 1976, the apartheid state began to face not only a weaker economy, but also the growth of internal opposition and sanctions from abroad. By the dawn of the 1980s the state was in crisis. Both from within the ranks of the business community, and from within the state itself, doubt emerged as to the long-term sustainability of the project of grand apartheid. Many within the business community believed that they could no longer afford to rely on cheap African labour.[34] In addition, the growth of resistance among African workers, especially in the form of politicized trade unions, suggested that the apartheid government no longer possessed the administrative strength to maintain an intricately controlled migrant labour system. By the time that government reform loosened control over the pass-law system and allowed African trade unions to organize in 1979, these were already a *de facto* reality. The recognition of African trade unions was a last-ditch cynical attempt on the part of the state to try and depoliticize these unions, premised on the hope that the trade unions, once they had gained access to lawful methods of protest and negotiation, would become depoliticized and would not provide yet another avenue of opposition to severely faltering government control. While the actual violence and brutality administered by the state in the 1980s seems to suggest its control of the forces of coercion, it belies its actual weakness in maintaining a system that had become both unsustainable and generally despised. Unlike the confident and well-organized state administration of the 1960s, the 1980s would see state administration over labour in total disarray, intervening at arbitrary and ad-hoc intervals in order to disrupt worker organization.

While there had been some degree of loosely defined union organization amongst stevedores in the 1940s and 1950s, this had been stamped out by the Labour Supply Company.[35] The two strikes by stevedores in Durban

34. Dan O' Meara, *Forty Lost Years: The Apartheid State and the Politics of the National Party, 1948–1994* (Athens, OH, 1996), pp. 176–178.
35. Hemson, "Dock Workers, Labour Circulation and Class Struggles in Durban", pp. 95–100.

in 1969 and 1972 had not been organized by any formal union body because African unions were illegal. During the early 1970s, benefit funds and advice bureaux were established across the country and were peripherally involved in the 1972 stevedore strike and the wider 1973 Durban strikes, when they attempted to highlight the immediate exploitation of workers in their particular workplaces.[36] Yet these organizations were not unions, and consisted primarily of white leftist intellectuals whose position was always to advise workers on the best course of action. These intellectuals had little experience of the realities of working under the difficult conditions that apartheid had constructed. While the intentions of these activists were often noble, their real significance in worker consciousness and action was limited. Furthermore, the danger of overemphasizing their role in the strikes removes much of the agency that workers themselves displayed both in organizing and leading the strikes.

The mid- to late 1970s witnessed not only a resurgence in worker militancy but also the beginnings of a new union movement in South Africa. Unions began to form tentatively in many workplaces, and a new trade-union federation, called the Federation of South African Trade Unions (FOSATU), formed in 1977. Although these unions often bore the hallmarks of the older benefit funds, unionists became more adventurous and open in their practices of organizing until their *de jure* recognition in 1979, following the Wiehahn Commission.[37] The Wiehahn strategies enjoyed very limited success, even in the early 1980s, and instead allowed trade unions to become a platform for anti-apartheid organization and widespread resistance to apartheid.

In the docks, trade unionism spread in the late 1970s. Senior management in the major stevedoring companies almost encouraged the development of trade unionism as part of a broader strategy to modernize the labour force.[38] Middle management were not comfortable with the

36. Another example of this type of involvement with the African working class was the wages commissions set up at white "liberal" universities across South Africa. A typical wages commission document would advise workers of their positions and encourage them to strike for high wages. These documents were available in both English and Zulu. For a University of Natal wages commission document on the stevedoring industry in Durban, see University of the Witswatersrand, Fosatu Collection, AH 1999 C3.19.12.1 Wages Commission, University of Natal. Also see Hemson's somewhat exaggerated account of the role of the Benefit Fund in the 1972 stevedore strike in *idem*, "Class Consciousness and Migrant Workers", pp. 605–670. For an account of involvement in the 1973 Durban strike, again somewhat overemphasized, see Gerhard Mare (ed.), *The Durban Strikes 1973: "Human Beings with Souls"* (Durban, 1976). pp. 69–76.
37. O'Meara, *Forty Lost Years*, p. 273.
38. Interviews: Captain Gordon Stockley, 25 June 2001; Siza Makhaya, 11 June 2001. Makhaya commented that many in middle management regarded senior management as taking "crazy and radical" steps in reforming the workforce.

development of trade unions during this initial period, with a number of recorded disciplinary incidents, and one in particular where a white foreman told union members "to collect their wages from the union".[39] Despite these incidents, the two early unions in the docks, the South African Allied Workers' Union (SAAWU) and the Transport and General Workers' Union (TGWU) were hardly able to claim anything near majority membership in the stevedoring industry. In 1980, the latter could claim a mere 300 members out of a possible 2,500 stevedores.[40] It was only in 1981 with the development of a relationship between SASSCO and a new union, the General Workers' Union, that unionism would become significant in the harbour at the same moment that containerization was beginning seriously to alter the harbour landscape.

LIBERAL COMPANIES AND TECHNOLOGICAL CHANGE

With the economic burden of the Labour Supply Company gone, and the influence of state policy significantly smaller, the remaining stevedoring companies set about forging a new system of industrial relations on the docks. For senior company officials, such as Stockley, it was critical that the industry became sustainable in the long term, and negotiated the technological change already at hand.[41] Central to this process was an attempt by SASSCO, and later SAS, to build a strong identity with its workforce. This was not simply a gesture – Stockley realized that the stevedoring workers in Durban had been "over-exploited", and that they were not equipped to deal with the new skills required for containerization. Of course, by developing a strong sense of identity in the company among the workforce, Stockley also hoped, and ultimately ensured, that he would not have to cope with a great deal of industrial strife. Contrary to many other workplaces in South Africa during the early 1980s, the major companies in the stevedoring industry also brokered deals and developed good relations with trade unions. Perhaps this was motivated to some extent by the power that European and American dockside unions had displayed through their independence – which Stockley and others in the companies must surely have known about – but it was also motivated by Stockley's self-proclaimed commitment to ensure a stable and well represented workforce.[42] At this particular time in South

---

39. University of the Witwatersrand Dept of Historical Papers, FOSATU Collection, AH 1999 C.1.9.12.8.3, Grindrods Discipline.
40. Jeremy Baskin, "The GWU and the Durban Dockworkers", *South Africa Labour Bulletin*, 8 (1982), pp. 18–33, 20.
41. Interview: Captain Gordon Stockley, 25 June 2001.
42. *Ibid.* By this time, Stockley was entirely in charge of operations in stevedoring nationally. He was determined to make stevedoring work, and declared at a speech at the Durban Country Club in 1982 that he was not prepared to move at the speed of the slowest ship.

Africa many industries were suspicious of trade unions and still had state
support, at least in principle, to clamp down on any "trouble" that might
have arisen.

Yet Stockley's embrace of the General Workers' Union was only one
aspect of his drive to modernize the stevedoring industry in South Africa.
A primary component of this policy was the introduction of "multiskilling" within the company. This involved teaching every member of the
work-gang new roles, in order that each could function in any place within
the gang, as specific work required.[43] While the company proclaimed
"multiskilling" as a progressive measure, eliminating "idle time", it set the
conditions in place to reduce the size of the gang and retrench workers. As
containerization developed in South Africa, the number of workers needed
in a work-gang would decline, as the skills required for securing a
container were substantially less labour-intensive than for loading break-
bulk cargo.

In addition, SASSCO aimed to reform the workplace and alter the
power relations by introducing two measures. Firstly, it attempted to
change the accommodation arrangements for stevedores. Stevedores lived
in company compounds that had been critical in the functioning of power
within the Labour Supply Company. By changing worker accommodation, the company could be relieved both of these older structures of
power and of the cost of maintaining them. Workers actually rejected the
company's attempt to move them into subsidized housing, with many
workers tending to remain in the compound until the 1990s.[44] The second
aspect of the company's liberalizing initiatives was to introduce language
classes in English in an ostensible attempt to prepare workers for the new
kinds of "open management" of the company. Part of the language
initiative was also to destroy the older hierarchical arrangement of power
within gangs that had developed during the time of the Labour Supply
Company. Yet the language policy was also a way of clearly individualiz-
ing workers, which was to be very useful in identifying particularly
productive or skilled workers, critical during a time of retrenchment.

Alongside these processes was the computerization of all stevedoring
work, showing which shifts had been worked and the various skill levels
individual workers possessed.[45] During the 1970s and before, this process

43. *Ibid.*
44. Lawrence Schlemmer *et al.*, "Future Dwelling Preferences of Hostel Dwelling Migrants", a
study of the housing needs of stevedores in the Durban metropolitan area and interviews with
Themba Dube, Les Owen, Gordon Stockley, and Mike Morris.
45. Interviews: Captain Gordon Stockley and Hugh Wyatt. Processes of surveillance at work
are nothing new, and even the gang structure of the Labour Supply Company monitored
individuals' performance, by the use of time clocks and rubber bands heatsealed on to workers'
wrists. Compare Harry Braverman, *Labour and Monopoly Capitalism: The Degradation of
Work in the Twentieth Century* (New York, 1974). p. 57.

had been coordinated by foremen through time cards, and subject to infinite abuse. It is crucial to understand the dual nature of this computerization process: on the one hand, it introduced perhaps a fairer system of industrial relations into the port. But on the other, it was very much part of a process of control, intimately connected, as Castells would suggest when referring to work in the information age generally, as "the individualization of work and the fragmentation of societies".[46] In this instance, the society undergoing fragmentation would be the work-gang.

In 1981, an agreement was negotiated between SASSCO and the GWU that introduced a guarantee system to the stevedoring industry. This meant that all workers employed in stevedoring in Durban would be paid for a certain number of days of work, regardless of whether there was actually work to be done. This agreement was fundamentally important since, following the collapse of the Labour Supply Company, there was no guarantee of permanent employment, especially in the context of the retrenchments that had begun in 1979. The guarantee initially provided for three and half days wages, and subsequently moved up to four.[47]

A further change to the structure of the stevedoring industry was the merger of the two remaining stevedoring companies. SASSCO and Rennies Grindrod entered into negotiations on a possible merger in late 1982.[48] At the end of the year, they submitted an application to the competitions board to create a single stevedoring company in the docks. In their submission, the two companies recognized the need for a stable and well-paid labour force, and the need for capital investment in the stevedoring industry that could only really occur with the suspension of the competition between the two companies for relatively meagre resources. A stable workforce could be trained and developed to meet changed industrial demands, and with the total cost of labour amounting to 40 per cent of both companies' costs, it seemed that continued competition would destroy any future for stevedoring. An additional factor in this decision was based on the decline by 6.3 million tons of break-bulk cargo, handled nationally, between 1976 and 1981.[49]

The merger brought immediate benefits and problems. Casual labour was once again eliminated throughout the port and workers were all given four-day guarantees. Through negotiations with unions, wages in the

46. Manuel Castells, *The Rise of the Network Society* vol. 1 of *The Information Age: Economy, Society and Culture* (London [etc.], 1996).

47. Interview: Les Owen, Senior Industrial Relations Manager, SASSCO and SAS 1979–1984, 5 June 2001.

48. In 1981, Rennies and Grindrods Cotts had merged into Rennies Grindrod, leaving only two stevedoring companies on the docks.

49. SASSCO and Rennies Grindrod, "Rationalisation of the Stevedoring Industry: Memorandum to Competitions Board", August 1982. This document does not come from an archive but rather was given to me by retired management of South African Stevedores.

industry increased at the end of 1982.[50] The merger also resulted in an oversized staff of both management and workers. Almost as soon as South African Stevedores (SAS) came into existence in August 1982, both management and workers were retrenched.[51] After the merger, almost there were almost two years of relative stability on the docks in Durban. As a monopoly, South African Stevedores ran a very efficient operation and there were few retrenchments. When there was a particular shortage of work, stevedores would take short periods of unpaid leave, but neverthe-less did not lose their jobs. Although there were still too many stevedores employed by the company, a quick solution would have destroyed the balance that the company and union had created in the harbour. And this would not simply have meant retrenchment, but ultimately a retreat from the industrial relations system itself.

THE HIDDEN HAND OF THE STATE: INTRODUCING COMPETITION

Yet this situation would not endure. As has been noted already, the early 1980s had seen the state undergoing tremendous strain in an effort to stay in power. Its retreat from the arena of workplaces had allowed South African Stevedores, in negotiation with the General Workers' Union, a relatively free hand in controlling stevedoring work in Durban. With a trimmed labour force, the company lasted through 1983 without competition. SAS management believed that the future was in their hands, and that they could build long-term sustainability in the industry.[52] But there was a crucial dimension that I have not yet mentioned: the state still owned the physical area of the harbour and controlled port operations and the railways. Although the state no longer had the capacity to intervene directly in stevedoring companies, state officials grew increasingly concerned about the "liberal" practices of SAS.

The 1983 Industrial Relations Report of the SAS Corporate Plan acknowledged the difficulties of the relationship and the potential for conflict with the South African Transport Services (SATS).[53] The report specifically highlighted the fact that SAS could not afford to intimidate SATS, which had sole control over stevedoring licences and protected the fact that SAS had no competition.[54] Even before the end of 1983, a major conflict had arisen between the two bodies. The General Workers' Union

50. *Daily News*, 23 December 1982, "Wage Increases for Stevedores".
51. *Ibid.*, 25 August 1982, "Managers Axed after Stevedoring Merger".
52. Interview: Captain Gordon Stockley, 25 June 2001.
53. South African Transport Services replaced the old South African Railways and Harbours in the early 1980s.
54. South African Stevedores Corporate Plan 1984–1987, Industrial Relations Report.

had attempted to expand and organize all workers in the harbour at Port Elizabeth. SATS had brought in the police to prevent any kind of unionization spreading beyond the stevedores, and forcefully told the GWU that in no way would it allow any kind of union organization to occur.[55] When a radio station interviewed Les Owen, the industrial relations officer of SAS, about the strike, Owen had explicitly said that South African Transport Services was in the wrong and that independent unions must be allowed to operate in the docks. Shortly after the interview, the directors of SAS were summoned to Pretoria and threatened with the loss of their stevedoring licence.[56]

While the state did not remove the operating licence, it did begin to issue a number of new licences to smaller operators, thus reintroducing competition into the port. The most significant of these occurred when the major iron and steel conglomerate in the country, ISCOR, publicly complained about the high rates that SAS was charging as the sole stevedoring provider. Keeleys Stevedoring was issued a stevedoring licence and specifically cut out a niche in the steel market by becoming the sole provider for ISCOR.[57] Keeleys employed casual labour "off the street" and paid these workers substantially less than SAS.[58] By having much smaller labour costs, Keeleys was also able to gain a foothold in many of SAS's other markets. GWU tried to organize in Keeleys and found that it had no conception of liberal industrial relations, and even attempted to make GWU a "sweetheart" union.[59] The union even complained to the state that, under the prescribed wage determination, Keeleys was paying its workers below the minimum rate.[60]

Crucially, the state had succeeded in recreating the casual labour system. As Keeleys developed, the guarantee system, the single most important measure of stevedore security, was undermined and SAS abandoned it as too costly. Furthermore, the added material pressure on the company and

55. Mike Morris, "Stevedoring and the General Workers' Union, part 2", *South African Labour Bulletin*, 11 (1986), p. 108.

56. Interview: Les Owen, 5 June 2001.

57. ISCOR, the major iron and steel conglomerate in the country, imported and exported large amounts of irregular-sized pieces of steel during the 1980s through Durban. Its relationship to the state stretched back to its formation in 1928, when the state considered it impossible to industrialize South Africa without an iron and steel industry. It was strongly tied to national (as opposed to colonial) capitalist interests and protected white workers. See Ari Sitas, "African Worker Responses on the East Rand to Changes in the Metal Industry, 1960–1980" (unpublished Ph.D. thesis, University of the Witswatersrand, 1984), pp. 68–77.

58. Morris, "Stevedoring and the General Workers' Union, part 1", pp. 112–114.

59. Interview: Mike Morris, 28 June 2001. Morris was an organizer for the GWU in Durban from 1981 to 1985. Company management, such as Stockley, concurred with Morris's description of Keeley's stevedoring. Stockley also suggested that many of those employed by Keeley's were retrenched stevedores.

60. *Financial Mail*, 3 August 1984, "Wage Determination: Payment Problems".

the growing emphasis on container trade saw the company retrench a
further 600 stevedores in February 1985.[61]

THE FAILURE OF THE UNION MOVEMENT AND THE
RE-EMERGENCE OF CASUAL LABOUR

The General Workers' Union stood on a knife-edge in early 1985. After
four years of maintaining a fragile but progressive industrial relations
system in the docks, building a guarantee system and controlling the
retrenchment of workers, suddenly it was all falling to pieces. As the
GWU's main organizer in Durban, Mike Morris, expressed his helpless
position:

> We couldn't actually deal with it. It drove me out of the union in the end. It was
> constantly disheartening, we tried to negotiate the best deal we could, and it was
> never good enough [...]. It was an impossible situation and I did not realise, until
> I did the research afterwards, what a worldwide trend this was [...] we spent our
> time negotiating retrenchments.[62]

The withdrawal of the General Workers' Union from the docks would
prove to be a decisive turning point. Although formally it merged with the
Transport and General Workers' Union, solid union support for the
workers was never the same. Morris claimed that its strategy as a union
proved incorrect, that it should that made a more sustained effort to
incorporate all harbour workers at every port.[63] Yet the union was fighting
a losing battle against technological change. Moreover, the union failed to
transcend its origins as a noble, yet ultimately paternalist structure.
Officials in the General Workers' Union were predominately white
intellectuals, and unlike other industries in South Africa, notably the
mining sector, there was never a transformation in the administrative
structure of the union towards a greater representation of workers among
the officials. It was only possible for the union to withdraw from the
workplace because its leadership was largely made up of people who did
not depend on stevedoring for their long-term security or livelihood.

The Transport and General Workers' Union (TGWU) was a much
larger national union, which had little experience of organizing stevedores.
It had always played a key role in the national organizations of trade
unions, first within the Federation of South African Trade Unions
(FOSATU), and from 1985 in the Congress of South African Trade
Unions (COSATU). The TGWU had a wide range of experience in the
transport sector, but was hamstrung not only by its lack of familiarity with
conditions in the harbour, but also by COSATU's overtly political aims of

61. *Natal Mercury*, 18 February 1985, "600 Durban Dockworkers to Lose Jobs".
62. Interview: Mike Morris, 28 June 2001.
63. *Ibid.*

overthrowing apartheid. In addition, like any other union in South Africa during this time, it had simply no idea of how to organize casual labourers.

The difficult political climate in South Africa during the later 1980s would also become a feature in the docks. Largely because of the political stance of TGWU, the Inkatha Freedom Party (IFP) formed a union that came to the docks in the hope of claiming the allegiance of the migrant workforce. What followed between 1987 and 1991 was a disastrous rivalry between the two unions, with both trying to claim political ground in a struggle that increasingly involved the intimidation of workers' families and threats to their rural homes. There were a number of instances where violence occurred, and even a couple in which workers were killed. The end result was that management was left essentially unchallenged. More retrenchment of stevedores followed in May 1987, seemingly unchecked by either union.[64] At the end of the political fracas, in July 1991, the majority of the stevedoring labour force found themselves casualized, unequipped in the latest technical skills, and often struggling for regular employment.

In contrast to the woes of the stevedores, Durban harbour was booming. In 1994 containerized cargo made up more than 30 per cent of the total operations of the harbour, and this percentage rose steadily.[65] In its framework for new port developments, the new government hardly considered the position of the stevedores at all, despite deliberate emphasis on redressing the imbalances of the past. It was far more concerned with issues of customer satisfaction, building new container terminals, and overall growth of the industry.[66] In government reports, the casual stevedoring industry was blamed for past inequalities. The government did make one serious attempt to regulate casual labour by recommending the establishment of a common labour pool for stevedores.[67] Unfortunately, this only functioned successfully for a year before employers withdrew, claiming the pool was too big, too expensive, and ultimately inefficient.[68]

Besides the obvious effects of retrenchment, the destruction of the gang structure that had for so many years been central to the labour process on the docks also affected worker morale. Stevedores no longer felt part of a

---

64. David Hemson. "Beyond the Frontier of Control", *Transformation*, 30 (1996), pp. 83–114, 97–99.

65. Jones, *The Port of Durban and the Durban Metropolitan Economy*, p. 17.

66. Dept of Transport, "White Paper on National Transport Policy, 20 August 1996". This can be found at www.gov.za/whitepaper/1996/transportpolicy1996.htm, accessed on 19 June 2002, 12.00; Dept of Transport, "Moving South Africa: A Transport Strategy for the year 2020". Located at www.transport.gov.za/projects/msa/msa.html, accessed on 18 June 2002, 14:00.

67. Best described in Simon Stratton, "The Implementation of the Dock Labour Scheme in the Port of Durban", (unpublished, 1999).

68. To some extent, employers were correct. The register of the pool was manipulated and even unionists admitted it was too big. Interview by the author: Tony Kruger, Chairman of Durban Stevedores' Association, 28 November 2000.

team of strong "buffalo" who made the harbour work. In a series of interviews with stevedores conducted by David Hemson in the early 1990s, he found that workers no longer had any pride in their work, and felt that the mechanization of the port made them "weak".[69] Even before the 1990s, many stevedores realized that the prospects of a long-term future in the industry were small. Their responses were to turn back towards the only area that they had any promise of security within the migrant labour system. For instance, Mr Ntshangase, an established stevedore who had been working in the industry since the 1950s, suggested, when interviewed in 1982, that the only thing the union could do was ensure a retrenchment package and then he would "go back home [...] to look after my cattle".[70] The majority of remaining stevedoring workers were over forty years old, a consequence of the Last-In-First-Out, (LIFO) policy of retrenchment negotiated by both the GWU and TGWU, and felt that the rural areas offered the only alternative for them after forced retirement or retrenchment.[71]

These views represented one of the bitter ironies of the migrant labour system in the stevedoring industry in Durban. In the 1950s, stevedores had claimed Durban as their home and engaged in a losing struggle against influx control with the apartheid state. By the end of apartheid, stevedores had so little hope left in the industry that they turned back towards the homeland areas that the apartheid state had designated as their homes.[72] Over a period of twenty years, the number of permanent workers in the industry had shrunk from 2,800 in the early 1970s to 1,200 in 1985 and to 300 in 1991. About 1,000 workers occupied the ranks of casual stevedores, but had absolutely no guarantees of work or security of employment whatsoever. Given that stevedores were highly exploited throughout the century, the final decade of the century saw their humiliation; they had become marginal and peripheral workers.

It is important to emphasize the form that casualization has taken in Durban. In most ports the trend has been away from de-casualization. As Klaus Weinhauer has suggested in his study of de-casualization in ports, this move has depended on the ability of the state and employers to "secure disciplined work", and has involved an intensification of control over the

69. David Hemson, "The Global Imperative? Containerization and Durban Docks" (n.p., 1996), pp. 10–12. For a more complete account of the interviews see *idem, Migrants and Machines: Labour and New Technology in the Port of Durban* (Pretoria, 1995).

70. Mr Ntshangase interviewed by Tina Sideris on 19 November 1982; Wits Historical Papers, SAIRR Oral History Project, interview #44.

71. Hemson, "The Global Imperative? Containerization and Durban Docks", pp. 8–14.

72. In a different context of industrial decline, Ferguson has shown that a "return to the land" is by no means unproblematic. See James Ferguson, *Expectations of Modernity* (Berkeley, CA, 1999), pp. 123–128.

stevedoring labour process.[73] In Durban, the state crudely attempted to control stevedoring work in the 1960s and early 1970s in order to fit the industry into its model of racial exclusion and "culturally defined" practice. When this model failed, stevedoring companies sought to recreate the industry in terms of new technologically defined imperatives and safeguard the future of the industry. Yet they failed – and casualization became the dominant mode of stevedoring work in South Africa.

THEORIZING THE TRANSFORMATION OF WORK IN DURBAN

How are we to situate the radical transformation that occurred in the stevedoring industry in Durban? Despite the fact that the evidence presented shows a particular story of the changing practices of labour administration over three decades, this is not merely a local story of change. By its very nature, a harbour is a connection to the rest of world. In an important sense, that connection is in constant dialogue with the rest of the world. In this case, the dialogue demanded a radical technological remaking of the port, which altered the manner in which work in the port was done. The denationalization of shipping lines in the 1970s, and the increased privatization in the port sector internationally, are additional factors that influenced both the speed of the move towards containerization and the shape that it took.[74]

There are also broader connections. Fordism around the world suffered a crisis in the mid-1960s, and the 1970s and 1980s were times of economic and political turmoil that marked an attempt to resolve the problems created by the rigidity of Fordism. What emerged, in David Harvey's terms, was a new regime of flexible accumulation that sought to create new sectors of production, new markets, and intensify the speed of technological innovation.[75] Flexible accumulation also created new working conditions, undercutting organized labour in areas with no well-established labour traditions, and rolling back the power of trade unions throughout the globe. Containerization was one such technological innovation. As Stephen Graham and Simon Marvin demonstrate, the rapid expansion of communication networks and the transport sector developed as necessary elements in this expanded consumer market. They show that flexible labour markets are key to this

---

73. Klaus Weinhauer, "Power and Control on the Waterfront: Casual Labour and Decasualisation", in Sam Davies *et al.* (eds) *Dock Workers: International Explorations in Comparative Labour History*, 2 vols (Aldershot, 2000), pp. 581–602.
74. Broeze, "Containerization and the Globalization of Liner Shipping", pp. 24–25.
75. David Harvey, *The Condition of Postmodernity: An Enquiry into the Origins of Cultural Change* (Oxford, 1990), pp. 147, 150–153.

expansion.[76] Given that four important features of containerization are the standardization of port facilities, the rapidly accelerated turnaround time of cargo, a flexible labour force, and the coordination of container ships through the use of integrated computer networking systems, it becomes clear that containerization was a key technological innovation in this global transformation.

If we consider the position of the stevedores in Durban, we find further parallels. They underwent processes of "multiskilling", saw their gang units destroyed, and became flexible workers. By 1990, the vast majority of the stevedores had no union organization, were super-exploited casual workers, and had lost all pride in their work and all faith in the future. This position, while not shared to the same extent by other dockworkers world-wide, is shared by many industrial workers, as Pierre Bourdieu has shown. In his edited volume of essays, *The Weight of the World*, he and other contributors probe the difficulties and suffering of contemporary society.[77] In an important section on the decline of industrial work, the book's contributors present first-hand accounts of the difficulties of flexible employment and the impossible task that trade unionists face in organizing under these conditions.[78]

While Bourdieu's book was largely based on conditions in France, his general conclusions about the nature of casual work can be extended to other societies. In an important sense, it reflects the position that stevedores find themselves in. We could say that they share the fate of workers in information societies whose struggles are not merely about the conditions of work, but the possibility of regular work itself. This parallels the suggestion, by Manuel Castells, that "the new economy does not create or destroy work, but rather reshapes the conditions of work".[79] Yet this reshaping has come with more of a loss that Castells acknowledges. Following Bourdieu, it is important to realize that the number of young computer experts is insignificant when compared to the number of industrial workers who face uncertain and difficult futures. Flexible work may have its advantages for the highly qualified technicians of the information age, but it has extremely serious repercussions for industrial workers.

The development of containerization thus carries important features of the contemporary world economy within it. Yet the transformation of work in Durban is not merely about machines replacing men, it is also

76. Stephen Graham and Simon Marvin, *Telecommunications and the City: Electronic Spaces, Urban Places* (New York, 2001), pp. 40–41, 286.

77. Pierre Bourdieu (ed.), *The Weight of the World: Social Suffering in Contemporary Society* (Oxford, 1999).

78. See articles by Michel Pialoux, Stéphane Beaud, Louis Pinto, and Bourdieu in *ibid.*, pp. 255–419.

79. Castells, *Rise of the Network Society*, p. 265.

about how this process happened. And a consideration of the effects of this transformation shows that a uniform result in every port simply did not occur. Instead, global technological innovation coincided with the local conditions of a port in South Africa, that is a port in a place where workers had a significantly different history, and a fundamentally weaker position. Where well-organized dockworkers in certain ports in the United States and in western Europe managed both to limit retrenchment and prevent casualization, in South Africa, containerization in conjunction with poorly organized trade unions, an unsympathetic government, and a legacy of racist and super-exploitative labour relations, produced retrenchment and casualization.

What is important about this consideration is that it prevents us from broadly characterizing the changes in ports world-wide as a process of "globalization" or in generalizing the nature of work in the "information age". Indeed, important recent work has signalled the difficulty of using these terms at all. In her study on the connections between Taiwanese investment and local communities in South Africa, Gillian Hart powerfully demonstrates that popular and academic discourse on globalization proves disabling, since it assumes the coherence of the notion of "globalization" itself.[80] Instead, she argues that new spatial interconnections develop within this moment of neoliberal capitalism in an entirely inconsistent manner, as a reflection of local contingencies. Above all, this study challenges the notion that it is possible to test "the level of globalization in any single economy". Frederick Cooper goes further by arguing that the discourse on globalization is entirely superficial, ignoring both the extent to which long-distance connections were forged over history and the endurance of uneven spaces of power in the global arena.[81] Citing a range of examples from the spread of Islam across the Indian Ocean from the eighth century, the Atlantic slave trade of the seventeenth and eighteenth centuries, and the decolonization of Africa in the postwar period, Cooper suggests that globalization theorists offer an entirely ahistorical picture of networks and connections that privilege the present as "unique" and malign the past.

To underscore the value of Cooper's argument, I present two important conclusions. Firstly, that containerization as a global process has produced different consequences: that Rotterdam has not followed the same trend as Durban suggests that these processes do not create homogenous results. Secondly, and crucially linked, is the suggestion that the reason why

---

80. Gillian Hart, *Disabling Globalization: Places of Power in Post-Apartheid South Africa* (Durban, 2002), pp. 14, 290.
81. Frederick Cooper, "What Is the Concept of Globalization Good For? An African Historian's Perspective", *African Affairs*, 100 (2001), pp. 189–213.

differences occur has much to do with local conditions, and within this, the particular choices made by states and bodies such as trade unions. Indeed, the particular trajectory of trade-union organization in Durban has not, except for a brief period, dealt with casualization in any satisfactory manner. But this is the result of the historical legacies of division, difference, and misunderstanding, and the decisions that have been made. In short, the local is decisive in the global. Technology changes environments, but the shape of these changes is decided by particular conditions in any given society.

CONCLUSION

In October 2002, longshoremen on the west coast of the United States, from Portland to Los Angeles, engaged in a three-week strike that crippled port operations.[82] The fact that dockworkers can still bring harbours to a standstill, and raise the attention of the entire country, shows that union organization can still be effective in the containerized shipping world. However, this stands in stark contrast to the position of the stevedores in Durban. Because of both fractured unionization and the legacy of apartheid, stevedoring workers in Durban have been entirely out-manoeuvred, casualized, and divided as a body of workers. While the occasional strike in Durban upsets operations, companies have no obligation or contract with casuals and can simply hire alternative workers. A major problem, as I have illustrated above, is that trade unions were not controlled by workers at any stage in the history of stevedoring in Durban. On the west coast of the United States, the legacy of strong worker-controlled organization has meant not only solidarity but also higher wages in relation to many other industrial workers.

In this paper, I have discussed the development of containerization and its implications for the stevedores working in South Africa. While in an important sense this development represents the emergence of the new economy, the experience of these workers suggests that we must not be too hasty in generalizing about the effects of technological change or claim that the new economy simply homogenizes difference. In many ways, dock-workers in Durban are today further from their European and American counterparts than they were before containerization. Because of their shared historical experience, the stevedores do in many ways resemble other industrial workers in South Africa. However, since the 1920s period when they enjoyed a privileged place in the city, the stevedores' experience has never been quite the same as that of other workers either.

Despite this, I have suggested that the experience of Durban stevedores

---

82. *New York Times*, 6 October 2002, "A Union wins the Global Game", pp. 1–3.

is not entirely unusual in the contemporary world. In the last twenty years, they have experienced precisely the disillusionment felt by workers in France described by Bourdieu. The dockworkers in Durban suffer from poor morale; they realize that their skills are worth less and less, and that their prospects in the new economy are extremely limited. Moreover, they no longer enjoy the benefits of full employment. Neither they themselves nor established trade unions have been able to organize them. They have become casual workers in an economy with an oversupply of workers and an undersupply of work. Perhaps we could say that the similarities are due to an experience of work in the "information age". Nevertheless, this paper has suggested that to stop at these similarities is misleading, since it would be to forget the historical circumstances in the development of these working conditions in different places. While in both contexts, workers are "flexible", it would too superficial to claim that their conditions are really the same.

It may appear here that I am valorizing the conditions of work that existed in the past. This is not my purpose. Throughout the world, both industrial and dock work were often highly exploitative, and many of the struggles throughout the world during the nineteenth and twentieth centuries were attempts to improve the difficult conditions of industrial work. Instead, my purpose is to show the relationship between past conditions and present ones. This is especially salient in the South African context, where the exploitation of workers was amplified by the racial policies of the apartheid state. The particular administration of stevedores in Durban was part of a wider form of societal exploitation of cheap African migrant labourers. At the height of apartheid, the Durban stevedores worked for low wages and were forbidden from organizing their workplace or protesting against the state. They enjoyed little protection from the dangers of harbour work and were frequently injured. These workers were not part of an industrial-relations system or a society that recognized their rights as citizens, but were instead part of an industrial relationship where they were treated more like subjects.

What is especially tragic about this part of the history of South Africa is that at the moment that workers began to gain rights at work similar to their European counterparts, global economic changes began to undermine the position of industrial workers as a whole. These changes were felt particularly acutely by the stevedores working in Durban, both because the harbour was a frontline of the new economy, and because the harbour could never really be as isolated as the rest of South Africa during apartheid. Mass retrenchments happened a decade earlier than in other industries. The changes to the industrial-relations system in South Africa, and the unionization of the stevedores came precisely at the moment when containerization threatened to, and ultimately did, decimate older forms of work. Unionists with little practical experience were confronted simultaneously with the impossible task of remaking the working relationships of the past and the spectre of mass retrenchment. The story of that failure makes a broader point about understanding work in the "information age": that this understanding can only be gained through both an analysis of general features such as flexibility and a coming to terms with local history and politics, which always play a significant part in global change.

IRSH 48 (2003), Supplement, pp. 123–152 DOI: 10.1017/S0020859003001299

Compressing Time and Constraining Space: The Contradictory Effects of ICT and Containerization on International Shipping Labour*

Helen Sampson and Bin Wu

INTRODUCTION

The twentieth century has been a period of rapid change in terms of production and consumption, work, and employment. Much of this change has been driven by developments in technology or the application of new technologies to existing production systems and ways of ordering and organizing work. In characterizing such change, Schumpeter popularized the term *innovation*.[1] In viewing innovation as the main engine of economic growth, Schumpeter was interested in the idea of the entrepreneur as innovator, not simply in terms of an agent for the introduction of new inventions but more broadly as an organizational innovator introducing new systems of work, new products, and new forms of production.

The early twentieth century saw the introduction of mass production systems, by entrepreneurs such as Henry Ford, and an associated growth in patterns of mass consumption. However, by the end of the century there had been a shift away from enterprises maximizing economies of scale through the mass production of individual goods towards more flexible "just-in-time" systems, increasingly demanding flexible workers,

* We are very grateful to the staff of the Tetra terminal in Rotterdam for their time and help and for allowing us to gain an insight into the operation of a deep-sea container terminal. We are also grateful to all the seafarers that took part in the research informing this paper over a three-year period. We would like to thank the staff of the anonymous short-sea terminal who allowed us to visit and observe their operations as part of the background research to the study. In terms of the writing of the paper we have appreciated the comments and encouragement of Huw Beynon, Aad Blok, and Greg Downey, and the inimitable critique of Tony Lane. We would like to thank the ESRC and SIRC for funding the research we have drawn on in producing this paper. Final thanks are due to Phil Belcher, Mick Bloor, and Erol Kahveci for their contributions to data collection. See also Erol Kahveci, Tony Lane, and Helen Sampson, *Transnational Seafarer Communities* (Cardiff, 2002).
1. Joseph A. Schumpeter, *Capitalism, Socialism, Democracy* (New York [etc.], 1942).

geographic flexibility in plant placement, and access to new and distant markets for less durable and more fashion dependent goods.[2]

The introduction of such forms of production and consumption (termed *postmodern* by some) combined with, and were to a great extent dependent upon, the technological revolution that accompanied them. Thus "just-in-time" systems required excellent information and communications systems to be effective. Similarly, in the search for flexible workers and access to new markets, many companies went "global", and the world of many workers and increasing numbers of citizens underwent a transformation resulting from what has been referred to as "time–space compression".[3] This phenomenon is said to leave individuals with a sense of the world getting smaller, as many are able to traverse space at ever increasing speeds, and send and receive information at the touch of a button, or more likely, the click of a mouse. Harvey illustrates the notion of *time–space compression* using the example of a shrinking globe; he explains:

> The time taken to traverse space [...] and the way we commonly represent that fact to ourselves [...] are useful indicators of what I have in mind. As space appears to shrink to a "global village" of telecommunications [...] and as time horizons shorten to the point where the present is all there is [...] so we have to learn to cope with an overwhelming sense of *compression* of our spatial and temporal worlds.[4]

Thus, for many people the accessible space of the everyday world can be seen to have expanded as a result of cheaper and more rapid systems of transportation. In addition, time may be perceived as having "speeded up", both in terms of the pace of everyday life, and the time it takes to communicate over long distances in the context of what is increasingly a twenty-four hour global society. Such changes cannot be seen as uniform, however, as they impact on different individuals and groups in varying ways. Most notably, poverty excludes many from the "global village" characterized by Harvey, whilst time horizons do not inevitably shrink for all, and indeed unemployment, imprisonment, or entrapment in tedious and monotonous work may do much to stretch them. Given such variability, and the centrality of transport in the process underpinning time–space compression, it seems apposite to consider the experiences of transport workers in the context of their work traversing the globe at incrementally increasing rates. Intriguingly seafarers, at the forefront of modernization, given their role in the mass transportation of freight, may be seen to have been pioneers in the process of time–space compression. Their experiences highlight the very ways in which time and space is

---

2. David Harvey, *The Condition of Postmodernity: An Enquiry into the Origins of Cultural Change* (Cambridge, MA [etc], 1990).
3. *Ibid.*
4. *Ibid.*, p. 240.

affected by the changes in systems of transportation, transforming both the spatial and the temporal world.

In the late twentieth century, the seafarer labour market, which was always, to some extent, global in scope, became increasingly *organized* on an international basis with the development of crew supplying agencies and management companies in developing countries such as India, the Philippines, Myanmar, Indonesia, and, most recently, China. Thus, whilst investment in shipping has remained largely in the "West" the supply of labour has increasingly moved "East". Movements away from labour markets in the developed world (including Japan) have been accompanied to some extent by a "deterioration" in the employment conditions of seafarers. Whilst differences exist in the opportunities offered to seafarers from different parts of the world, many of today's seafarers, including officers, are employed in relatively deregulated labour markets with little or no job security. They are increasingly employed by ship-management companies and paid on a per-voyage basis, thus increasing the ease with which they can be hired and fired. Thus, modern ships are generally populated by multinational crews of seafarers, many of whom are employed on short-term contracts, and all of whom operate in a highly time–space compressed environment. Modern vessels plough the seas at increasingly rapid rates. A container vessel today might be expected to travel at an average speed of 22 knots, whilst in the 1960s a similar ship would have had an average speed of approximately 15 knots. Thus, a new Filipino cadet today may find himself whisked away from his provincial home, flown halfway round the world to join a vessel, only to be sailing the coastal waters of his homeland within a month, having "visited" six or seven ports. Such mobility is deceptive, however, as the world cannot be seen as becoming more accessible to the seafarer even as it becomes *compressed*. Indeed, the evidence is of the opposite trend, and in many ways the spatial world of the seafarer can be seen to have contracted.

These phenomena and their underlying causes are amongst the issues considered in this paper. Time and space are experienced differently by people in different contexts, cultures, and circumstances. Whilst we might objectively measure both space and time, our sense of these and what they mean alter according to our situations. This paper will argue that, curiously, as a result of increased separation from shore and associated isolation, monotony, and boredom, in some respects modern seafarers have more in common with seafarers of the late nineteenth century than they do with seafarers in the 1950s and 1960s. In the days of early sailing ships, seafarers could be out at sea for months without sight of land or indeed another sail. They typically experienced feelings of isolation and boredom and could be tremendously uplifted by the sight of the shore or another ship, as Franklin described in 1726 when recounting his "tedious" voyage from Southampton to Philadelphia:

There is something strangely cheering to the spirits in the meeting of a ship at sea, containing a society of creatures of the same species and in the same circumstances with ourselves, after we had been long separated and excommunicated as it were from the rest of mankind. My heart fluttered in my breast with joy when I saw so many human countenances, and I could scarce refrain from the kind of laughter which proceeds from some degree of inward pleasure.[5]

For very different reasons, modern seafarers are similarly removed from land and often have a similar sense of space and time. Whilst working conditions, wages, and standards of health and hygiene have improved across the industry, seafarers in the twenty-first century once again find their lives at sea to be characterized by isolation, tedium, and confinement. They too experience a sense of "excommunication" and separation. As an oiler involved in our ethnographic study aboard one vessel explained: "[It's] like a prison. You eat and then you work [...]. Yes, like a prison. You don't go ashore."[6]

METHOD

This paper draws on the preliminary findings of a pilot study undertaken by Sampson in the Port of Rotterdam at two modern container terminals. The study involved the analysis of secondary data and visits to two modern container terminals – one engaged in short-sea, and one engaged in deep-sea trade. This was followed by an ethnographic study of the Tetra deep-sea container terminal,[7] incorporating in-depth tape-recorded interviews with terminal employees (largely in supervisory or management grades), with a terminal-based representative of the shipping line, and with senior officers aboard vessels calling at the terminal in the course of the week. Additionally, the paper draws on the findings of seven ethnographic research voyages undertaken as part of an ESRC-funded project on transnational seafarer communities (ESRC ref: L214252036). In the course of these, seafarers of all ranks and varying nationalities took part in detailed tape-recorded interviews focusing on life and work aboard, rigorous fieldnotes were maintained, and a photographic record kept. The paper draws on all of these sources in considering the technological and organizational changes in shipping that have been associated with the "speed-up" of voyages and/or cargo operations, and the impact these have had on the lives and work of seafarers.

5. Benjamin Franklin, "Journal of a Voyage", in Jonathan Raban (ed.), *The Oxford Book of the Sea* (Oxford, 1992) pp. 92–107, 100.
6. Oiler: interview with Sampson. NB – an oiler is the equivalent rank to an able-bodied seafarer but oilers work in the engine room rather than on deck.
7. The terminal name has been altered to protect anonymity and confidentiality.

BACKGROUND

Shipping has a long history inherently characterized by innovation and change. In Britain, for example, people first navigated waterways and sheltered seas in canoes.[8] Subsequently, sailing ships dominated ocean transport for several centuries. However, by the early part of the nineteenth century some had become steam-assisted, with the introduction of (increasingly efficient) coal-fired boilers. Full steam power followed on closely from these hybrid vessels and this mode of power persisted for approximately a century. By the mid-twentieth century, however, steam ships had generally been replaced by those with diesel-fed engines. The internal organization of the ship altered too, and in some dramatic ways. The introduction of an engine required radical transformations aboard, as engineers, firemen, and watertenders were added to the ranks of seafarers,[9] and a chief engineer was put in charge of them. This change affected the organization on board so dramatically that seafarers today still refer to a "divide" between engineers and navigation officers, making ironic use of the cliché that "oil and water don't mix". There were significant changes on the bridge too, with advances in navigation and the introduction of revolutionary pieces of equipment such as radar and, much later, satellite-assisted global positioning systems.

This process of transformation and the uptake of available innovative technologies in merchant shipping was both gradual and uneven. The first steam ship to cross the Atlantic was sail-assisted and was built in New York in 1819. She was rapidly followed by faster steam-powered vessels[10] and the development of more efficient systems of propulsion, (screw rather than paddle).[11] However, many companies were reluctant to invest in unproven new technologies. Sailing ships continued as deep-sea merchant traders until as late as 1929 and sailing barges known as "boomies" or "dandys" continued with continental trade right up until, and during, World War II, when diesel-fuelled motor coasters were already dominant in the same trades.[12] Thus, the transition from sail to steam and then to diesel ships, and from wooden to metal hulled vessels, was a slow one characterized by overlap rather than fracture.

Similarly, the up-take of innovation in navigation, information, and

---

8. Hubert Moyse-Bartlett, *From Steam to Sail: the Final Development and Passing of the Sailing Ship* (London, 1946).

9. Mariam G. Sherar, *Shipping Out: A Sociological Study of American Seamen* (Cambridge [etc.], 1973).

10. Alfred George Course, *The Merchant Navy: A Social History* (London, 1963).

11. The first screw-propelled ships came into service in the early 1840s, the largest of these early vessels combining sail and steam being *The Great Northern* and *The Great Britain*, launched in 1842 and 1843 respectively. See Stephen Fisher (ed.), *Innovation in Shipping and Trade* (Exeter, 1989).

12. Tristan Jones, *A Steady Trade* (London, 1984).

communication, technologies has varied. Today, a modern container vessel such as those included in the Rotterdam pilot study might have automated computer-monitored engines, sophisticated (ARPA) radar systems, satellite communications,[13] Global Positioning Systems (GPS), Electronic Chart Displays (ECDIS), internet access, e-mail, and access to satellite and mobile telephones. Additionally, it is likely to carry cargo-monitoring equipment, and software programmes for ballasting and stress calculations, replacing the requirement for seafarers to be directly involved in measuring cargo temperatures or taking soundings. This contrasts dramatically with what one might find aboard an older refrigerated vessel or a bulk carrier. Here, one ship included in the ethnographic research undertaken by Sampson did not have access to any satellite telephone communication and relied on VHS radio posts to make periodic telephone contact with the world. This vessel had few computers aboard, little software of any kind, and no e-mail. None of the five ships boarded by Sampson in the period 1999–2001 had electronic charts (ECDIS) and all relied on chief officers rather than shore-side staff for stress calculations and cargo planning. Thus, in the modern context it is also clear that, in terms of innovation, some companies lead whilst others lag behind. These differences between ships and shipping company practices are constrained to some extent by national, and increasingly international, regulation that requires certain standards, practices, and equipment on board deep-sea cargo vessels. This is not a new phenomenon. In the UK, for example, the requirement to maintain a radio watch on all British vessels was established in 1919 following the high-profile loss of the *Titanic*. Such national regulation has increasingly been supplemented and underpinned by international requirements, such as those introduced by the 1948 International Safety of Life at Sea Convention and, more recently, amendments to regulations relating to Standards in Watchkeeping and Certification (STCW '95) and the introduction of International Safety Management (ISM) systems.

The ship (like the factory) has therefore been transformed, and so too has the context in which it operates. The working lives and experiences of seafarers have altered and developed in line with changes in the organization of work both aboard and in port. Ships transport large amounts of materials between ports, and shipowners have always been aware of the significance of port handling for the profitability of their operations. The continuing pressure for shore-side automation and innovation has been driven by a number of concerns, and not least by pressure from shipowners who want their ships to be available to transport their next cargo at the earliest possible opportunity. A berthed ship is widely regarded by the industry as a waste of money, as it may incur expensive

13. Satellite communication was first introduced in the mid-1970s.

port dues (as in early twentieth-century Rotterdam) and it is languishing rather than actively transporting cargo. As a shipping line representative in Rotterdam explained:

> The [...] main thing is and the focus is always the vessel. That's our most expensive tool, apart from the people we have. So, if the [...] vessel's at sea, that's the only thing we aim at [...]. The vessel is the most expensive thing, and one of our [...] [particular vessel type] [...] is 3,500 US dollars an hour. So, if you keep a vessel idle for ten hours [...]![14]

Thus, in the twenty-first century the fast turnaround of a vessel is as much a priority as it was in the early and mid-twentieth century, when mechanization and then automation were increasingly introduced. The efficiency of a terminal remains critical in determining the success of its client shipping lines, and it can make the difference between profit and loss.[15] Alongside terminal operations, organizational innovation and change aboard ship has been required to ensure fast efficient shipping services and profitability in the global freight market. The experience of the Port of Rotterdam provides an excellent illustration of these processes.

INNOVATION IN PORTS AND CARGO HANDLING OPERATIONS: THE CASE OF ROTTERDAM

The city of Rotterdam is located in an important strategic position in terms of European trade and is currently the world's sixth largest container port (see Table 1 and Figure 1 overleaf).

Investment in the Port of Rotterdam began at an early stage, and in 1872 a waterway was constructed to facilitate shipping of increasing tonnage. In 1878, the construction and opening of the Binnehaven, the first basin on the south bank of the Maas, heralded the beginning of the seaward development of what is today a massive port, catering for a highly diverse range of ships and cargoes.[16]

The beginning of the twentieth century saw increasing mechanization within the port. Of major significance was the introduction of mechanized grain unloading. The consequences of this for the dock-labour force were immense. Many workers faced redundancy and unemployment and, as a result, organized a major strike against technical change.[17] This strike, the

14. Shipping line representative: interview with Sampson.
15. Edmund J. Gubbins, *The Shipping Industry: The Technology of the Economics of Specialisation* (London, 1986).
16. Rotterdam Europort, "Port of Rotterdam: Characteristics of Rotterdam Port", *Yearbook of Rotterdam Europort* (Rotterdam, 1978).
17. Dick van Lente, "Machines and the Order of the Harbour: The Debate About the Introduction of Grain Unloaders in Rotterdam 1905–1907", *International Review of Social History*, 43 (1998), pp. 79–109.

Table 1. *Top ten container ports – 2001*

Rank	Place	TEU*
1	Hong Kong	17,9000,000
2	Singapore	15,520,000
3	Busan	7,900,000
4	Kaohsiung	7,540,000
5	Shanghai	6,334,000
6	Rotterdam	6,129,000
7	Los Angeles	5,184,000
8	Shenzen	5,040,000
9	Hamburg	4,700,000
10	Long Beach	4,463,000

Source: ECT website 2002
* Twenty foot equivalent units

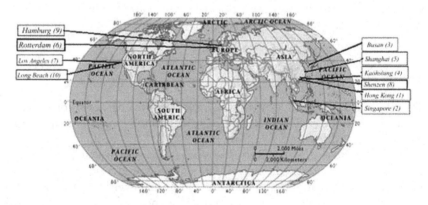

Figure 1. Map illustrating location of top ten container ports.

first of two in the period 1905–1907, enjoyed success, but ultimately the grain unloaders, like the first electric cranes a decade earlier, were introduced and accompanied by a loss of jobs and a reduction in ship turnaround times.

Following these upheavals, there was no further major industrial unrest in the Port of Rotterdam for over fifty years. At this time, the introduction of another revolutionary set of changes aimed at reducing vessels' turnaround time, and relating to containerization, threatened the work and lives of port workers once again.[18] Containerization was pioneered, in

18. *Ibid.*

its current form, by the trucker Malcolm McLean in the USA.[19] Traditional break-bulk ports in the 1960s took some time in unloading and loading, and ships could be "idle" in port for periods of up to two weeks.[20] Shipowners' dissatisfactions with such slow cargo-handling operations were exacerbated by the rising stevedore and port costs in the 1950s and 1960s[21] which were said to have resulted from wage inflation and rising port dues.[22] McLean was inspired by transportation methods adopted by the US military, which allowed cargoes to be moved fluently from land to sea transport without the need for loading and unloading, much reducing the time a vessel was required to spend in port. He set up a company that he called *Sea-Land* and within a short space of time large *Sea-Land* vessels were crossing the Atlantic at impressive speeds.[23] However, despite the rapid transition to containerization that took place on a world scale, the process had, and continues to have, a number of critics,[24] some of whom have questioned why shippers have not made greater use of alternative cargo unitization, for example palletization.[25]

Dock workers and their trade unions had problems with containerization from its inception and there were a number of strikes and container boycotts by workers across the world (e.g. La Guaira in Venezuela, Tilbury and Liverpool in the UK, and Rotterdam in the Netherlands) in the 1960s and 1970s. The basis for opposition was often not the fact of containerization (which many considered part of the "inevitable" trend of progress), but was around wages, and the renegotiation of what constituted *dock-work* and what was defined as *the docks*. Here, technical innovation had been accompanied by changes in the social organization of work, as haulage contractors were attempting to "stuff and strip" containers beyond the traditional confines of the port.[26] In this sense, such labour resistance cannot be regarded simplistically as a Luddite response to mechanization as Wilson explains:

> [...] these were not instances of mere Luddite intransigence; they were linked to a wider policy of job protection in a period of rapid change, and in London, the

19. However, containerization of various forms had previously been practised on a small scale in a number of world regions. See De Jong, *Is There Any Future in Conventional Cargo Handling?*.
20. Jeffrey Martin and Brian J. Thomas, "The Container Terminal Community", *Maritime Policy Management*, 28 (2001), pp. 279–292.
21. Robert Gardiner and Alistair Couper (eds), *The Shipping Revolution: the Modern Merchant Ship* (London, 1992).
22. Gubbins, *The Shipping Industry*.
23. The first container-only transatlantic voyage was undertaken by the Sea-Land vessel, *Fairland*, from the USA to Rotterdam.
24. See Rick Hogben, *A Sharp Look-Out: One Hundred Years of Maritime History as Reported by "Fairplay"* (London, 1983).
25. Gubbins, *The Shipping Industry*.
26. David F. Wilson, *Dockers: The Impact of Industrial Change* (London, 1972).

aims of the Tilbury ban were always clearly stated: it was to remain until a package deal was negotiated, providing security for all dockers in the port [...].[27]

Trade unions did not, therefore, oppose mechanization and automation *per se*, and were sensitive to international competition.[28] They did, however, challenge the detail of containerization and sought, where possible, to maintain workforce levels. These were subject to remarkable global variation, being as low as three workers per gang in Rotterdam and seventeen per gang in New York.

Today, in Rotterdam stevedores may utilize crane gangs of between five and two workers and may average between twenty-five to thirty crane moves per hour.[29] This is a significant increase in numbers of moves per hour on the early days of container terminals when productivity rates were averaging eighteen moves per hour. An experienced terminal manager described how this major increase in cargo-handling capacity directly results from computerization:

> In those days [thirty years ago] you were talking about a productivity of eighteen, and that was the accepted norm. Then you also see changes over the years but that is taking a long time – you don't take quantum leaps, it's a very slow process [...]. Basically, it worked exactly the same but you didn't have the computer systems of today [...], and that's unthinkable nowadays, but as I said the norm in those days were about seventeen or eighteen [moves per hour] and today is about thirty or thirty-five. So its almost double in thirty years.[30]

These changes have combined with technical changes aboard ships to alter radically the ways in which life and work on board is organized and experienced. Here, as ashore, innovation in technology has been accompanied by other patterns of change associated with the social composition of the workforce and its organization.

THE IMPACT OF INNOVATION IN THE TETRA TERMINAL

The Tetra terminal is located in a vast isolated area of the port of Rotterdam dedicated to container loading and unloading. Container terminals owned by other operators flank it left and right, and to find it

27. *Ibid.*, pp. 142–143.
28. The strike in the Port of Rotterdam in 1979 led to the diversion of cargoes and shipping lines to Antwerp and some custom never returned. See De Jong, *Is There Any Future in Conventional Cargo Handling?*.
29. Interestingly, fully automated straddle-carrier operations utilizing automated guided vehicles (AGVs) rather than human straddle-carrier drivers may be unable to increase their numbers of moves per hour to a level that would equate with slightly less automated operations using straddle-carrier drivers.
30. Tetra employee: interview with Sampson.

you have to look hard, driving down avenues formed by stacks of containers up to nine boxes high. The terminal building is itself dwarfed by the containers surrounding it. It is a three-storey construction that rather resembles a large "portacabin". A number on the side of the building is all that identifies it and sets it apart from its "siblings" dotted along the waterfront.

The Tetra terminal is owned and managed by a company whose "parent" also owns a similarly named shipping line. This shipping line and its conference[31] associates are the main clients for the terminal. As a result, within the one building reside the Tetra terminal staff (a number of whom are ex-seafarers) engaged in managing, operating, and supporting the container terminal, and a small number of Tetra shipping-line staff responsible for providing "agency" services to vessels alongside. Such services include the organization of, bunkering,[32] the provision of stores, crew changes, laundry etc. The area beyond the terminal building is known as the "yard", and it is here that reach-stackers and straddle-carriers[33] operate, moving containers from and to the large cranes servicing the ships, and to land-based vehicles of various types. Yard planning and organization are critical to the speed of the operation, and efforts are made to ensure that boxes are stacked as close as possible to the vessel or vehicle they are to be transported to next. Thus, the yard is divided into zones along the waterside for each incoming vessel, and zones along the roadside for other forms of transportation. At Tetra, two straddle-carriers work with one waterside crane which is operated by two workers alternating as *crane driver* and *radio man on deck*. A fifth worker completes the "gang" and is located with a radio on the quayside. Their functions were explained thus:

> One crane these days in our terminal consists of five people, so that's not a lot. So, its two crane drivers because one crane driver can only go for four hours and they have to change, and when the crane driver doesn't drive the crane he stays as *radio man deck*; and there are two straddle-carrier drivers and a *radio man wall* who does the administration and the coordination between carriers and crane, so its basically five men that can load and unload a ship [...]. The terminals next door are fully automated [...], that means only two people – the crane drivers – the rest goes automatic.[34]

31. It is not unusual for container shipping lines to establish agreements with competitors on service sharing etc., known as conferences.
32. Bunkering is the term used to refer to taking on fuel stores.
33. Reach-stackers can stack and unstuck boxes up to nine high. Straddle-carriers are driven over boxes and are used to lift them and transport them on to lorries or to or from the waterside. They are highly mobile and move rapidly around the yard.
34. Tetra employee: interview with Sampson.

Whilst not automated to the extent of its futuristic neighbour, whose yard is devoid of human life and is operated by driverless automated guided vehicles reminiscent of the aliens in the film *War of the Worlds*, the Tetra operation is high tech and highly computerized. The drive to reduce manual operations in favour of automation continues, and with it is an associated drive to reduce the overall number of employees. This situation appeared to be regarded pragmatically by interviewees. One manager explained:

> The future is definitely automation and less people. That is 100 per cent definite [...]. Technology is needed these days and improvements with that will continue, because the margins in this industry are extremely small and we have to make money to survive, so we don't want to stop our technical developments. I guess that's the future [...]. Training of course – you have to continuously adjust your organization, so maybe its putting a strain on people more so than before – but that's life. That's the world nowadays.[35]

Another whose job involved yard planning and supervision was actively involved in seeking ways to eliminate manual planning in favour of automation. He impassively explained: "If the settings are right you don't have manual planners. If a box arrives it should automatically go to an area somewhere, to a specific floorspace without human intervention. We are still facing two manual planners [...] because of the problems we have."[36] To facilitate the level of automation introduced at Tetra, considerable investment in ICT has taken place. The terminal has two main-frame computers running in parallel with each other to protect against down time and data corruption. Staff in the control tower[37] are equipped with PCs running off the shelf software packages designed for yard planning. Straddle-carrier and crane drivers communicate using two-way radios as do the radio men (deck and wall). The straddle-carrier drivers receive their instructions from small hand-held computers in their vehicles, and crane drivers are similarly equipped. Workers operating in the "yard" work as isolated individuals communicating with each other by radio or electronic means, and they are required to work under pressure and at speed. From the vantage point of the control tower, the straddle-carriers and cranes resemble a colony of ants, highly organized, highly mobile, and with a strong sense of purpose. It is quite obviously not a production line, yet it has this feel.

The scene is markedly different at a terminal dedicated to non-containerized goods. Here port workers swarm over a vessel in teams.

---

35. *Ibid.*
36. *Ibid.*
37. The control tower overlooks the yard and resembles a small air traffic control tower both internally and externally.

The workers communicate verbally and using sign language; they interact with each other and they interact with seafarers, and the scene resembles organized chaos more than organized production. In Brazil, in the course of ethnographic work aboard a bulk carrier, a stevedore foreman was encountered fishing from the side of the vessel, engaging in casual conversation with passing stevedores and seafarers, whilst observing his team loading forest products into the holds. Such a scene is not only unimaginable but quite simply impossible at a terminal such as Tetra, where encounters with and between workers are more likely to occur inside the terminal building than on the quayside. The workforce at Tetra is thus rendered invisible to the majority of seafarers, just as seafarers are rendered invisible to Tetra employees. The distance between them is relatively short and yet the yard itself acts as a chasm dividing them. The following interview extract is illustrative:

> *Interviewer*: What about the interaction between the sea staff and the terminal staff? Is there any?
> *Tetra employee*: Too little.
> *Interviewer*: You think it should be more?
> *Tetra employee*: I would like to see more, but the thing is that we are sitting here, and to go down to the ship you have to go around [gestures long route circumventing yard]. So it is a distance of [several] kilometres. People don't do it.

Thus, despite encouragement by the company, and even though some terminal staff are ex-seafarers themselves and know some of the senior officers aboard visiting vessels, contact between the two groups of employees is minimal. In the course of collecting ethnographic data aboard noncontainer vessels on relatively stable routes Sampson observed a number of occasions where sea staff (including ratings) were invited ashore by shore-based staff. These groups had come to know each other over a period of time, as a result of their contact in the course of their work. This did not happen at the Tetra terminal, where one employee illustrated the way in which the insulation of the container terminal from the ship discourages such social relations:

> Although it is encouraged from here that we have to take the captain out and the company pays, just so the master or the chief engineer has another face and he can talk [...], you don't do it [...] – you can always make time, but I don't go on board and say to a stranger come, we have a bite somewhere. I don't do that.[38]

Thus, the organization of work in container terminals militates against social contact between shore and sea-staff. The space around the ship, *the yard*, has become controlled, and unauthorized access is prohibited for

38. Tetra employee: interview with Sampson.

health and safety reasons, and to minimize disruption to operations. Equally, the ship has become a remote and unfamiliar space to shore-side workers, few of whom will touch a deck in the course of their work.

INNOVATION ABOARD AND THE AVAILABILITY OF WORK

Whilst Schumpeter's work emphasized entrepreneurship amongst individuals, others, in developing his ideas, have identified innovation and entrepreneurship at the level of the firm,[39,40] and have argued that innovation is essential for the survival of modern-day shipping companies.[41] In this, achieving reductions in employee numbers and increasing competitiveness are seen as primary drivers of innovation replacing the historical pressures of environmental and safety standards and regulation. Some have argued that innovation in shipping has indeed facilitated drastic reductions in crewing levels: "In more recent years, technological change has again become an important factor in shipping with the introduction of new information, computer control, and communications technology which facilitates drastic crew reductions with consequent savings in ship accommodations and other costs."[42] However, these changes in crewing practices are complex, and are consequently difficult to trace and precisely pinpoint.

The complexity of the relationship between innovation and crew size results from the changing nature and heterogeneity of the shipping industry, and the casualized nature of the seafarer labour market. Whereas the introduction of new labour saving technology or automated machinery at a fixed site ashore often results in sudden and dramatic downsizing,[43] aboard, it often takes place as a gradual process of attrition. Seafarers on short-term contracts are not generally "sent home" mid-contract but are simply not replaced after they return home for their vacation. Similarly, reductions in crew sizes are rarely obviously dramatic, as they have tended to either coincide with the introduction of new types of vessel (steamships or equally container vessels), or with a general trend of increasing vessel size and increasing freight movement. Thus crewing levels per gross ton

39. Jeffrey G. Covin, "Entrepreneurial vs. Conservative Firms: A Comparison of Strategies and Performance", *Journal of Management Studies*, 28 (1991), pp. 439–462.
40. Jan Inge Jenssen and Trond Randøy, "Factors that Promote Innovation in Shipping", *Maritime Policy & Management*, 29 (2002), pp. 119–133.
41. Ernst G. Frankel, "The Economics of Technological Change in Shipping", *Maritime Policy & Management*, 18 (1991), pp. 43–53.
42. *Ibid.*, p. 44.
43. Van Lente, "Machines and the Order of the Harbour".

may have declined over time,[44] but aboard a ship seafarers may be sailing with crews of similar size to those they are generally accustomed to. Equally, seafaring jobs may be periodically redefined by crew managers and ship owners as "cleaning jobs" or specialist tasks for "riding crew",[45] whilst, in reality, the tasks are the same as those that have traditionally been performed by workers classified as, for example, "wipers" or "fitters". As a result, seafarers themselves do not seem to have perceived "drastic" reductions in crewing levels as a quote from a senior officer of a container ship illustrates:

> Changes in technology mean [that] somebody thinks we can use less crew members, but that does not correspond to reality. We're still the same [number of] people on board but now they call it maintenance crew [...] and other repairmen and all that, but actually there's still the same number of people on board. The minimum safe manning was years ago, twenty-one [years ago] for example, [...] twenty-eight [people]. Are we twenty-eight people currently? I think so. OK, so we have a special job being performed but we are generally between twenty-one [...] and twenty-five people on board.[46]

This situation of gradual change on board ship contrasts starkly with the dramatic cutting of dock work in Rotterdam when mechanized grain unloaders were introduced. This difference (in experience and perception) was also apparent when containerization began to replace break-bulk cargo transportation. Thus, the Rotterdam dockworkers of the early twentieth century perceived technology as almost representing a "death-blow" for the harbour, as Van Lente in describing one of the strikers' protest songs explains: "The song said that it would make hundreds of workers lose their jobs. It called the machine the image of the employers who had introduced it: hard and cold, it would suck the lifeblood out of the workers even as it sucked the grain out of the ships."[47] By contrast seafarers, when they have staged industrial action, have tended to focus on wages rather than on employment issues connected to innovation, automation, or mechanization. Nevertheless, at sea, as ashore, a number of specific jobs can be seen to have been lost as a result of technological innovation within the maritime industry, and some estimates indicate that crew sizes have dropped by as many as thirty seafarers per ship in the

44. According to some sources, the ratio of seafarers to gross ton has dropped from three persons per 1,000gt in 1960 to one person per 1,000gt in 1980. See Hercules E. Haralambides, "An Economic Analysis of the Seagoing Labour Market", presented to the Fifth World Conference of Transport in Research, July 1989, and quoted in John Spruyt (ed.), *Ship Management* (London, 1994).
45. Riding crew are usually assigned to a ship in order to perform a particular maintenance or repair task. When the task is completed they are reassigned to a different ship.
46. Officer aboard container vessel: interview with Sampson.
47. Van Lente, "Machines and the Order of the Harbour", p. 80.

period 1950–1980.[48] Most twentieth-century changes can be linked to automation and the change from steam to diesel (e.g. the loss of donkeymen,[49] some engineers, firemen[50]). However, one recent change has been a direct result of innovation in communications technology and the mandatory introduction of GMDSS. This relates to the job of the radio officer, which has disappeared altogether from the vast majority of vessels.

The unwelcome loss of radio officers has much been regretted by many seafarers, and has had particular consequences for the workload of ship's captains. As one explained:

> Well it's [the captain's job] changed a lot because I'm now the radio officer. So we no longer have a radio officer as of three or four years ago [...]. We have an internet-based communication system, and that's new in the last three to four years – and that is a mixed thing for us. It's certainly – the communication is good, and is fast and it's reliable, but it's also provided them [shore-side operations] with the means to pour information at us and vast volumes of information, and sometimes [...] we wish we didn't have so much communication.[51]

Despite the associated changes to their work and the loss of radio officers aboard, many officers have responded to developments in ICT in positive if not entirely uncritical ways. The reasons for such response are multiple. Developments in information and communication technology have had a global impact which, whilst modulated by variations within and between societies and individuals, have had implications for an enormous segment of the world population. Developments in ICT have come to extend beyond age, employment, and gender distinctions in impacting on the lives of very many members of contemporary societies particularly, but not exclusively, in those societies characterized by affluence. Workers, including many seafarers, are integrated into such ICT-literate and rich societies, and are thus in a position to benefit from innovation as consumers, social actors, and employees. Similarly, however, they are not blind to the extent to which innovation can result in unwelcome change to labour processes and labour markets, particularly in terms of redundancy and deskilling (although the notion of deskilling in the merchant marine is challenged by some).[52] In this context, and given the rapid change brought about by technological innovation to the post-

---

48. CETS, *Crew Size and Maritime Safety* (Washington DC, 1990).

49. A donkeyman was an engine-room petty officer responsible for the maintenance and repair of the donkey boiler and engine which was used in providing power for a number of deckside mechanical pieces of equipment, e.g. winches.

50. Firemen were responsible for feeding the boilers with coal and maintaining the generation of optimum levels of steam.

51. Captain of container vessel: interview with Sampson.

52. Eric W. Sagar, *Ships and Memories: Merchant Seafarers in Canada's Age of Steam* (Vancouver, 1993).

industrial realm of work, the response of workers to date could be characterized as constrained. Certainly, within the shipping industry, mariners have taken a highly rational approach to mechanization, automation, and latterly the ICT revolution. They have not been blind to the disadvantages associated with such technologies, but neither have they generally been reactionary, given the introduction of innovative instruments, machines, or processes. Their attitudes can be gauged not only via interviews but additionally via comments made in the "trade" press. In response to the introduction of GMDSS, for example, with the consequent loss of radio officers, there has been much criticism from merchant officers. One master mariner, in a recent interview for a trade publication, expressed the views of many when he said:

> I have yet to be convinced that GMDSS has improved safety of life at sea. I believe that a dedicated radio officer, using the latest technology, would be safer [...]. The high number of false alerts speaks for itself – the equipment is not user-friendly [...]. GMDSS equipment should be simple to operate, user-friendly and intuitive. Equipment manufacturers should remember that deck officer GMDSS operators are *not* communications specialists.[53]

His thoughts were echoed by a captain interviewed in Rotterdam, who described how too many alarms on the bridge, including GMDSS false alarms, result in some of them being "screened out" by officers on watch, with the implication that important alarms could be ignored, resulting in the endangering of the lives of the ships' crew or others in distress at sea. She explained:

> All the alarms, a lot of alarms on the bridge [...] are just dressing. [They do] not need to be there [...]. They could make a blinking alarm [instead] [...] and you can't stop it [GMDSS] either. It has to go beep-beep for about five seconds; you can't stop it. That's not necessary either [...]. You just [end up in a situation where you] acknowledge all the alarms and you don't even know what they're for. Sometimes an important one goes by – [they're] pretty dangerous all these alarms [...]. It's like all these distresses that are false alarms. 99 per cent of them are false alarms.[54]

Nevertheless, despite their awareness of the impact of the loss of the radio officer on the workload of the captain, most serving seafarers accept this with pragmatism. Their criticisms thus tend to centre on issues of safety and operational concerns, rather than on changes to their personal job descriptions or workloads.

---

53. John Gorman-Charlton, quoted in *Ocean Voice*, 21 (2001).
54. Captain of container vessel: interview with Sampson.

INNOVATION ABOARD AND CHANGES IN THE NATURE OF WORK

In combining the findings from the pilot study of the Tetra container terminal in Rotterdam and the on-board ethnographic research, it becomes apparent that computerization and the communications revolution have combined in ways that not only make fast vessel turnaround a possibility but have also fuelled innovation and organizational change aboard. In general, ICT has impacted on the work of officers and has had little effect on the daily work of ratings who are mainly engaged in routine maintenance, cleaning, painting, and "chipping".[55]

In common with most modern vessels, Tetra ships do not carry radio officers but have replaced VHF emergency communication systems with Global Maritime Distress and Safety Systems (GMDSS) and have transferred much of the work of radio officers to captains, also known as *Masters*. Masters are thus far more concerned with paperwork and the preparation of records and documents for port officials, customs and immigration officers, charterers, inspectors, and company shore-side workers than they were hitherto. They have had to acquire rapidly a good understanding of computers and computer software, and have seen their role change to be less that of "master mariner" and more that of "vessel manager". Tetra ships carry a considerable number of computers loaded with a range of sophisticated software which monitors and/or controls ballasting, bunkering, freight temperatures, engine-related pressures and temperatures, as well as more prosaic functions such as the ordering of stores and equipment. All officers interact with such systems to some extent, and consequently all have seen a shift from being engaged in more practical manual tasks to carrying out more sedentary monitoring and administrative tasks. For example, the chief engineer of a Tetra "mother vessel" is able to monitor engine pressures and temperatures as well as other relevant information from his/her day room (office), and can thus retain a vigilant yet unobtrusive watch on the work of other engineers throughout the day or (in unusual circumstances) night. Remaining in the office, the chief is able to deal with the large volume of paperwork and record-keeping required by the shore-side office, and in terms of the routines of daily life has seen a shift in role from that of expert and often "hands-on" engineer to somewhat remote administrator. The chief officer's role has also been transformed. Previously, the chief officer had, as a central feature of his/her work, responsibility for cargo stowage and stress and stability calculations. Aboard the modern Tetra ship, however, the chief officer is merely required to check stowage plans and stability and stress calculations prepared ashore after they are presented,

---

55. Chipping rusting paint prior to repriming/painting is a common task for ratings.

on the vessel's arrival, on a floppy disk. An additional and surprising associated change in the role of chief officers aboard larger Tetra ships is the requirement for the chief officer to oversee bunkering, a job normally undertaken by a member of the engineering team and not traditionally regarded as associated with the work of chief officers at all.

Such changes in the organization of work have been accompanied by changes in the way in which tasks are carried out. These are perhaps most obvious on the bridge of modern container vessels where the Tetra ships are typical in carrying ECDIS and the most modern integrated navigation systems. These free the navigators from reliance on paper charts although, for the time being, these are still carried and manually corrected on board. Skills once the stock in trade of seafarers, such as using a sextant to take sights, and communicating to other vessels regardless of the nationality of their seafarers using Morse lamps, have been, or are being, lost whilst new skills relating to the use of information and communication technology are rapidly being acquired. Such changes have fuelled demand in some sectors of the industry for dual-purpose officers trained not for either the engine or the deck-side but for both. Such officers have been employed and trained for some decades, but innovation and change in the latter part of the twentieth century has led to a renewed interest in the production of dual-purpose officers and their introduction by an increasing number of companies, including the Tetra shipping line.

Seafarers may have more opportunities than many to participate in the introduction of innovative technologies aboard. Ships are relatively unique environments and it is often only in the real world of the ship that many maritime innovations can be truly tested (although simulators are increasingly used to test new navigational aids and equipment). The early limitations of radar and its implication in a number of maritime accidents is illustrative.

Many shipping companies are run by ex-seafarers who understand the importance of user feedback from the ships, and some companies have gone so far as to introduce websites where seafarers can comment on any aspect of their job or life aboard. That seafarers are willing and able to comment was apparent in our research. Their response to innovation and change was far from dismissively negative but was generally thoughtful and constructive. Some, who preferred more practical rather than computer-based activities, welcomed developments in radar, for example. Others saw the benefits of innovation whilst being concerned about what might be its "side effects", for example information overload. Several queried the wisdom of losing traditional skills of navigation, but equally recognized the extent to which mistrusted new equipment can soon be regarded as the norm and accepted and relied upon, whilst others differentiated between established reliable equipment and other hard and software that could not be trusted. The following remarks are illustrative:

There's more, yeah, more communication [...] [it's] not so good [...] no news is good news! There's too much and I'm an idiot with paperwork. More papers make me more an idiot. That's a personal thing. Some people are very good with papers. I'm lousy [...]. If I knew there was so much paperwork in this job I would never have chosen it. Never in my life [...]. When I first started I was in Coasters sailing round the Faroe islands, Malta, nobody looked at papers [...]. Never anybody! [...] How I see it with the paperwork, it's a jungle [...] which for me is not transparent. Too many systems, I can't oversee it [...]. Generally I like to sail. [The] best bits [of my job] are where you get in contact with the elements [...]. Seamanship. This is not seamanship [rustles papers] this is horseshit![56]

We can send a telex in the morning questioning about a reefer [refrigerated container] and then in the afternoon we have the answer. So that has been better because in the old days the radio officer, he couldn't get in touch of something ashore [...] now you can take this phone [indicates satellite telephone] and call directly to the person [...]. All the monitoring system, in the engine department you can monitor the main engine. This [pointing to a computer screen with gauges and diagrams] is the main engine, all the temperatures [are shown] here and the pressures all the time [...]. So it has been a little bit easier. On the other hand [...] you can have a lot of information now but not using them for anything.[57]

If it [a computer or other piece of ICT] doesn't work all of a sudden you can, might, make a mistake 'cos you've gotten used to it [...]. We don't trust it [indicating a refrigerated container monitoring computer on board] because we've always experienced it makes mistakes, so even though it works nobody trusts it completely. So we always check [physically using traditional measuring devices].[58]

The generally pragmatic response by seafarers to innovation in ICT is likely to be due partly to the fact that many historical technological changes have reduced the dangers that seafarers are exposed to, and have dramatically improved working and living conditions aboard. The transition from sail to steam removed a number of hazardous tasks (for example, those involving climbing highly unstable rigging to release or secure sails), and the move from steam to diesel engines must have surely been welcomed by the firemen who had to fuel the boilers on steam powered vessels. Sagar illustrates this point vividly in his account of such work explaining:

Firemen, who are sometimes called stokers, had one of the hardest jobs ever to be endured by human beings. Their job was to keep the boilers fired by keeping the coal fires burning as cleanly as possible. Working near the boilers, they came close to burning alive, especially in the tropics, where fresh air would not get

56. Container vessel officer: interview with Sampson.
57. *Ibid.*
58. *Ibid.*

down the ventilators, and temperatures could reach 130 or 140 degrees Fahrenheit. Trimmers worked in the dark, dusty coal bunkers, shovelling coal and moving it about in wheel barrows [...]. In the British merchant marine in 1893, forty-one firemen or trimmers committed suicide. In 1894 forty-nine firemen or trimmers committed suicide. Driven mad by the heat they would throw themselves into the sea.[59]

The introduction of information technology aboard and its subsequent improvement has similarly resulted in safety gains. It has also led to a decline in the number of repetitive and monotonous tasks officers routinely carry out. For example, aboard early container ships the manual entry of container numbers into a software programme was required. This is now fully computerized, pleasing many chief officers, as one container vessel captain explained:

> I've never been where the computers have broken down, because if the computers break down I think we would just have to go ashore and do our calculations. We couldn't possibly take every container and calculate the old fashioned way. But about three or four years ago we just had to put every container on the computer. That would take a long time for the chief officer and now he just gets a disk to check. That's much better.[60]

The advantages of new technology are therefore, generally appreciated by seafarers. However, many also highlight the extent to which new technologies have eroded some pleasurable aspects of their work. On container vessels, for example, load and stress calculations are done ashore and the ship is merely presented with a "soft" copy of a cargo plan on disk to check. Similarly, ship-board cranes are no longer utilized nor carried, removing responsibility for their maintenance from vessel crews. For many chief officers cargo handling, and stress calculations alongside crane "gear" maintenance are amongst the more interesting aspects of work at sea, and some go so far as to avoid working on container ships because the nature of the work has changed in this way. One captain of a Tetra container vessel, for example, tried to avoid being moved to container ships for a number of years for this very reason. Despite pressure from her company, she preferred to remain aboard her company's less prestigious vessels trading in and around Africa. She explained:

> I've been on the African boats – they're not as large as these – where we get to arrange a little bit where the cargo goes and we have a say in it when it's loaded, and that's more interesting than these boats [...]. Yes, I've been on those boats for about eight years and enjoyed very much. Here the Mate doesn't have very much to do with where they load and when, and on the Africa boats they have their own crane. So that's more like it's old-fashioned and I learned very much from

---

59. Sagar, *Ships and Memories*, p. 44.
60. Captain of container vessel: interview with Sampson.

that [...]. They [the company] always want to move us around and they tell me I'd better go and try these [container ships] and I think, "Oh No, I want to stay". That was because it was more interesting in port and we felt more useful.[61]

INNOVATION ABOARD AND THE EXPERIENCE OF TIME AND SPACE

Whilst changes to crewing levels brought about by innovation are difficult to pinpoint and may be largely un-noticed by seafarers, changes to the nature of work on board, the speed at which it is carried out, and its reorganization are far clearer, as is the impact of containerization on the turnaround time of ocean-going as well as coastal vessels. Evidence collected from the Port of Rotterdam suggests that increases in numbers of crane moves per hour achieved by modern container terminals have translated into faster vessel turnaround, and that this process is ongoing and relatively rapid. Thus over as short a period as five years it is possible to demonstrate a significant, though not dramatic, increase in the speed with which ships are able to get in and out of ports (see Table 2).

Kahveci's research in Sandhaven[62] also demonstrates the speed at which current vessels can load and discharge, arrive and depart, from modern port terminals. His data suggest that an average port stay today accounts for approximately 13 per cent of a vessel's working time, as opposed to 50 per cent thirty years ago.[63] This inevitably impacts not only on vessel operators and their profit margins but also on the work and welfare of dockers[64] and seafarers.

For seafarers, innovations that allow ships to turnaround in port faster impact on access to shore leave, and land-based facilities and amenities. This can prevent poorly paid ratings from accessing cheap telecommunications; it prevents seafarers from purchasing necessary items, which may have particular implications for women seafarers,[65] and it has more general implications for social isolation and associated mental health issues.[66] Our ethnographic work aboard ships of different types has revealed the extent

---

61. *Ibid.*
62. This is a fictitious name for an existing port facility.
63. Erol Kahveci, "Fast Turnaround Ships Impact on Seafarers' Lives", *Seaways*, (March 2000), pp. 8–12.
64. In Rotterdam, evidence is emerging of health problems such as back trouble amongst straddle-carrier drivers. This is believed to result from the "human-unfriendly" design of the carriers.
65. Phil Belcher *et al.*, *Women Seafarers: Global Employment Policies and Practices* (Cardiff, 2002).
66. Helen Sampson and Michelle Thomas, "Health and Safety at Sea: Social Factors, A Neglected Dimension", *Proceedings of International Symposium on Human Factors on Board 2001* (Bremen, forthcoming).

Table 2. *Vessel turnaround times in the Tetra Terminal: 1997 and 2002**

Year	Mean time (hours)	Median time (hours)	No. of vessels
1997	23.19	22.00	37
2002	20.50	19.00	26

Source: Port of Rotterdam Authority
* To facilitate comparison the port of Rotterdam supplied data for all vessels arriving and departing in the first and last weeks of March 1997 and 2002. The figures here are based on extrapolated data for Tetra vessels in these periods.

to which seafarers look forward to shore leave and the importance it holds for life on board. When seafarers are able to go ashore in groups, shore-leave acts to strengthen social solidarity aboard. Additionally, it breaks up the monotony of everyday life aboard and gives seafarers something to talk and laugh about once they are back at sea.

On container vessels, some companies have compensated for lack of shore leave by shortening lengths of contracts for sea staff. This leaves seafarers feeling more pragmatic about denied opportunities for shore leave than might otherwise be the case, as the following comments made by senior officers (who generally have the shortest contracts) aboard different vessels in Rotterdam show:

> We have one place in Long Beach where we're almost three days because they totally empty the ship and load [it again] [...] so that's very nice and people enjoy it [...] everybody gets the chance to go ashore [...]. When we are out for only three months at a time [the length of the transglobe voyage cycle and the senior officers' contracts] its not so important, but everybody looks forward to Long Beach and everybody also looks forward to Hong Kong because we're there for twenty-four hours [...]. They look forward to it but I don't know what it would be like if we didn't [have those shore-leave opportunities in the 13-week tour]. I guess I haven't thought about the importance of that.[67]

> I was always on liner services then [about twenty-five years ago when he was first at sea] [...] as opposed to tramp services [which usually spend longer in ports for a variety of reasons]. And the liner services had schedules and, at least in my experience, they pretty well maintained them. But the port time was certainly greater. Anywhere from one to three or four days [...]. I would say more typically the port times were three to five times longer and a lot less cargo and the ships were smaller and we might spend all day on eight or nine hundred tons of cargo, where in one hour [nowadays] one crane can load that [...]. The quality of life here [...] has evolved over time and we've adapted to it. [...] going ashore is something, it would be nice to do but you don't necessarily expect that it will happen [...]. I'm not saying that's a good thing but it's what's evolved [...] there's

67. Captain of container vessel: interview with Sampson

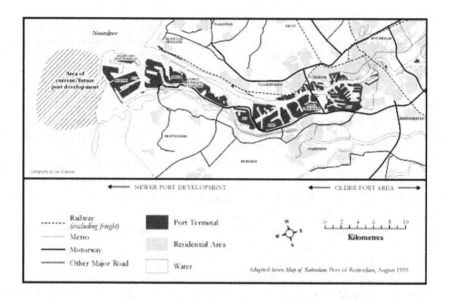

Figure 2. Map of Rotterdam Port showing "seaward drift" of modern development and public transport routes.
Adapted from Map of Rotterdam, *Port of Rotterdam, August 1999, cartography by Jan Edwards*

times when you think it's not [...] that it isn't very good from our side [...]. [But] we're well paid, we have generous vacation schedules so I think we're willing to put up with it.[68]

Whilst the lack of time available for shore leave is probably the major reason for seafarers remaining on board for most of their contract period, the location of terminals also frequently militates against shore leave. Modern terminals and their space-hungry requirements for water frontage and excellent transport infrastructure have driven change in the spatial layout of modern port cities. These have altered as newer port facilities have been constructed in increasingly geographically remote districts, often at a great distance from population centres. The port of Rotterdam provides a good example of this tendency. Its oldest port terminal buildings and berths, some of which have fallen into disuse, are located very close to the city centre, whilst its most modern container terminals have been constructed up to 60km away at the mouth of the river (See Figure 2).

Travelling from the new terminals to the centre of Rotterdam takes approximately one hour by car and costs around € 200 for a return trip.

68. *Ibid.*

The situation is compounded by a total absence of public transport with the result that seafarers report never going ashore there. As one explained:

> I would never consider going to shore in Rotterdam which I did before, because it is too far away [...]. Many years ago the terminal was in Rotterdam so maybe two hours sailing upstream [from the current terminal] [...]. At that time it would be ten to fifteen minutes [to get from the port to the city centre], [...] ten minutes by taxi, even a tram you could take [...] now I don't know probably three quarters of an hour [...]. It's too far away. It's too expensive![69]

These circumstances impact upon seafarers in different ways. Better-paid officers can probably afford to take taxis to the city centre, but are generally unable to leave the vessel as a result of their responsibilities. Whilst ratings may be granted shore leave but find such extravagance prohibitive. Thus, in varying ways, distance and time combine to prevent seafarers accessing the wider world when their ships berth at such modern terminals.

Fast vessel turnaround, facilitated by containerization and innovation in information and communication technology, would therefore seem to have a number of disadvantages for serving seafarers. For those working aboard vessels with short turnaround times, the *spatial sphere* accessible to them has shrunk as a result of their isolation from towns and cities and the speed with which they are in and out of port. Concurrently, changes in working practices and in the use of space in modern cargo terminals have combined to limit seafarers' contact with other related workers, widening the gulf between them and land-based society. Thus, the vessel has become more like a prison then ever.[70] The experience of *transnational* life has traditionally been a central feature of the lives of seafarers, as they have had the opportunity to interact with others of different nationality and culture in ports around the world. Such transnationality is disappearing, however, just at a time when it is becoming a major part of the lives of many others engaged in different occupations. Paradoxically, for a workforce engaged in an occupation driving the process of time-space compression, the lives of today's seafarers are becoming more inwardly focused, as they are increasingly trapped in the *hyperspace* characteristic of the internal territory of their vessels.[71]

Companies have attempted to ameliorate such disadvantages for some seafarers, particularly European/US officers, and have introduced shorter

---

69. *Ibid.*
70. Tony Lane, "Being on a Ship is Being in Jail", *Naftika Chronika*, November (1998), pp. 88–89.
71. Helen Sampson, "Transnational Drifters or Hyperspace Dwellers: An Exploration of the Lives of Filipino Seafarers Aboard and Ashore", *Ethnic and Racial Studies*, 26 (2003), pp. 253–277.

voyage contracts and longer leave-periods. For ratings, however, and seafarers generally drawn from world regions other than Europe, North America, Japan, and Australia, such provisions have not been adopted. These seafarers are put under some significant strain and risk as a result of the new processes introduced in shipping freight at fast speed around the world.[72] They describe long periods of boredom and monotony and a requirement for mental "toughness",

> I describe [a] seafarer's life as a boring one. I'd say boring [...] there is no excitement also [...] you have to, in seafaring you have to be tough, you [need] strength to be [...] [there is] pressure so you have to be tough, [...] [which] means you [...] are strength [strong] enough to stand by yourself. [It is] boring because you are very isolated. [You don't know] what happen [...] what is happening in your country [...], what is happening in your family? [73]

"Oh, a seafarer's life, a seafarer's life sometimes is boring and then boring and then [...] I cannot think, boring ahhh...".[74] And they suggest that it is very hard for people ashore to imagine the lives of people at sea. One seafarer approaching the end of a twelve-month contract described how:

> If you try to explain to them [ashore] that this is the situation they wouldn't believe you. They say that this man is lying [...]. I don't like to be explaining to people about my job – yeah – because if I started explaining to you, you wouldn't believe [...]. My job is very tedious, very hard working. [I] spend 365 days on board everyday working, everyday working, everyday working, until the end of the trip [...]. I am expecting now to go home any trip maybe next loading/discharging. [...]. My heart is now all at home. Now want to go I want to leave here [...] the sea so it's only time, it's only time now [...].[75]

Others described how they wouldn't recommend a seafarer's life to their friends or children: "If I talk to some stranger I don't influence him to come, to become a seafarer unfortunately its difficult you know. Every time you come alone, come alone, even my little boy when he grow up I don't like him to become a seafarer somehow."[76]

> I don't know if he [my son] will come on board. I would like it if he didn't have to because it's a hard life and I don't want him to suffer like me, I don't want him to suffer like I've suffered [...]. Life on ship is very lonely, so I don't want him to suffer like that – he is supposed to be with his wife and children not like me. When I am here I miss my children, it's hard working on ships, very hard.[77]

72. Sampson and Thomas, "Health and Safety at Sea".
73. Able-bodied seafarer: interview with Kahveci.
74. Able-bodied seafarer: interview with Sampson.
75. Ordinary seaman: interview with Bloor.
76. Bosun: interview with Sampson.
77. Electrician: interview with Sampson.

If seafarers have not recently benefited from the speed up of cargo operations or vessels themselves in the late twentieth and early twenty-first centuries, we might expect that they will at least have benefited from the revolution in telecommunications and the introduction of the internet. In some cases this seems to be the case. Whilst close to the shore, seafarers can use their own personal mobile phones, and "texting" is often popular with less well-off individuals. Officers, and particularly the captain, are most likely to benefit from access to company-funded communication systems. They can often access vessel mobile telephones, and may be granted free e-mail for their own personal use aboard. Aboard Tetra ships, all crew members were, in principle, granted free on-board e-mail access. Such access is being phased in by a number of companies and is clearly a positive development. However, even this kind of provision often fails to produce uniform access for a number of reasons. A significant number of seafarers' families do not have, or cannot afford, access to e-mail, and even where they can they may encounter further barriers. For example, Thai workers aboard Tetra vessels (also on the longest voyage contracts) were unable to read or write in English, and as a result of the difference between Thai and Roman script were unable to use English-language keyboards. Thus, even if their families had internet access they were unable to make use of the free e-mail provision aboard.

This, like the example of shore leave, highlights the differential impact of technological innovation upon seafarers and the contradictions inherent in a time–space compressed world. The compensation for slower forms of communication in the 1960s and 1970s was longer periods of shore leave, where seafarers could see and experience different countries and cultures and meet and interact with different peoples. Today, a seafarer working a nine-month contract aboard a fast-turnaround vessel, with three months vacation a year, may in his working life see less of the world than his nineteenth-century counterpart on voyages of months without sight of land, but ashore in different parts of the world for similarly extended periods.

CONCLUSIONS

Shipping, as a form of modern transportation, both drives and is itself effected by the forces that have been described by Harvey and others in producing time–space compression. Paradoxically, the workers employed on ships experience such compression as constraining rather than liberating, in terms of their access to the wider world. If the global village represents the notion of the world on your doorstep to some, for seafarers the village has become a remote one, largely inaccessible and imaginary. New technology has changed the world of seafarers in some positive ways, offering increased safety in navigation and, often, more comfortable working conditions. It has also impacted negatively upon their working lives. Seafarers aboard vessels utilizing modern container terminals are rarely able to go ashore, and have little direct contact with "outsiders" in the course of their voyage contracts. They have thus seen their spatial worlds diminish. Whilst aboard traditional vessels, seafarers today might still have the opportunity to "see the world" from time to time, the visible world of the seafarer aboard a container vessel is largely confined to the steel clad interior of his/her ship.

The response of seafarers to such changes aboard appears to be nuanced and complex. They may recognize some of the disadvantages of innovation (for example the loss of the radio officer, increased use of computers and paperwork), but like Tatsuno[78] and Yasuda's[79] workers in Japan, they nonetheless contribute to the process of technical and organizational innovation. In the case of seafarers, this is achieved in the forms of critiques of unsatisfactory change (such as the introduction of GMDSS) in the trade press, via professional bodies (e.g. the Nautical Institute), and directly to companies, suggestions for positive change (via company websites and direct interaction with shore-side personnel), and support for changes perceived as effective (e.g. better ship–shore communication, and the computerization of container records). Furthermore, the shipping industry is organized in such a way that it is often seafarers or ex-seafarers who drive change aboard ships from temporary or permanent positions ashore in shipping companies and in related services such as stevedoring. In this the Tetra terminal is illustrative:

> We have quite a lot of seafarers in the terminal, there are a lot of former seafarers. First of all seafarers, they normally like something close to the ships, like the waterfront industry. Many seafarers at some stage like to get ashore and then they get a job which relates to what they do. And the approach most seafarers have is very good because it is like being on a ship, when the ship is sinking you don't go for a coffee break. That's the approach we need in this business.[80]

The full complexity of the response of seafarers to the possibilities offered by new technologies is captured memorably in a poem written by a comparatively modern mariner (J.F.K.) and published in 1977. The poem is titled "Ships to Come", and incorporates the following verses:

Our engineers sleep by day.
The crew are drunk on lager.
The Mate on watch neglects his sight,
To read *The Forsyte Saga*.

78. Sheridan Tatsuno, *Created in Japan: From Imitators to World-Class Innovators* (New York, 1990).
79. Yuzo Yasuda, *40 Years, 20 Million Ideas: The Toyota Suggestion System* (Cambridge, MA, 1991).
80. Tetra employee: interview with Sampson.

What kind of ship is this? you say,
Where things seem so erratic.
Our craft is of some future day,
Entirely automatic.

Of rust you will not see a bit,
For everything is plastic.
And if by chance a rock is hit,
We'll bounce off like elastic.

Though work is nil, we still do rave
'Gainst sea life with each breath.
For if we aren't bored to the grave –
We'll drink ourselves to death.[81]

Here, the benefits to seafarers of less work, more leisure time, less stress, and increased safety are all humorously highlighted and attributed to various forms of innovation. Equally however, J.F.K. pinpoints some of the drawbacks of innovation at sea in terms of quality of life and job satisfaction. In this the potential for automation and the application of technology to deskill work[82,83] is brought into stark relief.

What the poet did not anticipate in his vision of the future, and we would argue to be of equal importance, is the extent to which innovation in shore-side cargo operations has impacted on the life and work of seafarers, and indeed port workers. The role of some seafarers has been changed by such innovation (for example the chief officer), but containerization and the fast vessel turnaround it has facilitated, along with the location of modern port terminals has impacted, albeit differentially, on all seafarers working aboard such ships. Speed up of cargo operations and changes in the utilization of, and access to, space have changed the working environment, spatial worlds, and temporal contexts of seafarers in unanticipated ways that have been negative more often than positive. Such change has had significant consequences for the lives of seafarers, as well as for their work, yet there has been little resistance to its introduction. This may be partly attributed to the fact that even amongst relatively small crews (of twenty to twenty-five) it is evident that the impact of technological innovation is experienced differently depending on both the rank and nationality of seafarers. Nevertheless, it would be inaccurate to suggest that ratings rather than officers suffer as a result of such change. The work of officers has been affected by innovation more than that of ratings, officer positions have been lost as a result of innovation, and it is

---

81. Abridged from Ronald Hope, *Voices from the Sea: Poems by Merchant Seamen* (London, 1977), p. 58.
82. Harry Braverman, *Labour and Monopoly Capital* (New York, 1974).
83. Mike Noon and Paul Blyton, *The Realities of Work* (Basingstoke, 1997).

frequently officers who, due to their responsibilities aboard, have the least opportunities for shore leave. As one first engineer aboard a tanker put it:

> Ah you see these days, these days when you approach a port you approach a problem [...] normally we discharge for twenty-four hours, and this twenty-four hours is my worst twenty-four hours because I have the entire plant working down below [...]. There is no way I can go outside [...]. It is not really worth it any more [...] too much hassle, too many problems, too many things, you know![84]

Nevertheless, officers (depending on nationality) have longer leave periods and work shorter voyages than ratings; their income is generally higher than ratings (although ratings in some companies may be paid more than junior officers in others), and they are more likely to have access to e-mail and mobile telephones aboard. They are thus more likely to experience the time–space compressed world they are operating in positively. For many ratings it would seem that time–space compression makes the world less rather than more accessible, limiting rather than expanding their spatial and communicative horizons whilst distorting time in such a way that periods spent aboard drag on interminably.

---

84. Engineer: interview with Sampson.

IRSH 48 (2003), Supplement, pp. 153–180 DOI: 10.1017/S0020859003001305
© 2003 Internationaal Instituut voor Sociale Geschiedenis

Letting the "Computer Boys" Take Over: Technology and the Politics of Organizational Transformation

NATHAN L. ENSMENGER

Most experts agree that another barrier to the most desirable use of the computer is the immense culture and communication gap that divides managers from computer people. The computer people tend to be young, mobile, and quantitatively oriented, and look to their peers both for company and for approval [...]. Managers, on the other hand, are typically older and tend to regard computer people either as mere technicians or as threats to their position and status – in either case they resist their presence in the halls of power.

T. Alexander, "Computers Can't Solve Everything", *Fortune*, (1969)

INVENTING THE COMPUTER PROGRAMMER

In the decades following the development of the first electronic digital computers, the computer industry in the United States grew from nothing into an important and expansive sector of the American economy. Whereas in the early 1950s electronic computers were generally regarded as interesting but extravagant scientific curiosities, by 1963 these devices and their associated peripherals formed the basis of a billion-dollar industry. By the beginning of the 1970s, more than 165,000 computers had been installed in the United States alone, and the computer and software industries employed several hundred thousand individuals worldwide.[1]

Co-evolving with these flourishing new information industries was a novel species of technical professional, the computer programmer. In 1945 there were no computer "programmers", professional or otherwise; by 1967 industry observers were warning that although there were at least 100,000 programmers working in the United States, there was an immediate need for at least 50,000 more.[2] "Competition for programmers", declared a contemporary article in *Fortune* magazine, "has driven salaries up so fast that programming has become probably the country's highest paid technological occupation [...]. Even so, some companies can't

1. Kenneth Flamm, *Creating the Computer Government, Industry, and High Technology* (Washington DC, 1988), p. 135.
2. Bruce Gilchrist and Richard Weber (eds), *The State of the Computer Industry in the United States* (New York, 1972).

find experienced programmers at any price."[3] By the end of the 1960s they had become the center of the "software crisis", a debate about the health and future of the computer industry that was to continue for the next quarter of a century.

It many respects it is the history of the computer programmer, rather than the computer itself, that is most important to our understanding of this crucial period of rapid and fundamental transformation in the history of information technology. While electronic computing held a certain high-tech appeal for many corporate executives in the late 1950s and early 1960s, few had any idea how to integrate effectively this expensive, unfamiliar, and often unreliable technology into their existing operations. It was the computer programmers who developed the applications software that transformed the latent power of a general-purpose computer into a specific tool for solving actual real-world problems. For many organizations, it was the availability of software that most determined the success or failure of their computerization efforts. As computer hardware became faster, more reliable, and less expensive, the relative importance of software – and software developers – became even more pronounced.

Despite their obvious importance to the history of information technology, computer programmers represent a perplexing problem for the historian. We know almost nothing about who they were, where they came from, or what their daily work lives were like. Neither laborers nor professionals, they defy traditional occupational categorizations. The ranks of the elite programmers included both high-school dropouts and ex-Ph.D. physicists. Originally envisioned as little more than glorified clerical workers, they quickly assumed a position of power within the corporation vastly disproportionate to their official organizational role. Defined by their mastery of the highest of high technology, they were often derided for their adherence to artisanal practices. Although associated with the emerging academic discipline of computer science, they were never widely considered to be either scientists or engineers. Even to this day, their occupational expertise remains difficult to clearly define or delineate.[4] The term "programmer" itself encompasses such a wide range of occupational categories – from the narrow and highly technical "coder" to the elite and influential "systems man" – that it is more useful as a rhetorical device than as an analytical category.[5]

3. Gene Bylinsky, "Help Wanted: 50,000 Programmers", *Fortune*, 75 (March 1967), pp. 445–556, 141.

4. Bruce Webster, "The Real Software Crisis", *Byte*, 21 (1996), p. 218.

5. Although many of the earliest programmers were women, by the beginning of the 1960s programming was generally considered a male profession. Certainly the elite ranks of "systems men" were, quite literally, men. As Margaret Rossiter and others have suggested, masculinity was a cultural resource that aspiring professionals could draw upon in order to improve the standing of their discipline. For many in this period the very concept of a professional was

It is precisely this ambiguous occupational identity that makes the computer programmer such a fascinating and controversial figure. Throughout the 1950s and 1960s, the identity of the computer programmer was negotiated and renegotiated in response to a changing social and technological environment. By virtue of their close relationship to the increasingly powerful technology of electronic computing, computer programmers became the subject of highly contested boundary disputes with traditional corporate employees. In the language of the contemporary management literature, programmers represented influential "change-agents". In their role as mediators between the technical system (the computer) and its social environment (existing structures and practices), computer programmers played a crucial role in transforming the computer from a scientific instrument into a powerful tool for corporate control and communication. As such, they also served as a focus for opposition to and criticism of the use of new information technologies. From the "programmer personnel" problem of the 1950s to the "software turmoil" of the 1960s to the "world-wide shortage of information technology workers" in the 1990s, the focus of debate about the software crisis has continued to center around the unique nature of computer programming as an intellectual and occupational activity.[6] The Y2K crisis, the H1-B visa debates, recent concerns about the loss of programming jobs to India and Pakistan, are all part of a much larger pattern of debate about the new structure of technical labor in the late twentieth and early twenty-first centuries. This paper will explore the emergence of the computer programmer as a central figure in an ongoing debate about the role of information technology in organizational transformation. It focuses on the conflict between the craft-centered practices of the computer programmers and the "scientifically" oriented management techniques of their corporate managers. It argues that the skills and expertise that computer programmers possessed transcended traditional boundaries between business knowledge and technical expertise, and that computer programmers constituted a substantial challenge to established corporate hierarchies and power structures. It suggests that the continued persistence of a "software crisis" mentality among industrial and governmental managers, as well as the seemingly unrelenting quest of these managers to develop a software development methodology that would finally eliminate corporate dependence on the craft knowledge of individual programmers, can best be understood in light of this struggle over workplace authority.

synonymous with an all masculine and thus high-status occupation. A more thorough discussion of the systems men can be found in Thomas Haigh, "Inventing Information Systems: The Systems Men and the Computer, 1950–1968", *Business History Review*, 75 (2001), pp. 15–61.
6. Office of Technology Policy, United States Department of Commerce, "America's New Deficit: The Shortage of Information Technology Workers", technical report (1997).

THE ORIGINS OF PROGRAMMING

The first clear articulation of what a programmer was and should be was provided in the late 1940s by Herman Goldstine and John von Neumann in a series of volumes on "Planning and Coding of Problems for an Electronic Computing Instrument". These volumes, which served as the principal textbooks available on the computer programming until at least the early 1950s, outlined a clear division of labor in the programming process that seems to have been based on the practices used in programming the ENIAC. These practices were themselves adapted from those used at the large manual computation projects at the nearby Aberdeen Proving Grounds. In these projects, the most senior women (by this point in time manual computation had become an almost exclusively feminine occupation) developed elaborate "plans of computation" that were carried out by their fellow human "computers". Since electronic computing was envisioned by the ENIAC developers as "nothing more than an automated form of hand computation", it seemed natural that similar plans could be constructed for their electronic counterparts.[7]

Drawing on their experience with the ENIAC, Goldstine and von Neumann spelled out a six-step programming process that clearly differentiated between the high-level conceptual activities involved in "planning" an algorithm and the tedious but straightforward work of "coding" it into machine-readable form. The planner would conceptualize the problem mathematically and physically, perform a numerical analysis to determine precision requirements and evaluate potential approximation errors, and design the overall algorithm. The coder would merely write out steps of a computation in a form that could be read by the machine, either by encoding them on punch cards, or in the case of ENIAC, by plugging cables and setting switches. Whereas the planners were typically scientists or engineers (and therefore also overwhelmingly male), the coders were low-status and almost inevitably female (at least at the ENIAC project).

The use of the designation "coder" in this context is significant. "Coding" suggested a highly specialized – and rigidly circumscribed – set of occupational activities that required little more than conscientious precision and a small degree of technical training. Like keypunch operators or stenographers, coders existed only to transcribe the thoughts of others. They merely operated the machinery designed by others. Coders obviously ranked low on the intellectual and professional hierarchy. As the historian Jennifer Light has suggested, coders were quite literally the "invisible technicians" of the ENIAC project: in press coverage of the

7. David Allan Grier, "The ENIAC, the Verb to Program and the Emergence of Digital Computers", *Annals of the History of Computing*, 18 (1996), pp. 51–55, 53.

project they were never referred to individually, and in many of the publicity photos they were cropped out entirely.[8]

The idea that the aspects of the programming process most intimately connected to the manipulation of the machine (rather than the definition of the problem) were both low-status and uninteresting carried forward into the commercial computer projects of the early 1950s. An early manuscript version of the UNIVAC "Introduction to Programming" manual, for example, highlighted the distinction between the managerial "programmer" and the technical "coder":

> [...] in problem preparation, the detailed work may be accomplished by two individuals. The first, who may be called the "programmer", studies the problem, determines the appropriate method of solution, and prepares the flow chart. This person must be well versed in the particular field in which the problem lies, and should also be able to fully exploit the flexibility and versatility of the UNIVAC system. The second person, referred to as the "coder" need only be familiar with the technique of reducing the flow chart to the specific instructions, or coding, required by the UNIVAC to solve the problem.[9]

By differentiating between these two tasks, one clerical and the other analytical, the manual reinforced the Goldstine/von Neumann model of the programming process. It is important to note that the versatile "programmer" referred to above was not a computer specialist. He was the planner, the provider of abstract knowledge, not the master of the machinery; the actual "computer" aspect of electronic computing was to be delegated to specialist technicians. In this model the real business of software development was analysis; the actual coding aspect of programming was trivial and mechanical. "Problems must be thoroughly analyzed to determine the many factors that must be taken into consideration", suggested the aforementioned manual, but the once this analysis had been completed, the "pattern of the [programming] solution would be readily apparent". Although this division of the programming process into two distinct and unequal phases did not survive into the published version of the UNIVAC documentation, its earlier inclusion highlighted the ubiquity of such distinctions.

Despite this general insistence of the planning/coding distinction, however, in actual practice it was often difficult to differentiate between the two functions. As the ENIAC project leaders themselves discovered to their dismay, controlling the operation of an automatic computer was nothing like the process of hand computation, and the "ENIAC girls"

---

8. Jennifer Light, "When Computers Were Women", *Technology & Culture*, 40 (1999), pp. 455–483.
9. Sperry Rand Univac, "Introduction to Programming", Programming for the UNIVAC, Part 1 (typewritten manuscript, 11 June 1949); Hagley Achives, Box 372, Accession 1825.

were therefore responsible for defining the first state-of-the-art methods of programming practice. Programming was a very imperfectly understood activity in these early days, and much more of the work devolved on the coders than anticipated. To complete their coding, the coders would often have to revisit the mathematical analysis of the problem at hand; and with their growing skills, some scientific users left many or all of the six programming stages to the coders. In order to debug their programs and to distinguish hardware glitches from software errors, they developed an intimate knowledge of the ENIAC machinery. "Since we knew both the application and the machine", claimed ENIAC programmer Betty Jean Jennings, "we learned to diagnose troubles as well as, if not better than, the engineers".[10] Like many later observers, Goldstine and von Neumann appear to have described the division of labor in the programming process as they would have preferred it to be, rather than how it existed in practice.

THE "BLACK ART" OF PROGRAMMING

The transformation of the computer programmer from clerical worker to technical specialist was not confined solely to the ENIAC project. In electronic computer installations all over the country the limitations of first generation hardware devices demanded of programmers the development of creative innovations and "work-arounds". For example, many of these machines did not have floating-pointing hardware, so the programmers had to do complicated calculations to ensure that the values of the variables would stay within the machine's fixed range throughout the course of the calculation. Little was known about the best algorithms and numerical methods to use for this purpose, so a programming problem could often turn into a research excursion in numerical analysis. Memory devices had very little capacity, and programmers had to develop great skill and craft knowledge to fit their programs into the available memory space. Devices were also slow, so tricks and intricate calculations were required to make sure to get every bit of speed out of the machines, such as carefully placing an instruction at a particular location on the drum memory so that the read head would be passing by that very location on the drum at the time when it came time to execute that instruction.

It is during this period that a peculiar cultural stereotype of the computer programmer emerges. The emphasis on individual creativity and idiosyncratic technique in contemporary programming practice suggested that computer programmers, like chess masters or virtuoso musicians, were endowed with a uniquely creative ability. Programmers were therefore selected for their intellectual gifts and aptitudes, rather than

10. W. Barkley Fritz, "The Women of ENIAC", *Annals of the History of Computing*, 18 (1996), pp. 13–28, 20.

their business knowledge or managerial savvy. "Look for those who like intellectual challenge rather than interpersonal relations or managerial decision-making. Look for the chess player, the solver of mathematical puzzles."[11] Because the presence of one of these gifted programmers could often determine the difference between the success and failure of an expensive electronic data processing (EDP) project, companies went to great lengths to identify and retain them.

The popular notion that good programmers were born, not made, was supported by a series of aptitude tests and personality profiles developed by employers and human resources experts. One widely cited IBM study determined that code produced by a truly excellent programmer was twenty-six times more efficient than that produced by his merely average colleagues.[12] Despite the serious methodological flaws that compromised this particular study (including a sample population of only twelve individuals), the 26:1 performance ratio quickly became part of the standard lore of the industry. Dr. E.E. David of Bell Telephone Laboratories spoke for many when he argued that large software projects could never be managed effectively, because "the vast range of programmer performance indicated earlier may mean that it is difficult to obtain better size-performance software using machine code written by an army of programmers of lesser average caliber".[13] Skilled programmers were thought to be effectively irreplaceable, and were treated and compensated accordingly.

It is during this period that most corporations stopped formally differentiating between "programmers" and "coders". The now common-place designation "programmer" was adopted to describe the entire process of application development. The verb "to program", with its military connotations of "to assemble" or "to organize", suggested a more thoughtful and system-oriented activity.[14]

Even the development of new "automatic programming systems" such as FORTRAN and COBOL, although originally intended to eliminate the need for skilled programmers altogether, had the unintended effect of elevating their status. For those interested in advancing the academic status of computer science, the design of programming languages provided an ideal forum for exploring the theoretical aspects of their discipline. More practical-minded programmers saw programming languages as a means of

11. Joseph O'Shields, "Selection of EDP Personnel", *Personnel Journal*, 44 (1965), pp. 472–474, 472.
12. Hal Sackman, W.J. Erickson and E.E. Grant, "Exploratory Experimental Studies Comparing Online and Offline Programming Performance", *Communications of the ACM*, 11 (1968), pp. 3–11, 3.
13. Peter Naur, Brian Randall, and J.N. Buxton, *Software Engineering: Proceedings of the NATO Conferences* (New York, 1976), p. 33.
14. Grier, "The ENIAC, the Verb to Program", pp. 51–55, 53.

eliminating the more onerous and error-prone aspects of software development. By eliminating much of the tedium associated with low-level machine coding, they allowed programmers to focus less on technical minutia and more on high-status activities such as design and analysis.

It is this last development that is most significant. Software development managers soon discovered that although automatic programming systems helped eliminate simple syntax and transcription errors, they did little to reduce the underlying complexity of the programming process. As the long-time industry analyst Willis Ware suggested in a 1965 editorial:

> We lament the cost of programming; we regret the time it takes. What we really are unhappy with is the total programming process, not programming (i.e. writing routines) per se. Nonetheless, people generally smear the details into one big blur; and the consequence is, we tend to conclude erroneously that all our problems will vanish if we can improve the language which stands between the machine and the programmer. 'Tain't necessarily so. All the programming language improvement in the world will not shorten the intellectual activity, the thinking, the analysis, that is inherent in the programming process. Another name for the programming process is "problem solving by machine", perhaps it suggests more pointedly the inherent intellectual content of preparing large problems for machine handling.[15]

Since so much of the programming process involved "intellectual activity, mathematical investigation, discussions between people", very often, individuals who were trained as programmers actually do the early stages of the programming process but do none of the actual writing. Ware estimated that at least one-half of the total programming man-hours in a project was occupied by analysis and definition of the problem.[16]

Willis Ware was not the only observer to argue for the expansion of the programmer's occupational bailiwick to include design and analysis. A 1959 Price-Waterhouse report on "Business Experience with Electronic Computers" argued that, whereas a knowledge of business of operations could usually be obtained by an adequate expenditure of time and effort, "innate ability [...] seems to have a great deal to do with a man's capacity to perform effectively in the fields of computer coding and systems design".[17] In fact, the study's authors suggested,

> [...] the term "programmer" [...] is unfortunate since it seems to indicate that the work is largely machine oriented when this is not at all the case [...] training in systems analysis and design is as important to a programmer as training in

15. Willis Ware, "As I See It: A Guest Editorial", *Datamation*, 11 (1965), pp. 27–28, 27.
16. *Ibid.*, p. 27.
17. B. Conway, J. Gibbons and D.E. Watts, *Business Experience with Electronic Computers: A Synthesis of What Has Been Learned from Electronic Data Processing Installations* (New York, 1959), p. 83.

machine coding techniques; it may well become increasingly important as systems get more complex and coding becomes more automatic.[18]

The clear implication of recent experience, in both scientific computation and business data processing, seemed to be that programmers should be given more responsibility for design and analysis, that the idea that coding could be left to less experienced or lower-grade personnel was "erroneous", and that "the human element [was] crucial in programming".[19]

The growing role of programmers in high-level design activities, combined with a continued emphasis on innate skills and ability, provided individual programmers with a certain degree of immunity from managerial imperatives. Indeed, throughout the 1950s software development projects were thought to be almost impossible to manage using conventional methods. [20] The general consensus was that computer programming was "the kind of work that is called creative [and] creative work just cannot be managed".[21] One industry observer went so far as to argue that the "major managerial task is finding – and keeping – 'the right people': with the right people, all problems vanish".[22] During this period, many corporate programmers enjoyed an unprecedented degree of personal authority and professional autonomy. Programmers were not only "encouraged to feel they are professionals", but they were included as active participants in all phases of application development, from design to implementation, in order to ensure their cooperation and enthusiasm.[23]. For the time being, the power to control the computer rested with the individual programmer, rather than with the management bureaucracy.

The ambiguous nature of their corporate identity proved to be something of a mixed blessing for programmers, however. The perceived lack of managerial control over the programming process provoked tension within the corporate structure. As the electronic computer became increasingly central to the social and economic life of commercial organizations, the exceptional status and practices the computers programmers began to attract increased an unwelcome attention. The same personality traits that were seen as indicative of genius could also be seen as antisocial and subversive. The lack of widely accepted formal methods for evaluating programmer aptitude and ability weakened their claims to "professional" status: if programming was indeed more art than science, its

---

18. *Ibid.*

19. *Ibid.*, p. 90.

20. Bylinsky, "Help Wanted: 50,000 Programmers", pp. 445–556, 141; Charles Lecht, *The Management of Computer Programming Projects* (New York, 1967), p. 9.

21. Robert Gordon, "Review of Charles Lecht, *The Management of Computer Programming Projects*", *Datamation*, 14 (1968), pp. 200–202, 200.

22. Robert Gordon, "Personnel Selection", in Fred Gruenberger and Stanley Naftaly (eds), *Data Processing [...] Practically Speaking* (Los Angeles, CA, 1967), p. 88.

23. Conway *et al.*, *Business Experience with Electronic Computers*, p. 81.

practitioners could hardly claim the same status as other white-collar professionals. [24] When John Backus (the IBM researcher best known as the inventor of the FORTRAN programming language) famously described programming in the 1950s as "a black art, a private arcane matter [...] [in which] the success of a program depended primarily on the programmer's private techniques and inventions", he did not intend it to be a compliment.[25] The same qualities that had previously been thought essential indicators of programming ability, such as creativity and a mild degree of personal eccentricity, could also be perceived as being merely unprofessional.

Nevertheless, the long-standing association of programming ability with creative genius provided individual programmers with a powerful claim to personal and professional authority. By the end of the 1950s it had become clear that computer programmers were anything but routine clerical workers. But what kind of employee did that make them, exactly? The possession of valuable technical expertise did not automatically translate into professional standing or even long-term occupational survival. Other similarly skilled craftsmen had seen their occupations deskilled or eliminated – a historical fact that computer programmers seem to be well aware of. Computer programmers in this period seem to have been aware of their own ambiguous status, and worked to established the structures of professionalism: academic computer science curriculum, certification programs, and professional societies.[26]

SOFTWARE TURMOIL

By the beginning of the 1960s, however, developments occurred in both the technical and social environment of electronic computing that

24. In 1955 IBM introduced its Programmer Aptitude Test (PAT), which correlated performance in training programs with subsequent performance ratings by project managers and served for many years as a *de facto* industry standard. The test was adapted from a psychological examination developed by the American Council on Education, and included questions about number series, figure analogies, and arithmetic reasoning. By 1962 an estimated 80 per cent of all businesses used some form of aptitude test when hiring programmers. Although the IBM PAT was used by almost 40 per cent of these businesses, numerous alternatives were developed, and the other 60 per cent used some combination of more than 60 different exams. Although aptitude tests were accused of being inaccurate, irrelevant, and susceptible to widespread cheating, many employers continued to use them well into the 1970s. No single test was widely accepted as being very accurate or definitive, however; they were simply one of the only tools available for dealing with the problem of programmer labor.

25. Nick Metropolis, J. Howlett and Gian-Carlo Rota (eds), *A History of Computing in the Twentieth Century : A Collection of Essays* (New York, 1980), p. 126.

26. Nathan Ensmenger, "The 'Question of Professionalism' in the Computer Fields", *IEEE Annals of the History of Computing*, 23 (2001), pp. 56–73.

prompted a re-evaluation and re-negotiation of the computer program-mer's proper place in corporate and professional hierarchies. In the first half of the decade innovations in transistor and integrated circuit technology increased the memory size and processor speed of computers by a factor of 10, providing an effective performance improvement of almost 100. The falling cost of hardware allowed computers to be used for more and larger applications, which in turn required larger and more complex software. As the scale of software projects expanded, they became increasingly difficult to supervise and control. They also became much more expensive. Large software development projects acquired a reputa-tion for being behind schedule, over budget, and bug-ridden.

Commercial software development projects changed not only in size but in character. Whereas the first electronic computers were produced for military and scientific purposes, the second generation of computers were designed explicitly for business. In addition to producing general purpose computers that were relatively reliable and affordable, manufacturers like IBM could also provide the services and peripherals necessary to integrate the electronic computer into existing systems and processes. As the computer became more of a tool for business than a scientific instrument, the nature of its use – and of its primary user, the computer programmer – changed dramatically. The projects that business programmers worked on tended to be larger, more highly structured, and less mathematical than those involved in scientific computing. The needs of business demanded a whole new breed of programmers, and plenty of them.

The "personnel problem" posed by the shortage of programmers quickly assumed crisis proportions. As early as 1961 observers were already warning of a "gap in programming support" that threatened to "get worse [...] before it gets better".[27] Five years later "one of the prime areas of concern" to EDP managers was "the shortage of capable programmers", a shortage which had "profound implications, not only for the computer industry as it is now, but for how it can be in the future".[28] Large corporations like IBM struggled to develop costly internal training programs. Fly-by-night vocational schools sprung up all over the country, promising golden opportunities but delivering little more than trained typists.

The widespread programmer labor shortage, combined with a series of highly publicized software disasters, including the software related destruction of the Mariner 1 spacecraft and the infamous IBM OS/360 debacle (which cost IBM more than half a billion dollars – four times the original budget – the single largest expenditure in company history),

27. Robert Patrick, "The Gap in Programming Support", *Datamation*, 7 (1961), p. 37.
28. Richard Tanaka, "Fee or Free Software", *Datamation*, 13 (1967), pp. 205–206, 206.

lent credence to claims that an industry-wide software crisis was imminent.[29]

The focus of much of the debate about the burgeoning software crisis was not so much the computer itself as the computer programmer. In the late 1960s the venerable consulting company McKinsey & Company issued a series of reports suggesting that the real reason that most data processing installations were unprofitable is that "many otherwise effective top managements [...] have abdicated control to staff specialists – good technicians who have neither the operation experience to know the jobs that need doing nor the authority to get them done right".[30] The reports helped redefine contemporary understandings of the nature and causes of the software crisis by suggesting that the real "personnel problem" was not shortage but mismanagement. The solution to "unlocking the computer's profit potential", according to McKinsey & Company, was to restore the proper balance between managers and programmers: "Only managers can manage the computer in the best interests of the business. The companies that take this lesson to heart today will be the computer profit leaders of tomorrow."[31]

Freed from some of the constraints of earlier technology and eager to take advantage of a less-skilled (and less-expensive) workforce, managers began to look for solutions to the software crisis that would eliminate corporate dependence on the craft knowledge of individual programmers. New perspectives on these problems began to appear in the industry literature.

> There is a vast amount of evidence to indicate that writing – a large part of programming is writing after all, albeit in a special language for a very restricted audience – can be planned, scheduled, and controlled, nearly all of which has been flagrantly ignored by both programmers and their managers,

argued Robert Gordon in a 1968 review of contemporary software development practices.[32] The professional journals of this period are replete with exhortations towards better software development management: "Controlling Computer Programming"; "New Power for Management"; "Managing the Programming Effort"; "The Management of

---

29. The Mariner I incident involved a software problem that resulted in the destruction of multi-million-dollar spacecraft. The IBM OS/360 project, delivered nine months late and riddled with errors, took an enormous toll on the company, in both personal and financial terms. Its failure was the subject of one of the most widely read books on software project management, Frederick Brook's *The Mythical Man-Month* (Reading, MA, 1975).

30. McKinsey & Company, "Unlocking the Computer's Profit Potential", *Computers & Automation*, 18 (1969), pp. 24–33, 33.

31. *Ibid.*, p. 33.

32. Gordon, "Personnel Selection", p. 200.

Computer Programming Efforts".[33] Although it was admittedly true "that programming a computer is more an art than a science, that in some of its aspects it is a creative process", this new perspective on software management suggested that "as a matter of fact, a modicum of intelligent effort can provide a very satisfactory degree of control".[34]

It was the 1968 NATO Conference on Software Engineering that irrevocably established software management as one of the central rhetorical cornerstones of all future software engineering discourse. In the fall of that year a diverse group of influential computer scientists, corporate managers, and military officials gathered in Garmisch, Germany, to discuss their growing concern that the production of software had become "a scare item for management [...] an unprofitable morass, costly and unending". "We build software like the Wright brothers built airplanes", complained one prominent participant: "build the whole thing, push it off the cliff, let it crash, and start over again".[35] The solution to the so-called "software crisis", suggested the conference organizers, was for software developers to adopt "the types of theoretical foundations and practical disciplines that are traditional in the established branches of engineering".[36] In the interest of efficient software manufacturing, the "black art" of programming had to make way for the "science" of software engineering.

By defining the software crisis in terms of the discipline of "software engineering", the NATO Conference set an agenda that influenced many of the technological, managerial, and professional developments in commercial computing for the next several decades. For a number of conference participants, the key word in the provocative NATO manifesto was "discipline". For example, in his widely quoted paper on "mass-produced software components", Douglas McIlroy forcefully articulated his plan for "industrializing" software production:

> We undoubtedly produce software by backward techniques. We undoubtedly get the short end of the stick in confrontations with hardware people because they are the industrialists and we are the crofters. Software production today appears in the scale of industrialization somewhere below the more backward construction agencies. I think that its proper place is considerably higher, and would like to investigate the prospects for mass-production techniques in software.[37]

33. C.I. Keelan, "Controlling Computer Programming", *Journal of Systems Management*, 20 (January 1969), pp. 30–33; D. Herz, *New Power for Management* (New York, 1969); Richard Canning, "Managing the Programming Effort", *EDP Analyzer*, 6 (1968), pp. 1–15; Charles Lecht, *The Management of Computer Programming Projects* (New York, 1967).
34. Keelan, "Controlling Computer Programming", p. 30.
35. R.M. Graham, quoted in Naur *et al.*, *Software Engineering: Proceedings of the NATO conferences*, p. 32.
36. *Ibid.*, p. 4.
37. *Ibid.*, p. 7.

McIroy's vision of a software "components factory" invokes familiar images of industrialization and proletariatization. According to his proposal, an elite corps of "software engineers" would serve as the Frederick Taylors of the software industry, carefully orchestrating every action of a highly stratified programmer labor force. And like the engineers in more traditional manufacturing organizations, these software engineers would identify themselves more as corporate citizens than as independent professionals.[38]

The turn towards management solutions to the software crisis that followed the 1968 Garmisch Conference reflected a significant shift in contemporary attitudes towards programmers and other computer specialists. Indeed, many of the most significant innovations in software engineering to be developed in the immediate post-Garmisch era were as much managerial as they were technological or professional. When a prominent adherent of object-oriented programming techniques spoke of "transforming programming from a solitary cut-to-fit craft, like the cottage industries of colonial America, into an organizational enterprise like manufacturing is today", he was referring not so much to the adoption of a specific technology, but rather to the imposition of established and traditional forms of labor organization and workplace relationships.[39]

By reconstructing the software crisis as a problem of management technique rather than technological innovation, advocates of these new management-oriented approaches also relocated the focus of its solution, removing it from the domain of the computer specialist and placing it firmly in the hands of traditional managers.

A NEW THEOCRACY – OR INDUSTRIAL CARPETBAGGERS?

Prior to the invention of the electronic digital computer, information processing in the corporation had largely been handled by conventional clerical staffs and traditional office managers. There had been attempts by aspiring "systems managers" to leverage expertise in the technical and bureaucratic aspects of administration into a broader claim to authority over the design of elaborate custom information processing systems.[40] In certain cases, strong-willed executives were able to use information technology to consolidate control over lower levels of the organizational hierarchy. For the most part, however, the use of such technologies did not

38. Ensmenger, "The 'Question of Professionalism'".
39. Brad Cox, "There is a Silver Bullet", *Byte*, 15 (1990), p. 209.
40. Thomas Haigh, "Technology, Information and Power: Managerial Technicians in Corporate America: 1917–2000", (unpublished Ph.D. thesis, University of Pennsylvania, 2002).

contribute to the rise of a class of technical professionals capable of challenging the power of traditional management.[41]

As more and more corporations began to integrate electronic computers into their data processing operations, however, it became increasingly clear that this new technology threatened the stability of the established managerial hierarchy. Early commercial computers were large, expensive, and complex technologies that required a high level of technical competence to operate effectively. Many nontechnical managers who had adapted readily to other innovations in office technology such as complicated filing systems and tabulating machinery, were intimidated by computers – and by computer specialists. As the electronic computer became an increasingly valuable source of institutional and economic power and authority, programmers and other computer personnel emerged as influential organizational "change-agents" (to use the management terminology of the era).[42] This was particularly true of business programmers. The systems they developed often replaced, or at least substantially altered, the work of traditional white-collar employees. Traditional corporate managers, not unsurprisingly, often resented the perceived impositions of the "computer boys", regarding them as threats to their position and status.[43]

The rising power of EDP professionals did not go unnoticed by other middle-level managers. In a 1967 essay on "The Impact of Information Technology on Organizational Control", management consultant, Thomas Whisler, warned his colleagues "it seems most unlikely that one can continue to hold title to the computer without assuming and using the effective power it confers".[44] A decade earlier, Whisler and his colleague Harold Leavitt had coined the term "information technology", and had predicted that within thirty years the combination of management science and information technology would decimate the ranks of middle management and lead to the centralization of managerial control.[45] His 1967 article suggested that EDP specialists were the direct beneficiaries of such centralization, which occurred at the expense of traditional managers. He quoted one insurance executive who claimed that "There has actually been a lateral shift to the EDP manager of decision-making from other

---

41. JoAnne Yates, *Control Through Communication: The Rise of System in American Management* (Baltimore, 1989).

42. John Golda, "The Effects of Computer Technology on the Traditional Role of Management", (M.A. thesis, Wharton School, University of Pennsylvania, 1965), p. 34.

43. For example, see T. Alexander, "Computers Can't Solve Everything", *Fortune* (October 1969), p. 169, and Thomas Whisler, "The Impact of Information Technology on Organizational Control", in Charles Myers (ed.), *The Impact of Computers on Management* (Cambridge, MA, 1967), pp. 16–48, 44.

44. *Ibid.*, p. 44.

45. Harold Leavitt and Thomas Whisler, "Management in the 1980s", *Harvard Management Review*, 36 (1958), pp. 41–48.

department managers whose departments have been computerized."
Another manager complained about the relative decline of managerial
competence in relationship to computer expertise:

> The supervisor [...] has been replaced as the person with superior technical
> knowledge to whom the subordinates can turn for help. This aspect of
> supervision has been transferred, at least temporarily, to the EDP manager and
> programmers or systems designers involved with the programming [...] under-
> neath, the forward planning function of almost all department managers has
> transferred to the EDP manager.[46]

Information technology, argued Whisler, "tends to shift and scramble the
power structure of organizations [...]. The decision to locate computer
responsibility in a specific part of an organization has strong implications
for the relative authority and control that segment will subsequently
achieve."[47]

Whisler was hardly alone in his assessment of the impending danger of
an organizational power shift. In her 1971 book, *How Computers Affect
Management*, Rosemary Stewart described how computer specialists
mobilized the mystery of their technology to "impinge directly on a
manager's job and be a threat to his security or status".[48] In his 1969 article
"Computers Can't Solve Everything", Thomas Alexander emphasized the
cultural differences that existed between "computer people" and business
managers: "Managers [...] are typically older and tend to regard computer
people either as mere technicians or as threats to their position and status –
in either case they resist their presence in the halls of power."[49] Authors
Porat and Vaughan listed several deprecating titles that managers used to
describe their upstart rivals, including "the new theocracy", "prima
donnas", "the new breed", "industrial carpetbaggers", and "other similarly
unflattering titles".[50]

It is not difficult to understand why many managers came to fear and
dislike computer programmers and other software specialists. In addition
to the usual suspicion with which established professionals generally
regarded unsolicited changes in the status quo, managers had particular
reasons to resent EDP departments. The unprecedented degree of
autonomy that corporate executives granted to "computer people" seemed
a deliberate affront to the local authority of departmental managers. "All
too often management adopts an attitude of blind faith (or at least hope)
toward decisions of programmers", complained one management-oriented

46. Whisler, "The Impact of Information Technology on Organizational Control", p. 44.
47. *Ibid.*, p. 48.
48. Rosemary Stewart, *How Computers Affect Management* (Cambridge, MA, 1971), p. 196.
49. Alexander, "Computers Can't Solve Everything", p. 169.
50. Avner Porat and James Vaughan, "Computer Personnel: The New Theocracy – or
Industrial Carpetbaggers", *Personnel Journal*, 48 (1968), pp. 540–543.

computer textbook.[51] As a result of the "inability or unwillingness of top management to clearly define the objectives of the computer department and how it will be utilized to the benefit of the rest of the organization", many operational managers "expect the worse and, therefore, begin to react defensively to the possibility of change".[52] The adoption of computer technology threatened to bring about a revolution in organizational structure that carried with it tangible implications for the authority of managers: "What has not been predicted, to any large degree, is the extent to which political power would be obtained by this EDP group. Top management [...] have abdicated their responsibility and let the 'computer boys' take over."[53]

As Thomas Haigh has suggested, it was during the late 1950s that the concept of management information (and computerized management information systems) was developed; by the beginning of the 1960s the computer had become not just a tool to be managed, but also a tool for management.[54] A whole host of new would-be management experts, including systems men, operations research experts, and management consultants emerged to threaten the professional authority of middle-level managers. The frequent association of "computer boys" with external consultants only compounded the resentment of regular employees.

There were other reasons why traditional managers felt threatened by computers and computer specialists. The continuous gap between the demand and supply of qualified computer personnel had in recent years pushed up their salary levels faster than those of other professionals and managers. It also provided them with considerable opportunities for horizontal mobility, either in pursuit of higher salaries or more challenging positions. These opportunities were often resented by other, less mobile employees. In addition, the unprecedented degree of autonomy that corporate executives granted to "computer people" seemed a deliberate affront to the local authority of departmental managers. In the eyes of many nontechnical managers, the personnel most closely identified with the digital computer "have been the most arrogant in their willful disregard of the nature of the manager's job. These technicians have clothed themselves in the garb of the arcane wherever they could do so, thus alienating those whom they would serve."[55]

In response to these perceived challenges to their authority, managers developed a number of interrelated responses intended to restore them to their proper roles in the organizational hierarchy. The first was to define

51. Michael Barnett, *Computer Programming in English* (New York, 1969), p. 3.
52. Porat and Vaughan, "Computer Personnel: The New Theocracy", p. 542.
53. Golda, "The Effects of Computer Technology", p. 34.
54. Haigh, "Inventing Information Systems".
55. *Datamation* editorial, "The Thoughtless Information Technologist", *Datamation*, 12 (1966), pp. 21–22, 21.

programming as an activity, and by definition programmers as professionals, in such a way as to assure it and them a subordinate role as mere
technicians or service staff workers. The rhetoric of management literature
reinforced the notion that computer specialists were self-interested,
narrow technicians rather than future-minded, bottom-line-oriented good
corporate citizens. "People close to the machine can also lose perspective",
argued one computer programming "textbook" for managers. "Some of
the most enthusiastic have an unfortunate knack of behaving as if the
computer were a toy. The term 'addictive' comes to mind [...]."[56]
Managers emphasized the youthfulness and inexperience of most programmers. They cited aptitude tests and personality profiles (often of
questionably scientific validity) that suggested that computer programmers were particularly antisocial, that they "preferred to work with things
rather than people", as examples of the "immaturity" of the computer
professions.[57]

Another common strategy for deprecating computer professionals was
directly to challenge their technical monopoly. If working with computers
was in fact not all that difficult, then dedicated programming staffs were
superfluous. One of the alleged advantages of the COBOL programming
language frequently touted in the literature was its ability to be read,
understood – and perhaps even written – by informed managers.[58] In its
"Meet Susie Meyer" advertisements for its PL/1 programming language,
the IBM Corporation asked its users an obviously rhetorical question:
"Can a young girl with no previous programming experience find
happiness handling both commercial and scientific applications, without
resorting to an assembler language?" The answer, of course, was an
enthusiastic "Yes!" Although the advertisement promised a "brighter
future for your programmers", (who would be free to "concentrate more
on the job, less on the language") it also implied a low-cost solution to the
labor crisis in software. The subtext of appeals like this were non-too-
subtle: If pretty little Susie Meyer, with her spunky miniskirt and utter lack
of programming experience, could develop software effectively in PL/1, so
could just about anyone.

Experienced managers stressed the critical differences between "real-
world problems" and "EDP's version of real-world problems".[59] The
assumptions about programmers embedded in the infamous McKinsey
reports – that they were narrowly-technical, inexperienced, and "poorly
qualified to set the course of corporate computer effort" – resonated with

56. Barnett, *Computer Programming in English*, p. 5.
57. For example, see Dallis Perry and William Cannon, "Vocational Interests of Computer
Programmers", *Journal of Applied Psychology*, 51 (1967), pp. 28–34.
58. Gordon, "Review of Charles Lecht", p. 85.
59. Harry Larson, "EDP – A 20-Year Ripoff!", *Infosystems*, 21 (1974), pp. 26–30, 28.

many corporate managers.[60] They provided a convenient explanation for the burgeoning software crisis. Computer department staffs, although "they may be superbly equipped, technically speaking, to respond to management's expectations", are "seldom strategically placed (or managerially trained) – to fully assess the economics of operations or to judge operational feasibility".[61] Only the restoration of the proper balance between computer personnel and managers could save the software projects from a descent into "unprogrammed and devastating chaos".[62]

In much of the management literature of this period, computer specialists were often cast as self-interested peddlers of "whizz-bang" technologies. "In all too many cases the data processing technician does not really understand the problems of management and is merely looking for the application of his specialty."[63] The 1969 book *New Power for Management* emphasized the myopic perspective of programmers: "For instance, a technician's dream may be a sophisticated computerized accounting system; but in practice such a system may well make no major contribution to profit."[64] Others attributed to them even more Machiavellian motives: "More often than not the systems designer approaches the user with a predisposition to utilize the latest equipment or software technology – for his resumé – rather than the real benefit for the user."[65] Calling programmers the "Cosa Nostra" of the industry, the colorful former-programmer turned technology management consultant H.R.J. Grosch warned managers to "refuse to embark on grandiose or unworthy schemes, and refuse to let their recalcitrant charges waste skill, time and money on the fashionable idiocies of our racket".[66] Like many of his management-oriented colleagues, he argued that programmers needed to "accept reality, not to rebel against it". Many of the technological, managerial, and economic woes of the software industry became wrapped up in the problem of programmer management.

The idea that the so-called "software crisis" could largely be attributed to mismanagement by technicians served a dual purpose for traditional middle-level managers. First of all, it placed them solidly in the role of corporate champion. Many of the most prominent software engineering methodologies developed in the immediate post-Garmisch-conference era

---

60. *Datamation* Editorial, "Trouble [...] I Say Trouble, Trouble in DP City", *Datamation*, 14 (1968), p. 21, 21.
61. Herz, *New Power for Management*, p. 169.
62. Robert Boguslaw and Warren Pelton, "Steps: A Management Game for Programming Supervisors", *Datamation*, 5 (1959), pp. 13–16.
63. W.R. Walker, "MIS Mysticism (Letter to Editor)", *Business Automation*, 16 (1969), p. 8.
64. Herz, *New Power for Management*, p. 169.
65. H.L. Morgan and J.V. Soden, "Understanding MIS Failures", *Data Base*, (Winter 1973), pp. 157–171, 159.
66. Herb Grosch, "Programmers: The Industry's Cosa Nostra", *Datamation*, 12 (1966), p. 202.

were management-related or driven. Secondly, this particular construction of the software crisis provided an unflattering image of the computer specialists vis-à-vis management. By representing programmers as short-sighted, self-serving technicians, managers reinforced the notion that they were ill-equipped to handle "big-picture", mission-critical responsibilities. After all, according to the McKinsey reports, "Only managers can manage the computer in the best interests of the business."[67] And not just any managers would do: only those managers who had traditional business training and experience were acceptable, since "managers promoted from the programming and analysis ranks are singularly ill-adapted for management".[68]

THE STRUGGLE FOR OCCUPATIONAL TERRITORY

To many observers of computer revolution of the late twentieth century – both historians and practitioners alike – the emergence of new, manage-rially-oriented, "rational" solutions to the software crisis marked "a major cultural shift in the perception of programming", the welcome beginning of a new era in which software development "started to make the transition from being a craft for a long-haired programming priesthood to becoming a real engineering discipline".[69] In this conventional and essentially Chandlerian interpretation, an important but immature industry, driven by the changing economics of commercial computing and guided by well-established managerial and organizational principles, simply restructured itself along the lines of traditional industrial manufacturing. In the internal language of the software engineering discipline, an "inversion in the hardware-software cost ratio curve" occurred in the mid-1960s that clearly demanded a managerial response.[70] Put more simply, the cost of the actual computers went down at the same time that the cost of using them (developing and maintaining software) went up. By the end of the decade the expenses associated with commercial data processing were dominated by software maintenance and programmer labor rather than equipment purchases. And since the management of labor fell under the traditional domain of the middle-level manager, these managers quickly developed a deep interest in rationalizing the practices of their computer programmers.

67. McKinsey & Company, "Unlocking the Computer's Profit Potential", p. 33.
68. J.L. Ogdin, "The Mongolian Hordes versus Superprogrammer", *Infosystems*, 20 (1973), pp. 20–23, 20.
69. Martin Campbell-Kelly and William Aspray, *Computer: A History of the Information Machine* (New York, 1996), p. 201.
70. Barry Boehm, "Software and its Impact: A Quantitative Assessment", *Datamation*, 19 (1973), pp. 48–59. See also Michael Mahoney, "Software: the Self-Programming Machine", in Atsushi Akera and Fred Nebeker (eds), *From 0 to 1: An Authoritative History of Modern Computing* (New York, 2001).

For labor historians and historians of technology the story is a little more complicated. If we take seriously the claim – widely accepted in both disciplines – that technologies and technological systems represent more than just the "one best way" to accomplish a particular function but are also the embodiment of very specific social, political, and power relationships, then the ongoing debate about the software crisis assumes a much larger significance. Computer programmers are in many ways the paradigmatic "knowledge workers" of postindustrial society.[71] At the very least, they play a central role in the development of the computerized information systems that have become ubiquitous components of the modern work environment, whether office building, retail establishment, mechanic's shop, or assembly line. Surely then it is crucial that we understand the nature of the computer programmer's work, if only to understand the politics of the technologies that they build. As Shoshona Zuboff argues in her book *In the Age of the Smart Machine: The Future of Work and Power*, "computer based technologies are not neutral; they embody essential characteristics that are bound to alter the nature of work within our factories and offices, and among workers, professionals, and managers".[72] What then are the "essential characteristics" of software and software development that shape our understanding of work, identity, and power in the information technology industry (and the many industries that rely on information technology)? How can we understand the social and occupational history of the computer programmer in terms of a larger debate about the role of information technology in organizational transformation?

One possible interpretation of the burgeoning software crisis of the late 1960s and the emergence of new management-oriented solutions to the problem of software production might situate these developments within the context of a larger struggle between labor and the forces of capital. Indeed, the few scholarly treatments of software workers that do exist adopt this approach. Building on the work of Harry Braverman and David Noble, the labor historian Philip Kraft argued in his 1977 book *Programmers and Managers: The Routinization of Computer Programming in the United States*, that "programmers, systems analysts, and other software workers are experiencing efforts to break down, simplify, routinize, and standardize their own work so that it, too, can be done by machines rather than people". Cloaked in the language of progress and efficiency, the imposition of increasingly rigorous management controls on the process of programming was envisioned primarily as a means of

71. Daniel Bell, *The Coming of Post-Industrial Society* (New York, 1973).
72. Shoshana Zuboff, *In the Age of the Smart Machine: The Future of Work and Power* (New York, 1988).

disciplining and controlling a recalcitrant work force.[73] Joan Greenbaum, in her 1979 study of "Management Theory and Shopfloor Practice in Data-Processing Work" arrived at a similar conclusion.[74]

A superficial reading of the management literature of this period, with its confident claims about the ability of performance metrics, development methodologies, and automatic programming languages to reduce corporate dependence on individual programmers, might suggest that this is indeed a straightforward story of the routinization and degradation of programmer labor. Certainly, the twentieth century is replete with such stories. In fact, many of the software management methodologies proposed in late 1960s do indeed represent "elaborate efforts" that "are being made to develop ways of gradually eliminating programmers, or at least reduce their average skill levels, required training, experience, and so on".[75] Their authors would have been the first to admit it.

If computer programming had remained, as was originally intended, a form of glorified clerical labor, then the deskilling hypothesis might serve a more useful interpretive function. There is an existing literature on the routinization and feminization of clerical work.[76] As we have seen, however, computer programmers in this period generally managed not only to maintain their status and autonomy, but also improbably to extend it. What began as low-status, clerical, and feminized labor emerged as one of the most well-paid, highly romanticized, and stereotypically masculine of white-collar occupations. Writing in 1971, the occupational sociologist Enid Mumford actually lauded data processing as one area "where the philosophy of job reducers and job simplifiers – the followers of Taylor – has not been accepted".[77] More than four decades after corporate managers first began their attempts to rationalize software development along the lines of traditional manufacturing, computer programming remains a distinctively craft-oriented and idiosyncratic discipline. Although complaints about the quality and reliability of software still plague software developers – the rhetoric of crisis continues to dominate discussions about the health and future of the industry – it is clear that computer programmers in the 1960s were active participants in the struggle to define the boundaries of their own professional competence and authority.

An alternative interpretation might view this history in terms of the

---

73. Philip Kraft, *Programmers and Managers: The Routinization of Computer Programming in the United States* (New York, 1977), p. 32.
74. Joan Greenbaum, *In the Name of Efficiency: Management Theory and Shopfloor Practice in Data-Processing Work* (Philadelphia, PA, 1979).
75. Kraft, *Programmers and Managers*, p. 26.
76. Sharon Strom, *Beyond the Typewriter: Gender, Class and the Origins of Modern American Office Work, 1900–1930* (Urbana, IL, 1992); Margery Davies, *Woman's Place is at the Typewriter: Office Work and Office Workers, 1870–1930* (Philadelphia, PA, 1982).
77. Enid Mumford, *Job Satisfaction: A Study of Computer Specialists* (London, 1972).

professionalization literature. During the 1950s and 1960s many white-collar occupations attempted to professionalize, and computer programmers were no exception.[78] They established professional societies, codes of ethics, and certification and curriculum standards.[79] Belonging to a profession provided an individual with a "monopoly of competence", the control over a valuable skill that was readily transferable from organization to organization.[80] Professionalism provided a means of excluding undesirables and competitors; it assured basic standards of quality and reliability; it provided a certain degree of protection from the fluctuations of the labor market; and it was seen by many workers as a means of advancement into the middle class.[81] Programmers in particular saw professionalism as means of distinguishing themselves from "coders" or other "mere technicians". Corporate managers generally embraced the concept of professionalism. It appeared to provide a familiar solution to the increasingly complex problems of programmer management: "The concept of professionalism", argued one personnel research journal from the early 1970s, "affords a business-like answer to the existing and future computer skills market".[82] The rhetoric of professionalism was ideologically neutral, and appealed to a wide variety of individuals and interest groups. Professionalization was one of several widely adopted strategies for dealing with the software crisis.[83]

Thinking in terms of professionalization provides several benefits. It allows us to locate the history of computer programming in a familiar literature, and it provides a number of useful explanatory devices. One of the most useful is the sociologist Andrew Abbott's "ecological" model for understanding professional change and development. In *The Systems of Professions: An Essay on the Division of Expert Labor*, Abbott describes the "jurisdictional struggles" that occur among groups of professionals struggling for control over a particular occupational territory.[84] In Abbott's model, professions are fluid organisms able to adapt and expand when occupational niches become available to them and to respond and defend themselves when their particular territory becomes threatened by

78. Harold Wilensky, "The Professionalization of Everyone?", *American Journal of Sociology*, 70 (1964), pp. 137–158.
79. Ensmenger, "The 'Question of Professionalism'".
80. Magali Sarfatti Larson, *The Rise of Professionalism: A Sociological Analysis* (Berkeley, CA, 1977).
81. Robert Zussman, *Mechanics of the Middle Class: Work and Politics Among American Engineers* (Berkeley, CA, 1985).
82. *Personnel Journal* Editorial, "Professionalism Termed Key to Computer Personnel Situation", *Personnel Journal*, 51 (February 1971), pp. 156–157.
83. Nathan Ensmenger, "From 'Black Art' to Industrial Disciple: The Software Crisis and the Management of Programmers", (unpublished Ph.D thesis, University of Pennsylvania, 2001).
84. Andrew Abbott, *The Systems of Professions: An Essay on the Division of Expert Labor* (Chicago, IL, 1988).

competitors. Disruptive new technologies often allow for the creation of new niches or the expansion of existing occupational territory. It is clear that this is in part what happens with the electronic computer in the late 1950s. As the electronic digital computer technology became an increasingly important tool for corporate control and communication, existing networks of power and authority were uncomfortably disrupted. The conflicting needs and agendas of users, manufacturers, managers, and programmers all became wrapped up in highly public struggle for control over the occupational territory opened up by the technology of computing.

This professionalization narrative is not entirely satisfactory, however. Despite their best efforts to establish the institutional structures of a profession, computer programmers were never able to achieve widespread professional recognition. They were unable, for example, to develop two of the most defining characteristics of a profession: control over entry into the profession and the adoption of a shared body of abstract occupational knowledge – a "hard core of mutual understanding" – common across the entire occupational community. They failed to convince employers sufficiently of the value of professionalism, and were often divided among themselves over issues involving academic standards and certification requirements. Complaints about the lack of professional standards among computer programmers continue to play a central role in discussions about the nature and causes of the software crisis. Despite the widespread adoption of the rhetoric of software engineering, most computer programmers are not engineers and would not identify themselves as such. Although the "question of professionalism" continues to be a very live issue in the programming community, in general computer programmers are not in general considered to be professionals.[85]

So if not professionals, managers, or clerical support staff, what exactly are computer programmers? How can does their unique history tell us about larger patterns in work practices and the organizational of labor in the late late twentieth century?

Perhaps the most useful way to think about the computer programmer is as a technician. As the organizational theorist Stephen Barley has suggested, technicians are a relatively recent addition to the pantheon of occupations.[86] Although technicians do not fit easily into the interpretive framework of either labor history or the sociology of professions, they represent the fastest growing sector of the American labor force. They include such occupations as radiological technicians, science technicians, engineering technicians, and medical technicians. Their work often

85. Ensmenger, "The 'Question of Professionalism'".
86. Stephen Barley, "Technicians in the Workplace: Ethnographic Evidence for Bringing Work Into Organization Studies", *Administrative Science Quarterly*, 41 (1996), pp. 404–441.

transgresses traditional occupational boundaries; according to Barley, technicians "often wear white collars, carry briefcases, and conduct sophisticated scientific and mathematical analyses. Yet they use tools, work with their hands, make objects, repair equipment, and, from time to time, get dirty."[87] They are often – albeit at times grudgingly – granted a great deal of autonomy by their employers.[88] Like computer programmers, technicians occupy an ambiguous occupational space that is difficult to categorize.

Also like computer programmers, technicians serve as mediators between the technological and social architectures of the organization. Technicians are often responsible for building, repairing, and monitoring the complex systems that keep a company running. Because they play a support role that is tangential to the core business of the organization and generally possess skills radically different from those of their colleagues, they are often seen as foreigners to the worksite.[89] Traditional employees often resent their dependence on technicians and consider them insufficiently subservient.[90]. Like the "computer boys" of the late 1960s, technicians often wield power disproportionate to their official position in the occupational hierarchy.

There are a number of other similarities between Barley's description of technicians and the history of the computer programmer. Although they are generally well-educated and rely heavily on scientific or engineering training, technicians also value intuition and craft knowledge. They tend to learn on the job, rather than from formal academic or vocational training programs. They make extensive use of social networks and community-based systems of information exchange. Their expertise is often local and idiosyncratic and difficult to communicate or define as a set of abstract principles.[91]

It seems clear from these descriptions that computer programmers can be considered as a type of technician. In fact, this seems to be the most useful way to make connections between software workers and other forms of technical labor. It captures the tension inherent in the practices of software development: the curious coexistence of high technology and artisanal sensibilities; the inability of programmers to conform to conventional professional, scientific, or engineering categories; the persistent attempts by corporate managers to restructure software

---

87. *Ibid.*, p. 412.
88. Stacia Zabusky and Stephen Barley, "Redefining Success: Ethnographic Observations on the Careers of Technicians", in Paul Osterman (ed.), *Broken Ladders: White Collar Careers* (Oxford, 1996), pp. 185–214.
89. Barley, "Technicians in the Workplace", p. 422.
90. *Ibid.*, p. 430.
91. *Ibid.*, p. 427.

development along the lines of traditional manufacturing; the remarkable persistence of the forty-year-old software crisis.

By looking beyond simplistic explanations of computer programmers as either degraded "software factory" workers or failed software engineers – or as *sui generis* exceptions to larger historical patterns – we can recapture the broader relevance of the history of information technology to social and labor history. Thinking of computer programmers as technicians allows us to locate them in a larger historical context. They are both like and unlike traditional workers, and both the similarities and differences are revealing.

At the very least, the history of computer programmers provides a reinterpretation of what has generally been treated as a purely technical debate; it suggests that corporate workers, managers, and computer programmers have been active participants in shaping the technology of electronic computing. Like any new technological innovation, the computer could not simply be inserted, unchanged and unnoticed, into the well-established social, technological, and political systems that comprised modern corporate and academic organizations. Just as the computer itself was gradually reconstructed, in response to a changing social and technical environment, from a scientific and military instrument into a mechanism for corporate control and communication, modern businesses and universities had to adapt themselves to the presence of a powerful new technology. Over the course of the 1950s and 1960s, the identity of the computer programmer was continually invented and reinvented in response to a changing social and technical environment. Embedded into all of the major technical innovations of period was a particular model of what the users/programmers of these inventions should look like. Was the idealized computer programmer a routinized laborer in a Taylorized "software factory" or a skilled, autonomous professional? Should programmers base their occupational identity on the model of the engineer/scientist or the certified public accountant? Should they emphasize craft technique or abstract knowledge? Did they need to be college educated or simply a vocational school graduate? Should they be male or female? The answers to each of these questions had significant implications for the role of electronic computing – and of computing professionals – in modern corporate and academic organizations. It is no wonder, therefore, that they were not readily resolved in this, or for that matter any other, period in the history of computing.

EPILOGUE

In the years since the 1960s the software industry has only continued to expand. A recent study by the Bureau of Labor Statistics shows that, since 1972, employment in the computer services industries (which includes software and associated services) has grown 300 per cent.[92] There are now at least 1.9 million computer services workers in the United States alone. Even discounting the recent boom (and subsequent bust) in the information technology sector, software and its associated services remains one of the largest and fastest growing industries in the United States.

The obvious importance of the industry to the national and global economy suggests that computer programmers are a worthy object of continued study. The recent debate over the information technology worker supply, which has implications for a wide range of funding, education, and immigration policy issues, revealed a surprising lack of basic information about the size and structure of the information technology labor market.[93] It is clear, however, that many of the institutional structures that continue to inform our understanding of information technology and information technology workers – academic, professional, and technological – took their shape in the period discussed in this paper. In many ways the basic framework of the debate about the software crisis has remained essentially unchanged in the decades since the 1960s. In an industry characterized by change, the rhetoric of crisis has proven remarkably persistent.

In recent years the debate about the software crisis has gone global. Competition from Asia, both in terms of an influx of Asian programmers entering the United States on H1-B and L1 visas, as well as the movement of software development projects to offshore "software factories", has created new tensions within the computing community. Many of the questions about certification, professionalization, and workplace control that dominated discussions about software workers in the 1960s have re-emerged, this time around couched in terms of fears of foreign competition and national security. These are discussions that have occurred in the past, but always in regard to blue-collar manufacturing jobs, not skilled white-collar occupations. Many of the organizational tensions associated with computerization projects have been further complicated by questions of race and nationalism. There has been a renewed interest in unionization among information technology workers, a development that had previously been strongly resisted by both employers and aspiring technical professionals.[94]

Because computer programmers confound so many of the traditional

92. William Goodman, "The Software and Engineering Industries: Threatened by Technological Change?", unpublished technical report (1996).

93. Peter Freeman and William Aspray, *The Supply of Information Technology Workers in the United States* (Washington DC, 1999).

94. From the 1960s onward, movements to unionize computer programmers emerge periodically, but none acquired any significant momentum. Like many aspiring professionals, programmers generally resisted unionization efforts, and the constantly expanding demand for new programmers discouraged any attempts to erect barriers of entry to the occupation.

categories of historical and sociological analysis, they suggest new ways to re-evaluate the role of the computer in late twentieth-century society. Much of the literature on the computer, from the earliest days of computing to the present, has focused on its "revolutionary" potential. And yet, more than thirty years after the first NATO Conference on Software Engineering, advocates of a more industrial approach to software development still complain that the "vast majority of computer code is still handcrafted from raw programming languages by artisans using techniques they neither measure nor are able to repeat consistently".[95] The study of the computer in the context of work practices, occupational conflict, and organizational politics allows us to explore not only change but continuity, and to link the history of the computer to a larger body of labor and social history, as well as to contemporary issues of concern to a broad range of audiences.

95. W. Gibbs, "Software's Chronic Crisis", *Scientific American*, (September 1994), p. 86.

IRSH 48 (2003), Supplement, pp. 181–204 DOI: 10.1017/S0020859003001317
© 2003 Internationaal Instituut voor Sociale Geschiedenis

"Computers in the Wild": Guilds and Next-Generation Unionism in the Information Revolution*

CHRIS BENNER

> There's a great deal of practical experience that is required to be a senior system administrator – not just being trained. You have to understand the idiosyncratic way that computers behave in the wild.
>
> Hal Pomeranz
> *Board Member, System Administrators' Guild (SAGE)*

INTRODUCTION

One of the aspects of the information revolution that has had negative implications for many workers is the erosion of the workplace as a basis for long-term security and collective solidarity. The dramatic pace of technological change, complex restructuring of firms, and continual competitive pressures for rapid innovation that are a central component of the information economy are contributing to fundamental transformations in work and employment. As part of this transformation, the trend towards the centralization of production in large enterprises that was the dominant feature of the industrial era is being superseded by production organized around smaller workplaces connected together in complex, constantly shifting networks operating at multiple spatial scales, from the local to the global. For many workers, one result is greater insecurity, as they increasingly have to update their skills, change jobs and even change careers more frequently. Some analysts have gone so far as to characterize the typical information age worker as a "free-floating individual, connected on-line to a variety of task-performing organizations, ever-competing for resources and personal support, and assuming limited responsibilities towards limited people for a limited time".[1]

In this context, industrial unions, which were the dominant form of worker collective organization throughout most of the twentieth century,

* Thanks are due to Steve Sawyer and the editors of this volume for extremely useful comments and suggestions on earlier drafts of this paper.
1. Martin Carnoy *et al.*, *Sustainable Flexibility: A Prospective Study on Work, Family and Society in the Information Age* (Paris, 1997), p. 35.

have been declining, with unions now representing less than 10 per cent of the private sector workforce in the US. As "traditional" unions have declined, however, there has been a surprising (re)emergence of occupational communities – groups of workers who are linked more closely by their similar skills, social bonds, and labor market experiences than by their position in their employing organization. In many information technology occupations in particular, workers have been coming together to create occupation-based associations, frequently using a "guild" terminology with names like the System Administrators' Guild, the HTML Writers' Guild, and the Silicon Valley Web Guild. Once thought to be remnants of a pre-industrial social order all but wiped out by the development of mass production, new forms of guilds now seem to be re-emerging as workers come together to share knowledge, build contacts leading to their next jobs, and try to protect themselves from the insecurity and volatility of information-age labor markets.

Why are these occupational associations emerging now, and how are they organizing and trying to protect their members' interests? What motivates these organizations frequently to adopt a "guild" terminology in their names and organizational activities? How effective are these organizations at protecting workers' interests? Are they likely to become more prominent, and how can they become more effective in improving workers' conditions?

This paper addresses these questions by analyzing the activities of various guilds and occupational associations in Silicon Valley in the 1990s, the region at the core of innovation in global information-technology industries and an important context for examining the role of labor in the information revolution more broadly. In discussing the activities of these organizations, this paper will argue that, while they provide some important benefits for certain technical workers in the region, these contemporary "guilds" are limited in important ways. Most importantly, these organizations lack the ability to exercise monopoly control over access to skilled labor, or to enforce restrictions on production standards in their industries. These monopoly powers were a critical component of the influence wielded by medieval guilds, but are nearly impossible to achieve in the contemporary economy, given the rapidly changing skill requirements associated with the technological change and volatility of the information economy. Nonetheless, these contemporary guilds have improved their members' career opportunities, through improving skill development, facilitating access to new job opportunities, and organizing advocacy efforts. Thus, given that the factors that have given rise to these new occupational communities are unlikely to change, efforts to build collective action through occupational solidarity can be an important component of broader strategies aimed at building security for workers in the information economy.

This paper proceeds in the following way. The next section provides a brief review of the erosion of workplace stability in Silicon Valley, providing an important context for understanding the rise of occupation-based associations. The following section provides an empirical analysis of a range of guilds and occupational associations in Silicon Valley that grew quite rapidly in the 1990s, highlighting their activities in skill development, job networking, and political advocacy. This is followed by a discussion comparing these recent efforts with the medieval guilds that form an inspiration for their activities, while also comparing these structures with other forms of workers' collective action, particularly professional associations and new forms of occupational unionism. The final section analyzes the strengths and weaknesses of these contemporary guild-like forms of collective solidarity, and discusses the implications for broader strategies to improve workers' positions in the information economy.

LABOR FLEXIBILITY AND THE INFORMATION ECONOMY IN SILICON VALLEY

In the past thirty years, the economy has been dramatically restructured through a variety of processes, including most prominently the rapid development and diffusion of information technologies and rapid economic globalization, with dramatic implications for work, employment, and labor market dynamics.[2] Silicon Valley provides a useful context for examining these new trends in labor. Like studying work in the textile industry in England in the early 1800s in order to understand the first industrial revolution, or studying work in the auto industry in Detroit in the early 1900s in order to understand the second industrial revolution, studying work in Silicon Valley in the 1990s provides insights into ways the information revolution is transforming work globally. This is true for two fundamental reasons. First, Silicon Valley's very origins as an industrial region lie in information-technology industries, which have developed primarily in the last half-century. The relative newness of Silicon Valley's industrial structure, at least compared to older industrial regions, makes especially visible patterns of work and employment that are associated with the rise of information technology. Second, Silicon Valley is a global center of innovation and production in these information-technology industries, which are linked together in complex networks of production, customer and supplier relations. Product and process innovations are adopted in the region rapidly, allowing firms to develop

2. See Chris Benner, *Work in the New Economy: Flexible Labor Markets in Silicon Valley* (Oxford, 2002); Manuel Castells, *The Rise of the Network Society*, vol. 1 of *The Information Age* (London [etc.], 1996); Alan Burton-Jones, *Knowledge Capitalism: Business, Work, and Learning in the New Economy* (Oxford [etc.], 1999).

innovative management and human resource practices. These practices then often diffuse onto world markets and into other industries.

One of the prominent characteristics of labor markets in Silicon Valley is the relative lack of the workplace as a basis of long-term stability or solidarity for workers. Regional labor markets are characterized by rapidly changing skill requirements and volatile employment conditions. The Silicon Valley region has twice the national percentage of the workforce employed in temporary agencies, with up to 40 per cent of the region's workforce involved in nonstandard employment relationships.[3] Rapid turnover has become the norm, even for people classified as having "permanent" employment.[4] A recent random survey of workers in Silicon Valley, for example, found a median job tenure of just under thirty months, with only 46 per cent of respondents having had the same job for the previous three years, and 23 per cent reporting having had three or more different jobs in that time.[5] Even for those staying in the same job, skill requirements change rapidly, resulting in high levels of uncertainty and insecurity.[6]

The volatility in the region's labor markets is fundamentally tied to the nature of competition in the high-tech industries. Competitive success for firms and industries in information-technology industries depends on constant innovation in both developing new products and services, and in improving production processes.[7] As David Angel describes,

> In an era of intensified global competition, it is the ability to anticipate and create new market opportunities, to develop new products ahead of competitors and to reconfigure production processes rapidly in response to changing production requirements that offers the best prospect for long-term profitability of firms and industries.[8]

3. Chris Benner, *Shock Absorbers in the Flexible Economy: The Rise of Contingent Employment in Silicon Valley* (San José, CA, 1996).

4. See Martin Carnoy *et al.*, "Labour Markets and Employment Practices in the Age of Flexibility: A Case Study of Silicon Valley", *International Labour Review*, 136 (1997), pp. 27–48; AnnaLee Saxenian, "Beyond Boundaries: Open Labor Markets and Learning in Silicon Valley", in Michael Arthur and Denise Rousseau (eds), *The Boundaryless Career: A New Employment Principle for a New Organizational Era* (Oxford, 1996), pp. 23–39.; Kathleen Gregory, "Signing-Up: The Culture and Careers of Silicon Valley Computer People", (unpublished Ph.D. dissertation, Northwestern University, Evanston, IL, 1984).

5. Manuel Pastor *et al.*, *Economic Opportunity in a Volatile Economy: Understanding the Role of Labor Market Intermediaries in Two Regions. Report to the Ford Foundation* (San José, CA, 2003).

6. Benner, *Work in the New Economy.*

7. Carl Shapiro *et al.*, *Information Rules: A Strategic Guide to the Network Economy* (Boston, MA, 1998).

8. David Angel, *Restructuring for Innovation: The Remaking of the US Semiconductor Industry* (New York, 1994), p. 4.

This drive for constant innovation leads to a continual cycle of creative destruction, with new products, firms, and even entire industries replacing existing products, firms, and industries, while surviving firms are forced to restructure their operations and products. Lay-offs in the midst of economic growth are not unusual, but, in fact, have been a common experience in Silicon Valley throughout its history.[9] Indeed, flexible employment practices, with open labor markets and widespread circulation of skilled personnel among multiple firms, has been a key component in the long-term competitive success of firms and industries in the region.[10]

THE EMERGENCE OF SILICON VALLEY OCCUPATIONAL COMMUNITIES

In this context of rapid change and volatility, traditional unionization strategies which are rooted in workplace organizing have proved largely ineffective in protecting workers' livelihoods in information-technology industries.[11] In contrast, however, communities of technical workers in information-technology industries have become an important structure in regional labor markets and in many workers' lives. In the earlier days of the region's development, most of these social networks operated informally. Frequently social networks were built and sustained through a combination of informal and formal gatherings entirely outside firm boundaries. Various users groups and hobbyists' clubs brought people with similar interests and experiences together, while trade-association meetings and industry conferences provided a more formal organizational infrastructure supporting the development of these social networks.[12]

9. In 1998, for example, in the midst of an economic boom and a year in which total employment in Santa Clara County (the core of Silicon Valley) grew by over 3 per cent, many Silicon Valley firms were in the midst of laying off significant portions of their workforce due to restructuring. Prominent Silicon Valley firms that announced lay-offs included the following: Seagate (10,000; 10 per cent of their global workforce); Applied Materials (4,200; 30 per cent); Intel (3,000; 5 per cent); National Semiconductor (1,400; 10 per cent); Silicon Graphics (1,000; 10 per cent); Silicon Valley Group (900; 26 per cent); Lam Research (700; 15 per cent); Netscape (400; 12.5 per cent); Komag (480; 10 per cent); Cypress Semiconductor (100; less than 5 per cent); S3 (100; 15 per cent); Spectrian (200; 25 perc ent); Read-rite (250; 10 per cent); Adaptec (250; 7 per cent); and VLSI (10 per cent). See Benner, *Work in the New Economy*. For a discussion of similar dynamics in the 1970s, see John Keller, "The Production Worker in Electronics: Industrialization and Labor Development in California's Santa Clara Valley", (unpublished Ph.D. dissertation, University of Michigan, Ann Arbor, MI, 1981).
10. AnnaLee Saxenian, *Regional Advantage: Culture and Competition in Silicon Valley and Route 128* (Cambridge, MA, 1994).
11. See Chris Benner, "Win the Lottery or Organize: Economic Restructuring and Union Organizing in Silicon Valley", *Berkeley Planning Journal*, 12 (1998), pp. 50–71; Karen Hossfeld, "Divisions of Labor, Divisions of Lives: Immigrant Women Workers in Silicon Valley", (unpublished Ph.D. dissertation, University of California, Santa Cruz, CA, 1988).
12. Saxenian, *Regional Advantage*, pp. 30–34.

Dense social networks among workers serve as pathways for information about jobs, changing technologies, and shifts in industry dynamics. As the region has grown larger and more complex, workers in the regional production complex have become more conscious of the importance of this informal information sharing for their career success. As a result, they have more deliberately tried to create the formal infrastructure to support these "networking" opportunities. Organizations of skilled workers have become an important collective basis for improving worker's career paths, building stability and opportunity in the midst of uncertainty and change.

Frequently, these new occupation-based associations find inspiration for their activities in the activities of medieval guilds. Many information-technology workers view their occupation as a true craft, and see guilds as a model for promoting shared information, knowledge, and collective solidarity. Kynn Bartlett, Founder and then President of the HTML Writers Guild, put it this way:

> The name "guild" was chosen in order to look back at the older, medieval-type guilds. What we liked from that model was the notion of sharing knowledge – that building web design was something of a craft – not purely artistic or purely technical. Both are necessary to make an effective web site. For many people it is not just a technical exercise, but a creative outlet, [they are] expressing themselves through the work they do. The term "guild" calls to mind a certain way in which [the organization] supports the industry, as a support mechanism for web designers. We are a network, a helping hand, an educational resource. If they need something, they come to the guild and they are asking their peers. [The term "guild"] keeps in mind the main purpose [...] sharing information to make everyone successful.[13]

Specific guilds and guild-like associations that emerged or grew strongly in the 1990s include the following.[14]

Systems Administrators' Guild

The Systems Administrators' Guild (SAGE) has its origins in a large trade association called USENIX, which was founded in 1975 to bring together engineers, scientists, technicians, and systems administrators. USENIX sponsors numerous national conferences a year on various topics related to information technology development, one of which is large installation (more than 100 computers) systems administration (LISA). These LISA conferences have been held annually since 1986, and typically draw over 2,000 people. During the 1991 LISA conference, a group of systems administrators from the Bay Area decided to form an organization devoted exclusively to systems administrators, which came to be known as

13. Interview conducted July 1999.
14. These initiatives are all described in more detail in Benner, *Work in the New Economy*.

BayLISA. They formed this users' group because they were looking for a forum for networking on a regular basis, to help them stay up on technical issues, and to provide each other with moral and practical support. The core of people who formed BayLISA was also critical in the formation the following year of the Systems Administrators' Guild (SAGE) as a national organization with local chapters. SAGE was organized in order to "advance the status of computer system administration as a profession overall". It was founded as a special-interest group within USENIX, but over time SAGE has come to increasingly dominate USENIX functions as well, with SAGE membership totaling nearly 5,000 in 1999, over 50 per cent of the total USENIX membership.[15] BayLisa is now the Bay Area Chapter of SAGE, and is the largest single chapter.

Silicon Valley Web Guild

This organization was founded in 1996 and had grown to over 1,000 members by 2000. The organization has a strong presence of employers, not just of web-designers. Monthly meetings are held at different companies who co-sponsor the meeting, providing food and meeting space for free. Companies view this as good public relations and a potential marketing tool, while also providing good links to a network of workers in high demand. Part of the reason for the greater corporate involvement in the Web Guild is its relationship to the national Association of Internet Professionals, of which Silicon Valley Web Guild is the local chapter. The AIP nationally acts much like an industry lobby organization, and was not started by individual professionals, but by a company whose rapid growth was apparently strongly linked to the adult entertainment industry.[16] Nonetheless, the AIP sees its mission as providing benefits and programs that allow both its individual and corporate members to compete better in today's industry, serving as the voice of Internet professionals and industry corporations before the public, press, and within the online community on issues shaping the future of the Internet.

15. Hal Pomeranz, SAGE Board Member, Interview, July 1999.
16. The company that was instrumental in founding the AIP is R.J. Gordon & Co., an electronic business services and e-commerce company based in Los Angeles, CA. R.J. Gordon & Co. is principally known for its subsidiary creditcards.com, a processor of credit-card transactions over telephone or the internet. R.J. Gordon grew rapidly with the growth of the World Wide Web – it was named to the *Inc.* magazine list of 500 fastest growing companies in the United State for five years in a row (1994–1998). Its revenue jumped from under $5 million in 1994, to nearly $20 million in 1995, with much of this initial growth due to the rapid expansion of the on-line adult entertainment industry. R.J. Gordon & Co. wanted to help create an association to improve their image and make the World Wide Web more legitimate, so they put $1 million into the founding and creation of AIP (Hans Cathcart, Silicon Valley Web Guild Coordinator, Interview, May 1999).

HTML Writers' Guild

This organization was formed in 1994, and is probably the largest international organization of Web authors – it had over 123,000 members in more than 150 nations worldwide in April 2001, at the peak of the Internet boom. The leadership of the Guild is based in both southern California and in Florida, but the largest portion of the membership is in Silicon Valley. The organization was founded with the purpose of sharing information and knowledge, while increasing the visibility and prominence of web design as an occupation. The HWG has grown so rapidly in part because there are almost no barriers to entry into the guild. One-year trial memberships are free, and to retain membership requires simply receiving the minimum HWG correspondence: one general newsletter e-mail a month. Full membership costs $40 a year, but in 1999, only 2,500 of the members were full members. Nonetheless, the HWG has developed a wide range of active e-mail lists, with topics ranging from basic and advanced techniques of HTML, to business practices, standards, and ethics in the industry. There are only three part-time staff who maintain the core functions of moderating the e-mail lists, managing finances and membership lists, and building the organization. Their extensive web page of resources is maintained largely by a group of volunteers.

Silicon Valley Webgrrls

This organization was founded in 1997 with the goal of providing a forum for women in or interested in new media and technology "to network, exchange job and business leads, form strategic alliances, mentor and teach, intern and learn the skills to help women success in an increasingly technical workplace and world".[17] At its peak, Silicon Valley Webgrrls had a membership of over 1,000, monthly meetings that drew over 200 people regularly, and had a vibrant on-line listserv.

Society for Technical Communication

The Silicon Valley Chapter of the Society for Technical Communication (STC), with over 2,000 members, was established in 1971. The core of its activity is "advancing the arts and sciences of technical communication". Members include technical writers, editors, graphic artists, multimedia artists, Web and Intranet Page Designers, translators, technical illustrators, and others whose work involves making technical information understandable and available to those who need it. As in many of the Silicon

17. http://www.webgrrls.com.

Valley professional associations, members include employers and recruiters, as well as people working in the occupation.

Technical Writers' Trade Group

The Tech Writers' Trade Group was started in the mid-1980s, initially to develop a code of conduct for tech writers. This is an initiative of the National Writers' Union, and their membership is made of people in the same occupation as the Society for Technical Communication, but they advocate more explicitly for their members' interests, rather than focusing on technical communication more broadly. There are approximately 300 members of the Tech Writers' Trade Group in Silicon Valley. Key activities include a job hotline, training, and continued advocacy around legislative issues.

Graphic Artists' Guild

The Northern California Chapter of the Graphic Artists' Guild was formed in October 1995. Services to local members are primarily provided through the national offices. The Graphic Artists' Guild actually began in Detroit in 1967, when a group of illustrators in a local ad agency originated what they thought would be a typical strike to gain union recognition. The ad agency was able to break the strike by getting their artwork through mail order, and thus the members began to restructure the organization in more of a guild format, focusing on services to members that could be provided even in the absence of a collective bargaining agreement. For most of its history, GAG has been an independent union, but in 1999 it decided to affiliate with the United Auto Workers/AFL-CIO. Most of the activities of GAG are focused on a variety of services for members that help them improve their working conditions and career opportunities. The lack of a collective bargaining agreement means that essentially GAG has to convince its membership every year that being part of the organization is worth it, which helps ensure that the organization is responsive to the changing needs of its membership.

Working Partnerships Membership Agency

This is an initiative organized by the local AFL-CIO Central Labor Council. It is an effort to assist temporary clerical workers in the Valley, by linking a membership association with a nonprofit staffing services firm. Working Partnerships Membership Association is an association that brings temporary workers together for a variety of common interests, providing access to improved benefits, organizing advocacy efforts, such as a code of conduct for temporary agencies, and improving temporary workers' access to state unemployment benefits. The staffing agency puts workers in jobs paying a living wage, and offers them greater access to benefits and skills training.

These examples are only a portion of the occupational associations that play an important role in regional labor markets. One effort to count guilds and similar occupational associations active in the Valley identified nearly thirty organizations with active regular local meetings, including associations for database developers, Linux operating systems programmers, multimedia programmers, and help-desk professionals.[18]

There are a number of labor-market conditions that are common to all of these occupations in which guilds and similar associations have been emerging:

(1) They are all in occupations that require some significant level of technical skills. However, these skills are not company-specific, but are rooted in changing software, hardware and networking systems that are used across organizational contexts.

(2) These occupations also require a significant level of practical work experience, not just formal training, in order to understand how these complex information systems actually operate in practice. Thus, in order to understand "computers in the wild", workers in these occupations need far more than formal, classroom-based technical knowledge. Instead, informal mentorships and apprenticeship opportunities are an important part of becoming proficient in the field.

(3) The skills required to perform the work change rapidly over time, requiring high levels of ongoing learning

(4) Employment conditions change rapidly over time, with workers being more connected with their occupation and trade, rather than a particular employer.

In order to address these conditions, these occupational associations have developed broadly similar activities to assist their members in their own career development and improve their position in the regional labor market. Specifically, their activities can be divided into three broad categories.

First, all these organizations spend significant amounts of time trying to improve their members' opportunities for finding employment in the regional labor market. Sometimes this is done through a formal job listing or placement service. Technical Writers' Trade Group, for instance, has a jobs hotline, while the Society for Technical Communication runs a formal web-based job board. The Working Partnerships initiative goes the farthest in this regard, actually operating a staffing services firm. More

18. Benner, *Work in the New Economy*.

frequently, however, these guilds try to strengthen their members' employment opportunities through more informal channels of social networking. Most associations have regular monthly meetings, in which a significant portion of time is devoted specifically to sharing job leads. Many employers and recruiters attend these meetings as well, attracted by a concentrated group of people in a particular skill or occupation. On-line e-mail listservs provide another important source of job leads. All of these efforts go far beyond simple job listings in classified advertisements or on-line job boards, such as monster.com or hotjobs.com. Instead of being anonymous job listings, the job matching activities are closely linked with the social networks within these occupational communities. This is important, since it means that workers are able to gain much more information not just about available jobs, but about the quality of particular job opportunities. This includes the quality of the company offering the jobs, the nature of management practices, opportunities for advancement, specific skills and experience required, and so on. Furthermore, frequently job seekers learn about job opportunities through other members of their guild/association who are currently working in the company doing the hiring. This provides job seekers with valuable personal references and makes them more likely to be hired.

The second major activity these associations are engaged in is helping their members to improve their skills. Again, sometimes this is done through formal channels, such as organized training programs. The HTML Writers' Guild, for example, offers a range of on-line courses in writing skills, web-page management, and various specific software programs. Similarly the Technical Writers' Trade Group provides training in technical writing and career development, to help people get into the field. More important than these formal training programs, however, is the informal sharing of skills and experience. In all of these technical occupations, skills requirements are either difficult to identify, change rapidly, or both. As in the quotation at the beginning of this paper about the need for practical skills in systems administration, many of these occupations require high levels of tacit knowledge and practical experience. Changing software and hardware technologies require workers continually to upgrade their skills, and employers rarely provide adequate levels of training for employers to keep up to speed. Many workers, especially in new media industries, must spend a significant portion of their time making sure their skills are up-to-date.[19] These occupational communities help workers identify which skills are valued in the labor market, and helps identify ways of improving their skills. Even on a

19. Rosemary Batt *et al.*, *NetWorking: Work Patterns and Workforce Policies for the New Media Industries* (Washington DC, 2001).

day-to-day level, these occupational communities can play an important role in helping people learn on the job. Cross-firm communication, through phone calls, direct e-mails and e-mail listservs, provide an important resource for technical workers in problem-solving.[20]

Finally, these guilds also play an important role in improving their memberships' negotiating positions in the labor market. Again, sometimes this is done in a formal manner. Working Partnerships, for example, developed a campaign to upgrade conditions of temporary workers in the region by promoting a code of conduct for temporary agencies. The Technical Writers' Trade Group engaged in a major lobbying campaign in the state capital to help preserve overtime pay for tech-writers who were threatened with losing their hourly status. Other associations engage in this activity in more informal ways, primarily by providing information to help their members advocate for themselves individually in the labor market. These associations may provide training in individual negotiating strategies, provide detailed salary information based on surveys of the profession, and ultimately try to empower workers through strengthening their information, knowledge, and skills in negotiating.

STRUCTURES OF WORKERS' COLLECTIVE ORGANIZATIONS

The initiatives described in the previous section are somewhat limited in their capacity to impact employment conditions. Despite providing some important career benefits for their members, their impact on employers' behavior, firm human resource practices, and even skill and training systems at the moment are quite limited. They do, however, represent some intriguing organizing efforts and their increasing prevalence raises interesting questions about whether they are likely to be strengthened in the future. Are these guild-like associations likely to become more prominent? Can they be more effective in improving workers' conditions? To help answer these questions, it is useful to compare these initiatives to other historical patterns of collective organization. Since these organizations so specifically appeal to an idyllic image of medieval guilds, I turn first to an examination of the historical sources of strength and influence of guilds. I then compare these with other forms of worker collective solidarity, particularly professional associations and new forms of occupational unionism, discussing how contemporary Silicon Valley-based guild initiatives compare with these other efforts.

---

20. See Chris Benner, "Learning Communities in a Learning Region: The Soft Infrastructure of Cross-Firm Learning Networks in Silicon Valley", *Environment & Planning A* (forthcoming); Julian Orr, *Talking About Machines: An Ethnography of a Modern Job* (Ithaca, NY, 1996).

Guilds

Guilds have been defined as social groups or institutions created by workers around their work, skill or craft.[21] Most writers trace the beginning of guilds to early in the twelfth century in Europe, though there are antecedents in ancient Rome, and guilds have existed in many precapitalist economies, including in India, China, and Japan.[22] Though highly varied in strength, structure, operations, and influence, guilds continued to have significant strength throughout Medieval Europe for at least four centuries. Their power and influence waned in the seventeenth century, and by the late eighteenth century had been outlawed in France and much of the rest of Europe.[23] Guilds are most frequently associated with the development of apprenticeships and control over workplaces employing skilled craftsmen, and it is this popular image that the guilds in Silicon Valley appeal to. The activities of medieval guilds, however, were not limited to skills training and work activities, but in fact combined juridical, political, religious, and social aspirations, along with their basic concerns around economic activity. It was only with the combination of the workplace and broader societal activities that there were able to monopolize the practice of certain professions in medieval towns.

It is important to note that the internal governance structure of most guilds was dominated not by skilled crafts workers, but instead by master craftsmen who were typically owners of their own shops and had strong ties with local public authorities. While journeymen were members of the guild, their influence was significantly less than that of master craftsmen. In many cases, in fact, journeymen organized their own independent associations to try to influence governance of the guilds themselves. Apprentices were essentially indentured workers – sometimes paid in cash, but often in kind in the form of food and lodging – providing essential labor services for masters in their workshops, with few opportunities to escape unpleasant working conditions. Thus, Malcolm Chase is more accurate when he says, "the medieval guild was primarily an employers' organization, but with extensive responsibilities for what would now be termed vocational training and consumer protection".[24]

21. Elliott Krause, *Death of the Guilds: Professions, States, and the Advance of Capitalism, 1930 to the Present* (New Haven, CT, 1996), p. 2
22. See Steven Epstein, *Wage Labor & Guilds in Medieval Europe* (Chapel Hill, NC, 1991); Bo Gustafsson, "The Rise and Economic Behaviour of Medieval Craft Guilds", in *idem* (ed.), *Power and Economic Institutions: Reinterpretations in Economic History* (Brookfield, VT, 1991), pp. 69–106.
23. Interestingly, they survived in Germany through the mid-nineteenth century, and the corporatist structure of contemporary German labor relations apparently owes a great deal to this strong guild survival. See Krause, *Death of the Guilds*.
24. Malcolm Chase, *Early Trade Unionism: Fraternity, Skill and the Politics of Labour* (Aldershot, 2000), p. 9.

It is still instructive to understand how medieval guilds were able to be so effective, surviving over four centuries in the midst of significant economic change. They essentially combined the "mystery" of their craftmanship with the dynamics of a pressure group to create their monopoly power over their given craft in the region controlled by their particular town. Their source of influence was essentially rooted in four broad arenas.[25]

(1) Association: This included control over the process of who entered the craft and how they were to operate. There were rules about who might enter an apprenticeship, how an apprentice should be trained, the process of moving from apprentice to journeyman to master to craftsman, how the workplace would be controlled, how the product and skill would be monopolized and so on. The guild had the power to levy dues and assess fines for breaking the guild rules.

(2) Workplace: Guild masters owned the means of production, which in this case were the tools and the workshop itself required to make the particular product. As a group, masters could limit production to a pace that all could maintain, and that would not debase the quality of the product. For one guild master to profit at the expense of another, by charging more or less for the product than the guild price, by hiring more employees than the guild maximum, or by upping productivity above guild standards, was in theory prohibited.

(3) Market: Through the guild's monopoly over the product made and the skill required to make the profit, guilds were also able to control heavily the market price of the goods they made. Prices were generally set at a level the guild thought was fair, though of course there is evidence that consumers frequently thought the price too high.

(4) State: A critical component of the guilds' ability to exercise power was in their strong relationship with the local state. The Guilds' monopoly over a certain craft was only possible through the power invested in them by local authorities – typically at town level, though later in developing regional governments. To function, guilds generally aimed to obtain a written charter from the local power, which, in exchange for the payment of appropriate fees, gave them the right to regulate the particular craft. Loss of monopoly was the price for nonpayment of fees.

In each of these areas, it is clear that the power contemporary guilds wield is only a pale shadow of the power of their medieval namesakes. In terms of the power of association, contemporary guilds have little ability to control who enters their occupation and how they operate. The formal training and skills people need to enter these technical occupations comes from a wide variety of educational institutions and training programs that

---

25. Krause, *Death of the Guilds.*

are difficult to influence. On-the-job experience is developed through informal mentoring relationships and practical experience across multiple organizational contexts that would be extremely difficult to organize into a formal apprenticeship system. Furthermore, the rapid pace of technological change, and the associated rapid change in skill requirement, would make any single formal system nearly impossible to maintain, even were it to be created. Thus, gaining monopoly control over the supply of labor in this context is nearly impossible. Certainly workers in these associations do exercise some influence over labor market and workplace conditions. This is primarily through the positive benefits provided to members through improved skill development and employment opportunities, rather than through regulation of the workplace or the market for the goods and services they provide. The majority of contemporary guild members are not self-employed or independent contractors, instead being in traditional hourly or salaried positions, subject to the supervision of their employer. Admittedly there are some who are self-employed and thus may be said to "own the means of production" – the various pieces of software and hardware required to perform their work. Nonetheless, even in these situations, their work is only meaningful within the context of the broader network-production relationships that characterize the regional economy. In this broader production context, they have little influence over working conditions or the market for their products and services. This was painfully evident, for instance, for many technical workers in Silicon Valley, as the economic downturn in 2000 reduced wages dramatically for many skilled occupations. Furthermore, most of these associations have very weak ability to influence state regulation, which was a critical component of the power of medieval guilds. Lobbying efforts remain limited and weak and the few advocacy efforts that exist have had only a minimal impact.

In essence, these contemporary guilds are limited by the same economic conditions that undermined the power of traditional guilds – conditions associated with the rise of a large-scale, complex, capitalist society. This does not mean, however, that guilds can't play an important role even in the context of a capitalist economic structure. Recent scholarship, for example, suggests that medieval guilds may have played an important role in actually building a large-scale capitalist economy. Prior to the 1990s, most scholars agreed with the standard analysis originally established by Adam Smith and Karl Marx among others, that guilds were inefficient institutions that hindered the development of more productive ways of organizing production. Their strict regulation over the process of producing craft goods was seen to stifle innovation. Furthermore, as industrial capitalism began to take hold, with the development of a more complex division of labor and larger employment in a concentrated setting, the ability of industrial producers to take advantage of economies of scale and improve production systems eventually eroded the power that guilds had been able to exercise in the economy. In essence, guilds were seen as outdated social structures that hindered economic growth and prosperity by stifling innovation and constraining new production techniques.

More recent scholarship, however, has begun to question this view. Epstein,[26] for instance, argues that guilds played a critical role in ensuring the development and expansion of skills and thus were in fact critical in actually *creating* the conditions for capitalist expansion. He argues that guilds survived for so long because they played a critical economic role, sustaining interregional specialized labor markets, ensuring skills development for large portions of the workforce. It is estimated that in the sixteenth and seventeenth centuries in western Europe, roughly two-thirds to three-quarters of the male labor force had spent significant time in apprenticeship programs. Without the long time-period (most frequently five to seven years) of apprenticeships, Epstein argues, individual craftsmen were unlikely to invest significantly in training new artisans, who could relatively easily leave the training shop and set up as a direct competitor. Through apprenticeships, master craftsmen could reclaim their costs of training by requiring that the apprentice work for below-market wages for a period of time after gaining a set level of skills. Region-wide standards for skills and training programs were developed and transmitted relatively easily in these relatively small-scale labor markets with low rates of migration. Epstein also argues that guilds and associations of journeyman linked together in networks throughout western Europe also played a critical role in disseminating technological invention through the region. Rather than being inefficient organizations, he argues, guilds disappeared not through adaptive failure but because developing nation-states abolished them by decree, largely at the behest of large-scale producers who were constrained by the production and market regulations guilds had managed to get passed. The decline of craft production was as much about capitalists gaining control over labor processes and growing markets as it was about efficient production. Guilds, in fact, played an important role in ensuring skills development in a way that facilitated economic growth and dynamism.

For contemporary guilds in Silicon Valley, even though they don't have the monopoly power of medieval guilds, they have been able to play a significant role in improving the skills and knowledge development of their members. This role is important not just for the members of these guilds, but for employers in the region as well. Guilds play a critical role in ensuring the rapid diffusion of information through the regional labor market, and in the process contribute to the overall economic vibrancy of

26. S.R. Epstein, "Craft Guilds, Apprenticeship, and Technological Change in Preindustrial Europe", *Journal of Economic History*, 58 (1998), pp. 684–714.

the region.[27] Through their contribution to skills development and regional innovation, these guilds do have some potential ability to develop greater leverage within regional labor markets to improve conditions for their members. In evaluating the potential of this leverage, it is useful to compare these initiatives with the activities of professional associations, which are in fact the most direct descendent of medieval guilds. Classic professions – lawyers, doctors, professors, and to a lesser extent engineers – have employed many of the same strategies that guilds pursued in building their "guild-power" but clearly in the context of a growing capitalist economy. Examining trends in professional associations provides additional insights into the role contemporary guilds in Silicon Valley are playing in the economy.

Professional Associations

Professional associations arose in the late nineteenth and twentieth centuries, most prominently in a series of occupations – physicians, lawyers, engineers, administrators, and executives – that are widely recognized as having certain characteristics that distinguish them from other occupational categories, including: a claim to represent, to have a level of mastery over, and to practice a particular discipline, skill, vocation, or "calling"; advanced learning, usually represented by higher-education qualifications, showing an ability to learn and amass knowledge; high-level intellectual skills, showing an ability to grasp new events quickly and to respond effectively; independence and discretion within the working context, showing allegiance to an ethical framework and often to specific codes of practice which govern relationships between the profession, the professional, his/her clients and the wider society.[28]

Even in these classic professions, however, these occupations did not attain professional status without a struggle. Instead, the social status and financial rewards that professionals enjoy were obtained through long periods of collective mobilization and the exercise of political power.[29] Typically, the ability to gain professional status involved the ability to control access to the occupation, requiring that new practitioners be licensed according to procedures and regulations determined by, or at least heavily influenced by, the leading professional association. Furthermore, especially for lawyers and doctors, this professional status is heavily dependent on the required certification being entrenched in law and

27. Benner, "Learning Communities in a Learning Region".
28. Robin Middlehurst *et al.*, "Leading Professionals: Towards New Concepts of Professionalism", in Jane Broadbent *et al* (eds), *The End of the Professions? The Restructuring of Professional Work* (London [etc.], 1997), pp. 50–68.
29. Magali Sarfatti Larson, *The Rise of Professionalism: A Sociological Analysis* (Berkeley, CA, 1977).

regulated by the state. Nonetheless, the status of these occupations continues to be shaped by a complex interplay of market dynamics and political struggles. This status is heavily contested, both within particular professions, and between competing occupations in the labor market.[30] Recent unionization efforts by members of the medical profession, concerned about threats to their independence and professional status, highlights the fact that there is no linear movement towards increased professionalization, and that occupational status depends critically on changing power dynamics in the labor market.[31]

Professional associations, however, are not limited to these classic professions but in fact have also emerged in a range of technical and craft occupations as well. Here, the struggle for improved social status and financial rewards is both more difficult to achieve and less stable once attained. Yet membership in associations in these "semi-professions" remains both an individual strategy for people to improve their career opportunities and a collective strategy to improve the status of the occupation as a whole. There are a range of factors that shape the extent to which different professional and technical occupations are able to gain improved social status, including: the nature of the knowledge and skills required to perform the work; the system for entering and practicing in the occupation (certification and licensing); and the nature of employment relations in the occupation. Though part of the social status of people in traditional professions is linked to the specialized knowledge they have, how access to that knowledge is socially organized is also critical. The truly high-status occupations are those which are able to organize themselves to limit the supply of skills and knowledge. Doctors, for example, monopolize not only their practice of medicine, but their licenses and the sale of medical drugs by legal prescriptions. If medical knowledge were not so strongly monopolized, the prestige and rewards of doctors would be much less. Thus, the formation of a monopolistic practitioner group has historically been a central component of occupations gaining professional status. These groups are able to determine the nature of knowledge required for the occupation, formally certify those who are fit to practice, and limit practice to those who have been appropriately certified. In semi-professions, however, it is much harder to create a truly monopolistic practitioner group and thus more difficult to raise the status of members of the occupation through this strategy. As a result,

30. See Charles Derber, *Professionals as Workers: Mental Labor in Advanced Capitalism* (Boston, MA, 1982); Charles Derber et al., *Power in the Highest Degree: Professionals and the Rise of a New Mandarin Order* (New York, 1990).

31. See David Riccardi, "LA County Doctors Vote Decisively to Unionize", *Los Angeles Times* (29 May 1999), p. A1; Emily Yellin, "American Medical Association to Form a Physician's Union: Some Doctors See Relief in Plan to AMA Union; Others Call Move an Inadequate Solution", *New York Times* (25 May 1999), p. A18.

professional associations in these occupations tend to be more decentralized and democratic, placing less emphasis on the certification of their members and more emphasis on actively intervening in the labor market on behalf of their members.[32]

Thus, contemporary guild initiatives in Silicon Valley can be thought of as efforts to organize professional associations in semi-professional occupations, but in information-technology-related occupations that have particular characteristics that shape their ability to increase their members' economic and social status, along with their power in the labor market. The power of these information-technology workers is rooted in their capacity to cope with rapidly changing technology and to deal with uncertainty – to tame the "computers in the wild". This kind of power, however, is clearly less tangible than institutional bases in truly self-regulating professions, rooted in a monopolistic practitioner group. Information-technology workers derive considerable status from being associated with cutting-edge technological and economic change, but at the same time they are constantly being market-tested for the relevance of their skills, and the organizational problems they claim to be able to solve.[33] Ultimately, the ability of mid-level workers in information-technology industries to attain and retain their high status in the labor market requires dealing with rapid change. It requires the ability to stay on top of industry trends and changing skill demands, to find access to multiple employment opportunities when needed, and to build career mobility over time across multiple organizational contexts. Workers in these occupations solve these problems of maintaining the market relevance of their skills by taking advantage of networks of information exchange in communities of workers who share similar types of expertise. Groups of users become resources for each other in maintaining knowledge about skills that are in demand. As a result, the guilds and occupational associations that have emerged in these occupations tend to be more decentralized and democratic, placing less emphasis on the certification of their members and more emphasis on actively intervening in the labor market on behalf of their members. These associations rarely focus on licensing or certifying members, or otherwise restricting access to the occupation. Instead, they focus on networking, providing various services to their members, and helping their membership anticipate and capitalize on changing industry trends. To do this requires building closer ties with employers than traditional professional associations (in which

32. Randall Collins, "Changing Conceptions in the Sociology of the Professions", in Rolf Torstendahl and Michael Burrage (eds), *The Formation of Professions: Knowledge, State and Strategy* (London, 1990), pp. 11–23.
33. Robin Fincham, "Introduction: Problems and Perspectives for the Organised Professions", in *idem* (ed.), *New Relationships in the Organised Professions* (Aldershot, 1996), pp. 1–18.

members are often self-employed) and frequently providing placement services for their members.

These associations also recognize that their members are by-and-large in employment situations where they are being paid by an employer, rather than being self-employed. They thus also have various activities and services aimed at strengthening their members' ability to negotiate a strong contract for themselves. In so doing, they also begin to converge with important new directions in the labor movement and union organizing strategies, which have been increasingly focusing on occupationally based organizing. Examining the reasons for the growth and development of this new unionism also provides important insights into the potential of these guild efforts to become more effective.

CHANGING UNION STRUCTURES AND NEW UNIONISM

Unions obviously have a long history, while the dominant form of unionism has changed and their relative strength has ebbed and flowed over time. Prior to the 1920s, craft unions and less formal, community-based unions played the greatest role in representing workers' interests. Craft-based unions in many occupations were able to set standards of fair rates that their members individually demanded from their employers. Community-based unions, such as the Knights of Labor and the IWW, had a broad social-movement character, building on community solidarity to defend workers' interests across a broad spectrum of industries.[34] Since the 1930s, however, industrial unionism has become the dominant form of unionism in this country. This model emerged out of the organizing strategies of the Congress of Industrial Organizations in the 1920s and 1930s, and became embodied in labor legislation with the 1935 Wagner Act. Organizing in the core of the growing mass production enterprises, workers in the CIO argued the importance of representation on an industry-wide basis, with collective bargaining carried out between company leaders and leaders of appropriate unions. At the core of this strategy is organizing based on long-term stable employment with a single employer who largely controls the conditions of employment. Workers and their unions agreed in practice to negotiate primarily over issues of compensation and work practices, leaving to company management the larger, more strategic issues of corporate investment, technological development, and other issues of competitive concern in the market.

Collective bargaining in this model, especially as it became entrenched into labor law, is based on individual worksites or with single employers.

---

34. See David Montgomery, *The Fall of the House of Labor: The Workplace, the State, and American Labor Activism, 1865–1925* (Cambridge, [etc.], 1987); Charles Craver, *Can Unions Survive? The Rejuvenation of the American Labor Movement* (New York, 1993).

This structure of representation worked fairly well in large manufacturing industries, where a majority of workers were organized. Pattern bargaining amongst unionized firms, along with efforts of nonunion firms to match union compensation packages (partly in order to avoid unionization), meant that, in practice, workers were often represented similarly across whole industries. Stable markets in mass-production enterprises, and well-developed internal labor markets that existed in many firms, provided a solid support for union structures.

As the economy has changed, however, with more service-sector employment and higher levels of volatility, uncertainty, complex networking, and outsourcing production arrangements, representation that is based on a single work-site or single employer has proven increasingly inadequate for defending workers' interests. For workers who move frequently from employer to employer, or whose working conditions are not primarily determined by a single employer (such as temporary workers, and many workers in subcontracting relationships), there are few opportunities in the current industrial-relations system for adequate representation. As a result, unions now represent less than 10 per cent of the private-sector workforce.

In recent years, however, the union movement has been experimenting with a range of innovations that extend beyond bargaining over wages and working conditions in a single enterprise, to becoming involved in issues of labor supply, labor quality, placement, and career advancement. The initiatives include alliances with employers and community groups, as well as other unions. They can focus on strengthening internal career ladders, as well as creating new external career ladders within an industry and across industries, expanding labor involvement in job matching as well as the design and delivery of training.[35] In many ways, these initiatives are similar to the structure of unions in construction trades, where hiring halls and apprenticeship training programs have been common for many years. In industries where "project-based" employment is the norm, such as in the television and movie production industry, an active intermediary role for unions is accepted practice.[36] The fact that these initiatives are emerging in other industries, however, indicates the growing recognition amongst unions that standard industrial-model unionism is no longer adequate for

35. See Laura Dresser *et al.*, *Rebuilding Job Access and Career Advancement Systems in the New Economy*, Center on Wisconsin Strategy Briefing Paper (Madison, WI, 1997); Stephen Herzenberg *et al.*, *New Rules for a New Economy: Employment and Opportunity in Postindustrial America* (Ithaca, NY, 1998); Eric Parker *et al.*, "Building the High Road in Metro Areas: Sectoral Training and Employment Projects", in Lowell Turner, Harry Katz, and Richard Hurd (eds), *Rekindling the Movement: Labor's Quest for Relevance in the 21st Century* (Ithaca, NY, 2001), pp. 256–273.
36. Lois Gray *et al.*, *Under the Stars: Essays on Labor Relations in Arts and Entertainment* (Ithaca, NY, 1996).

addressing the labor market concerns of a wide range of the American workforce. This has led to increased interest in models of occupation-based associations as potential alternatives.

This trend is clearly evident in Silicon Valley. Of the guild-like initiatives described here, three of them are directly linked with unions: the Technical Writers' Trade group, the Graphic Artists' Guild, and the Working Partnerships Membership Association. All three initiatives are trying to build power for workers in the absence of collective bargaining, through a variety of methods. This new model of unionism involves more of a focus on career development through training, services, and advocacy efforts. The organizational cohesion is rooted in specific occupational communities, primarily rooted in the regional labor market. The Working Partnerships Membership Association is particularly significant in that it is trying to build a similar organizational model for a group of workers (temporary clerical workers) who lack many of the technical skills and occupational cohesion that holds together the other guilds and occupational associations. This initiative started in the last 1990s, and is still too young to evaluate fully, but it shows interesting promise.

It is clear that occupational associations are not nearly as powerful in their ability to impact employment conditions as traditional unions operating in the context of a collective bargaining agreement. Nonetheless, in the absence of such an agreement and in the context of volatile, rapidly changing labor market, such occupationally based associations can clearly be important support for workers. This is particularly true in occupations with significant technical skills, but as the case of Working Partnerships demonstrates, it may also be relevant for a significantly wider group of workers as well. Furthermore, if such occupational associations are linked with the broader union movement, creating alliances with the stronger unions operating in more traditional industries and in the public sector, their ability to significant impact employment conditions through advocacy efforts and political intervention would be greatly increased.

Most of the guild initiatives in Silicon Valley have no involvement with the formal union movement in the Valley. They have grown independently, focused primarily on the needs of their own membership, and not envisioning themselves as part of a broader labor movement. This is largely due, however, to their impression of unions as inflexible organizations limited to collective bargaining in the public sector and traditional industries. The significant gap between these guilds and the formal labor movement seems to be shrinking in recent years, as the local labor movement in Silicon Valley has provided prominent leaders in a string of non-traditional activities, ranging from advocating for universal children's health insurance, to improved transportation systems, to more accountable redevelopment initiatives. The AFL-CIO Central Labor Council has begun approaching a number of these guild initiatives to become associate members of the council, and in the process trying to develop more effective advocacy efforts that can address the needs of the guild membership. While still in its infancy, such efforts do suggest that there may be significant room for strengthening guild efforts through building closer ties with the stronger union movement.

CONCLUSIONS: LESSONS FOR A COLLECTIVE REPRESENTATION IN THE NEW ECONOMY?

In comparing the activities of contemporary guilds in Silicon Valley with the experiences of medieval guilds, and with professional associations and new unionism, as a model of collective mobilizing, certain strengths and weaknesses become clear. The weaknesses are most readily apparent. Contemporary Silicon Valley guilds lack significant influence in the arenas of power that medieval guilds were able to exercise, including controlling labor supply and regulating the market for their products and services. Similarly, they lack the ability to create a monopolistic practitioners' groups, which is a critical basis of power for true professional associations. Likewise, without the protection of a collective bargaining agreement, as in a traditional union context, the power of these guilds to influence employer behavior and protect their wages and working conditions are severely limited.

Nonetheless, it is also clear that these guilds do have certain strengths that provide important benefits to their members. They help improve their members bargaining position vis-à-vis their employers, by providing advice and training in their individual negotiations, and by engaging in broad advocacy initiatives. They help their members improve their employment prospects, by improving access to new jobs and career opportunities. Perhaps most importantly, they provide an important learning infrastructure, helping their members increase their own skills and learning opportunities over time. In the environment of rapid change and volatility that characterizes the information-based economy of Silicon Valley, it is this ability to help their members deal with rapid change that is most critical. Furthermore, because employers gain from the improved skills of guild members, it is likely that these guilds and occupational associations will continue to be significant in the regional labor market and perhaps grow. The incremental, informal, and cross-firm character of the learning communities that these guilds help create are valuable and fill a role in the regional production complex that both formal training programs and worksite-based learning cannot fill.

This role in building strong learning communities also highlights the broader significance of these Silicon Valley case studies. The information revolution is resulting in a growing proportion of people in the United States working in occupations with characteristics similar to those in which these Silicon Valley guilds have emerged. Whether referred to as "symbolic analysts",[37] semi- and highly-autonomous workers,[38] or knowledge-workers,[39] an increasing number of people are working in jobs that require a combination of technical skills, practical work experience, and a significant amount of independent decision making. When this is combined with a high-degree of nonfirm specific knowledge, and volatile employment conditions, guilds can likely provide important assistance to a wide number of people.

If such guild initiatives are to play a more significant role in influencing labor market conditions, however, they cannot remain isolated in their small occupational niches. Having a broader impact on working conditions will require building broader alliances and engaging in more significant political advocacy efforts. To date, signs of such a broader perspective are minimal. Nonetheless, there do exist important convergences between these guild initiatives and the new occupation-based organizing efforts of the labor movement – convergences that are rooted in the changing structure of work and employment in the information economy. This suggests that guild-like structures are likely to continue to grow and potentially become an important component of a broader set of initiatives aimed at improving workers' livelihoods.

---

37. Robert B. Reich, *The Work of Nations: Preparing Ourselves for 21st-Century Capitalism* (New York, 1991).
38. Herzenberg, *New Rules for a New Economy*.
39. Burton-Jones, *Knowledge Capitalism*.

IRSH 48 (2003), Supplement, pp. 205–223 DOI: 10.1017/S0020859003001329
© 2003 Internationaal Instituut voor Sociale Geschiedenis

Emerging Sources of Labor on the Internet: The Case of America Online Volunteers

HECTOR POSTIGO

INTRODUCTION

In 1995 AOL announced that it would be converting its pricing plan from an hourly rate that ranged from $3 to $6 an hour to a flat monthly rate of $15.95. The increase in member subscription was expected to be significant, and a wave of concern swept through the large remote-staff volunteer population, whose duties included monitoring electronic bulletin boards, hosting chat-rooms, enforcing the Terms of Service agreement (TOS), guiding AOL users through the online community, and even creating content using the AOL's own program, RAINMAN (Remote Automated Information Manager), the text scripting language and the publishing tool that allows remote staffers to update and change content on AOL. Chief among remote-staff volunteer's concerns was the initiative to convert many of the volunteer accounts from overhead accounts, which had access to tools and privileges that made remote-staff volunteers' duties on par with in-house employees, to unbilled or discounted accounts. In a meeting meant to address the emerging concerns of remote-staff volunteers held over electronic chat, Bob Marean, a representative for AOL, confronted over 450 remote-staff volunteers. One of those present described events at the meeting as follows:

> [...] we were all upset [...] I am even pointing to myself and saying "Guide Strike". All of a sudden, Guide Strike becomes a reality. As we are talking about it, we become serious. There were ten [guides] [...] I drafted a letter encouraging all guides to strike. Guide USN [the screen name of another guide] was in the row with us. He had already tendered his resignation and he volunteered to send the letter. [...] Nothing happened for a few days. AOL released me from the guide program. I got a letter when I signed on for a shift and I was given seven days to delete my screen name [...]. They never told me why I was fired, just that I was released from the program.[1]

Other guides involved in the attempted "strike" were let go as well. Some were told that their behavior during the meeting violated their TOS

---

1. Unknown author, interview, "Former Guide RRP's Story". Available at http://www.observers.net/guiderrp.html; last accessed November 2002.

agreement, while others were never given any reasons. Some were allowed to return but only after mandatory "behavioral training [...] and a three to six month probation".[2]

Postindustrialism and the Internet have come together to draw value from cultural labor produced on the Internet; the case of AOL will show that management practices seeking to control the work process have helped define volunteers as workers. This is the central irony of the volunteer's story. In response to the increase in member numbers and a lone lawsuit filed by ex-volunteer Errol Trobee for back wages, AOL tried to restructure the remote-staff volunteer organization to gain control over it, and by so doing AOL positioned some of its volunteers to see themselves as employees.[3] This article draws from the sociological literature that explains the postindustrial shift and situates emergent forms of work within the technologies of postindustrialism. Historically, this article situates the AOL volunteers as part of the hobbyists and volunteers that have traditionally been part of the rise of the information commu-nication technologies, generally, and the Internet specifically.[4]

---

2. *Ibid.*

3. It is important to note that this paper discusses two lawsuits for back wages against AOL. The first lawsuit filed by Trobee in 1995 is part of what influenced AOL to change its relationship with its volunteers. The second suit was filed by Kelley Hallisey *et al.* in 1999, and is a class-action lawsuit following the changes made by AOL to the volunteer organization.

4. Here, it is worth noting that the primary data reviewed for this piece was gathered in the archives of www.observers.net, an organization founded by a number of ex-volunteers, some of whom are suing AOL for back wages. This fact poses some problems concerning the primary data since the archives cannot be cross-referenced against another source. Potentially, this may bias the data in favor of viewing AOL volunteers as workers. However, since the primary data present in the Observers website is not generate by AOL volunteers or ex-volunteers alone but also contains internal documents leaked to the press, interviews with management, chat logs with management leaked on the Net, and a collection of glossaries that help the user in navigating the AOL communities, it is possible to generate a thorough picture of the volunteer experience at AOL from the point of view of management and as well as volunteers. While it is true that this is a single archive, the fact remains that this is the only public archive that holds records of AOL's dealings with its volunteers. Because of ongoing litigation, other potential sources remain inaccessible. For example, at AOL's request, the court documents for an ongoing lawsuit filed by ex-volunteers under the Fair Labor Standards Act remain sealed, and the plaintiffs and defendants in the case are no longer commenting on the case. Complicating matters further is the common practice of many members of Internet communities not to use their real names; this, combined with the gagging order issued by the court, prevents us from knowing the identities of many of the principle players in this story. Where possible, I have supplemented accounts of events or analyses of the story of AOL volunteers with corroborating commentary from media and news sources and an interview I conducted with the lead plaintiff in the class-action lawsuit prior to the court's order. Unfortunately, these limitations are part and parcel of the study of distributed Internet communities taking shape in recent history. We should note, however, that media coverage of the events concerning AOL volunteers and management's commentary, also reported on by media sources, strongly support the story of AOL volunteers as it evolves in the archives of www.observers.net, and therefore I remain confident the these sources can generate a complete story of the experience of those volunteers who chose to see themselves as employees.

AOL AND ITS VOLUNTEERS

The "Guide Strike" or "The Row 800 Incident", discussed above, represents a turning point in the relationship between AOL and its volunteers. Quantum Computer Services, as AOL was known prior to 1989, was founded to provide Internet service to early personal computer users. AOL negotiated exclusive deals with Commodore Corporation, Tandy Corporation, and Apple Computers to provide Internet service for users of the Commodore 64, the Deskmate, and the Apple II respectively. Subsequently, Quantum changed its name to America Online and combined all of its online services under the AOL trademark, expanding its user base to any personal computer user with a modem. When it entered the Internet-service-provider business, AOL had approximately 75,000 users that it had attracted through its partnership with Apple, Tandy, and Commodore. By the early 1990s volunteers were an integral part of AOL's community and did much work to establish content and help new members. In the early days of AOL, the company never specifically set out to create a volunteer organization but it welcomed the fact that the communities could maintain themselves through the work of volunteers.[5]

The relationship between AOL and its volunteers in the early 1990s had been established under the influence of the early Internet community spirit present in other Internet communities, such as Howard Rheingold's Whole Earth 'Lectronic Link (WELL)[6] and the various Usenet groups of hobbyists and information enthusiasts engaging in what has been described by some observers as a gift economy of information exchange.[7] Volunteers that maintain communities on the Internet have been around since the Internet's early years; however Netizen's giving of their time and energy has its true roots in the hacker history that was an essential component of the formation of the Internet. The idea of freely giving up one's time and knowledge is rooted in the academic, collaborative efforts that shaped the Internet as a project for the United States Defense Department's Advanced Research Projects Agency (ARPA). Many of the early Internet and software pioneers believed in working for the pleasure of tinkering and for the reputation they derived from coming up with innovative solutions to technical problems. They engaged much of their work with a passionate zeal that has come to by immortalized in Steven

5. Kara Swisher, *AOL.Com: How Steve Case Beat Bill Gates, Nailed the Netheads, and Made Millions in the War for the Web* (New York, 1998).
6. Howard Rheingold, *The Virtual Community*, available at http://www.rheingold.com/vc/book/; last accessed November 2002.
7. Richard Barbrook, "The High-Tech Gift Economy", available at http://www.firstmonday.org/issues/issue3_12/barbrook/index.html; last accessed November 2002.

Levy's "hacker ethic".[8] Combined with aspects of 1960s communitarian ideology, the Internet became infused with a collaborative ethos where commodification and sale were not the primary concern. William Gates Jr, for example, enraged early Netizens by suggesting that users should pay for his Altair Basic. As will be discussed later, this was not the only force influencing volunteers to contribute their time. By the time AOL started to become an important player on the Internet, the hype surrounding computers and their business potential began to surface. Thus, many volunteers became involved with the Internet to acquire the increasingly valuable computer capital that they hoped would propel them to better lives.[9]

The collaborative ethic that surrounded the early Internet involved both hardware and software. The work of Paul Cerruzi on the early electronics hobbyists is especially relevant as an example of work on the hardware side of hacking. As the microprocessor made its transition to the personal computer, Ceruzzi suggests, the electronics hobbyist had already set up a support network that "neither the minicomputer companies had or the chip makers could provide".[10] Thus, when personal computer makers began to release their wares, they had a "tech-support" department already waiting for them in the form of electronics magazines aimed at providing technical advice and hardware.

AOL volunteers are direct descendants of the early Internet contributors that played such a significant role in the rise of the Internet and computing. AOL volunteers in many ways represent those early collaborators as they have come to confront the commodification of the Internet. Many AOL volunteers still wax romantic about the early days of the AOL community. According to them, the structure of the AOL community was relatively simple. Those first joiners of AOL were given "charter member accounts" and a reduced service rate for the length of their stay. The initial work that volunteers did for AOL was to help other members learn how to navigate and interact in the community. The volunteer designations included hosts for those hosting online chat-rooms, bulletin board monitors, and guides. Guides were the most experienced

---

8. In Steven Levy, *Hackers: Heroes of the Computer Revolution* (Garden City, NY, 1984), Levy coins the term "hacker ethic", which he describes as composed of the following six tenets: "(1) Access to computers – and anything that might teach you about the way the world works – should be unlimited and total. Always yield to the Hands-On Imperative. (2) All information should be free. (3) Mistrust Authority – Promote Decentralization. (4) Hackers should be judged by their hacking, not bogus criteria such as degrees, age, race, or position. (5) You can create art and beauty on a computer. (6) Computers can change your life for the better."
9. For more on this history see Janet Abbate, *Inventing the Internet* (Cambridge, MA, 2000), Katie Hafner and Matthew Lyon, *Where Wizards Stay Up Late: The Origins of the Internet* (New York, 1996), and Douglas Thomas, *Hacker Culture* (Minneapolis, MN, 2001).
10. Paul Ceruzzi, "Inventing Personal Computing", in Donald MacKenzie and Judy Wajcman (eds), *The Social Shaping of Technology*, 2nd edn (Buckingham, 1999), p. 71.

volunteers, and were the staffers given access to overhead accounts and the associated tools, employee areas, and the power to enforce the TOS agreement. Members became volunteers by being recommended by other volunteers, the training was informal, and they were not generally organized under any central division within the AOL organization. Volunteers were given two hours credit time for every hour they volunteered and were able to "bank" those hours for future use. Many who became volunteers did so because they had been spending thousands of dollars on monthly service fees, and exchanging work for time on the system was a way to keep the bills down.[11] Still others logged on and became volunteers because they believed that AOL would provide them with the needed computer experience to be employable in the emerging tech-economy or even by AOL. Kelly Hallisey, a volunteer since the early 1990s, recalls explaining to her husband why she stayed online for such long hours, "We were having major arguments over it [staying on line] and I said, 'You know [...] this is the way things are going to go, I can see this turning into a really good paying job."[12] Still others felt compelled to volunteer by the "community" spirit they encountered on AOL, and thus many of the accounts of why remote staffers volunteered so many hours are permeated with references to "online families" and go so far as to create a kinship system based on mentor/mentored relationships. The mentor would be considered the mother or father of the mentored volunteer, and the grandparents were the mentor's mentors.[13] This sense of "family" was not only created as a marketing tactic by AOL but existed and was propagated among some volunteers in the very early days of the "community".

AOL was wildly successful at marketing its online services, primarily because of a central vision articulated by Steve Case that crafted the services as facilitators of communication, not as a sales service, such as the services of CompuServe, a chief competitor, came to be viewed. Thus, for the company, online chat, e-mail, and bulletin boards were its main form of content early on. "Chat was a compelling form of content that the cash-poor AOL did not even have to pay for. With thousands of people chattering away nightly, AOL subscribers could entertain themselves", wrote a Wall Street reporter when commenting on AOL strategy.[14] Even in the name it gave its volunteers, AOL implicitly expressed the value of the type of relationship it had with early volunteers helping to create content. They were called "remote staff", with no designation separating

11. Unknown author, interview, "Interview with Guide Tom D", available at www.observers. net; last accessed November 2002.

12. Hector Postigo, phone interview with Kelly Hallisey, 15 February 1999.

13. Unknown author, interview, "Reflections of a Guide", available at http://www.observers. net/fxguide3.html; last accessed November 2002.

14. Swisher, *AOL.Com*, p. 94.

them from the remote staff that were paid for their services. Some remote-staff volunteers saw their relationship to AOL as a work relationship even in this early period, primarily because they felt that in exchange for services they were getting significant savings in online-provider costs. One remote-staff volunteer, upon learning that AOL would be converting to a flat service fee and that guides might be required to pay a discounted monthly fee, stated,

> Yeah, I'll guide for $3.95 a month if they only make us work one shift [...]. I'm a teacher and it warms the cockles of my heart when I look into a kid's face and see that he "gets it" [...] but I sure as hell wouldn't keep going to work each day if I wasn't getting paid.[15]

By mid-1995 tensions developed between AOL and its volunteers, even before the switch to a flat rate later that year. The primary causes of emerging tensions were an already-increasing membership and a lawsuit filed by an ex-volunteer, both of which culminated in a reorganization of the volunteer groups. The volunteers had already started voicing their concerns that they could not handle the volume of members frequenting chat-rooms and bulletin boards, and that therefore many were going unattended. To accommodate the rise in members, AOL had taken in more volunteers to begin filling in where current volunteers could not. This irritated current volunteers, because their once small community began to see large increases in numbers. Some complained that they no longer recognized those in the volunteer community, and others chafed at having to admit new members who had not been recommended, as was the tradition. The element of elitism in this scenario is easy to spot: along with volunteering came certain powers that admittedly some volunteers were not willing to share. Additional tension came from AOL's change in attitude. Since, at that time, the volunteers were not clearly organized under any one internal division, AOL now realized that it had little control over how volunteers were representing AOL in the various public forums. As one manager put it, "There was this sudden light-bulb moment where they [management] said, 'Oh, my God, we have thousands of people out there acting as our representative, and we don't even know who they are'."[16] This prompted AOL to begin restructuring in order to get a handle on the activities of its volunteers.

An even more important catalyst for reorganization was ex-volunteer Errol Trobee's decision to sue AOL for the value of the "banked" hours he had earned prior to his release. As stated earlier, AOL volunteers, under the hourly-pricing plan, could earn two free hours for every hour they

15. Chat log, "Log of Row 800 Incident", available at www.observers.net/row800.html; last accessed November 2002.
16. Robert Grove *et al.*, "The People vs America Online", *Forbes ASAP*, available at http://www.forbes.com/asap/2001/0219/060.html; last accessed June 2002.

volunteered. Trobee demanded less than $600 for his work and claimed that, under the technical definition within AOL's own employee handbook, he was an employee. Trobee was able to produce a manual given to volunteers that proved to the court that he could be classified as an employee. AOL was forced to settle the lawsuit to avoid facing charges of violating labor law. The lawsuit jarred AOL management, who commissioned an internal analysis of the company's relationship with its volunteers. Following the study, an internal memo written by AOL counsel John Gardiner stated, "Notwithstanding AOL's classification and structure, there are [sufficient] elements of an employer/employee relationship between AOL and the remote staff to warrant internal review of the relationship and appropriate action by AOL."[17] Gardiner suggested three options for AOL: first, that AOL restructure the relationship to be more consistent with that of an independent contractor relationship; however, Gardiner suggested that such restructuring would compromise AOL's ability to control the volunteers. Second, he suggested that AOL completely outsource the remote staff to a third party; however, the third party should not be a proxy or shell, since this would not relieve AOL of its employer responsibilities. And thirdly, he suggested that AOL hire the remote staff outright.[18]

Reorganizing the volunteers: what's in a name?

In retrospect, it is clear that AOL chose two of the three options presented by Gardiner. As Bob Marean, a manager for AOL, fielded questions about the new pricing plan for monthly services and the restructuring of the volunteer relationships, AOL was preparing to hire some of the volunteers. It also decided to create a proxy organization, AOL Communities Incorporated (ACI), to handle the volunteers as well as to serve as a source of temporary employees. The volunteers would no longer be called remote staff but community leaders and would be housed in the Community Leader Organization (CLO) managed by ACI. AOL chose not to give more control over content and community management to the volunteers; rather, it placed control over communities and content production more squarely in the hands of the company. AOL did this in a number of ways.

Firstly, the dissolution of overhead accounts took away some volunteers' ability to design content for AOL. To many of the volunteers this was seen as a deskilling process. With access to RAINMAN, volunteers not only had the ability to change content, but could also attain the kinds

17. John D. Gardiner, "Summary of Legal Issues and Options Related to Remote Staff", available at www.observers.net/oalmemo.html; last accessed November 2002.
18. *Ibid.*

of programming skills that they felt made them viable for future employment. Many suggested that without access to RAINMAN they essentially became TOSCops (Terms of Service enforcers).[19] Furthermore, the CLO required that volunteers serve one to two three-hour shifts per week to remain in the Community Leader Program (CLP). This practice was in place prior to the formation of the CLO but now became centralized and enforceable through a single management entity.

The CLP was not only composed of volunteers: at certain levels volunteers and ACI employees were working together. And there seemed to be much speculation as to who was getting paid for the work they were doing. Many felt that teams were composed of both volunteers and paid staff. One area of the new organization was of particular concern to those volunteering as guides. The Community Online Support Team (COST) within the CLO was composed of four teams of volunteers, guides, people connection hosts, road trip hosts and rangers. The management team at the level of COST (coordinating the four COST teams) was clearly ACI paid staff, yet many speculated that at the level of team managers, those actually managing guides or rangers, there was a mix of paid and volunteer staff.[20] When one guide tried to request a list of who was paid and who was not paid within a certain team, her request was denied. She describes her frustration as follows:

> I wanted to know who'd been paid [...] so I put in my request for who had been [...] promised paychecks and who was receiving paychecks. They refused to answer that [...] now why refuse to answer that [...], and you know people that were paid that were management from my area refused to answer the question, but all of a sudden I started getting jumped on by these other people and I know for a fact that three out of four of those other people got paychecks [...]. I understand it's a corporation and it has a right to make money but I think even a corporation has to have some sense of morals and what is proper behavior [...] it's very underhanded.[21]

For this particular volunteer it was necessary to know who was paid on her team, because she had also been promised a paycheck when the transition to ACI took place. This silence created a level of division among the volunteers and also made it more difficult for individuals to demand payment.

Other policies implemented by management at this time also became disruptive to the community of volunteers. One such policy involved a

19. Unknown author, interview, "Interview with Guide Tom D".
20. Unknown author, "Response 2", available at www.observers.net/response2.html; unknown author, interview, "Reflections of a Guide", available at www.observers.net/fxguide3.html; unknown author, "AOL Glossary", available at www.observers.net/index/glossary.html: Observers.net; and Hector Postigo, phone interview with Kelly Hallisey, 15 February 2001. Websites last accessed November 2002.
21. *Ibid.*

"Names and Initials" folder posted to the community leader forum, the Community Leader Headquarters (CLHQ). The folder itself was a repository of screen names that current volunteers used when not on a shift. Thus, it was possible for volunteers to browse through this folder and see when a fellow volunteer was in a chat area under his or her "play-name". That way other volunteers would be able to recognize them and engage them in conversation about work without fear of violating their nondisclosure agreement. The official use for the folder was so that some employees and specific volunteers would be able to update carbon copy lists for e-mailing purposes. But since access was not restricted to only those volunteers with an official use, other volunteers appropriated the list for their own social purposes. However, in a letter to staff, one of the ACI COST managers informed the community leaders that access to the "Names and Initials" folder would be restricted to only those who had an officially sanctioned reason. The community leaders responded with a series of e-mails and postings protesting the restriction.

The primary reason for the protest was that if a community leader was released from the program, as was often the case during this period, then the remaining volunteers would have no way of knowing that person had left. The "fired" community leaders would, as one volunteer put it, "[slip] into the night, quietly".[22] CLHQ did have at this time a "Goodbye" folder which departing community leaders could post to when they left; however, this folder was only available to those who left voluntarily. Community leaders who had been let go by AOL would usually get an e-mail when they logged on to AOL informing them that their access to places like the CLHQ had been terminated; therefore, unless they contacted other community leaders via another method, there was no way for these released community leader to address the community-leader population in general. Before losing access to the "Names and Initials" folder, community leaders could check for the "play-names" of individuals they had not seen in a while and inquire about their status. Now that level of access was gone. Some community leaders were quick to speculate that this was a form of damage control, since it was known among them that those volunteers who criticized AOL while in "uniform" (a term referring to being logged on with a name that identified the user as a volunteer, such a GuideRRP or HostAtom) were often removed from service.[23]

22. Unknown author, forum log, "Inside AOL Guide Program Pt. 2", available at www.observers.net/response2.html; last accessed November 2002.
23. Almost every log and interview reviewed for this article, including those posted from internal AOL sources, mentioned this point. These include "Inside AOL Guide Program Pt 2", "Interview with Guide Tom D", "Reflections of a Guide", "Former Guide RRP's Story", and unknown author, interview, "Interview with HostAtom", available at http://www.observers. net/host_atom.html; last accessed November 2002. See also Robert Ablon, "Was America Online Out of Line?", *New Jersey Law Journal* (4 December 1995).

Community leaders complained bitterly that this change would disrupt their means of communicating, but management proceeded with the change anyway. The results of this particular act of restructuring are an immediately obvious and salient example of what Lawrence Lessig meant when he said that in cyberspace "code is the law".[24] By simply changing the access permissions to the "Names and Initials" folder, management easily made it much more difficult for volunteers to communicate with potentially dissenting members.

The incident concerning the "Names and Initials" folder is of particular interest because it brought out much of the frustration the community leaders were feeling with management. Among other things, this incident was a disruption to the sense of community within the volunteer group and was emblematic of the process by which some community leaders began to see themselves as employees. One particular post put it in these terms: "Frankly I admit that there are times where I feel like we volunteers are now work in cubicles, where before it was an auditorium."[25] Yet this was not the only outcome of the "Names and Initials" incident. What also surfaced was the declaration of a general fear among some community leaders that speaking out against changes would have repercussions. During the exchange over the folder, some of the community leaders confided that they normally did not talk about their feelings of demoralization as a result of the structural changes because of fears that they would be released, or because they generally found management inattentive to their concerns.[26] The rift that was present at this juncture in the history of the CLO contrasts dramatically with the stories recounted by some community leaders of the early days of AOL.

Things did not seem to be going smoothly for the management of the CLO either. Management seems to have been under pressure to keep the community leaders in line and out of litigation as the restructuring occurred. As one manager put it, "The mantra that came down from on high was, 'Keep them [volunteers] out of the newspapers, out of the courtrooms, and get as much out of them as you can'."[27] To this end, some volunteers were consistently promised paying jobs that were continuously moved out of reach.[28] One particular guide, for example, was promised a job as a RAINMAN programmer and waited from January of 1998 until April of that year to get his first check.[29] When it eventually came, it was for a lower pay-scale and only covered part of the time he had worked; the

---

24. Lawrence Lessig, *Code: And Other Laws of Cyberspace* (New York, 1999).
25. "Inside AOL Guide Program Pt. 2".
26. *Ibid.*
27. Grove *et al*, "The People vs America Online".
28. Unknown author, interview, "Interview with Guide 29", available at www.observers.net/g29.html; last accessed November 2002.
29. "Former Guide RRP's Story."

remainder of the time he had worked was still considered volunteered time. The volunteers were not AOL's first priority, and even some members of management found themselves in tough positions concerning the community leaders. An ACI manager, responding to this particular guide's complaints, wrote:

> ACI staff and community leaders "were out of site out of mind" to most AOL employees [...]. Frequently, VPs with budgetary responsibility deferred decision-making regarding ACI, and on some occasions reversed decisions after the results of ensuing policies were already being implemented. This caused those of us managing ACI to go back on promises we had made based on approvals we had in hand from our VPs. My whole experience with ACI was painful [...]. I did not want to be in a position of managing people who I treated as colleagues but who the company treated as second class citizens.[30]

As the ACI structured the CLO, it also initiated a program called "member empowerment". The thrust of that initiative was to make the member experience as free from volunteer intervention as possible. Prior to the restructuring process, members who had been hacked or were being harassed in a chat-room or via instant message could contact a guide to either "nudge" the offending member (gently inform him or her of the Terms of Service contract and of proper online etiquette) or remove the offender altogether. Under the member empowerment program any TOS action (an action that resulted in expelling a member for violation of TOS) was highly discouraged, and members were encouraged to contact the TOS department themselves via e-mail. According to guides working the chat-rooms and in the TOS department, these e-mails went largely unanswered unless the violation was so egregious that the TOS mailbox was flooded.[31] The guides most affected saw their positions further compromised. First they had lost the overhead accounts with access to RAINMAN and bankable hours, and now they could do very little except corroborate the complaints about the offending behavior of a member and hope that enough members complained. Many guides saw this as an attempt by AOL to boost their member base by simply not enforcing the TOS agreement.

All told, the restructuring of the volunteer program at AOL after 1996 resulted in AOL having a much greater degree of control over what the community leaders did and how they interacted online, especially those serving as guides. Guides now had to adhere to minimum shift requirements, engage in the corporate bureaucracy when they needed to act against a member, enter a structured two-week training session, fill out

---

30. *Ibid.*
31. See "Interview with Guide Tom D"; unknown author, interview, "Inside AOL Guide Program Pt. 1", available at www.observers.net/response1.html (last accessed November 2002); and "Interview with Guide 29".

extensive shift reports, and deal with a management that increasingly appeared to be unresponsive to their needs. AOL accomplished all of this by setting up ACI as the organizing proxy for its volunteers, and it managed to get a hold on its content by taking a larger role in the activities of community leaders. AOL, however, had inadvertently ignored Gardiner's recommendations: the proxy organization did not seem to create enough space between AOL and its volunteers, and by taking such an active role in the work volunteers did, AOL may have contributed to volunteers appearing more like employees should the court apply the law's Right to Control test for determining employment relationships. "The Right to Control test focuses on a factual determination of whether the employer controls principle aspects of the individual's work efforts."[32] These include "(1) amount of training; (2) set work hours; (3) oral or written reports required; (4) order of work set and significant investment by the worker."[33] By 1999, as many of the CLO's changes became entrenched, various community leaders began to see their volunteerism in a different light.

The volunteers today

It's clear that not all community leaders were dissatisfied with the turn that volunteering for AOL took, following the creation of ACI and the CLO. The majority, in fact, were either silent on the matter or echoed one community leader's sentiment, "I knew I was volunteering and what the work would be and the benefits would be. It was still my choice to do so. If I wanted to be an employee of AOL, I would apply for one of those positions [...] I got what I bargained for."[34] Yet, the few that did change their attitudes about AOL did so in a dramatic fashion: To them, AOL was no longer a family affair but an exploitative relationship, no longer fun but drudgery.

When, in 1999, a group of ex-volunteers filed a class-action lawsuit against AOL under the Fair Labor Standards Act, most had been released from service for allegedly criticizing the CLO. When asked to list reasons why they were willing to work such long hours for so long and only now chose to file a grievance, they invariably recounted stories of community and of feeling good about their volunteer work. While there is little doubt that many did volunteer for the altruistic rewards, many came to AOL with other expectations. Some thought that volunteering would be a springboard to employment in a lucrative Internet company; others

---

32. Gardiner, *Summary of Legal Issues and Options Related to Remote Staff.*
33. *Ibid.*
34. Unknown author, "Fighting the Truth, Kicking and Screaming", available at www.observers.net; last accessed November 2002.

wanted to gain experience with computers; and still others simply wanted a price break on the hourly rates that were driving their service bill beyond their budgets. As their expectations failed them, the reorganization process positioned some of the volunteers to begin reassessing the meaning of volunteering and community at AOL. Whether as a means of revenge or as a means of empowering themselves against organizational and institutional forces that took from them work they valued, these few ex-volunteers chose to reconstitute themselves as employees and began viewing community as a commodity.

Kelly Hallisey is one of the lead plaintiffs in the 1999 lawsuit. Following her release from AOL, she joined a group of ex-guides and founded Observers.net, a website dedicated to critiquing AOL's business practices. From Observers.net, Hallisey launched her lawsuit for back wages and gathered much media attention for her role as an ex-guide. The lawsuit contends that AOL volunteers are employees of the company, and that AOL is in violation of the Fair Labor Standard Act because it failed to classify it's 15,000 volunteers as employees and pay them a federal minimum wage. Should Hallisey win this case, it would dramatically restructure the way AOL, and any other portal that uses volunteers to maintain its technical and social infrastructure, does business. Today, community leaders who are suing AOL readily recognize their role in the production process for community, and make direct links between their work and the profits garnered by AOL. The ex-volunteers have a long road ahead of them, because they must convince the court and their many critics that community production online is no mere hobby or leisure activity, but an organized process yielding a valued commodity. If they succeed, the value of what they do will no longer be hidden under the rhetoric of hobby or leisure. As they engage in this next phase of defining themselves as workers, the story of AOL volunteers becomes a story of occupational formation.

DISCUSSION

The large socio-economic changes of the past thirty years are of significant importance to an analysis of unwaged labor on the Internet, because they create the context within which such activities as forming and supporting community, volunteering, and pursuing hobbies can be tapped as a source of revenue. Tiziana Terranova first put forth the thesis that unwaged labor on the Internet is an aspect of the postindustrial economy in an article entitled "Free Labor: Producing Culture for the Digital Economy".[35] My paper, first and foremost, adds to that work by investigating examples

---

35. Tiziana Terranova, "Free Labor: Producing Culture for the Digital Economy", *Social Text*, 18 (2000), pp. 33–57.

originally pointed out by her. While her work convincingly situated the phenomenon within the context of postindustrial society, it did not explain how the labor-exploitative relationship developed specifically between free-content providers and commercial interests, such as AOL.

In her analysis, Terranova identifies the emerging phenomenon of unwaged labor on the Internet as an extension of an ongoing project of cultural appropriation and commodification. She borrows from the Italian autonomist analysis of late capitalism the concept of the social factory, which "describes the process whereby 'work processes have shifted from the factory to society'",[36] and uses it to explain both the harnessing of "Netizens'" work by corporations, and the giving and "channeling" of such work, freely, by "Netizens" themselves. Taken collectively, the work of volunteers, content makers, website posters, and all others who add content to the World Wide Web constitute a "network of immaterial labor", comprised of a collective intelligence that is the self-organized, principle productive force of the digital economy. "Capital's problem", Terranova states, "is how to extract as much value as possible",[37] from this collective.

Terranova is correct in her analysis of the relationship between post-Fordist production and the cultural production on the Internet. David Harvey, in *The Condition of Postmodernity*, points out the emergence, since 1973, of a new productive regime from the aftermath of the economic failures of Fordist production. In the wake of the devastation of the world's industrial centers following World War II, America stood alone as the single industrial giant from the 1950s until the early 1970s. During this period, America's economy underwent a Golden Age, driven by Fordist production processes, goods, and patterns of consumption. The Fordist model relied upon the mass consumption of mass-produced products. Within this model, various sectors of society came together to form a total regime of capitalist accumulation dependent on the state, the consumer, and the laborer.

Signs of a crisis in this regime of accumulation began as European and Japanese reconstruction reached completion. Increasing levels of competition destabilized the Fordist regime that had been built out of investments on rigid, fixed capital infrastructures presupposing "stable growth and invariant consumer markets".[38] Flexible accumulation emerged as a new regime after 1973. Organizational structures became more fluid, with the emergence of outsourced and flex-time labor markets. The flexible production process of the post-Fordist state depends on constant

36. *Ibid.*, p. 33.
37. *Ibid.*, p. 46.
38. David Harvey, *The Condition of Postmodernity: An Enquiry into the Origins of Cultural Change* (Oxford, 1990), p. 142.

innovation and product development driving fast-paced markets and competition. Under flexible accumulation, businesses employ their flexibility to stay ahead of their competition, and consumption is dependent on rapid turnover of goods. Goods such as software, computers, and other technologies, whose production is driven by rapid and continuous innovation and short market life, have become staples of the new consumption. Generally then, production patterns have shifted toward the production of knowledge goods and services.

As David Harvey points out, the economy could not be sustained by flexible accumulation if consumption had not been restructured as well, primarily by the cultural forces of the "fleeting qualities of the post-modernist aesthetic that celebrates difference, ephemerality, spectacle, fashion and the commodification of cultural forms".[39] The ephemeral nature of today's jobs can hide labor in the context of leisure. In the case of the Internet, this labor is always in plain site (we see the wealth of information on the Web) yet those who do the work of generating and maintaining the Web remain hidden away under the rhetoric of volunteer-ism or hobby. Terranova tries to get at that "hiddenness", and explains it as a complex relationship between cultural production, or the social factory, and the technologies and methodologies of postindustrialism.

Ultimately, however, I part ways with Terranova over her analysis of individuals within this technological/economic vortex; in her desire to explain the nature of unwaged labor and its relation to the broad historical shifts of postindustrialism, she too quickly dismisses the AOL volunteers and other content producers. When discussing AOL volunteers, she writes, "Out of 15,000 volunteers only a handful turned against it", and suggests that they work for "the excitement and dubious promises of digital work". Portraying them so powerlessly leads to a hopeless vision of what these "hidden workers"[40] may accomplish. While some may have come to AOL in hopes of attaining what Joe Sullivan has called computer capital,[41] that "dubious promise", this alone cannot disqualify them from earning a wage, especially if they so directly contribute to the success of a company like AOL. Furthermore, when Terranova wrote her analysis in 1999, it is true that only a "handful" had turned against AOL by filing a

39. *Ibid.*, p. 156.
40. Here, I mean hidden in the way Greg Downey suggests when he writes "Labor is crucial not just in setting up internetworks but in operating them as well. This kind of ongoing, flexible labor is hard to see. Indeed the very advantage of constructing an information network can be that the commodification of the virtual serves to mystify the material"; Greg Downey, "Virtual Webs, Physical Technologies, and Hidden Workers: The Spaces of Labor in Information Networks", *Technology and Culture*, 42 (2001), pp. 209–235, 224.
41. Joseph Sullivan, "Understanding Computerization: Sociological Concepts for a Phenom-enological Approach", (paper presented at the 1999 Meetings of the Eastern Sociological Society), p. 26.

lawsuit, but many more were frequenting sites such as Observers.net, posting stories about their fallout with AOL. In 2002, the number of volunteers filing suit has increased and lawsuits have cropped up in California and New Jersey, as well as in New York State. One cannot dismiss such attempts at recognition now. AOL thought its volunteers were contributing to its content as a form of leisure, but today these contributors no longer seem like passive "cultural producers" in an economy that extracts value from them while they passively continue to produce it.

Staking out an occupation

The transition of AOL community leaders from volunteers to workers is one mediated by both self-reconfigurations and responses to institutional changes. In a sense, the case of AOL community leaders is a classic study of the process by which an occupation is born from unpaid work. At an early level of development, an occupation lacks the institutional and social recognition that helps the early "occupational pioneers" convince society that they are worthy of compensation. The problem is compounded when the services they provide are tasks that are generally perceived to be the work of families and communities, or hobbies and leisure. At the core of this difficulty are ideological perceptions of the relationships between those who do care-taking work, such as creating communities, the service itself, and the recipients of the service.

One way of better understanding how these ideological perceptions came about is to look at women's labor history. In response to the rapid growth of capitalism during the nineteenth century, there was a growing apprehension of the sale of labor power to strangers.[42] This preoccupation, even obsession, as Nancy Folbre has called it, lead to the prevalent antebellum concept of gender spheres, which designated maintenance of the home and the associated housework as a woman's sphere. The notion of gender spheres suggested that, through women's self sacrifice and altruism, civilization would be saved from the evils of emerging materialistic capitalism. Jeanne Boydston further explains how this concept became entrenched in the popular consciousness by describing how "ideology of spheres" gained a foothold through prescriptive literature and romanticism. Ultimately, women's housework disappeared in the popular consciousness as a form of labor by being romanticized, "pastoralized" as she puts it, into a form of leisure. Boydston writes:

> The metaphors of ideology were transformed into the data of behavior. With no loss of prescriptive power – indeed, with the enhancement that arises from the

42. Nancy Folbre, *The Invisible Heart: Economics and Family Values* (New York, 2001).

immediacy of lived experience – the symbolic assumed the garb of daily experience [...]. As romantic narrative played against lived experience, the labor and economic value of housework ceased to exist in the culture of Antebellum Northeast. It became work's opposite: a new form of leisure.[43]

Community making, as an extension of family maintenance, falls under the influence of the same type of rhetoric that "pastoralized" women's housework. American society continues to see volunteer work of the kind that generates and maintains communities (both on and offline) as market inalienable, as a noble and altruistic pursuit, even as companies like AOL commodify community.

In the case of community making, community as a commodity requires a degree of de-pastoralization. AOL volunteers must force a reconceptualization of community making as no longer altruistic or an act of familial responsibility, but rather as a commercial service. They must also force a reconceptualization of the relations between the service providers and recipients. That shift must reconfigure service relations compelled by family and community ties to a relationship compelled by employment and contract. The community leaders involved in the AOL lawsuit have started thinking of their work along these lines. They recognize community as a commodity and understand the key role it played in the making of AOL. One community leader put this way: "We were creating community, community which is what they [AOL] sell themselves as."[44] Ultimately, the volunteers' lawsuit is an attempt at forcing a new understanding of community making.

While the case of AOL community leaders itself follows the pattern of previous groups' attempts to stake out new occupational territory, recognition is not certain. Unlike other groups attempting to make similar transitions, AOL volunteers lack much institutional support. AOL refused its volunteers access to its content-creation tools when it became clear that AOL did not have control over content production. In addition, by renaming the volunteers from remote staff to community leaders, AOL moved out of reach much of the institutional rhetoric that would have helped volunteers shape themselves as being involved in the occupation of community making. Comparatively, other volunteer groups that did make the transition to an occupation had considerable institutional support. Take for example the volunteer IBM user group "Share", founded by IBM and some of its customers to develop applications for IBM mainframes. Participation in the Share group was on a volunteer basis, but it is clear that the group had at its disposal considerable resources to help establish programming as an occupation. While working on developing applications

---

43. Jeanne Boydston, *Home and Work: Housework, Wages, and the Ideology of Labor in the Early Republic* (New York, 1990).
44. Hector Postigo, interview with Kelly Hallisey, 15 February 2001.

for IBM hardware, it was the availability of resources, such as access to the company's computer centers, and the support of supervisors, that made occupational formation possible.[45] Ultimately Share programmers did not stake out their occupational claims through the formation of professional societies and other tactics typical of occupational formation,[46] but rather through a process of interaction with their large institutional "customers".

Apart from ideological and institutional hurdles, volunteers engaged in community making online, must ironically transcend their own history. As stated earlier, community making online has its roots in hacker culture, and its tradition of free information exchange. AOL community leaders hoping to recategorize themselves must transcend the history that has defined them as volunteers and hobbyists. Howard Rheingold in *The Virtual Community*, for example, is most often cited as the spokesperson for understanding online communities. Rooted in the counterculture of the 1960s, online communities have been described by Rheingold in romanticized and ideal terms. The work of Pekka Himanen, Eric Raymond, Peter Wayner, and others involved in the open-source movement has also presented hacking and community making in idealized terms by giving production of software and content online the aura of the "gift economy".

CONCLUSIONS

The process of value production on the net continues to be hidden. Even as the class action lawsuit against AOL goes to court, many content producers and volunteers in other venues continue their work. Certainly they have chosen this path, and one does not wish to patronize them with claims of false consciousness. Their reasons for contributing are their own. Some truly find it rewarding, and that is payment enough. But for those who feel cheated by the experience, perhaps the course that the AOL volunteers have taken is appropriate. Such a course does not seem easy, however, and it comes about through painful realizations about prior conceptions of contributions to an idealized Internet. For the AOL community leaders who eventually filed a lawsuit, it was a process marked with a sense of loss of the promises that the Internet seemed to hold. Community turned out to be for sale and the AOL "family" turned out to be alienating as the membership grew. While a "self-organizing",

---

45. Atsushi Akera, "Voluntarism and the Fruits of Collaboration", *Technology and Culture*, 42 (2001), pp. 710–736.
46. Examples of these tactics include "linking practice to formal knowledge, teaching recruits, acquiring rights to self-discipline, and securing legal authority to license and credential practitioners"; Bonalyn Nelsen and Stephen Barley, "For Love or Money? Commodification and the Construction of an Occupational Mandate", *Administrative Science Quarterly*, 42 (1997), pp. 619–653.

harnessable labor force may be a postindustrial dream come true for corporations, it also proves to be intractable. Attempts to bend the collective intelligence of the Internet to the will of corporate organization withers its versatility and its willingness to continue to contribute to the social factory. In that case, businesses like AOL seem to be facing a double bind. They need the kind of dynamism that spontaneous cultural production and organization engender, yet they must avoid the alienating control structures that often have to be established to operate multibillion-dollar media conglomerates.

The course that the AOL volunteers have chosen seeks to grasp the "ephemerality" of cultural production, a project made all the more difficult by the historical baggage that work such as community making seems to carry. It is further complicated by the ironic trends within Internet history that situated production within a gift economy. Staking out an occupational claim is tricky business, because it opens AOL up to a new host of exploitative practices, such as outsourcing, a process made all the easier by the nature of ICTs and globalization. Ultimately, however, the AOL volunteers represent an example, small as it may be, of the possibility of breaking out of the "social factory" and making visible the new sources of value in an emerging media world.

IRSH 48 (2003), Supplement, pp. 225–261 DOI: 10.1017/S0020859003001330
© 2003 Internationaal Instituut voor Sociale Geschiedenis

Commentary: The Place of Labor in the History of Information-Technology Revolutions

GREG DOWNEY

INTRODUCTION

As co-editor of this *IRSH* supplement "Uncovering Labour in Information Revolutions", I have to begin this commentary with a confession. Before I entered the world of abstract knowledge production, commodification, and consumption known as academia, I was myself a worker in a world of much more concrete information processing: I was a computer programmer in the US from the mid-1980s to the mid-1990s, a time we might now consider the nostalgic heyday of desktop-office information technology (IT).[1] In the spirit of full disclosure, before I leap into an analysis of how we might more broadly conceptualize information technology together with information labor in different historical contexts, I have decided to work through my own historical narrative a bit. After all, if historical practice teaches us nothing else, it teaches that each of us makes sense of the world through the lens of personal experience, leaving historians (among others) with the daunting task of interpreting, translating, and finding patterns of meaning in those experiences. Thus I offer this candid admission: "I was a teenage information worker!"

And I really was a teen. I began my own IT labors in the early 1980s, not as a producer but as a consumer – buying a home computer and accessories while still in secondary school, and supplementing my lack of in-school exposure to technology with how-to books, so that I could move myself from "computer literacy" to "computer programming". Following the examples I saw in hobbyist magazines, I wrote half a dozen BASIC programs which I then submitted for publication (sadly, all were rejected). Although on one hand I was pursuing valued, high-tech production skills

---

1. For simplicity's sake, I'm using the shorthand "information technology" to stand in for a set of tools, algorithms, and infrastructures which might more accurately (but not completely) be described as "information production, storage, communication, and processing technology". In other words, the "revolution" is in the way technology enables (and sometimes compels) humans to manipulate, conceptualize, and value information in new ways, whether that information is being transmitted or transported, produced or consumed, stored or processed.

– fully endorsed by my middle-class parents and my public-school educators – on the other hand I was happily engaged in a nascent consumption community of "geek chic" which remains crucially important to the PC industry today.

I continued this consumption after secondary school through an increasingly prevalent form of technical education (masked as academic education) combined with contingent labor (masked as apprenticeship): I was a computer-science major at a large US public university during the school year, and a "summer intern" at various arms of the US military-industrial-academic complex in the summer. One of these summers, due to a labor strike at a defense-contracting aerospace plant where I was working, I was pulled from my 9-to-5, first-shift office job – sitting in front of a computer terminal, cleaning up FORTRAN programs – and placed into a 3-to-11 second-shift factory job, instead – this time standing in front of a computer terminal, manually relaying machine parts that were automatically supplied to me from a robotic rack storage system into the correct little boxes on a passing conveyor belt. I had moved, for a short time, from the white-collar realm of "informatization" to the blue-collar realm of "automation."

Finally, after university, I wove a professional IT career of my own through the US information industry: first as an in-house "analyst" within a large advertising agency, helping multinational consumer-products firms efficiently buy time in increasingly fragmented global mass media; and later as an in-house "programmer" within a small research laboratory, claiming to bridge the gap between psychology, education, and machine intelligence for the benefit of military and corporate training. At the advertising agency, the technical division of labor was coupled with an organizational division of labor: in-house analysts were trained to act (toward other employees) as a sort of outside consulting firm; however, we were valued (by management) precisely because we held secret knowledge about the firm and could supposedly build better IT systems faster than an outside contractor. At the research lab, on the other hand, the technical division of labor ran hand in hand with a social division of labor: programmers (who coded knowledge using programming languages) were almost entirely male, and "indexers" (who coded knowledge using representational languages) were almost entirely female. But male or female, we were nearly all under the age of thirty, and were expected to either quit of our own accord or apply to the lab's spin-off, for-profit consulting company at some point before our job tenure grew too long. Thus did this IT worker, exposed by now to the military and the corporate, the white-collar and the blue-collar, the contingent and the professional aspects of software labor, finally decide to abandon his high-tech career altogether and pursue instead the academic analysis of technology in society. (Well, only after realizing that the 100 résumés I had sent to new,

stock-option-laden "dot-com" companies in Silicon Valley hadn't generated a single response. As I said, full disclosure.)

Today, in my academic capacity, I am still an information worker. I am
paid (quite generously, really) to read and research, to teach and Web-surf,
to "publish or perish". In the course of my labors, I consume information,
I organize information, I communicate information (the old-fashioned
word is "teaching"), and if all goes well, I produce information. As an
employee of a large US public university, my salary is paid by a historically
shifting combination of taxpayer funds, federal grants, student-tuition
dollars, and intellectual property royalties. My position is expected to
serve a variety of political-economic goals: building curious, informed, and
media-savvy citizens; imparting employer-demanded job skills to new
labor force entrants; and enhancing the "competitiveness" of my city, state,
region, and nation. Yet I continue to believe, somehow, that I am
motivated in this complex situation mainly by the noble pursuit of truth.

So in writing this essay I am vexed with the personal question: do I now,
or did I ever, qualify as "information labor" in any sort of useful analytical,
structural, or even Marxian sense? Surely my story is not representative of
any sort of universal education or career experience through the IT
revolution. And perhaps all my story really does is help to explain (though
not to excuse) the rather severe bias in what follows toward recent IT
history, toward computerized IT labor, toward IT as it has been
experienced in the US context, and toward the experience of rather
privileged actors within that context. Yet, I am struck by the fact that my
personal history maps quite well with the tripartite division of information
labor proposed by Aad Blok in the introduction to this volume: (1) labor in
producing and reproducing information infrastructures; (2) labor in
producing the information which exists in and through these infrastructures; and (3) labor of other sorts which is irrevocably changed through the
application of information and its infrastructures. I think we each need to
use such personal stories to ask: during moments of profound technological change, how can historians bring individual, contingent, anecdotal
histories into wider frameworks? How might we finally begin to define
"the labor history of the information technology revolution"?

DEFINING INFORMATION-TECHNOLOGY REVOLUTIONS

For something said to be so far-reaching, so transformative, and so
unprecedented as this information-technology revolution, it might come
as a surprise to anyone except historians that there are few if any agreed-
upon frameworks for conceptualizing, periodizing, explaining, and
evaluating that revolution (if in fact "revolution" is the proper term at
all). Though the Internet and World Wide Web occupy much of our
discussion today – the Pew Internet and American Life Project has

counted that, in the US, some 37 per cent of all full-time workers (and 18 per cent of part-time workers) are now equipped with Internet access in their workplace – few would limit the IT revolution to the early 1990s combination of CERN's HTML protocols and the NCSA's free browser software that so soon spawned new definitions of social processes like "e-commerce" and "digital divides".[2]

Many assume instead that the latest IT revolution began some time in the mid-1970s, mainly in the US, with the application of microprocessors to a new category of small calculating machines first called "home computers" but later renamed "personal computers" (PCs) as they moved out of the home and into the office.[3] This marking of the IT revolution is attractive since it seems to correspond with the oft-cited date of 1973 as the herald of a societal shift from "modernity" to "postmodernity".[4] Quite a few social scientists – from geographers and sociologists to economists and even "futurists" – have pointed to this shift as involving new ways of applying information to global capitalist accumulation: the intensified application of knowledge to production, the increased use of communications to coordinate production at a distance, and the growth of a nonmaterial sector of the productive economy based on services and spectacles rather than on goods and materials. The result is often a new geography of capitalism, whether at the scale of a "megalopolis" or a "new industrial state".[5] For example, Manuel Castells has argued for conceptualizing an "informational society", writing that even though "information, in its broadest sense, e.g. as communication of knowledge, has been critical in all societies", today we are witnessing "a specific form of social organization in which information generation, processing, and transmission become the fundamental sources of productivity and power, because of new technological conditions emerging in this historical period".[6]

2. Pew Internet and American Life Project, http://www.pewinternet.org, last accessed 3 September 2000); Janet Abbate, *Inventing the Internet* (Cambridge, MA, 1999); Tim Berners-Lee with Mark Fischetti, *Weaving the Web: The Original Design and Ultimate Destiny of the World Wide Web by its Inventor* (San Francisco, CA, 2000).

3. Ted Nelson, *The Home Computer Revolution* (South Bend, IN, 1977); Paul Freiberger and Michael Swaine, *Fire in the Valley: The Making of the Personal Computer*, 2nd edn (New York, 1999); Steven Levy, *Hackers: The Heroes of the Computer Revolution*, updated edn (New York, 2001).

4. David Harvey, *The Condition of Postmodernity: An Enquiry into the Origins of Cultural Change* (Cambridge, MA, 1989). Others push this date back into the 1960s or even 1950s, e.g. Fredric Jameson, *Postmodernism, or the Cultural Logic of Late Capitalism* (London, 1991).

5. Jean Gottmann, *Megalopolis: The Urbanized Northeastern Seaboard of the United States* (Cambridge, MA, 1961); John Kenneth Galbraith, *The New Industrial State* (New York, 1967); Daniel Bell, *The Coming of Post-Industrial Society: A Venture in Social Forecasting* (New York, 1973); Robert B. Reich, *The Work of Nations: Preparing Ourselves for 21st Century Capitalism* (New York, 1992).

6. Manuel Castells, *The Rise of the Network Society*, vol. 1 of *The Information Age: Economy, Society and Culture* (New York, 1996), p. 21, n. 33.

Castells went on to tie this new society, a geography at the scale of the "space of flows", directly to the technologies of the PC era.

Yet such claims aren't unique to our own historical period. Others trace the key IT revolution not to personal computers but to what we might call "organizational computers", the transistor-powered "glass-house" corporate mainframes of the 1950s and 1960s.[7] If we abandon computers entirely, we can point instead to early advances in electromechanical punched-card data processing and typewritten record keeping, beginning with the Gilded Age firm.[8] This date can be pushed back further still, for example to the 1840s birth of electromagnetic communication-at-a-distance in the first working telegraphs in the US and Britain.[9] Even defining the start of the information-technology age in terms of non-electrical knowledge production techniques is no less valid (and has spawned a cottage industry of research all its own).[10]

Of course, we historians expect claims of "revolution" to be full of ambiguity and debate; our careers turn on our ability to define and defend change as either evolutionary or revolutionary, expected or surprising, universal or time- and place-specific. The technological transition commonly known today as the "second industrial revolution", involving electrical power, industrial chemistry, and fossil-fuel combustion around the turn of the twentieth century, also inspired a crisis of historical reperiodization, from Lewis Mumford's "eotechnic, paleotechnic, and neotechnic" ages to Stephen Kern's assertion that these new technologies ushered in a "crisis of abundance".[11]

Furthermore, there are plenty of good reasons to believe that other forces, which cannot be reduced to the effects of information technology, are at play in dialectical motion with our current IT revolution. For example, much of the affluent industrial world has for the last two decades been governed under an increasingly powerful ideology of neoliberalism

---

7. James W. Cortada, "Progenitors of the Information Age: The Development of Chips and Computers", in Alfred D. Chandler, Jr and James W. Cortada (eds), *A Nation Transformed by Information: How Information Has Shaped the United States from Colonial Times to the Present* (Oxford, 2000), pp. 177–216.

8. JoAnne Yates, "Business Use of Information and Technology during the Industrial Age", in Chandler and Cortada, *A Nation Transformed by Information*, pp. 107–136.

9. Richard R. John, "Recasting the Information Infrastructure for the Industrial Age", in *ibid.*, pp. 55–106.

10. Daniel Headrick, *When Information Came of Age: Technologies of Knowledge in the Age of Reason and Revolution, 1700–1859* (Oxford, 2002); Michael E. Hobart and Zachary S. Schiffman, *Information Ages: Literacy, Numeracy, and the Computer Revolution* (Baltimore, MD, 2000); Asa Briggs and Peter Burke, *A Social History of the Media: From Gutenberg to the Internet* (Oxford, 2001); Peter Burke, *A Social History of Knowledge: From Gutenberg to Diderot* (Cambridge, 2000).

11. Lewis Mumford, *Technics and Civilization* (San Diego, CA, 1934); Stephen Kern, *The Culture of Time and Space: 1880–1918* (Cambridge, MA, 1983).

or, as geographers Jamie Peck and Adam Tickell describe it, "a commitment to the extension of markets and logics of competitiveness [combined] with a profound antipathy to all kinds of Keynesian and/or collectivist strategies".[12] These governance strategies of privatization, "deregulation" (inevitably followed by reregulation), and market liberalization, when combined with global computer-mediated communications networks, may indeed herald a new form of "digital capitalism" as Dan Schiller has argued.[13] Similar cases might be made for macro-processes of globalization, urbanization, and even, perhaps, democratization.

But others point out that, regardless of intervening forces, the IT revolution does not represent a fundamental change in the global capitalist economy. In the UK, geographers Ash Amin, Doreen Massey, and Nigel Thrift countered the government-sanctioned "Rogers Report" vision of twenty-first century informational cities by arguing that "the urban economic mainstream – in and beyond the knowledge economy – will continue to require traditional resources such as caterers, cleaners, tangible goods, part-time and seasonal work, and age-old means of communication".[14] Even one of the most vocal advocates of recent IT in popular culture, cyberpunk novelist, Bruce Sterling, has viewed our current notions of living through "revolutionary" times as quaint: "The Radio Age, the Aviation Age, the Atomic Age, the Space Age [...] all of these so-called 'ages' are history. Soon our much-trumpeted 'Information Age' will have that same archaic ring", to the degree that "what is called new media would be better described as temporary media".[15] If we can't even agree that our own times are revolutionary, how can we hope to make similar judgements about history?

CONSIDERING THE PLACE OF LABOR IN IT REVOLUTIONS

I think the greatest challenge in first periodizing, then describing, and finally analyzing information revolutions is that in the case of information technology, the moment of labor required for technological innovation has received the most attention, but the moments of labor dealing with technological production, distribution, and daily use have consistently been overlooked.

For example, historian of technology, Thomas Hughes, created a

12. Jamie Peck and Adam Tickell, "Neoliberalizing Space", *Antipode*, 34 (2002), pp. 380–404.
13. Dan Schiller, *Digital Capitalism: Networking the Global Market System* (Cambridge, MA, 1999).
14. Ash Amin, Doreen Massey, and Nigel Thrift, *Cities for the Many, Not the Few* (Bristol, 2000).
15. Bruce Sterling, "The Digital Revolution in Retrospect", *Communications of the ACM*, 40 (1997), p. 79.

framework for understanding US technological history in particular by referring to entrepreneurial "system-builders" like Thomas Edison and Elmer Sperry: historical actors who combine engineering expertise with management insight to build profitable and pervasive technological infrastructures.[16] In the twentieth century, such an explanation of historical change is often tied into the military-industrial-academic complex (the production of ENIAC, SAGE, and ARPANET come to mind).[17] Even in the nineteenth century this framework can be deployed: one can explain the innovation of the telegraph by analyzing the system-building efforts of either individual entrepreneurs (Samuel Morse, Royal House, Alfred Bain) or corporate entities (Magnetic Telegraph, Western Union, AT&T). Yet if one studies instead the labor of telegraph operators, one can see that important innovation took place on a daily basis in the space of the local office as well as in the space of the central electrical shop, not by professional engineers but by operators "on the key".[18]

Innovation does not only occur in the production of technology, however; often the consumers of technologies must innovate as well, especially business consumers who are using technology to gain a competitive edge in the capitalist marketplace. Here again, technology purchasers and managers are studied more readily than less powerful technology users, under a historical practice which turns its eye to the "visible hand" of corporate management under capitalism.[19] This framework continues to be applied to a myriad of information technologies in the office workplace, both in the US and in Europe.[20] But even the most well-executed "scientific office management" strategies rarely work as planned, and studies of those who labor under such systems can reveal the social innovations which often accompany technical ones.[21] As Sharon Hartman Strom argued, "without an expanded army of clerks, managers, and business professionals, modern economic and government organization would have been impossible", since "an office hierarchy based on class and gender produced the paperwork, bookkeeping, and managerial

---

16. Thomas P. Hughes, "Machines, Megamachines, and Systems", in Stephen H. Cutcliffe and Robert C. Post (eds), *In Context: History and the History of Technology* (Bethlehem, PA, 1989), pp. 106–119.
17. Thomas P. Hughes, *Rescuing Prometheus* (New York, 1998).
18. Paul Israel, *From Machine Shop to Industrial Laboratory: Telegraphy and the Changing Context of American Invention, 1830–1920* (Baltimore, MD, 1992).
19. Alfred D. Chandler, Jr, *The Visible Hand: The Managerial Revolution in American Business* (Cambridge, MA, 1977).
20. Richard L. Nolan, "Information Technology Management since 1960", in Chandler and Cortada, *A Nation Transformed by Information*, pp. 217–256; Onno de Wit, Jan van den Ende, Johan Schot, and Ellen van Oost, "Innovation Junctions: Office Technologies in The Netherlands, 1880–1980", *Technology and Culture*, 43 (2002), pp. 50–72.
21. William H. Leffingwell, *Scientific Office Management* (Chicago, IL, 1917).

expertise that propelled the machinery of scientific management and the integration of economic functions", a machinery and integration too easily ascribed to a management administrative revolution.[22]

Studies of how labor is involved in IT innovation illustrate an important point: it is the very ability of information technology to help us redefine the temporal and spatial parameters of our social existence that makes this kind of technology (and the times in which it exists) "revolutionary". We might think in terms of the "time-space distanciation" which Anthony Giddens has ascribed to modernity – the ability to act at a distance using formalized social and technical arrangements.[23] Or we might consider the "time-space compression" which David Harvey has offered as a hallmark of postmodernity – the inability to act in isolation given the increasing spatial and temporal interdependence of different local sites, again through formalized political-economic and technical infrastructures.[24] Either way, seeing IT revolutions as revolutions in social time and social space is a crucial (and productive) analytical strategy, revealing the production of a "fractured geography" that human and economic geographers have only begun to explore.[25] But only when combined with the creative, productive, and ongoing presence of human labor (itself always situated in space and time) can information technologies – or, really, any technologies at all – have such a transformative effect upon human society.

DIFFERENT UNITS OF ANALYSIS WITHIN IT REVOLUTIONS

One of the arguments I have tried to make in my own research is that the need to analyze the place of labor in this "revolution of time and space" is all the more pressing because labor is, almost by definition, the least obvious aspect of the information technology revolution to analyze.[26] Simply put, labor is too often overshadowed by alternative units of analysis – the "information" or the "technology".

For example, ever since mathematical theorists Alan Turing, Claude Shannon, and Norbert Wiener operationalized concepts of "computability", "signal/noise", and "cybernetics" in the early twentieth century, the standard unit of analysis in IT revolutions has been taken to be

---

22. Sharon Hartman Strom, *Beyond the Typewriter: Gender, Class, and the Origins of Modern American Office Work, 1900–1930* (Urbana, IL, 1992).

23. Anthony Giddens, *The Consequences of Modernity* (Stanford, CA, 1990).

24. Harvey, *Condition of Postmodernity*.

25. James O. Wheeler, Yuko Aoyama, and Barney Warf (eds), *Cities in the Telecommunications Age: The Fracturing of Geographies* (New York, 2000).

26. Greg Downey, "Virtual Webs, Physical Technologies, and Hidden Workers: The Spaces of Labor in Information Internetworks", *Technology and Culture*, 42 (2001), pp. 209–235.

"information".[27] Indeed, although the "information science" of cybernetics has not proven to be the universal paradigm shift that its proponents once hoped, "information studies" has instead emerged to pursue the social concerns surrounding how information is organized and retrieved, commodified and consumed. Lively debates over electronic copyright, digital libraries, and online privacy may be found in this research stream.[28] But while historians have followed social information through its life in "print culture", cultural-studies scholars are the ones primarily analyzing cyberspace as a hypertextual "virtual culture".[29]

How might labor be incorporated into such a focus? If the unit of analysis remains information itself, we might ask how information is brought to bear in the unequal relations between political-economic actors – not just the relationship between labor and capital, but competitive relations between individual laborers and cooperative relationships within labor organizing as well. Information in the form of propaganda and advertising has long been a tool by which capital has attempted to control its external environment, and information channels with labor are embodied both in corporate newsletters and factory reading rooms.[30] As authors in the *Journal of Labor Research* and elsewhere have noted, labor's information exchange in the service of collective action faces both promises and risks in an environment of instantaneous but perhaps impersonal e-mail.[31] And since information about job openings is crucial to waged labor, as new IT infrastructures supplant personal word of mouth, new divides in the labor market may be opening.[32] But while such issues are gaining the attention of sociologists, economists, geographers, and activists, synthesizing historical studies of these phenomena are hard to find.

27. Alan Turing, "On Computable Numbers, with an Application to the *Entscheidungsproblem*", *Proceedings of the London Mathematical Society*, series 2, 42 (1936–1937), pp. 230–265; Claude Shannon, "The Mathematical Theory of Communication", *Bell System Technical Journal* (July and October 1948); repr. in Claude Shannon and Warren Weaver, *The Mathematical Theory of Communication* (Urbana, IL, 1949); Norbert Wiener, *Cybernetics, or Control and Communication in the Animal and the Machine*, 2nd edn (Cambridge, MA, 1961 [1948]).
28. Lawrence Lessig, *Code and Other Laws of Cyberspace* (New York, 1999); Christine Borgman, *From Gutenberg to the Global Information Infrastructure: Access to Information in the Networked World* (Cambridge, MA, 2000).
29. Adrian Johns, *The Nature of the Book: Print and Knowledge in the Making* (Chicago, IL, 1998); James P. Danky and Wayne A. Wiegand (eds), *Print Culture in a Diverse America* (Urbana, IL, 1998); Steven G. Jones (ed.), *Virtual Culture: Identity and Communication in Cybersociety* (Thousand Oaks, CA, 1997).
30. Stuart D. Brandes, *American Welfare Capitalism, 1880–1940* (Chicago, IL, 1976).
31. *Journal of Labor Research*, special issue on IT and unions (Spring, 2002); Eric Lee, *The Labour Movement and the Internet: The New Internationalism* (London [etc.], 1997).
32. Susan Hanson, "Reconceptualizing Accessibility", in Donald G. Janelle and David C. Hodge (eds), *Information, Place, and Cyberspace: Issues in Accessibility* (New York, 2000), pp. 267–278.

Most recent historical studies of IT have, in fact, followed a different unit of analysis than information, echoing Marshall McLuhan's famous 1964 declaration that "the medium is the message".[33] Around this time, new "historians of technology" began to suspect that perhaps the proper unit of analysis in technological revolutions should be the technology itself.[34] Here the questions revolve around how technology is devised, commodified, and consumed in society; historical "household diffusion" and "social effects" studies, such as Claude Fischer's *America Calling*, are legion for any information technology we might identify, from the telephone and the radio to the television and the personal computer.[35] In some places, such as the journal *Technology and Culture*, authors have uncovered fascinating cases where IT laborers have been hidden from the historical record.[36] But too often with IT, studies still record only the actors of innovation and/or the actors of consumption, leaving laborers out entirely.

Here again, though, we could certainly incorporate labor into a technology-based focus. We might ask not who devises and markets information technologies, but who produces and reproduces them on a daily basis? What kind of service labor knits these technologies together into systems, networks, or even internetworks? And what kind of technical labor keeps increasingly complex technologies functioning on round-the-clock schedules? For example, the UK journal *New Technology, Work, and Employment* has in the last few years offered a forum for the discussion of IT and labor in contexts as diverse as welding, commercial broadcasting, and telephone call-centers.[37] But adapting such sociological studies to historical contexts still proves elusive.

In each of these two ways of slicing the IT revolution – in terms of information or in terms of technology – labor lurks as a hidden unit of analysis. Information itself can be defined as the commodified surplus of centuries of labor. Technology has been alternately defined as the tool

33. Marshall McLuhan, *Understanding Media: The Extensions of Man* (New York, 1964).
34. John Staudenmaier, *Technology's Storytellers: Reweaving the Human Fabric* (Cambridge, 1985).
35. Claude S. Fischer, *America Calling: A Social History of the Telephone to 1940* (Berkeley, CA, 1992).
36. Jennifer S. Light, "When Computers Were Women", *Technology and Culture*, 40 (1999), pp. 455–483; Richard Lindstrom, "'They All Believe They Are Undiscovered Mary Pickfords': Workers, Photography, and Scientific Management", *Technology and Culture*, 41 (2000), pp. 725–751.
37. A. Mutch, "The Impact of Information Technology on 'Traditional' Occupations: The Case of Welding", *New Technology, Work and Employment*, 13 (1998), pp. 140–149; A. McKinlay and B. Quinn, "Management, Technology and Work in Commercial Broadcasting, c.1979–98", *New Technology, Work and Employment*, 14 (1999), pp. 2–17; V. Belt, R. Richardson, and J. Webster, "Women, Social Skill and Interactive Service Work in Telephone Call Centres", *New Technology, Work and Employment*, 17 (2002), pp. 20–34.

of the skilled laborer, the engine behind the productive laborer, or the automation which should replace the expensive or intransigent laborer. And almost every historical periodization of the IT revolution has involved some sort of broad shift to "knowledge work", explicitly valorizing a certain set of (supposedly new) mental labors while relegating a parallel set of physical labors to the dustbin of history. Yet overall the notion of "information labor" as a historical unit of analysis is lacking any secondary synthesis or coherent body of theory.

NORMATIVE ASSUMPTIONS ABOUT INFORMATION LABOR

I won't pretend to offer such a synthesis here – that is a project not only beyond the scope of one article, but beyond the scope of one individual scholar. However, I would like to discuss some possible components of such a synthesis, because so many of the studies of IT labor which do exist are grounded in *a priori* (and often normative) assumptions which are only now coming under more nuanced scrutiny. These assumptions fall into three groups: assumptions about the productivity consequences of applying IT to manufacturing and services labor; assumptions about the characteristics of labor in industries which use IT to sell information itself; and assumptions about the spatial and temporal effects of IT-based production on society as a whole.

Assumptions about IT and the productivity of labor

First of all, like any technological change within a context of capitalist production, the goals of increased labor efficiency, productivity, and profitability have all been used to sell information technologies of all sorts. Yet in the specific case of IT, such quantitative gains may often come at a qualitative price. As Shoshana Zuboff argued after reviewing early-1980s IT investments in firms as diverse as paper mills and insurance offices, "Information technology not only produces action but also produces a voice that symbolically renders events, objects, and processes so that they become visible, knowable, and sharable in a new way", a process she called "informating" to indicate that it was the inevitable (and hopeful) flipside of "automating".[38] But as more and more information becomes available about production processes – especially increased surveillance over the presumably unproductive activities of labor within those processes – a situation of "information overload" may occur, necessitating a vicious

---

38. Shoshana Zuboff, *In the Age of the Smart Machine: The Future of Work and Power* (New York, 1988).

cycle of further IT investment in order to store, process, and make sense of the increased volume of surveillance data itself.[39]

Another widely-popularized example of the risks of informating has been dubbed the "productivity paradox". Since new personal computers were viewed as "general purpose technologies" on par historically with the steam engine and electricity, economists in the early 1980s expected large and easily-measurable productivity gains across nearly all aspects of the economy. But, in 1987, Morgan Stanley economist Steven Roach defined "America's technology dilemma" as increasing spending for IT coupled with flat productivity, and the race was on in academia to either explain or debunk this seeming paradox.[40] Today the paradox is often declared solved by arguing that the "IT payoff" was merely delayed in its appearance: "As IT continues to displace labor, factory, and equipment throughout the production system [...] and IT investments approach 10 to 15 per cent of GDP, the economic contributions of IT will be more visible and the productivity issue will no longer be a matter of debate."[41]

Both the debates over "information overload" and "productivity paradoxes" are contested in terms of theory, measurement, and normative focus (overload for whom? productivity of whom?). But each case, expectations of the corporate benefit from IT are structured by competition, as capital collectively adopts a new "socially necessary" set of labor processes. New IT is bound up with images of progress, success, and power such that for both organizations and individuals, the question is no longer whether to use IT in the workplace, but how best to use IT for both organizational and personal goals. Yet such choices are not automatic for historical actors – economists have long observed that under changing spatial and temporal conditions of competition, firms may display "industrial rigidity". Economic geographer, Erica Schoenberger, has studied how such coping strategies are formed, linking corporate actions to the self-identities (and firm-identities) of high-level decision makers themselves. Using case studies from Lockheed and Xerox, she argued that managers don't resist all forms of change, but are constrained in the kinds of change they will attempt or accept.[42] Thus as historians we might ask: is such a pattern of "inevitable" but constrained IT adoption, filtered through the eyes of actors trying to both envision new strategies and

39. Andrew Urbaczewski and Leonard M. Jessup, "Internet Abuse in the Workplace: Does Electronic Monitoring of Employee Internet Usage Work?", *Communications of the ACM*, 45:1 (2002), pp. 80–83.
40. Erik Brynjolfsson and Lorin M. Hitt, "Beyond the Productivity Paradox", *Communications of the ACM*, 41:8 (1998), pp. 49–55.
41. Sanjeen Dewan and Kenneth L. Kraemer, "International Dimensions of the Productivity Paradox", *Communications of the ACM*, 41:8 (1998), pp. 56–62.
42. Erica Schoenberger, *The Cultural Crisis of the Firm* (Cambridge, MA, 1997).

measure current risks, found consistently in capitalist economies whenever the space/time "rules of the game" change due to new technology?

If historical assumptions about the productivity of new workplace technologies have been overly optimistic, then perhaps they are balanced by pessimistic assumptions about the elimination of labor altogether due to that same technology. For example, in the US, worries over wholesale "deindustrialization" after the oil price shocks of 1973 and 1979 quickly followed the original enthusiasm over the "postindustrial" society, especially given the dramatic loss of profitability in the US auto industry and the equally dramatic governmental attacks on organized labor in the 1980s.[43] Information technology, along with the new globalization which it seemed to be enabling, was one of the culprits in this analysis. According to one estimate, in 1970 there were under 1,000 industrial robots in operation worldwide, but only a decade later there were more than 30,000.[44] This situation led social critics Stanley Aronowitz and William DiFazio to predict a "jobless future" in 1994 and Jeremy Rifkin to declare that "the end of work" was near in 1995.[45] For the editor of *CPU: Working for the Computer Industry*, the idea that "latter-day capitalism asymptotically approaches 'laborless production'", was self-evident in the new "dark factories": fully-automated factories so named because the interior lights were left turned off, since there were no humans present inside.[46]

As historians, we first need to remember that such debates are not new. Amy Bix has effectively shown that questions over technological job loss have waxed and waned throughout the twentieth century, especially during hard economic times: "During the Depression decade, 1930 to 1940, many citizens worried that stubbornly high unemployment rates signified a deep imbalance in the Machine Age system."[47] In this context, Elizabeth Baker first documented "[t]he displacement of men by machines" in the printing industry (1933).[48] Second, historical precedent shows that job loss is not necessarily the only result of new technology (if it is a result at all). Stuart Blumin reminded us that

43. Barry Bluestone and Bennett Harrison, *The Deindustrialization of America: Plant Closings, Community Abandonment, and the Dismantling of Basic Industry* (New York, 1982).

44. Tessa Morris-Suzuki, "Robots and Capitalism", in James Davis, Thomas Hirschl, and Michael Stack (eds), *Cutting Edge: Technology, Information Capitalism, Social Revolution* (London, 2000), pp. 13–28.

45. Stanley Aronowitz and William DiFazio, *The Jobless Future: Sci-Tech and the Dogma of Work* (Minneapolis, MN, 1994); Jeremy Rifkin, *The End of Work: The Decline of the Global Labor Force and the Dawn of the Post-Market Era* (New York, 1995).

46. Jim Davis and Michael Stack, "The Digital Advantage", in Davis, Hirschl, and Stack, *Cutting Edge*, pp. 121–144.

47. Amy Sue Bix, *Inventing Ourselves Out of Jobs? America's Debate over Technological Unemployment, 1929–1981* (Baltimore, MD, 2000).

48. Elizabeth Faulkner Baker, *Displacement of Men by Machines: Effects of Technological Change in Commercial Printing* (New York, 1933).

The number of office workers (bookkeepers, cashiers, accountants, office clerks, stenographers, and typists) increased ninefold in the last thirty years of the [nineteenth] century, from fewer than 70,000 to more than 600,000, and, though fully one-third of this increase is accounted for by the entrance of women into all types of clerical office work, [...] the multiple increase for men was nearly three times as great as the multiple for the male work force as a whole.[49]

In seeking meaningful patterns of historical change, we may find it most useful to trace not aggregate job losses or gains, but a more subtle shift from higher-wage manufacturing jobs to lower-wage service jobs – many with an information-processing component or context. This "contingent economy" has grown together with the rise of office IT, yet cannot be reduced to that IT (especially in light of overt neoliberal state policies which encourage such an economy).[50] For example, a recent review of the division of labor in the US construction industry concluded that "Introduction of computer technology in the past two decades has occurred concurrently with a 40 per cent reduction of support staff as a percentage of total construction employment, and a doubling of management as a fraction of the construction work force", although "[t]he fraction engaged in craftwork has remained relatively stable".[51] Here again, attending to changing divisions of labor – technical, social, and spatial/temporal divisions which embody both obvious industrial restructuring together with more subtle shifts in responsibility, status, and career security – is a useful analytical strategy.

Somewhere between debates over increased productivity or increased unemployment are the questions over the effects of technology on the aggregate skill level (and, according to neoclassical economics, the justifiable wage level) of labor. Much of this debate came in the 1980s as a response to Harry Braverman's early 1970s "degradation thesis" that shifts into service occupations didn't necessarily mean greater skills, better wages, or less tedium.[52] His arguments drew upon a history of Taylorist "scientific management" which recognized that if nothing else, the hyper-rationalized management systems of Taylor, Ford, and others were information technologies themselves.[53] By the early 1990s, more optimis-

49. Stuart Blumin, "The Hypothesis of Middle-Class Formation in Nineteenth-Century America: A Critique and Some Proposals", *American Historical Review*, 90 (1985), pp. 299–338.
50. Richard S. Belous, *The Contingent Economy: The Growth of the Temporary, Part-Time and Subcontracted Workforce* (Washington DC, 1989); Polly Callaghan and Heidi Hartmann (eds), *Contingent Work: American Employment Relations in Transition* (Ithaca, NY, 1998).
51. James W. Platner and Xiuwen Dong, "Impacts of Digital Information Networks on Construction Contractors and Unions", *Journal of Labor Research*, 23 (2002), pp. 575–590, 588.
52. Harry Braverman, *Labor and Monopoly Capital: The Degradation of Work in the Twentieth Century* (New York, 1974).
53. Robert Kanigel, *The One Best Way: Frederick Winslow Taylor and the Enigma of Efficiency* (New York, 1997).

tic analysts like Paul Adler had swung away from Braverman's deskilling thesis to a new upgrading thesis:

> There are, of course, some cases where deskilling occurs. But an emerging body of research suggests first, that the use of new technologies will in general be more profitable when entrusted to more highly skilled employees, and second, that as a result, firms generally, although not always, "muddle through" to an implementation approach premised on upgraded skills and broader jobs.[54]

Like the questions over productivity and job loss, the deskilling/ upgrading debate was mainly argued in terms of manufacturing automation and the twin concepts of deindustrialization and postindustrialization. But the issue was also applied to office automation, though measuring this has been notoriously difficult. One early 1990s study in the US, using mid-1980s data, argued that employees who used computers at work were paid up to 15 per cent more than those who didn't.[55] A more recent US study claimed to support these findings, now citing Internet use at work (rather than plain old computer use) as the factor motivating an average wage difference of 13.5 per cent.[56]

But instead of looking simply at deskilling or upgrading, perhaps the place to look for historical change is in the contextual redefinition of skills themselves (and of the status associated with those skills). For example, there has been much debate over the existence of "digital divides" between those who have access to IT and those who do not, not only on a global scale but even within affluent states such as the US.[57] Usually digital divides are defined at the scale of the individual household or the individual school district; but defining them at the scale of the workplace as well might offer a new way for historians to unpack the meaning of "skill" together with other aspects of labor conditions, especially the ability to weave one's roles as consumer, citizen, and family member together with the role of worker.[58] Interestingly, Braverman's 1974 work was already beginning to wrestle with such combined redivisions of labor:

> [...] the employment of machinery pushes the office installation toward the warehouse and industrial districts of the cities. This is facilitated by the development of remote terminals and other communications devices which

54. Paul S. Adler (ed.), *Technology and the Future of Work* (New York, 1992), p. 3.
55. Alan Krueger, "How Computers Have Changed the Wage Structure: Evidence from Microdata, 1984–1989", *Quarterly Journal of Economics*, 108 (1993), pp. 33–60.
56. Ernest P. Goss and Joseph M. Phillips, "How Information Technology Affects Wages: Evidence Using Internet Usage as a Proxy for IT Skills", *Journal of Labor Research*, 23 (2002), pp. 463–475.
57. Pippa Norris, *Digital Divide: Civic Engagement, Information Poverty, and the Internet Worldwide* (Cambridge, 2001).
58. Greg Downey, "Differing Views of the Digital Divide: Social Justice and Spatial Justice in Cyberspace", in progress.

annihilate distance and do away with almost all the inconveniences of separate installations, so that executive offices can be maintained in the more expensive and accessible locations while the mass of clerical workers can be moved into lower-rent districts, often together with warehousing or production facilities. Thus the convenience and cachet of working in the central part of town, with its greater shopping interest and more varied lunching facilities, etc., begins for many clerical workers to disappear.[59]

This linking of new divisions of production with new divisions of social reproduction is another crucial strategy for tracing the information age historically.

Assumptions about labor in the information industries

Within the (often internalist) historical study of particular information industries, we can trace a second set of normative assumptions, this time concerning the workers rather than the work performed. The first of these assumptions dates back to the late nineteenthth century, when the first electrically-powered infrastructures for communication were consolidated under increasingly vast and increasingly centralized corporate structures: railroads, telegraphs, and telephones. These new networks of rails, wires, and offices, requiring such visible investments in the built environment, were subject to a pair of intertwined assumptions. First, the presence of these infrastructures was deemed a collective social good – just as postal delivery was seen as a fundamental component of republican democracy, so would rail access and wired communication be thought of as essential components of social and economic participation in the nation, regardless of the differing level of profit which firms might extract from one site versus another.[60] Second, the redundant construction of these infrastructures by different firms in the same place was seen as wasteful of social resources, an example of "ruinous competition" which detracted from the goal of "universal service". Out of these two sentiments came the idea that information infrastructure industries were somehow "natural monopolies", best organized under centralized control and subject to specific regulation for the social good.[61]

In such a realm of monopoly information infrastructures, laborers were often seen as technological components subject to a similar kind of regulation and rationalization – an ideal which affected organizing efforts in the telegraph and telephone industries even across differences of race,

59. Braverman, *Labor and Monopoly Capital*, p. 353.
60. Richard R. John, *Spreading the News: The American Postal System from Franklin to Morse* (Cambridge, MA, 1995).
61. This pattern worked out a bit differently in the US, where private interests such as Western Union and AT&T were allowed to reap profit from communications monopolies; nevertheless, they were theoretically subject to state regulation.

gender, and age.[62] Issues of national security and government accountability worked their way into communications industry labor battles
across national contexts; as a result, in most places these information jobs
were part of a civil service, though in the US they evolved through
successive periods of "benefit associations", company unions, and finally
independent labor unions. For example, even though it took the lowly
messenger boys (a historical archetype of contingent, piecewage labor)
nearly a century to be folded into the US telegraph unions, the timing of
that recognition was profoundly affected by the timing of two world wars
– and by the telegraph's strategic importance in both.[63]

In contrast, the case in the growing media industries over the same
period – not only print, but later radio and television – was one of more
varied constructions of labor. On one hand, these industries required
traditional industrial labor in order to function – paper had to be milled,
printing presses had to roll, resistors and vacuum tubes had to be soldered
into consumer radios and television sets. Such activities, some unionized
and some not, were generally not seen as "information labor" – however,
they could valuably be analyzed as such, especially as these extractive and
manufacturing jobs were among the first to be marched across both
regional and national borders.[64] On the other hand, the creative talent
behind the growing mass media – writers and actors, advertisers and
musicians – was often considered a professional and independent elite, not
a category of "labor" at all. Owning their own typewriters, finding their
own clients, submitting their own work over and over again for payment
by the piece, these individuals were often seen as entrepreneurs, even down
to the newsboys who "purchased" papers from distributors in the morning
and "resold" them for pennies on the dollar well into the night.[65] Jeremy
Tunstall noted that the media professions have for at least a century been
associated with a "moral division of labor", whether embodied in the
distinction between respectable vs. bawdy theater, family vs. adult
filmmaking, or serious vs. sensational journalism (with all of those
normative definitions subject to contemporary debate and historical
change). Significantly, even by 1900, this moral division of labor was
profoundly structured by space and time (in North American and
European cities at least): "Larger cities already had their distinctive theater

62. Edwin Gabler, *The American Telegrapher: A Social History, 1860–1900* (New Brunswick, NJ, 1988); Venus Green, "Race, Gender, and National Identity in the American and British Telephone Industries", *International Review of Social History*, 46 (2001), pp. 185–205.
63. Greg Downey, *Telegraph Messenger Boys: Labor, Technology, and Geography, 1850–1950* (New York, 2002).
64. Jefferson Cowie, *Capital Moves: RCA's 70-Year Quest for Cheap Labor* (Ithaca, NY, 1999).
65. Vincent R. DiGirolamo, "Crying the News: Children, Street Work, and the American Press, 1830s–1920s", (unpublished Ph.D. thesis, Princeton University, NJ, 1997).

and newspaper districts, whose employees typically worked at unusual times (especially in the evening) and tended to intermix socially; in these fairly insecure and irregular types of employment, social life also became a network for finding work."[66] This moral and spatial division of labor was also a gendered division of labor, a characteristic which persisted into media broadcasting on radio and TV.[67]

Various moral, spatial, and gender divisions of labor persist in the "media monopolies" of today, under new conditions of digital and economic convergence.[68] While new technology and new neoliberal policies affect media landscapes around the globe, their effects are by no means homogenous over this differentiated geography. For example, Ellen Hazelkorn's study of changes in the occupational structure of Ireland's television industry highlighted the special case of a smaller-population European country with a strong public broadcaster of its own competing with a powerful set of neighboring international broadcasters (BBC and ITV).[69] The more varied environments we can find for such studies – especially the formerly state-controlled media spheres of eastern Europe – the better we might understand how the laborers within media production systems are both constrained by and help set the limits of national media norms and practices.[70]

Although the communication infrastructure and media content industries are sometimes considered sites of "information labor" by scholars, the education industries rarely are. This is partly because education tends to be state-funded rather than market-based (though current neoliberal state policies aim to change this). But another reason can be found in the historical division of labor in the education industries. In the US, a polarization exists between primary/secondary education and college/ university education. At the grade levels, education labor is highly unionized, highly feminized, and (arguably) undervalued both economically and socially; at the college levels, education labor is rarely unionized, more gender balanced, and contradictorily valued with large research universities both charging high tuition fees and maintaining a culture in which education is secondary to publication in terms of hiring and

---

66. Jeremy Tunstall (ed.), *Media Occupations and Professions: A Reader* (New York, 2001), p. 2.
67. Donna L. Halper, *Invisible Stars: A Social History of Women in American Broadcasting* (Armonk, NY, 2001).
68. Robert W. McChesney, Ellen Meiksins Wood, and John Bellamy Foster (eds), *Capitalism and the Information Age: The Political Economy of the Global Communication Revolution* (New York, 1998).
69. Ellen Hazelkorn, "New Technologies and Changing Work Practices in Irish broadcasting", in Tunstall, *Media Occupations and Professions*, pp. 214–226.
70. Julie Kay Mueller, "Staffing Newspapers and Training Journalists in Early Soviet Russia", *Journal of Social History*, 31 (1998), pp. 851–874.

retaining faculty. As a result, questions over the proper place of new IT in each realm lack any connection to each other.[71] Furthermore, the tricky realm of technical/vocational education – where two-year training as a "Microsoft-certified network technician" might be more valuable than a liberal arts education – fits neither of these stereotypes. Here, many of the institutions are for-profit entities, and most of the content is overtly related to the long-standing aim of labor to find high-wage, high-tech careers (and of capital to externalize its own training costs).[72] Libraries offer a third set of sites where educational information management takes place in society, historically in a highly gendered division of labor.[73] Again, although today the notion of digital libraries is bringing some of this labor more into focus (often within the same debates of productivity, job loss, and deskilling as described earlier), we should not forget that the creation and honing of card- and shelf-based cataloging systems a century ago were no less valid forms of information work.[74]

Finally, a fourth category of information industry developed with the increasing bureaucratization and rationalization of the capitalist firm (and the state administrative unit) through the nineteenth and twentieth centuries: office work. This is one area in which not only historians but sociologists have made numerous contributions, tracing a history from the "Victorian clerks" in the nineteenth century to the legions of "white-collar" workers in the twentieth.[75] Much of this work has been motivated by three theoretical imperatives: attempting to define the "middle class" through the shift to office-based, symbol-processing service labor; tracing the polarization between professional white-collar workers and clerical white-collar workers (with that middle class being divided starkly along lines of power, wages, and tasks); and attempting to understand the way gender, race, and ethnicity are involved in these labor polarizations – especially how white-collar work becomes feminized into "pink-collar"

71. Larry Cuban, *Oversold and Underused: Computers in the Classroom* (Cambridge, MA, 2001).

72. Nina E. Lerman, "From 'Useful Knowledge' to 'Habits of Industry': Gender, Race, and Class in Nineteenth-Century Technical Education" (unpublished Ph.D. thesis, University of Pennsylvania, 1993); B.P. Cronin, *Technology, Industrial Conflict, and the Development of Technical Education in 19th-Century England* (Aldershot [etc.], 2001).

73. Dee Garrison, "The Tender Technicians: The Feminization of Public Librarianship, 1876–1905", *Journal of Social History*, 6 (1973), pp. 131–159; Joanne Passet, "Men in a Feminized Profession: The Male Librarian, 1887–1921", *Libraries & Culture*, 28 (1993), pp. 385–402.

74. Borgman, *From Gutenberg to the Global Information Infrastructure*; Wayne A. Wiegand, *The Politics of an Emerging Profession: The American Library Association, 1876–1917* (Westport, CT, 1986).

75. Gregory Anderson, *Victorian Clerks* (Manchester, 1976); Jürgen Kocka, *White Collar Workers in America, 1890–1940: A Social-Political History in International Perspective*, trans. by Maura Kealey (London, 1980).

work.[76] Even environmental history, as it has moved from the study of outdoor recreation spaces to indoor work places, has profited from the key insight that office labor history is structured by power and gender.[77]

Assumptions about IT and the space and time of the production process

In Alvin Toffler's 1980 manifesto *The Third Wave* (a sequel to his 1970 *Future Shock*) he spoke of the way computer-mediated communications would enable the rise of "electronic cottages" – a metaphor meant not only to evoke the unproblematic high-tech wiring of the sylvan, suburban home, but also to draw upon the idea of "cottage industry" where petty capitalists carved careers based on various information skills, selling those skills on a virtual market while avoiding long commutes and watching the kids at home.[78] Clearly, such a scene has not come to pass; however, with twenty years of intervening technological innovations such as cell phones and laptop computers, the focus of the wired household has arguably shifted to that of the wired individual (or in the US, perhaps, the wired sport utility vehicle). We have neither escaped our long commutes nor nested in our safe homes; however, with technology actually attached to the body, we have fragmented our daily existence so that the "separate spheres" of work and home blur together. An original vision of "telecommuting" as our new labor norm has been replaced with a more flexible vision of "teleworking".

Of course, the "we" here provides the key question. Put aside the statistics on digital divides which show that in the US, for example, even in 2002 only around 50 per cent of all households reported having Internet access.[79] Even within privileged "wired" households, which persons are able to fragment their work in space and time, from paper to bits, away from the congeniality of colleagues but still under the watchful eye of management? Empirical studies have found polarizations – highly-paid purveyors of business services go "hoteling" from office to client to home

76. C. Wright Mills, *White Collar: The American Middle Classes* (New York, 1951); Rosabeth Moss Kanter, *Men and Women of the Corporation* (New York, 1977); Heidi I. Hartmann (ed.), *Computer Chips and Paper Clips: Technology and Women's Employment*, vols 1–2, (Washington DC, 1987); Francisca Maria de Haan, *Gender and the Politics of Office Work: The Netherlands 1860–1940* (Amsterdam, 1998).

77. M. Murphy, "Toxicity in the Details: The History of the Women's Office Worker Movement and Occupational Health in the Late-Capitalist Office", *Labor History*, 41 (2000), pp. 189–213.

78. Alvin Toffler, *The Third Wave* (New York, 1981); Langdon Winner, "Whatever Happened to the Electronic Cottage?", *Netfuture* #, 121 [www.netfuture.org] (2001).

79. US Department of Commerce, National Telecommunications and Information Administration, *A Nation Online: How Americans are Expanding Their Use of the Internet* (Washington DC, 2002).

to hotel and back again, always in touch; struggling home entrepreneurs plug their business plans into both virtual broadband Internet subscriptions and local Mail Boxes Etc. shipping addresses; and most of all, low-paid data-entry workers use century-old typing or stenography skills to translate information from printed forms to computer screens, from tape recorders to text files, sometimes out in the next suburb and sometimes halfway around the world.[80] In too many cases, and in ways structured by the same old categories of gender, age, ethnicity, language, and family status, the virtual worker of tomorrow looks more and more like the piecewage homeworker of yesterday.[81]

Speculations about the space/time fragmentation of labor do not always start with the laborer, however. They also start with the firm itself. Especially in America, characterizing the days of US dominance over the global manufacturing market as over, the business press urges entrepreneurs and managers to make their firms more "agile", their work teams more "flexible", their responses to market conditions executable "just in time".[82] A whole field of study has arisen under these normative assumptions, combining the disciplines of organizational psychology and computer science to build the best performing systems for "distributed work" – an ideal situation where individual professionals, all of equal status and equal motivation, participate in global "teams" which are constantly shifting in size and composition.[83] Though the term "distributed" suggests that space is the most important consideration, it is really time that matters – turnover time in assembling teams, executing effective business plans, and then just as quickly disassembling teams (avoiding the pesky time scales of vacations, promotions and pensions).

These intertwined visions of the proper model for the individual and the corporation in the new economy (or, we could argue, the neoliberal political economy) come together in predictions of the changes which will accrue in social space itself as these models are increasingly instantiated. The old notions of cities withering into garden communities have been abandoned for a more Darwinian model: entrepreneurial cities which become "wired" – not only by investing in electronic infrastructure, but by attracting the "right" sorts of workers and venture capitalists – will transcend the limits of their states to become "cities of bits", linked into the

---

80. C. Stanworth, "Telework and the Information Age", *New Technology, Work and Employment* 13:1 (1998), pp. 51–62; Carla Freeman, *High Tech and High Heels in the Global Economy: Women, Work, and Pink-Collar Identities in the Caribbean* (Durham, NC, 2000).
81. Eileen Boris and Cynthia R. Daniels (eds), *Homework: Historical and Contemporary Perspectives on Paid Labor at Home* (Urbana, IL, 1989).
82. N. Fredric Crandall and Marc J. Wallace, *Work and Rewards in the Virtual Workplace: A "New Deal" for Organizations and Employees* (New York, 1998).
83. Pamela Hinds and Sara Kiesler (eds), *Distributed Work* (Cambridge, MA, 2002).

global networks of information, capital, and spectacle.[84] On the other hand, cities which don't (or can't) become wired will be left to fight for the scraps of the old economy under conditions of increasing state support, shrinking tax bases, declining services, and decaying infrastructure.[85] Sadly, both models abandon an earlier definition of wired cities, drawn from the promise of interactive cable television in the late 1960s, which envisioned such places as mustering information technology – and labor – for the social good of all.[86]

Besides their normative (and often ahistorical) assumptions about the proper models for individuals, organizations, and urban areas, the biggest problem with these three separate theories is that the spatial scales of the household, the firm, and the city interact dialectically with any social process we might investigate – not just production, but consumption and reproduction as well.[87] When "big-box" retail stores like Wal-Mart enter new markets, they do more than shift the spatial division of consumption from main streets; they shift a spatial division of labor from other employment opportunities and they shift a spatial division of capital out of the community. Such stores are increasingly involved in e-commerce in two ways: first, they require massive investments in information infra-structures to coordinate the tension between large-scale purchasing power (which drives costs down and profits up, taking market share from resellers who can't purchase as much or as quickly) and local fragmented consumption (channeling products to specific stores in specific places for specific consumer groups, restocking shelves "just in time"); second, they often involve a web presence which leverages the physical network of store sites as generators of local print and broadcast advertising, sites for "pick-up" stock to avoid shipping costs, and sites for merchandise return – consumption processes which, when handled in a physical site and not through the mail, may spin off into additional impulse sales. Thus should we consider the service labor upon which these stores rely as "information labor"? Should we be concerned about labor organizing efforts in rural strip malls as well as in Silicon Valley? If so, we should apply these same ideas to the previous turn-of-the-century, and reconsider the labor implicated in the then high-tech catalog retailing ventures of, in the US

84. David Harvey, "From Managerialism to Entrepreneurialism: The Transformation in Urban Governance in Late Capitalism", *Geografiska Annaler*, 71:B (1989), pp. 3–17; William J. Mitchell, *City of Bits: Space, Place, and the Infobahn* (Cambridge, MA, 1995).
85. Joel Kotkin, *The New Geography: How the Digital Revolution Is Reshaping the American Landscape* (New York, 2000).
86. Ralph Lee Smith, *The Wired Nation: Cable TV, the Electronic Communications Highway* (New York, 1972); William H. Dutton, Jay G. Blumler and Kenneth L. Kraemer (eds), *Wired Cities: Shaping the Future of Communications* (Boston, MA, 1987).
87. Neil Wrigley and Michelle Lowe, *Reading Retail: A Geographical Perspective on Retailing and Consumption Spaces* (New York, 2002).

case, Sears and Wards as a sort of "informational labor" as well, iterated not over the web but through the printing presses, postal roads and telephone lines.

Such issues are finally gaining attention with the recent push to synthesize the relationships between IT, the city, and social processes.[88] Urban planning scholar, Laura Wolf-Powers, recently pointed out that

> In advanced urban economies, scholars and policymakers argue, measures conventionally pursued to attract firms – tax incentives, urban infrastructure, mega-projects focused on drawing tourists or convention-goers – are increasingly less effective, because human capital, not physical capital, has become the twenty-first century's key competitive advantage. Thus, policies to attract desirable workers, in addition to policies aimed at increasing the skill level of the existing workforce, have gained priority among economic development planners."

But she pointed out a crucial flaw in this "community-upskilling" logic: "the majority of new jobs created in the 'knowledge economy' will continue to be low-status and low-paid".[89] In analyzing these relationships, many still argue simply that "Networked computing deterritorializes labor, rendering irrelevant the location on Earth of the work being done", and "retemporalizes labor by introducing a register of instantaneousness that is comprehensible as computer time but not as human or even machine time".[90] If we are to decide whether or not IT can "deterritorialize" labor completely, then attention to territory is precisely what is needed most.

What links each of these differing normative frameworks – involving assumptions about productivity and job loss, industrial and occupational character, and spatial/temporal reorganization of production – is that they all suggest that a universal, natural trend of technological development is somehow at work in the economy (and in society). Technology will inevitably trivialize labor; information industries will inevitably embody certain kinds of employment relations; and information labor of all sorts will inevitably decentralize throughout society. Thus what these frameworks all share more than anything else is a thread of technological determinism.

The idea of technological determinism doesn't have to be expressed as starkly as a teleological "progress narrative" of continually increasing mechanization, automation, and informatization to which society must

88. Stephen Graham and Simon Marvin, *Splintering Urbanism: Networked Infrastructures, Technological Mobilities and the Urban Condition* (London, 2001).
89. Laura Wolf-Powers, "Information Technology and Urban Labor Markets in the United States", *International Journal of Urban and Regional Research*, 25 (2001), pp. 427–438, 428.
90. Mark Poster, "Workers as Cyborgs: Labor and Networked Computers", *Journal of Labor Research*, 23 (2002), pp. 339–354, 340.

inevitably adapt. Instead, we as historians implicitly draw upon technological determinism when we are unable (or unwilling) to explore how
diverse historical actors – not just the producers of technology, not even
just the consumers of technology, but also those who reproduce that
technology on a daily basis – made their many different choices to
embrace, accept, ignore, or contest those technologies. At times we seem to
assume that labor history is a socially constructed history, but technological history is a materially determined one.

Fortunately, recent history of technology research contradicts this idea,
with the most fruitful and provocative work taking the position that
technology operates dialectically in society: both a product of human
thought and action, and a powerful structural force enabling and
constraining human thought and action.[91] From the point of view of
labor, processes of work are inevitably mediated by technologies, whether
those technologies are defined in the classical dichotomy between "tools"
and "machines" (each of those carrying normative assumptions about the
enskilling and deskilling of labor) or whether technologies are defined
more abstractly as "knowledges" and "systems" (where efforts to turn
human skills and experience into Taylorist algorithms are themselves
powerful technologies). From the point of view of technologies, dialectical
processes of technological innovation, production, distribution, and daily
use all depend on human labor, though each stage involves different kinds
of labor from different groups of actors in different proportions (and often
resulting in differing rewards). Over a decade ago, Phil Scranton argued for
closer cooperation between historians of labor and historians of technology. However, Scranton specifically called for more study of "efforts to
discern the relationships between shop-floor practice and technical change
in American industry", rather than, among other topics, studies of
information labor.[92] Filling this gap is even more important today.

THE INVISIBILITY OF INFORMATION LABOR

After reviewing this (partial) historiography of how information technologies and practices have been linked to labor so far, we need to ask at this
point: why is the labor history of the information revolution such an
elusive topic even to find, let alone to synthesize? Is it because information
labor, unlike other forms of labor, is somehow "invisible?". Is it because
information labor, even when recognized as such, does not involve the
exploitation of a working class? Or is it because information labor, even

91. Merritt Roe Smith, "Technological Determinism in American Culture", in Merritt Roe
Smith and Leo Marx (eds), *Does Technology Drive History? The Dilemma of Technological
Determinism* (Cambridge, MA, 1994), pp. 1–36.
92. Philip Scranton, "None-Too-Porous Boundaries: Labor History and the History of
Technology", *Technology and Culture*, 29 (1988), pp. 722–743.

when involving uneven and unjust social relations, has neglected to understand itself as labor and to organize collectively?

First, consider the many kinds of "invisibility" which we wrestle with in labor history. The Marxian concept of "commodity fetishism" has long suggested that all labor retains a degree of invisibility under capitalism, since all a consumer ever witnesses is a commodity's final, momentary price. All sorts of unwaged labor, especially by women, have also been invisible to the workings of the capitalist market (treated as "household reproduction" or "economic externalities").[93] Sociologist, Erving Goffman, has referred to the difference between "front-stage" and "back-stage" social processes, and most information labor may be contained in that back-stage space as workers seek out, assemble, and organize information out of view of peers, managers, or customers.[94] Historian of science, Steven Shapin, has pointed to the invisibility of low-status technical labor in the production of scientific knowledge.[95] And management's desire to formalize and rationalize labor processes has always been balanced by the fact that some work inevitably and invisibly escapes systematization, an idea which has gained currency again as work has been distributed in space and time due to information technology.[96]

Information technology adds another degree of invisibility to the mix. The virtual characteristics of the "information commodity" itself may help to obscure the labor necessary in its production – especially when those information commodities are apparently stored, located, duplicated, and exchanged (in the case of Napster, some might say stolen) so quickly and effortlessly from the vantage point of the consumer.[97] At the former Xerox Palo Alto Research Center – arguably the birthplace of the modern office-technology environment – one researcher regretted that "work has a tendency to disappear at a distance, such that the further removed we are from the work of others, the more simplified, often stereotyped, our view of their work becomes".[98] If we value the history of this work, we must help these workers to reappear.

But even when made visible, information labor is sometimes not even accorded the status of "labor" – at least labor of a certain kind. An actor in the informational society theorized by Manuel Castells is either privileged

93. Ruth Schwartz Cowan, *More Work For Mother: The Ironies of Household Technology from the Open Hearth to the Microwave* (New York, 1983).
94. Erving Goffman, *The Presentation of Self in Everyday Life* (London, 1969).
95. Steven Shapin, "The Invisible Technician", *American Scientist*, 7 (1989), pp. 554–563.
96. Susan Leigh Star and Anselm Strauss, "Layers of Silence, Arenas of Voice: The Ecology of Visible and Invisible Work", *Computer Supported Cooperative Work*, 8 (1999), pp. 9–30.
97. Dan Schiller, "The Information Commodity: A Preliminary View", in Davis, Hirschl, and Stack, *Cutting Edge*, pp. 103–120.
98. Lucy Suchman, "Representations of Work: Making Work Visible", *Communications of the ACM*, 38:9 (1995), pp. 56–68.

to be in the space of flows (as an individual, an entrepreneur, a city, or a region) or is placed on the other side of the "dual city" in a "black hole of the information economy" (where the standard labor history of industrial and service exploitation still applies).[99] Yet sociologists of work have called such stark dualities into question. While not denying that polarizations of income, status, and career prospects are being produced, they nevertheless argue that many new technology tasks, jobs, and careers blur any polarizing categories. For example, Peter Whalley and Stephen Barley argued that "technical work" (such as computer-support labor) transcends two common dichotomies: first, it involves both "mental" and "manual" labors simultaneously; second, it is both occupationally structured (worker as independent craftworker or professional) and organizationally structured (worker as bureaucratic company employee) at the same time.[100] In this way, information labor might be recognized as actually serving an important mediating role between other more homogenous organizational and occupational groups.

Even if information labor is made visible as such, the assumption that information laborers do not take collective action could be a barrier to critical analysis of their history. Perhaps the best example of this difficulty in recent years has been the question of the relationship between IT and trade unions. In the US, for example, overall union membership has declined dramatically under conditions of neoliberal governance, economic restructuring, and capitalist globalization just as personal computers, personal communications, and the World Wide Web have all entered the workplace. One group of management information systems researchers recently argued that,

> Information technologies make knowledge and information into a transportable commodity, which in turn transforms an organization from a factory into a body of ideas and skills. The "real" firm no longer exists in its machinery and production space, but in the knowledge and information systems that enable production. Thus, there is no factory to organize, no critical assembly line to strike, no organizational lynchpin on which a union can apply effective leverage.[101]

Although finding causal links is problematic, there is clearly a need to connect projects dealing with the "new unionism" to conditions of the "new economy". First, we might ask: can labor unions use IT to better

99. Castells, *Rise of the Information Society*.
100. Peter Whalley and Stephen R. Barley, "Technical Work in the Division of Labor: Stalking the Wily Anomaly", in Stephen R. Barley and Julian E. Orr (eds), *Between Craft and Science: Technical Work in US Settings* (Ithaca, NY, 1997), pp. 23–52.
101. Anthony M. Townsend, Samuel M. Demarie, and Anthony R. Hendrickson, "Information Technology, Unions, and the New Organization: Challenges and Opportunities for Union Survival", *Journal of Labor Research*, 22 (2001), pp. 275–287.

motivate nonunion workers to organize? Alistair Mutch has recently suggested that historically information access has been crucial to trade-union effectiveness, especially in times of technological change.[102] Yet Gary Chaison recently feared that in the present information environment,

> As unions deepen their Internet presence to compete against employer-controlled intranets, they can begin to do through their web pages what they would otherwise do through personal contact with members. Union resources and effort can be shifted away from activities requiring personal contact such as meetings, rallies, and social activities and toward the faster and less expensive promotion of an Internet presence. The union web page can become the primary means to communicate with members. Organizing can simply mean developing a website to attract potential members, connect them with online organizers, and collect digital signatures on union authorization cards.[103]

Thus the active union member might be reconstructed along neoliberal lines as simply a consumer of value-added services.

Secondly, we might ask: can IT workers in particular be motivated to organize at all? In one recent exploratory study of the attitudes of programmers, systems engineers, and software engineers toward labor unions, the researcher found that

> When asked about whether they had ever thought of joining a union, every high-tech worker interviewed responded with silence, and in several instances with prolonged silence. To a person, they said that they had never thought, even once, of ever joining a union or engaging in collective action to improve their working conditions.[104]

This study only dealt with a handful of respondents, but it reflects the general tone of the technical and business literature in suggesting that IT workers are an unnatural fit for traditional labor organizations. Yet if we expand our definition of "information workers" along the lines above – involving workers from the communications, media, education, and office administration fields – suddenly unions are everywhere. Information workers in the "physical internetwork" of information communication (UPS, FedEx, and the Post Office in the US) have been involved in organizing efforts throughout the 1990s, culminating in a UPS strike which shocked the nascent world of e-commerce with demands to end part-time labor, reduce overtime, and extend health benefits to all.[105]

---

102. Alistair Mutch, "Unions and Information, Britain 1900–1960: An Essay in the History of Information", *International Review of Social History*, 44 (1999), pp. 395–417.
103. Gary Chaison, "Information Technology: The Threat to Unions", *Journal of Labor Research*, 23 (2002), pp. 249–259.
104. Laurie P. Milton, "An Identity Perspective on the Propensity of High-Tech Talent to Unionize", *Journal of Labor Research*, 24 (2003), pp. 31–53.
105. Richard Rothstein, "Union Strength in the United States: Lessons from the UPS Strike", *International Labour Review*, 136 (1997), pp. 469–492.

Finally, we might ask: how have labor unions themselves changed with the introduction of IT? A senior research analyst with the International Brotherhood of Teamsters recently pointed out that his organization uses "a database of contract information for over 200,000 Teamster collective bargaining agreements (both expired and current)" through which they track "nearly 40,000 separate employer-union relationships".[106] In the US, even under the return of a labor-hostile conservative administration in 2000, such efforts have generated great enthusiasm for an IT-driven New Labor movement, with some longtime activists hoping that "Ongoing efforts by the AFL-CIO and its 66 affiliates to maximize their creative use of computer power may help slow, stem, and finally reverse Labor's decline in union density."[107] But it may be in reaching out beyond union members themselves that labor organizations use IT most effectively. Consider again the case of global retailing leader Wal-Mart Stores, Inc. – a firm so effectively enmeshed in the space of flows of consumer commodities that it did $218 billion in sales in 2002 among its 4,300 outlets worldwide. Potential Wal-Mart workers, consumers, or even hosting communities concerned about the health care benefits offered to the firm's 1.3 million employees don't have to simply rely on the claims on the company's website that "[t]he company contributes to the cost of health benefits" such that "60 per cent of our Associates tell us they joined Wal-Mart because of our benefits".[108] They can also explore the website, Wal-Mart Watch, maintained by the United Food and Commercial Workers Union (UFCW), to discover that "[s]trict eligibility requirements, huge employee co-pays, and big deductibles keep participation in Wal-Mart's health plan to 38 per cent of employees", leaving "425,000 employees – most of them women workers – who don't get health coverage from Wal-Mart".[109] Each site makes Wal-Mart labor visible in a different way. Web-surfers with access to both sites – theoretically from anywhere around the globe – can thus make their own decisions about the accuracy and import of these contested claims.

MAKING INFORMATION LABOR VISIBLE IN THE HISTORICAL RECORD

In a similar way, this supplement has been an attempt to correct the historical narrative in which information labor is left invisible – assumed to be technologically determined, deemed unimportant to historical

---

106. Robert E. Lucore, "Challenges and Opportunities: Unions Confront the New Information Technologies", *Journal of Labor Research*, 23 (2002), pp. 201–215, 208.
107. Arthur B. Shostak, "Today's Unions as Tomorrow's Cyberunions: Labor's Newest Hope", *Journal of Labor Research*, 23 (2002), pp. 237–249, 237.
108. Wal-Mart Stores website, http://www.walmartstores.com; last accessed 10 June 2003.
109. Wal-Mart Watch website, http://www.walmartwatch.com; last accessed 10 June 2003.

explanation, or somehow not cast as "labor" at all. We were surprised and delighted with the broad range of methodological approaches our authors took in challenging this narrative, including the exploration of diverse historical contexts, the use of ethnographic methods, and the engagement with important geographic concepts of space and time.

In the sense of context, the sites of IT labor discussed in this supplement range from eighteenth-century Germany, and nineteenth-century India, to twentieth-century South Africa and twenty-first-century Silicon Valley, pointing out the diverse ways in which IT revolutions are enacted, experienced, and contested on the ground in different times and places. In identifying just what kind of IT-related work was being performed in those contexts, our authors illustrate a consensus out of this diversity: the proper definition of information labor is not simply "knowledge work", but also the labor involved in producing and reproducing information infrastructures themselves, as well as more traditional production and service work under any new regime of informatization. For example, Eve Rosenhaft's "Hands and Minds" piece, in describing the eighteenth-century German survivor's pension funds, shows how pension clerks were implicated in two important new informational processes: the application of state-gathered mathematical statistics to profit-making business, and the advertising of investment opportunities to a population through the mass media.[110] Bernard Dubbeld, in his article on "Breaking the Buffalo", considers the containerized commodity-shipping network and its manifestation in Durban, South Africa. His narrative describes a key turning point in both a nation and an industry, on one hand representative of a shift to a global, real-time, networked information economy, but on the other hand quite historically, geographically and culturally contingent on a cultural legacy of apartheid and a local history of stevedoring.[111] And in their article "Compressing Time and Constraining Space", Helen Sampson and Bin Wu offer another lens on the story told by Dubbeld, using a focused study of the port of Rotterdam to explore the shifts in the spatial/temporal division of labor in the global shipping industry due to both on-board information/communication technology and in-port container/transport technology. Their history and interviews reveal how IT has transformed the physical calculating and monitoring of hull stresses and loads, both in terms of who does the work (officer or engineer) and where it is done (ship or shore).[112]

In the case of sources, too, our authors prove innovative. Though all the

---

110. Eve Rosenhaft, "Hands and Minds: Clerical Work in the First 'Information Society'", pp. 13–43.
111. B. Dubbeld, "Breaking the Buffalo: The Transformation of Stevedoring Work in Durban between 1970 and 1990", pp. 97–122.
112. Helen Sampson and Bin Wu, "Compressing Time and Constraining Space: The Contradictory Effects of ICT and Containerization on International Shipping Labour", pp. 123–152.

articles in this volume rely on traditional historical methods of archival research and subject interview to one degree or another, many employ ethnographic interview, observation, and participation methods as well. The opportunity to employ such first-hand techniques is rare in historical research, but when dealing with a contemporary subject like the IT revolution, in which social and spatial conditions are changing so rapidly, attention to recent history is a must. After all, one of the goals of history is to provide a sort of cultural anthropology of the past.[113] For example, in studying the recent changes in global shipping labor, Sampson and Wu talked to laborers of varying status, both on the shore and on the ship, and in the process were able to analyze how those very spatial categories of "ship" and "shore" were themselves in flux due to the way IT was put to use. Similarly, Chris Benner's essay on "Computers in the Wild" follows, first hand, the changing nature of labor "guilds" in Silicon Valley, through tumultuous years of Y2K fear and fervor, dot-com boom and bust. His study reveals not just the historical views of his actors in a specific time and place, but the changing geographical sense of what that place itself means, as both a labor market and a home. "Information" in Benner's view is not simply a commodity produced and consumed in the for-profit "content industry". Rather, information of another sort – tacit knowledge of the way complex technologies perform on the job "in the wild" – is also traded throughout a diffuse but active labor market.[114]

Finally, in applying historical and ethnographic methods to these contexts, many of our authors have also developed a keen sense of geographic awareness, which is often missing from work in the humanities and social sciences. In an obvious sense, these articles range over many different spatial locations of information labor – not just laboratories of IT innovation and offices of IT application, but places like those "electronic cottages" where individuals blur the lines between home and factory, and the docks and ships where the infrastructures of immaterial and material commodities merge to enable our current wave of globalization. But in a more subtle sense, our authors have taken the notion of space/time transformation as a key principle of IT labor itself. Deepak Choudhury in particular uses spatial analysis to understand the labor actions of telegraph workers under a regime of global empire in his story of the turn-of-the-century multi-stage telegraph strike in colonial British India and Burma.[115] Choudhury illustrates how a "virtual community" of labor, separated over regional distance but connected by electromechanical communication,

---

113. Anthony F.C. Wallace, *Rockdale: The Growth of an American Village in the Early Industrial Revolution* (New York, 1972).

114. Chris Benner, "'Computers in the Wild': Guilds and Next-Generation Unionism in the Information Revolution", pp. 181–204.

115. D. Choudhury, "India's First Virtual Community and the Telegraph General Strike of 1908", pp. 45–71.

could mobilize to act. Further, he argues that membership in that virtual community overcame (if only momentarily) persistent boundaries of race, class, and ethnicity – divisions which have historically been mobilized quite effectively by capital to reinforce less costly and more docile divisions of labor. The fact that Choudhury's tale took place nearly a century ago both contradicts and gives hope to the views of present-day Internet advocates such as Mark Poster, who recently claimed "the only way a movement can be constructed of workers on a global scale is through the Internet".[116] Still, we must remember that however virtual it may have seemed, the strike was important precisely because it was grounded in particular physical places – places of strategic and economic importance to the wider British Empire.

Given the varied historical, ethnographic, and geographic perspectives of the pieces in this volume, then, I would like to point to four general and dialectical themes which emerge from these articles as working hypotheses about information labor:

It takes technological labor to build and sustain new labor-saving technological infrastructures

In theorizing the production and reproduction of the urban built environment under capitalism, David Harvey has argued that "Under capitalism there is [...] a perpetual struggle in which capital builds a physical landscape appropriate to its own condition at a particular moment in time, only to have to destroy it, usually in the course of a crisis, at a subsequent point in time." To Harvey, this process represents a dialectic, a contradiction which capitalism as a whole needs to resolve continually, time and again, in order to continue to be profitable and productive:

> In order to overcome spatial barriers and to annihilate space with time, spatial structures are created that themselves act as barriers to further accumulation. These spatial structures are expressed in the form of immobile transport facilities and ancillary facilities implanted in the landscape. We can in fact extend this conception to encompass the formation of the built environment as a whole.[117]

Something similar happens in the application of technology to production, especially information technology. In order to innovate a new technological environment for the purposes of making labor more efficient, more productive, more easily managed, more flexible, or even less necessary, capital must invest labor in the production of new standards, new infrastructure, and new skills. But these technological innovations are rapidly taken on by all competitors and then become a

116. Poster, "Workers as Cyborgs", p. 349.
117. David Harvey, *The Urban Experience* (Baltimore, MD, 1989).

barrier to further innovation – until, that is, additional labor is mobilized to modify or replace those barriers once again.

Aristotle Tympas's insight into "Computing Electric Power Transmission Before the Electronic Computer" illustrates this dialectic by describing how complex, networked infrastructure systems of all sorts are necessarily underpinned by similarly complex information systems, both during their design and in the course of their functioning.[118] The human "computors" that Tympas discusses have been absent from recent information history, but are much on the minds of contemporary writers. In bringing them to our attention, Tympas effectively weaves the stories of three kinds of technologies: the electrical infrastructures normally conceptualized as solely the work of "system builders"; the ad-hoc electromechanical tools such as "network analyzers" which were built explicitly to solve mathematical and physical problems of infrastructure construction and operation; and the individual laboring "computors" embedded in both of these technological webs, whose expertise in operating the analysis tools was both necessary and undervalued.

The article by Nathan Ensmenger on "Letting the 'Computer Boys' Take Over" considers the next chapter of this innovation saga: the birth of the new-job category of "computer programming" within the for-profit firm, where programmers mediated between the new technology of electronic computers and the existing corporate social environment.[119] According to Ensmenger, programmers were caught in a bind: while they acted as enablers of a new, highly-valued corporate practice – electronic data processing – they also served as a lightning rod for criticism of the feared consequences of that same practice – organizational restructuring. This very tension in the new programming occupation helps to explain the historical origin and subsequent reproduction of the idea of a "software crisis" – both a recurring justification for rationalizing the labor of programmers under management control, and a constant lure for attracting more job-seekers to the field of computer programming itself.

Any changing technological division of labor is involved in a changing social division of labor as well

This idea is not meant to invoke technological determinism (as discussed above), but is meant instead to suggest the complex relation between technology and culture. For example, Ensmenger hits on just such a relationship when he observes that computer programming, the act of

118. Aristotle Tympas, "Perpetually Laborious: Computing Electric Power Transmission Before the Electronic Computer", pp. 73–95.
119. Nathan L. Ensmenger, "Letting the 'Computer Boys' Take Over: Technology and the Politics of Organizational Transformation", pp. 153–180.

instructing machines to act in deterministic ways in order to rationalize human business processes, was itself as a "craft" skill which apparently demanded a new "science" of the management of computer programming. This contradiction structured the different ways that managers attempted to exert control over their new and necessary computer-programmer labor force – from screening out all but the (supposed) best programmers, and paying higher salaries for only the most innately talented designers, to purchasing programming language packages which would allow the most unskilled programmer to produce adequate code, and learning a new systems-oriented management style themselves.

Similarly, Dubbeld describes how the Durban stevedores moved from "permanently casual" workers (in that they forged an intermittent work life in a single city) to "permanent apartheid" workers (their labor administered centrally and controlled by the state), to unionized workers (under conditions of increasing containerization), and finally back to "casual and flexible" workers (especially under new IT-enabled labor management systems). In the end, unions failed to protect these workers' interests: space was rationalized, time compressed, ownership consolidated, industrial links (between shipping, rail and road companies) tightened, and work-gangs (with their level of control over the labor process) first reduced in size, then subject to "multiskilling", and finally abandoned. This story reminds us that large-scale economic restructurings of international telecommunications, shipping, road, and rail infrastructures are global but not homogenous; when combined with the legacy of apartheid, the outcome was necessarily contingent. In the case of the US, for example, Ann Schwarz-Miller and Wayne K. Talley recently argued that the combination of transport technology, information technology, and neoliberal de- and reregulation have cut the number of railroad industry employees by half, vastly weakening their bargaining power, but have had "a positive effect on the demand for dockworkers", rather improving their bargaining position.[120] (Though this strong position was not enough to avoid a major West-Coast longshoreman lockout in Autumn 2002 – just before the e-commerce holiday rush.)[121]

Any changing technological and social division of labor is involved in a changing spatial and temporal division of labor as well

Even in industries which don't produce informational products or services, the application of information technologies almost always creates

120. Ann Schwarz-Miller and Wayne K. Talley, "Technology and Labor Relations: Railroads and Ports", *Journal of Labor Research*, 23 (2002), pp. 513–534.
121. Steven Greenhouse, "Labor Lockout at West's Ports Roils Business", *New York Times* [online] (1 October 2002).

new time-space conditions (just as the application of mechanized technologies created new time-space conditions in the Fordist factory). Commenting on the recent history of the trucking industry in the US, Michael Belzer has argued that under government deregulation (and driver/union reregulation), "advances in information technology have been adopted throughout the trucking industry to enhance carriers' competitiveness and meet customers' demands. This new technology increased the performance pressure on drivers and dockworkers who must meet more stringent time schedules under adverse conditions." Such technology is now so sophisticated that it "can be used to track driver activities as well, changing a formerly unmonitored job (suited to piece work and efficiency wages) into a monitored one. Carriers now know the location of their truck to within a few hundred feet".[122]

On the surface, the technological changes at work between ship and shore labor in Sampson and Wu's account of Rotterdam might seem to fit unproblematically with the historical narrative of "automation" described above: cranes, containers, and computer-mediated communications all help to decrease turnover time and decrease labor requirements, resulting in the capitalist's increase in both productivity and profit. Yet Sampson and Wu point out that not only are shore-based workers still required, but their spatial/temporal relationship to the ship-based staff has changed dramatically, with contact between the two groups now kept to a bare minimum. Aboard ship, the duties of various grades of officers have been redefined to incorporate new kinds of information management required by the shore office. But this routinized communication of data helps keep the ship-based staff out of casual communication with the dock staff. With new time and information requirements linked to computerization and containerization, and with the most modern ports (like Rotterdam) located far away from old city centers, the laborers themselves experience space/time horizons which are perhaps more constrained than ever before, even as the commodities they carry and the capital they generate both move more freely.

Information laborers from diverse social categories find their positionalities become bound up in the cultural understanding of the information technology itself

This final point considers how the qualities of laborers become attached over time to the qualities of a certain kind of labor – and vice versa. Tympas describes a dialectic between the roles of "analyst" (often male)

122. Michael H. Belzer, "Technological Innovation and the Trucking Industry: Information Revolution and the Effect on the Work Process", *Journal of Labor Research*, 23 (2002), pp. 375–396, 376, 390.

and "computor" (often female), arguing that with each advance in electromechanical calculating technology, the two labor categories were continually redefined to valorize the one and deemphasize the other. Not only was there a gendered division of labor in network analyzer work; but conceptions of analog devices and manual labors were devalued hand-in-hand with the feminization of those tools – arguably a fundamental step in the development of today's assumption that digital technology is (by definition) naturally superior to analog. Rosenhaft, in the most biographical of our articles, puts particular focus on key career moments of three "minor functionaries" of her information economy – male workers with foothold in the "middle class", relying not only on important numeracy and literacy skills, but on a tenuous web of social obligations. Rosenhaft illustrates that the importance of the rapid and accurate processing of information (not to mention the advertising of that informational power) was not only recognized by the eighteenth-century actors themselves, but was wrapped up in negotiations over personal reputation, the definition of a just living wage, the demands of absolute secrecy, and the fears of clerks using their informational capital to set up shop themselves.

What these examples share is a notion that "class" is a relation, a process, a positionality with respect to capital; not a thing.[123] Certainly class involves abstract Marxian social relations between the purchaser of labor power and the seller of labor power. But it also involves abstract cultural categories like "middle-class", "urban", and "professional" – all historically-specific social constructions of who is "valued", who is "educated", who is "high-tech" in any given economy and society. Thus, technologies become naturalized in difference-specific ways – for example, the masculinization of computer programming and the feminization of content production which I witnessed in my own career.

Hector Postigo's article describing "The Case of America Online Volunteers" addresses this question of positionality by exploring the creation of a labor identity in the case of the "volunteers", who both consumed and produced content in the nascent for-profit online service AOL.[124] Instead of considering the programmers of Ensmenger's study or the content designers of Benner's study, Postigo looks at a hybrid category of content producers – they neither programmed the infrastructure that made AOL work, nor designed the elements of AOL's "look and feel", but they did take on responsibility for the content which populated this infrastructure, and for the crucial ad-hoc communication with new subscribers (not just subscribers new to AOL, but subscribers new to

---

123. David Harvey, *Justice, Nature, and the Geography of Difference* (Cambridge, MA, 1996), p. 359.
124. Hector Postigo, "Emerging Sources of Labor on the Internet: The Case of America Online Volunteers", pp. 205–223.

the entire idea of computer-mediated communication). The historical changes that these AOL volunteers experienced illustrate the thorny social relations at work: there was a consumption aspect, where AOL volunteers received reduced subscription prices or "free hours" to spend at their leisure; there was a training aspect, where volunteers hoped to learn marketable skills and advertise their experience with AOL on a résumé to other firms; and there was a labor aspect, since AOL volunteers worked long hours and demanded at least recognition and respect if not remuneration. Postigo's story shows how these intertwined social relations of training, production, and consumption worked to build another social relation: virtual solidarity of a sort between members of the volunteer community itself. But this community was distinct from other organizations of laborers because of its invisible nature: it was unclear how many members there were; an alternate site, outside of AOL itself, was required to access the community; and only certain computer-mediated actions could easily occur there. Now that it has been made visible, we can ask whether this community gained its identity from AOL or in opposition to AOL.

NOT A CONCLUSION, BUT A BEGINNING

The articles in this volume illustrate that tracing the history of complex, parallel, and intertwined changes among technologies, spatiotemporalities, and human labors is no easy task – and trying to do so in real time is even harder. Information labor often doesn't map easily on to any single category of "class", and information technology itself is often dialectically involved in redefining social norms not only of class membership but of other social categories as well. I would argue that academics (and activists) need all the tools they can get to meet this challenge of interpretation and understanding. Historical contextualization, ethnographic interpretation, and geographical awareness are three sets of tools which I try to use in my own work, and which, I am pleased to see, have been put to good use in the articles of this volume.

But where do such snapshots of the "IT revolution" leave us? Some find it tempting to predict a new social revolution arising from this technology and labor revolution:

> Marx and many other writers have pointed out that social relations eventually must correspond to the level of productive forces. We now live in a time when productive forces have raced far ahead of social relations. The knowledge-intensive productive forces are straining against the chains of private property relations. The qualities of knowledge, to be fully maximized, require a system based on cooperation and sharing, because cooperation and sharing generates more information and social wealth. Such a system would emphasize education, because education builds the infrastructure for expanding social wealth. Such a

system would require the distribution of goods on the basis of need, because the [low] cost of production eliminates scarcity and wages. This, of course, is a radically different system.[125]

Yet others have argued against such naturalized change, fearing "the 'new knowledge/service economy' produces its own proletariat – in call centers, on assembly lines for producing high-tech products, and to service the continuing need for cleaners, security guards, waitresses and waiters".[126] As this volume illustrates, such debates are not new. But can we as historians offer any kind of new response?

I hope we can. Today's digital-divide discussions – whether focused on inequalities between households, schools, regions, or nations – inevitably encompass normative claims (overt or hidden) about the state of labor in the current and future information age. Our historical narratives can help reveal some of the contradictions found between the public investment in the development of information infrastructures (from semiconductors and programming languages to satellite communications and the Internet) versus the private monopoly on profit from the services and commodities that are subsequently developed using these infrastructures. Thus might we both write a labor history – with laborers themselves as units of analysis – and use that labor history as a lever for wider societal changes.

125. James Davis and Michael Stack, "Knowledge in Production", *Race & Class*, 34:3 (1993), pp. 1–14; repr. in Philip E. Agre and Douglas Schuler (eds), *Reinventing Technology, Rediscovering Community: Critical Explorations of Computing as a Social Practice* (Greenwich, CT, 1997), pp. 56–71.
126. Amin, Massey, and Thrift, *Cities for the Many*, p. 22.

International Review of Social History
PUBLISHED FOR THE INTERNATIONAAL INSTITUUT VOOR
SOCIALE GESCHIEDENIS, AMSTERDAM

SUBSCRIPTIONS
International Review of Social History (ISSN 0020–8590) is published in three parts in April, August and December plus one supplement in December. Three parts plus one supplement form a volume. The subscription price (excluding VAT) of volume 48 (2003) which includes postage and delivery by air where appropriate is £95 net (US$151 in the USA, Canada and Mexico) for institutions; £42 net (US$64 in the USA, Canada and Mexico) for individuals ordering direct from the publisher and certifying that the journal is for their own personal use. Single parts and the supplement are £25 (US$39 in the USA, Canada and Mexico) plus postage. An electronic only price available to institutional subscribers is £85 (US$135 in USA, Canada and Mexico). EU subscribers (outside the UK) who are not registered for VAT should add VAT at their country's rate. VAT registered subscribers should provide their VAT registration number. Japanese prices for institutions are available from Kinokuniya Company Ltd, P.O. Box 55, Chitose, Tokyo 156, Japan.

Orders, which must be accompanied by payment, may be sent to a bookseller, subscription agent or direct to the publisher: Cambridge University Press, The Edinburgh Building, Shaftesbury Road, Cambridge CB2 2RU; or in the USA, Canada and Mexico: Cambridge University Press, Journals Fulfillment Department, 100 Brook Hill Drive, West Nyack, New York 10994–2133. Periodicals postage paid at New York, NY and at additional mailing offices. Postmaster: send address changes in USA, Canada and Mexico to International Review of Social History, Cambridge University Press, 100 Brook Hill Drive, West Nyack, New York 10994–2133.

Information on International Review of Social History and all other Cambridge journals can be accessed via http://www.cambridge.org

GUIDELINES FOR CONTRIBUTORS

Manuscripts are considered for publication on the understanding that they are not currently under consideration elsewhere and that the material – in substance as well as form – has not been previously published. Two copies of the manuscript should be submitted. Each article should be accompanied by a summary, not exceeding 100 words, outlining the principal conclusions and methods in the context of currently accepted views on the subject. All material – including quotations and notes – must be double-spaced with generous margins. Use of dot-matrix printers is discouraged. Notes should be numbered consecutively and placed at the end of the text. Spelling should be consistent throughout (e.g. Labour and Labor are both acceptable, but only one of these forms should be used in an article). Turns of phrase using masculine forms as universals are not acceptable.

Sample Citation Forms

Book: E.P. Thompson, *The Making of the English Working Class* (London, 1963), pp. 320–322. Journal: Walter Galenson, "The Unionization of the American Steel Industry", *International Review of Social History*, 1 (1956), pp. 8–40. Detailed guidelines are available from the editor on request. Twenty-five free offprints of each article are provided, and authors may purchase additional copies provided these are ordered at proof stage.

Printed in the United States
by Baker & Taylor Publisher Services